The BIBLICAL WORLDVIEW

—

CREATION, FALL, REDEMPTION

Other works by Dr. Surrendra Gangadean & The Logos Foundation:

Philosophical Foundation: A Critical Analysis of Basic Beliefs

History of Philosophy: A Critical Analysis of Unresolved Disputes

Theological Foundation: A Critical Analysis of Christian Belief

Philosophical Foundation: Trivium Study Guide

The Logos Papers: To Make the Logos Known

The Westminster Confession: A Doxological Understanding

*The Westminster Shorter and Larger Catechisms:
A Doxological Understanding*

*On Natural and Revealed Theology:
Collected Essays of Surrendra Gangadean*

*The Logos Curriculum:
Grammar Catechisms: Philosophical, Theological, and
Historical Foundations*

Fundación Filosofica: Un Análisis Crítico de Creencias Básicas

DOXOLOGICAL REFORMED SERMON SERIES:

*The Book of Revelation: What Must Soon Take Place
Doxological Postmillennialism*

*The Unity of the Church: That They May Be One That the
World May Believe*

PHILOSOPHICAL FOUNDATION DIALOGUE SERIES:

Introduction to Philosophy: The Basic Things Are Clear to Reason

DOXOLOGICAL REFORMED SERMON SERIES

The BIBLICAL WORLDVIEW

CREATION, FALL, REDEMPTION

Genesis 1–3: Scripture in Organic Seed Form

SURRENDRA GANGADEAN

LOGOS PRESS PAPERS

LOGOS

A DIVISION OF THE LOGOS FOUNDATION
Phoenix, Arizona

The Biblical Worldview: Creation, Fall, Redemption
Genesis 1–3: Scripture in Organic Seed Form

Copyright © 2003, 2010, 2024 Surrendra Gangadean

Logos Papers Press 2024
Phoenix, Arizona
logospaperspress.com
thelogospapers.com

Cover Design: Beth Ellen Nagle
Typesetting: Matthew P. Hicks & Brian J. Phelps

Library of Congress Cataloging-in-Publication Data pending

Gangadean, Surrendra, 1943–2022.
    The biblical worldview: creation, fall, redemption
    genesis 1–3: scripture in organic seed form
    Includes index
    ISBN: 979-8-9898295-2-1 (hbk.)
    ISBN: 979-8-9898295-3-8 (pbk.)
    ISBN: 979-8-9898295-4-5 (e-book)

1. Biblical Worldview 2. Commentary—Genesis 1–3 3. Creation–Fall–Redemption 4. Doxological Reformed 5. Theology—Reformed I. Title

For those looking for
the city whose architect
and builder is God

APPENDICES

CONTENTS

SERIES PREFACE

THE *DOXOLOGICAL REFORMED SERMON SERIES*[1] is a collection of Pastor Surrendra Gangadean's sermons during his over two-decade tenure as the founder and senior pastor of Westminster Fellowship church. During this period, he delivered over 1,000 sermons, preserved through audio recordings, handwritten outlines, and congregants' notes. These sermons now form the basis of dozens of books, offering a Doxological Reformed exposition of the Scripture, the moral law, and foundational theological doctrines.

The significance of this collection lies in its pioneering nature—in seeking to advance the kingdom of God—providing the groundwork for future hermeneutical works. Pastor Gangadean developed and applied Rational Presuppositionalism[2] to general revelation in his work *Philosophical Foundation*,[3] addressing enduring challenges of the modern and postmodern world. Similarly, he tackled central questions concerning the content and application of Scripture. Recognizing the impracticality of writing full commentaries, Pastor Gangadean used sermons to engage the meaning of Scripture, foundational doctrines, and the moral law as applied to all of life.

Consequently, The Logos Foundation Editorial Board has unanimously decided to present the sermon series in its original form. Minor grammatical changes aside, the content remains untouched, accurately reflecting Pastor Gangadean's ongoing thought process. We aim to prepare the way for future generations to connect directly with the mind that shaped these doctrines. Preservation of the original will also aid

1. Surrendra Gangadean, *The Westminster Shorter and Larger Catechisms: A Doxological Understanding* (Phoenix: Logos Papers Press, 2023), xv-xxxii.

2. Surrendra Gangadean, "Paper No. 101: Rational Presuppositionalism: Critically Examining Assumptions for Meaning," in *The Logos Papers: To Make the Logos Known* (Phoenix: Logos Papers Press, 2022), 521–526; "Paper No. 52: Common Ground (Part III)," 281–282; "Paper No. 2: Common Ground," 9–13; "Paper No. 95: Rational Presuppositional Apologetics," 503–506; "Paper No. 96: The Project of Rational Presuppositional Apologetics," in *The Logos Papers*, 507–508.

3. Surrendra Gangadean, *Philosophical Foundation: A Critical Analysis of Basic Beliefs*, Second Edition (Phoenix: Public Philosophy Press, 2022).

the Editorial Board in capturing the diverse contexts in which his ideas were expounded. These sermons, coupled with foundational work in philosophy, theology, the humanities, and history, form the basis for forthcoming biblical commentaries. While each book is not exhaustive in itself, the series collectively reflects Pastor Gangadean's distilled wisdom throughout his body of work. As more books are published, a complete tapestry of his understanding will gradually unfold.

We regard the content of these sermons as invaluable contributions to the Next Reformation.[4] They illustrate how contextual thinking can illuminate the organic content of Scripture, reaching across every book and addressing even the most disputed passages that have troubled the Church throughout history. Through these sermons, the perspicuity of Scripture is meticulously brought into focus, shedding light on the clarity derived from general revelation, special revelation, and the cumulative insights of the Historic Christian Faith.[5] The convergence of the doxological focus, the doctrine of clarity and inexcusability, the knowledge of God as the good, and Rational Presuppositionalism collectively work to unveil the profound meaning of Scripture and encapsulate the essence of its truth.

Pastor Gangadean's preaching approach unfolds with a discernible progression. In the earlier sermons from 1993 to 2004, the emphasis rests on biblical exposition of the books of Scripture, laying a robust foundation by elucidating fundamental doctrines such as clarity and inexcusability, the divine image in man, the knowledge of God, church authority, and worship. Delivered with rapidity, these sermons were densely packed with content aimed at a comprehensive exposition.

From 2005 to 2014, a pronounced shift occurred in Pastor Gangadean's sermons, with a heightened focus on the need for sanctification within the context of discipleship. This period aimed to equip the congregation to grasp the interplay between foundational truths and personal application, fostering maturity. These sermons naturally evolved from the preceding foundational exposition of Scripture. After a decade of delving into the objective and subjective facets of biblical

---

4. Gangadean, "Paper No. 62: The Next Reformation," in *The Logos Papers*, 335–337.

5. Surrendra Gangadean, *The Westminster Confession of Faith: A Doxological Understanding* (Phoenix: Logos Papers Press, 2023); Gangadean, *The Westminster Catechisms*.

truths and their integration, the imperative to address remaining sin within the congregation became increasingly apparent.

The subsequent phase of preaching, spanning 2015 to 2022, witnessed a shift towards existential hermeneutics, emphasizing the moral law, the unity of the Church, public witness, and adopting a more deliberate and rhetorical expository style. While his pace slowed, his focus intensified on discerning how to apply truths to dismantle self-deception and self-justification among congregants and within the broader Church. The doctrine of repentance of root sin and an in-depth analysis of the doctrine of clarity and inexcusability assumed central significance.

The essence of these sermons constitutes the most profound exposition of the Word of God in its fullness to date. The expositor lived an exemplary life, building upon the cumulative insights from the three foundations, and endeavored to equip God's people with a clear understanding of Scripture amidst its myriad challenges, facilitating enduring responses.

Anticipating that this sermon series will serve as an essential source for crafting a biographical account of Pastor Gangadean's life and work, it becomes evident in these sermons how providence in his life, the challenges inherent in shepherding the flock, the practical application of doctrinal principles to the life of the Church, and a continuous response to the prevailing state of the Church and culture are interwoven. They stand as a testament to the life of a faithful servant who fought the good fight, finished the race, and kept the faith.[6]

These sermons, given initially to the congregants of Westminster Fellowship over the years, are deemed blessings that must be shared with the broader body of Christ. We consider it imperative to extend these blessings to our fellow brothers and sisters, and view it as our duty to contribute to the spiritual enrichment of the larger Christian community.

May the Lord bless the preaching and hearing of His Word, and may this compilation serve as the foundation for the contextual interpretation of Scripture for generations to come, and persist until the fulfillment

---

6. *2 Timothy 4:7–8.*

of the dominion[7] and mission[8] mandates in the earth being filled with the knowledge of the glory of the Lord as the waters cover the sea.

—THE LOGOS FOUNDATION
EDITORIAL BOARD
Phoenix, Arizona
February 2024

---

7. *Genesis 1:26–28.*

8. *Matthew 28:18–20.*

PREFACE

THE BIBLICAL WORLDVIEW: CREATION, FALL, REDEMPTION is the foundational, and therefore the inaugural book in the *Doxological Reformed Sermon Series*. Creation–fall–redemption are the foundational themes of biblical revelation and are best introduced in the first three chapters of Genesis. The truth of special revelation is encapsulated in Genesis 1–3 in an organic seed form, a unity that grows, encompassing all essential elements in summary. This unity progressively unfolds organically, and grows in fullness throughout redemptive history from Genesis to Revelation. Scripture *builds on*, is to be *understood by*, and is *the development of* what is revealed in Genesis 1–3. Understanding the beginning is necessary to understand all that follows.

As the reader becomes more familiar with the content of the biblical worldview, they will become increasingly aware of its foundational and pervasive role. Genesis 1–3 is the most quoted and exposited portion of Scripture in Pastor Gangadean's sermons. It serves as the paradigm for understanding, illustrating, and explaining the breadth and depth of the unfolding of biblical revelation. In keeping with the Westminster Confession of Faith in the use of clearer passages to understand less clear passages,[1] the content of the biblical worldview serves as the basis by which to interpret subsequent passages. "Those things which are necessary to be known, believed, and observed for salvation" (WCF. 1.7) are contained in this portion of Scripture. The emphasis on the centrality of Genesis 1–3, as well as his philosophical development of historical/creedal interpretations of the text, stands as one of Pastor Gangadean's profound contributions to the history of ideas. Upon comprehending the objective revelations in Genesis 1–3, the reader gains insight into the unity, clarity, harmony, continuity, sufficiency, and fullness of Scripture to a degree and depth not previously elucidated by other expositors.

The themes of creation–fall–redemption (biblical foundation in narrative form), and the subsequent development of the Seven Pillars of the

---

1. *WCF. 1.7.*

Faith[2] (biblical foundation in theological form), mark a revolutionary hermeneutical advancement to settle longstanding disagreements in the history of interpretation.[3] Since the true and full sense of any Scripture is not manifold but one,[4] and since thinking is presuppositional (the less basic in light of the more basic), understanding the content of the biblical worldview will enable the elucidation of meaning and the resolution of disputes. When the framework of the biblical worldview is used in conjunction with contextual interpretation (the use of good and necessary consequences in light of clear general revelation and the Historic Christian Faith), *then* will the fullness of the Word of God burst open to overcome objections to the truth of God in special revelation; *then* the perspicuity of Scripture will be asserted in making challenging books like the Gospel of John, Romans, Hebrews, and even Revelation accessible to all—in a due use of ordinary means;[5] *then* the implications of the biblical worldview will extend far beyond hermeneutics in Scripture to their larger missiological[6] and eschatological[7] purpose of deepening the revelation of God in creation and providence.

Creation–fall–redemption are the basic themes of biblical revelation. The latter assumes the former and is unintelligible without understanding the former. Redemptive revelation in the Scriptures assumes the existence of clear general revelation in the creation, as well as the existence of moral evil (sin) in the denial of clear general revelation. The movement in history is from good to evil to a restoration to what is good. The restoration from evil to good is gradual. Evil affects the understanding of good and evil itself,[8] and only gradually, through much conflict and suffering, do we overcome our denial of what is clear and come to understand the true nature of good and evil. The redemptive restoration to what is good, through long, intense conflict with evil,

---

2. Clarity and inexcusability, sin and death, curse and promise, repentance and faith, justification and sanctification, baptism and calling, resurrection and reward. For a fuller exposition see: Gangadean, "Paper No. 37: The Seven Pillars," in *The Logos Papers*, 207–210.

3. *Isaiah 40:3–5.*

4. *WCF. 1.9.*

5. *WCF. 1.7.*

6. *Genesis 1:26–28; Matthew 28:18–20.*

7. *Isaiah 11:9; Habakkuk 2:14.*

8. Gangadean, "Paper No. 103: The Noetic Effect of Sin," in *The Logos Papers*, 531–528.

serves only to deepen the good in a way otherwise impossible. Good does not merely overcome evil, but causes evil to serve the good.

The themes of creation–fall–redemption are best introduced from the first three chapters of Genesis, with the following caveats:

First, the reading of any text will reflect the reader's assumptions. This is as it should be. What is needed is a critical awareness of one's assumptions. To say that there are many different interpretations is not the end of all discussion, but an invitation to begin critical philosophical reflection on the different interpretive frameworks. The less basic assumes the more basic; special revelation assumes general revelation. If there is agreement on general revelation, there will be agreement on special revelation.

Second, there are many degrees of the use of reason and of understanding among those who broadly agree on general and special revelation. Popular levels of understanding do not reflect what has been achieved in the historical process of creedal definition of doctrine—what the best minds agree upon after much discussion. And historical/creedal understanding does not reflect some of the philosophical responses to challenges made since the last period of creedal definition, a period sometimes lasting for centuries.

What follows is a philosophical development of historical/creedal interpretations of the text of the first three chapters of Genesis. Reason is being used to understand general revelation, and reason and general revelation are being used to understand the text. At every step, the reader is called to engage diligently with the assumptions, implications, inferences, and arguments presented to arrive at conclusions that will serve as the basis for an ever-increasing understanding of the fullness that there is in God.

—THE LOGOS FOUNDATION
EDITORIAL BOARD
Phoenix, Arizona
February 2024

INTRODUCTION

In the Beginning: The Biblical Worldview

THE FOLLOWING IS A CONCISE ARTICULATION of the central doctrines and ideas expressed throughout the sermon series on the biblical worldview. The Logos Foundation Editorial Board crafted this introduction to orient the reader and to serve as a guide and reference for analyzing the content of Genesis 1–3. Additionally, for convenience, both a *concise* and *expanded* outline are included as appendices at the conclusion of this book.

CREATION: MAN IS CALLED TO ETERNAL LIFE IN KNOWING GOD

The Doctrine of Revelation

Revelation is of two kinds: general and special revelation. General revelation is what can be known about the nature of God and man, and good and evil, by all persons, everywhere, at all times. Knowledge of general revelation is necessary to answer two preliminary questions regarding special revelation concerning its necessity and existence. Why do we need special revelation, and how do we know that special revelation exists? The answer lies in clear general revelation,[1] which is prior to special revelation and is needed to show the necessity and existence of special revelation. Clear general revelation is objective revelation given in the creation and is therefore present from the beginning, since creation; it has deepened throughout history in providence and presently bears witness to each of us.

---

1. Gangadean, "Paper No. 102: The Clarity of General Revelation: God's Eternal Power and Divine Nature, and the Moral Law," 527–529; "Paper No. 41: What is Clear About God," 225–229; "Paper No. 112: Why General Revelation Is Basic in the Christian Worldview," in *The Logos Papers*, 583–585.

Why Do We Need Special Revelation?

Clear general revelation is necessary for meaning versus skepticism and fideism. Skepticism is the epistemological position that knowledge is not possible and that nothing is clear.[2] In contrast to skepticism, the principle of clarity affirms that at least something is clear.[3] It affirms that the basic things are clear and that the basic things about God and man, and good and evil, are clear to reason.[4] Clarity is necessary for meaning, knowledge, and truth. The opposite of "something is clear" is "nothing is clear." Consistently held, if nothing is clear, then no distinction is possible, including the distinctions between being and non-being, good and evil, and true and false. Intelligibility breaks down. Skepticism, consistently held, leads to nihilism, the loss of all meaning.

Clear general revelation is necessary for morality: If there is no clarity, then there is no inexcusability; without inexcusability, there is no basis for accountability in moral choices.[5] Without clarity, there is no sin and death, and therefore no morality. Fideism is holding a belief without proof based on understanding. Fideists affirm sin and death, but they lack content and justification. Sin can only be understood in light of inexcusability. Suppose there is no clear objective revelation. In that case, it follows that there can be no inexcusability for not knowing, no basis to know good and evil in which morality is grounded, and therefore no sin and ultimately no need for redemption through Christ. If there is no clarity, then all believers are fideists (believing without proof or understanding). Fideism, consistently held, empties belief of meaning.

Clear general revelation in connection with the problem of evil—the existence of moral evil (justice) and natural evil (mercy)—shows the necessity for special revelation.[6] The problem of evil is universal—ex-

---

2. Surrendra Gangadean, *History of Philosophy: A Critical Analysis of Unresolved Disputes* (Phoenix: Public Philosophy Press, 2022), 9–12.

3. Gangadean, *Philosophical Foundation*, 3–5, 287–292; Gangadean, *The Westminster Confession of Faith*, 1–13; Gangadean, "Paper No. 53: Common Ground (Part IV)," in *The Logos Papers*, 283–286.

4. Gangadean, *Philosophical Foundation*.

5. *Romans 1:18–20.*

6. Gangadean, *Philosophical Foundation*, 145–161; Surrendra Gangadean, *On Natural and Revealed Theology: Collected Essays of Surrendra Gangadean,* (Phoenix: Logos Paper Press, 2023), 141–147; Gangadean, "Paper No. 7: The Problem of Evil," in *The Logos Papers*, 33–39.

perienced by all existentially. It is an *intellectual* problem, not a practical one. The concern is to make sense of things and to know why evil exists, not how to avoid or remove evil. It is a problem for man as a rational being made in the image of God. The problem of evil is an *expectational* problem, for we intuitively sense that things could have been different—without misery, wickedness, and waste. The problem of evil states: *If God is all good and all powerful, why is there evil?* Understanding the problem of evil entails that natural evil is not original. Natural evil is imposed, not as punishment, but as a call back (mercy) from moral evil. By understanding natural evil as a merciful call back, we see the need for special revelation: How will God be both just and merciful to man in sin? Only special revelation can answer this question.

Special revelation assumes the clarity of general revelation. Common Ground (reason, integrity, Rational Presuppositionalism, and the Principle of Clarity) is the set of conditions necessary for thought and discourse.[7] Common Ground is necessary to understand general and special revelation. Clear general revelation is needed to understand the opening lines of the creation account in Genesis. The existence and nature of God, the nature of time, creation *ex nihilo,* substance, and subsequent creation have their basis in general revelation.

Special revelation teaches that clear general revelation expresses the divine nature and the moral law written in the hearts of all men.[8] Clear general revelation is assumed throughout all of Scripture, and answers the question of the necessity for Scripture. The clarity of general revelation requires the need for Scripture, and Scripture assumes and teaches the clarity of general revelation.[9] In recognizing and interpreting Scripture, we must begin with clear general revelation.

---

7. Gangadean, "Paper No. 2: Common Ground," 9–13; "Paper No. 50: Common Ground (Part I)," 275–276; "Paper No. 51: Common Ground (Part II)," 277–279; "Paper No. 52: Common Ground (Part III)," 281–282; "Paper No. 53: Common Ground (Part IV)," in *The Logos Papers,* 283–286.

8. *Romans 1:18–20, 2:14–15; Psalm 19.*

9. Gangadean, "Paper No. 112: Why General Revelation Is Basic in the Christian Worldview," in *The Logos Papers,* 583–585.

How Do We Know That Special Revelation Exists?

Special revelation must be consistent with clear general revelation. There is no inherent conflict between clear general revelation and Scripture, just as there is no fundamental conflict between philosophy, religion, and science. The apparent conflict arises from misunderstandings within science, religion, and philosophy rather than among these domains. When each discipline is understood, conflict is not possible among them. There is an order among them with philosophy being the most basic. *Philosophy*, as an area, is foundational to all other disciplines. The question of proof and origins belongs exclusively within the realm of philosophy.[10] *Religion* should assume the answers given in philosophy instead of professing belief in God or the soul without proof. *Science* should confine itself to understanding how things operate versus how things originate. In settling the question of what is clear from general revelation, philosophy is to provide the answer by engaging in natural theology.[11]

Special revelation has a redemptive focus. It must show how God's justice and mercy are connected with moral and natural evil. Special revelation must show how God is both just and merciful to man in sin. When engaging in the reading and interpretation of the Scriptures, it is essential to keep in mind its redemptive focus. Special revelation is only from God, who alone can redeem. Our sin is primarily and fundamentally against God. Given God's nature and attributes, only He can forgive, and knowledge of how God will forgive us can only come from Him; it is a revealed truth—only by Scripture can we know God's redemptive plan. It can be inferred that since God provides Scripture within the framework of moral and natural evil, the preservation of Scripture by God also occurs within the context of fallen humanity. Since it must be given in light of sin in man, and is given to restore man from sin, it therefore must be preserved from sin. In short, since it is given by God, it is preserved by God. Other scriptures claiming to be special revelation disregard the question of redemption. They begin with teachings that do not answer the question of redemption, and therefore do not qualify as special revelation.

---

10. Gangadean, *Philosophical Foundation*, 6–10; Gangadean, *History of Philosophy*, 3–9.

11. Gangadean, *On Natural and Revealed Theology*, 149–165.

Special revelation exists only in the biblical worldview of creation–fall–redemption contained in Genesis 1–3 and what builds on these chapters. Numerous alleged revelations, such as the Vedas, do not subscribe to the concept of creation. If they acknowledge creation, they may omit affirmation of the Fall, as seen in the Quran. Furthermore, these revelations often neglect to address the covenant representation in Adam or the imputation of sin. Therefore, these revelations do not see the need for a redeemer, a second Adam, to *undo* what Adam did and *do* what Adam failed to do. Only in the worldview of creation–fall–redemption do we find Scripture, and only Genesis 1–3 and what builds on this is Scripture—nothing else.

Special revelation originates from God, emphasizing His perspective rather than the perspective of men, and is intended for all individuals rather than a select few, with the primary purpose of redeeming man from sin and death. While initially given to the Hebrews, special revelation was not intended exclusively for them. They were the firstborn of all nations to be redeemed.[12] Redemption is intended for all the elect throughout history: for all the families of the earth.[13] Scripture as redemptive revelation keeps the context of human anthropology in mind (sin compounded to the third-degree—unbelief, self-deception, and self-justification—as well as the curse) even when the reader may not keep it consistently in mind.

The Doctrine of Creation

Why did God create?[14] In Himself, God is fully sufficient; this is known as the aseity of God.[15] "God hath all life, glory, goodness, blessedness, in and of himself; and is alone in and unto himself all-sufficient, not standing in need of any creatures which he hath made, nor deriving any glory from them, but only manifesting his own glory in, by, unto, and upon them" (WCF. 2.2).[16] God created because He is. To be is to reveal one's being. One cannot be without expressing one's being. In creating, God is being God. "It pleased God the Father, Son, and

---

12. *Exodus 19:6.*

13. *Genesis 12:1–3.*

14. Gangadean, *Philosophical Foundation*, 144.

15. Gangadean, *The Westminster Confession*, 53–56.

16. *The Westminster Confession of Faith.*

Holy Ghost, for the manifestation of the glory of his eternal power, wisdom, and goodness" (WCF. 4.1).

> God the great Creator of all things doth uphold, direct, dispose, and govern all creatures, actions, and things, from the greatest even to the least, by his most wise and holy providence, according to his infallible foreknowledge, and the free and immutable counsel of his own will, to the praise of the glory of his wisdom, power, justice, goodness, and mercy (WCF. 5.1).

Creation is revelation in a triple sense: *necessarily* (the acts of a being reveal the nature of that being), *intentionally* (it was deemed very good by God),[17] and *exclusively* (there is no direct knowledge of God apart from creation and providence). God's revelation in creation is *full* and *clear*; all of creation and providence serves this purpose. The question may be asked: Why did God create this world? The sufficient answer is that there is no better world (theodicy) to reveal God's nature and to deepen His revelation. Is there a better world than one full of God's glory as the waters cover the sea?[18] One in which His justice and mercy are deepened through sin and redemption? No—although this world does not exhaust infinitude, nevertheless, it is full.

The Doctrine of Creation *Ex Nihilo*[19]

"In the beginning" (Gen. 1:1a) speaks about a beginning in the ordinary sense of the word. Time began with creation. Time involves change; if there is no change, there is no time passing.[20] Matter is in constant change, and finite minds change in having one thought after another. Finite beings exist in time. Since God is unchangeable, there was no time before creation, for only God existed from eternity. God created from no preexisting matter. God created the substance of the universe, initially without form. The substance was in the form of a vast body of water consolidated in one place. Immediately after creation, providence begins: "the Spirit of God was hovering over the waters" (Gen. 1:2b).

---

17. *Genesis 1:31.*

18. *Isaiah 11:9.*

19. Gangadean, *Philosophical Foundation*, 141–143.

20. Gangadean, *History of Philosophy*, 35–40.

The doctrine of providence accompanies the doctrine of creation. God is both creator and ruler.

The Doctrine of Providence

Creation *ex nihilo* is to be distinguished from providence. Bringing into being (creation) and sustaining in being (providence) are distinct yet complementary acts. Theism affirms both creation and providence, unlike deism, which affirms creation yet denies God acting in creation. Providence assumes the distinction between first and second causes.[21] The first cause is God, and the second cause is the nature of things created. Man discovers the nature of things created through the work of dominion (naming and ruling). Providence is an active work beginning with special creation (subsequent creation). All was created by forming and filling from the original substance (the vast body of water). The work of creation is accompanied by the work of providence and both have the doxological purpose of glorifying God. Divine providence extends to the Fall and redemption and serves the purpose of creation. In creation, God reveals His glory; in providence, God deepens the revelation.

The Doctrine of Special Creation/Subsequent Creation

Original creation without form implies formation in subsequent creation. Subsequent creation builds upon the conditions brought into existence by the original creation.[22] Subsequent creation is sequential and cumulative. The following is a breakdown of the creative process:

Day 1: The creation of light initiates the sequence from darkness to light, marking the first day (without a specified 24-hour duration yet). Evening and morning are to be understood in the context of day and night, which in turn should be understood in light of light and darkness. The visible creation reveals the invisible nature of God, who is a God of light; in Him, there is no darkness at all.[23] Some revelation occurs through analogy—through signs and causality. The timeframe

---

21. Gangadean, *The Westminster Confession*, 61–63.

22. Gangadean, "Paper No. 143: The Biblical Worldview (Part III)," in *The Logos Papers*, 719–724.

23. *1 John 1:5.*

is not specified in a unit of measure other than *evening and morning*[24] constituting the first day.

Day 2: The creation of the heavens, firmament, and space occurs through a separation of the waters. Everything is initially created in one place and then expands, forming interstellar space, including galaxies and solar systems.

Day 3: The appearance of dry land and the division between land and sea is accompanied by the creation of vegetation. Each element is specially created after its own kind.

Day 4: The creation of the sun, moon, and stars establishes a 24-hour day with signs, seasons, days, and years.

Day 5: The creation of living creatures in the waters and the birds of the air takes place, each according to its kind, refuting the concept of theistic evolution.[25] These living creatures are meant to multiply and fill the earth.

Day 6: The creation of living creatures on the earth occurs, again emphasizing the distinct creation of kinds, which cannot be collapsed or blurred.

The Doctrine of Man in the Image of God[26]

Man, created in the image of God as a unity of diversity, consists of seven levels of human nature. Listed below, they proceed from the more basic to the less basic. Each aspect of human nature is to be understood in light of the prior levels, which are more inclusive:

(1) Larger aspect: Man is a finite, temporal, and changeable person in being wisdom, power, holiness, justice, goodness, and truth. All human beings have these qualities, always.

(2) Narrower aspect: Man is changeable. He can change in knowledge, holiness, and righteousness. In knowledge, he can change from belief to unbelief and from understanding to misunderstanding (and vice versa). In holiness, he can change from seeking the good (the knowledge of

---

24. *Genesis 1:5.*

25. Gangadean, *Philosophical Foundation*, 98–100.

26. Gangadean, *The Westminster Catechisms*, 133–135; Gangadean, "Paper No. 144: The Biblical Worldview (Part IV)," in *The Logos Papers*, 725–732.

God) to seeking his own glory. In righteousness, he can change from obeying God's law to obeying autonomous, man-centered laws.

(3) Triune personality: Man is created with a triune personality (intellect, emotion, and will) in the image of the Triune God. Man is to love God with the whole heart: mind, soul, and strength.[27]

(4) Body/soul unity: The visible body reveals the invisible soul. Body and soul are a unity, and they affect each other. There is an order; the soul rules and leads the body.

(5) Male/female unity: Fundamentally, male and female are differences of spiritual qualities grounded in the being of God. Man is a male/female unity reflecting the unity and order of those qualities in God. The visible differences between male and female reveal the invisible, spiritual realities of masculine and feminine. What was one nature (in Adam) became two persons (Adam and Eve), which were to become one flesh.

(6) Background: Man is historically situated, influenced, and developed. However, he is not historically, geographically, or genetically determined. Instead, man is covenantally determined—whether in Adam under the covenant of works or in Christ under the covenant of grace.

(7) Uniqueness: Man's uniqueness is irreducible to other aspects and factors of his being. It is a revelation of God in a unique way. Man's unique personality is continuing forever.

The Doctrine of Dominion—the Cultural Mandate

Man, made in the image of God, is called to exercise dominion over the creation, in which he is entrusted with *naming* things created (comprehending the essence) and *ruling* over them according to their nature. There are two realms of creation. Dominion in the natural world is by science (the study and naming of creation and the underlying laws by which things operate) and technology (applying those laws to exercise rule). Dominion in the human world is by the humanities (the study and naming of human nature) and the arts (an expression of the human condition and the rule of man over himself). Therefore, from the beginning, man engaged in the work of naming and ruling. The work of dominion will require all of mankind throughout all of history

---

27. *Mark 12:30–31.*

to accomplish. The work of dominion is *corporate* (achieved by individuals working in cooperation), *cumulative* (increases by transmission from generation to generation), and *communal* (it must be shared with others). Through the work of dominion, man comes to understand the nature of God by grasping the *Logos* revealed in the creation. Dominion is for God's purpose—the revelation of His glory. Dominion is for man's chief end—to glorify God by knowing Him and making Him known. Both God's and man's purpose coincide in the call to exercise dominion. The outcome of the completion of dominion is that the earth will be filled with the knowledge of God as the waters cover the sea. The sixth day is the last part of the creation account.

The Doctrine of the Goodness of Creation

The original creation was very good;[28] it was what God intended and what we should have expected, given the nature of God. There was no moral or natural evil. The creation is full of His glory.[29] We could and should have known the doctrine of the goodness of creation from clear general revelation by analyzing the very terms involved in the problem of evil. If God is all good and all powerful, why is there evil? The *could–would–must–did* argument shows that God created the world without evil:

> If God is all powerful, He *could* create a world without evil.
>
> If God is all good, He *would* create a world without evil.
>
> If God could and would, He *must* have created a world without evil.
>
> If God could, would, and must, then He *did* create a world without evil.

The Doctrine of the Good[30]

The good is the highest value, man's chief end,[31] eternal life,[32] the knowledge of God. The goal of dominion for man, as created in God's

---

28. *Genesis 1:4, 10, 12, 18, 21, 25, 31.*

29. *Isaiah 6:3.*

30. Gangadean, *Philosophical Foundation*, 208–211.

31. *The Shorter Catechism, Question 1.*

32. *John 17:3.*

image, is the knowledge of God. The good is the end in itself (vs. virtue and happiness).[33] The good is one, the source of unity in a person and among persons, and the same for all persons. The good is clear; it is grounded in human nature and therefore easily knowable. The good is perpetual; the same for all time since it is based on human nature. The purpose of dominion, its final outcome, extends from the Garden to the City of God (kingdom and culture) until the earth is filled with the knowledge of the Lord as the waters cover the sea.[34]

The Doctrine of Hope and the Sabbath[35]

The Sabbath is original (instituted from the beginning) and permanent (entails work and rest). As God worked and rested, man, as the image of God, will likewise complete the work of dominion and rest. Hope is maintained through all judgments on moral evil, including the universal judgment in Noah's day. The Sabbath in redemption restores man to the purpose of creation versus setting it aside through an otherworldly view of the good. Observing the Sabbath is a continual and perpetual reminder of man's purpose and hope. The Sabbath is the single greatest, continuing affirmation of hope for mankind.

FALL: MAN CHOOSES THE WAY OF SIN AND DEATH

The Doctrine of the Covenant of Creation[36]

A covenant is a voluntary condescension on the part of God to bless man. The covenant of creation is an additional blessing to that of being created in the image of God and being called to exercise dominion over the creation.[37] The purpose of the covenant is to establish man in a permanent (positive) relationship with God through the representation of one man. Since man in himself is changeable, all his descendants will be represented through the act of one man, a covenant head, in

---

33. Gangadean, *Philosophical Foundation*, 171–174.

34. *Isaiah 11:9*.

35. Gangadean, *Philosophical Foundation*, 211–219.

36. Gangadean, "Paper No. 145: The Biblical Worldview (Part V)," in *The Logos Papers*, 733–739.

37. *Genesis 1:26–28 KJV.*

the first man, Adam. All of life and history flows from one source by covenant representation.

The scriptural reality of the covenant is communicated in the expression used for God in Genesis 2—*The* LORD *God* (Yahweh/Jehovah Elohim), the Covenant-Keeping God. The covenant is further affirmed in the centrality of the Garden, from which all else flows—history, water, and life, with the two trees being at the center of the Garden. The decision to eat from either of the trees will affect the rest of the earth: the choice between good and evil, life and death, and the knowledge of God as the good versus anything else as the good. The creation of man and woman culminates with the covenant of marriage. The covenant of marriage is a major theme throughout Scripture, culminating in the consummation of history in the marriage supper of the Lamb. The visible marriage between one man and one woman becomes a revelation of the invisible reality of a permanent covenant relationship between God and man.

Adam undergoes a period of probation followed by manifestation through testing. Adam is being tested to see if he will obey or not, just as the Second Adam (Christ) was later tested and obeyed (the temptation in the wilderness and throughout His ministry, until declaring: "It is finished").[38] The temptation becomes manifest in the two trees and what they represent. They are not in and of themselves the reality, but represent it. The tree of life represents the way of life, the good as the knowledge of God, as determined by God. The tree of the knowledge of good and evil represents the way of death rooted in autonomy—man determining good and evil for himself over and against God's created order. The outward visible response to the command concerning the trees reveals the inward spiritual condition of our first parents.

There are several errors to be avoided in understanding the covenant of creation. First, the denial that there is a covenant. The absence of the term "covenant" has been used to set aside the essential elements of the covenant present in Genesis 2. This misunderstanding and denial of the covenant of creation is rooted in the conflict between literalism (unless the explicit word is present, the concept is not there) and conceptualism (the concept is present, and therefore, the term can be used). Second, the identifying of two separate covenants with

---

38. *John 19:30.*

the two testaments (the Old Testament representing the covenant of works and the New Testament the covenant of grace). Third, the belief that there are many covenants, as in the case of dispensationalism, which postulates that there are seven or nine covenants. Whether two or many, the underlying assumption is that there is a discontinuity between the covenants. Fourth, all is covenant. If Adam had obeyed, everything would have been completed, history would have ended, the entire universe would have been destroyed, and God would have taken Adam to a new place (two-kingdom view).[39] In this view, the work of dominion is not relevant.

The denial of the covenant has systematic implications. If there is no covenant of works, then there is no representation, no imputation, and we cannot speak of representation in redemption. The curse is no longer understood as connected with the covenant of representation or the promise (the seed of the woman). Therefore, there is no covenant of grace (no Adam and no Christ). By contrast, the covenant affirms representation by a new head, who is to *undo* by vicarious atonement what Adam did and *do* what Adam failed to do (fill the earth with the knowledge of God). The doctrine of triple imputation follows from covenant representation.[40] (1) The sin of Adam is imputed to mankind. (2) The sin of the elect is imputed to Christ. (3) The righteousness of Christ is imputed to the elect.

The Doctrine of Temptation

A temptation is a trial of faith and a test of understanding. It is original in Adam, and it is personal and continuing in all. Trials of faith reveal whether we are seeking God diligently or not, whether we believe the knowledge of God is the good or not, and whether we persevere in the way of life or in autonomy by determining good and evil for ourselves. Our faith and understanding are revealed through the temptation. Faith is the substance of things hoped for, the evidence of things not seen.[41] Faith is a shield that protects us, and it leads to trust. Trust is

---

39. David VanDrunen, *Living in God's Two Kingdoms: A Biblical Vision for Christianity and Culture* (Wheaton: Crossway Books, 2010).

40. Gangadean, *The Westminster Confession*, 149–151; Gangadean, *The Westminster Catechisms*, 197–198.

41. *Hebrews 11:1 KJV.*

the action that comes out of our understanding of the nature of God. We overcome temptations and trials by faith; faith is what pleases God.

The tempter was present in the Garden and is present today. He is our ancient foe described under four names. First, the devil, the dung hurler, the accuser of the brethren. Second, Satan comes as an angel of light, bringing deception. Third, he comes camouflaged as the serpent in cunning and craftiness. And fourth, he reveals himself boldly and fiercely as the great enormous red dragon. Part of his craftiness is to come concealed as a wolf in sheep's clothing,[42] and he also comes like a roaring lion seeking whom he may devour.[43] If we are not watchful and vigilant, we can be overcome. He is a liar and the father of lies; it was so from the beginning.[44] He is not the cause of sin but the occasion. He makes sin manifest.

The temptation itself is an attack against the Word of God in all its forms.[45] Here, it is against the Word of God spoken: "Did God really say, 'You must not eat from any tree in the garden'?" (Gen. 3:1b). An argument is presented and supported by a process of reasoning. To identify the self-contradictory nature of the statement, one must engage in reasoning and analysis. The temptation is aimed at challenging the character of God by accusing Him of limiting human potential in withholding access to wisdom. The argument is as follows:

Conclusion: "You will not surely die" (Gen. 3:4a).

Premise: "For God knows that when you eat of it your eyes will be opened, and you will be like God, knowing good and evil" (Gen 3:5).

The particular claim is that we will be like God, knowing good and evil. How does God know good and evil? God does not discover good and evil; He determines it by creation. The good for a being is according to the nature of that being. Man knows good and evil by discovery, not by creation. Only an infinite being can create—this is self-evident. Man is confined to manipulating substances that already exist. Being like God entails being infinite, eternal, and unchangeable, which we

---

42. *Matthew 7:15.*

43. *1 Peter 5:8.*

44. *John 8:44.*

45. Gangadean, "Paper No. 30: The Word of God," in *The Logos Papers*, 179–180.

clearly are not. The most basic truth about God is not kept in mind: His eternality over and against our temporality. The argument appeals to the deep needs of our nature—truth/wisdom (you will be like God, knowing good and evil),[46] beauty (pleasing to the eye), and goodness (good for food).[47] The decision to eat marks the pursuit of the way of death without God and ultimately placing ourselves above God.

The Doctrine of Sin from General Revelation, Special Revelation, and Historic Christianity

Sin, defined from general revelation, is an act contrary to one's nature. Sin is to neglect (by not seeking), avoid (by self-deception), resist (by self-justification), and deny (hardening oneself by denying our nature as rational beings) reason in the face of what is clear. The failure to see what is objectively clear is inexcusable. We are rational, made in the image of God, with the freedom to use reason to see what is clear. Reason, as the laws of thought, is most basic; it is a test for meaning, and it is self-attesting—it cannot be questioned but makes questioning possible.[48] The good for man as a rational being is the knowledge of God through the work of dominion (naming and ruling over the creation).[49]

Sin, as defined from special revelation, is autonomy. In autonomy, man puts himself in the place of God to determine good and evil. Man acts upon what pleases him, the love of the world, motivated by the lust of the eyes, the lust of the flesh, and the pride of life.[50] Man does what is right in his own eyes and he holds happiness or virtue as the good in place of the knowledge of God. Man puts self-love above the love of God.

Sin is expressed in not glorifying God as God;[51] all have sinned and come short of the glory of God.[52] In sin, man fails to know and glorify God. Coming to know the glory of God entails that God will enable us to glorify Him, in all that by which He makes Himself known, in

---

46. *Genesis 3:5.*

47. *Genesis 3:6.*

48. Gangadean, *Philosophical Foundation*, 10–15.

49. Gangadean, *Philosophical Foundation*, 207–219.

50. *1 John 2:16 KJV.*

51. *Romans 1:21.*

52. *Romans 3:23.*

all His works of creation and providence.[53] Glorifying God involves knowing God and making God known. The knowledge of God is attained through the work of dominion.[54] The earth shall be filled with the knowledge of God.[55]

The universal condition of man in sin is that no one seeks, understands, or does what is right.[56] Unbelief is sin, and ignorance is culpable. The fool does not seek because he thinks he knows, and the simple does not think he needs to know. Not seeking (root sin) leads to not understanding, and both lead to not doing what is right (fruit sin). Fruit sin is the outward expression of root sin. Fruit sin accepts degrees of depravity; it progresses (senseless, faithless, heartless, ruthless).[57]

The law of God is comprehensive.[58] The Ten Commandments encompass all of life—all choices, stations, and relationships. We are to meditate on the law day and night. It must be applied to every area. Sin affects our understanding of sin—the darkening of the mind. This is known as the noetic effect.[59]

Sin, as defined from Historic Christianity, is any want of conformity unto, or transgression of, the law of God.[60] The law of God is to be understood doxologically (focused on the good as the knowledge of God). When the law is not understood doxologically, we err (e.g., legalism or antinomianism). Sin stands in contrast with the good. Rather than glorifying and enjoying God forever, sin is the failure to glorify God as God and worship Him accordingly.

The Doctrine of Death

There are two kinds of death: spiritual and physical. In Scripture, descriptions of death are found in: John 11:25–26—"Jesus said to her,

---

53. *SCQ. 1, 46, 101.*

54. Gangadean, *The Westminster Catechisms*, 321–325.

55. *Isaiah 11:9.*

56. *Romans 3:10–12.*

57. *Romans 1:21–32.*

58. Gangadean, *Philosophical Foundation*, 171–284; Gangadean, *History of Philosophy*, 61–69; Gangadean, *The Westminster Catechisms*, 227–267; Gangadean, *On Natural Revealed Theology*, 127–139, 166–178.

59. Gangadean, "Paper No. 103: The Noetic Effect of Sin," in *The Logos Papers*, 531–528.

60. *SCQ. 14.*

'I am the resurrection and the life. He who believes in me will live, even though he dies; and whoever lives and believes in me will never die. Do you believe this?'"; John 5:28–29—"Do not be amazed at this, for a time is coming when all who are in their graves will hear his voice and come out—those who have done good will rise to live, and those who have done evil will rise to be condemned"; Revelation 20:14—"The lake of fire is the second death"; Ephesians 2:1—"As for you, you were dead in your transgressions and sins." Death is assumed in the sacrament of baptism, which signifies regeneration (resurrection from spiritual death). Physical death is removed from all, believers and unbelievers, in the general resurrection. Spiritual death remains for the unbeliever forever.

The wages of sin is spiritual death, not physical death. There is a necessary and inherent connection between sin and death versus the popular view of hell as future and imposed. Physical death is a call back from spiritual death. Spiritual death, present in this life, is to be understood as meaninglessness, boredom, and guilt, increasing without end. Spiritual death is a state of being—that of meaninglessness—and out of it arises error and misunderstanding. With meaninglessness comes a lack of satisfaction. Enjoyment of the creation without the Creator does not satisfy or provide lasting satisfaction. Out of meaninglessness comes boredom, from boredom comes excess, and from excess comes guilt. Boredom is inherent in meaninglessness, and guilt is inherent in the excess of boredom.

The Scripture speaks of spiritual death in visible ways: outer darkness, unquenchable fire, burning without satisfaction; the worm that does not die as the torment of conscience in guilt; and the endlessness of this condition in the bottomless pit. There is an essential continuity between spiritual death now and into the future.

There are common errors in the misconceiving of hell: Hell as a physical place in the future; purgatory as payment of justice through natural evil; annihilation as the extinguishing of the soul; in the naturalist view, there is no afterlife; in reincarnation, there are many afterlives; in universalism, all are eventually saved. All of these are to be contrasted with the revelation of the glory of God in justice (spiritual death) and mercy (physical death).

There are implications that follow the denial of the connection between sin and death. (1) If there is no sin and death and instead, the connection is made between sin and hell, we will believe that in the day we eat, we will not surely die. (2) We will fear hell rather than fear God. Since sin brings the noetic effect, we will continue in ignorance and error. (3) Out of our misunderstanding, we will not see the need for Christ our Savior. (4) Inexcusability in light of clear general revelation will not be seen. (5) Sin and death will not be seen since no repentance of root sin will take place. (6) As a consequence, we will not go on to maturity, teach others, or have lasting fruit. If there is no repentance, there will be no cleansing. (7) If the connection between sin and death is not seen, we will not see the connection between justice and mercy as a deepening of the glory of God.

The Doctrine of Theodicy: If God Is All Good and All Powerful, Why Is There Evil?

God is sovereign and was pleased to permit evil, having purposed to order it to His own glory.[61] Evil serves the purpose of God in deepening His revelation, specifically of His divine justice and mercy.

Gratuitous evil is an instance of intense suffering that God could have prevented without thereby losing some greater good or permitting some evil equally bad or worse. Only the doxological focus provides an answer to the objection of gratuitous evil (Job, Lazarus, and the man born blind from birth). Job was brought to repentance of root sin[62] through the increase of the curse to bear a lasting witness for all time, to all the intelligent order, regarding our failure to know and acknowledge God as we should. Lazarus' death was permitted, "for God's glory so that God's Son may be glorified through it" (Jn. 11:4b). The man born blind from birth was not punished for his sin or his parents' sin.[63] The curse was brought on him "so that the work of God might be displayed in his life" (Jn. 9:3b).

Original creation was very good, without natural or moral evil. From the terms used in the problem of evil, we can know that the original creation was very good (could–would–must–did argument). The problem

---

61. *WCF. 6.1.*

62. *Job 42:3–6.*

63. *John 9:1–3.*

of evil is a natural question that should occur to all since all are affected by it, and therefore all should seek to answer it.

Natural evil is due to moral evil. Death entered the world through Adam. Physical death is the third, continuing, and final call back to make us stop and think. Its purpose is to restrain, recall from, and remove moral evil. There is a corporate dimension of evil in war, famine, and plague.

The gradual removal of evil allows all forms and degrees and combinations of evil to come to expression in world history and be overcome. This is entailed in the doctrine of fullness. Evil is removed gradually by a spiritual war that is age-long and agonizing, in which good overcomes evil. Evil serves to deepen the revelation. The whole earth is full of the glory of God.[64] And the earth shall be full of the knowledge of God as the waters cover the sea.[65] The fullness doctrine is carried out by Christ, who is to fill everything in every way.[66]

REDEMPTION: MAN IS CALLED BACK BY THE CURSE AND THE PROMISE

Redemption presupposes the Fall, and the Fall presupposes creation. Redemption is the purpose of God to restore man to righteousness and life from sin and death, yet in such a way that evil will serve to deepen the original divine purpose of self-revelation in the creation. Evil objectively reveals the nature of the creation and the nature of God in ways not otherwise disclosed apart from evil. Evil is allowed to come to full expression in human history, in every form and degree of conflict and admixture with the good. In this conflict, good gradually, fully, and finally overcomes evil. Man's original rule is enlarged to include rule over evil in himself and others.

Redemption begins with God's call to man to repentance. Although resisted at first, this call persists and deepens. When man responds to this call in repentance and faith, he is forgiven and justified by God in a way that frees him from guilt and self-justification. And man is restored to his divine purpose by a gradual process of sanctification in

---

64. *Isaiah 6:3.*

65. *Isaiah 11:9.*

66. *Ephesians 1:23.*

which he learns to overcome evil in himself and the world. In doing so, mankind comes to know God and to fill the earth with the knowledge of God as the waters cover the sea.

The First Call Back to Repentance: Shame

> When the woman saw that the fruit of the tree was good for food and pleasing to the eye, and also desirable for gaining wisdom, she took some and ate it. She also gave some to her husband, who was with her, and he ate it. Then the eyes of both of them were opened, and they realized they were naked; so they sewed fig leaves together and made coverings for themselves (Gen. 3:6–7).

The first call back begins immediately after eating the forbidden fruit. The concept is present, although the word "call back" is not used. The feeling of shame came in because of sin. Previously, they were naked and felt no shame.[67] Genesis 3:7 must be understood in light of Genesis 2:25. The call back comes from their conscience. Conscience is an inward moral sense in man, created by God, that judges the moral action of man according to the moral law written on the heart.[68] Conscience includes the notion of being blameworthy and deserving of punishment. The feeling of shame is an inward recognition by one's conscience that one has sinned, is blameworthy, and deserves to be cut off (punished) for one's sin.

The failure to repent leaves one with guilt objectively and shame subjectively. One cannot remain in the state of shame given its powerful feeling of unworthiness—one has to either repent or relieve the shame through self-deception. Man avoids the first call to repentance by seeking to avoid shame. Adam and Eve sought to avoid shame by covering their physical nakedness. They sowed leaves together to cover their physical nakedness, which is a reminder of their spiritual nakedness. Sowing the covering of leaves involved a deliberate effort, showing intentionality on their part. They failed to recognize that while physical nakedness can be covered, the covering itself cannot be covered. Only by an ongoing effort of precarious self-deception can the first call back

---

67. *Genesis 2:25.*

68. *Deuteronomy 30:11–14; Romans 2:14–15.*

through shame be, at best, tentatively and temporarily avoided. The feeling of shame will be recurrent and will lead to the second call back.

The Second Call Back to Repentance: Self-Examination

Any manifest presence or reminder of God and the standard of His Word is avoided by man in the state of sin and self-deception. Adam, in sin, heard God and feared (immediate feeling) and hid from His presence, revealing the noetic effect of a darkened mind—hiding from God, who is infinite in knowledge, is self-contradictory to the point of being absurd—this shows the precarious nature of self-deception. God calls to Adam: "Where are you?"[69] This question is the second call back. God, who is infinite in knowledge, knows where Adam is, physically and spiritually. God is calling Adam to self-examination and to recognize his alienation from God—which has led him to hide from God. This second call is external, going beyond the internal call of conscience; it is through another person (in this case, God Him-self); the call comes in the form of a question (vs. declarative) calling to spiritual self-examination.

Adam exhibited existential honesty by confessing the effect of his sin: "I was afraid . . . so I hid."[70] Nevertheless, this is not a confession of sin since repentance requires the acknowledgment of sin as such. When confronted with sin, "Have you eaten?",[71] in his state of sin and self-deception, with his autonomy and self-centeredness, man justifies himself by blaming others: "The woman you put here with me—she gave me some fruit from the tree, and I ate it."[72] The blaming of his wife is not only ungentlemanly of Adam, but it is much more, for he excuses himself by blaming God. Adam is insinuating that he would not have sinned if God had not created the woman. The woman, when confronted, blames the tempter: "The serpent deceived me, and I ate."[73] While it may be true that the craftiness of Satan deceived her, he is only the occasion and not the cause of believing the lie. Blaming Satan is not an adequate justification in light of clear general revelation.

---

69. *Genesis 3:9.*

70. *Genesis 3:10.*

71. *Genesis 3:11.*

72. *Genesis 3:12.*

73. *Genesis 3:13.*

Adam and Eve could and should have known that Satan's claim was incoherent, and therefore false. Human self-justification attempts to excuse what is inexcusable. Only God's justification can provide the righteousness that God requires of man by the covenant of creation. Added to the root sin of not seeking is the sin of self-deception, and now, the sin of self-justification. These three realities and their extent (going to the point of blaming God) are necessary to understand the third call to repentance—the curse and the promise.

The Third Call Back to Repentance: The Curse and the Promise

God does not leave man in the state of sin, self-deception, and self-justification. God calls man back a third time. The third call back presupposes the rejection of the first two call backs. The purpose of the first two call backs was not frustrated by man's response in self-deception and self-justification. The third call back is lasting and final; it is for all human beings, everywhere, at all times. All men live and die under the curse. No nation, no tribe, no tongue, no class—rich or poor, high or low, Jew or Gentile, believer or non-believer, past or present—not one person is exempt. There is no further call back after death, for it is the culmination of the curse.

The third call back consists of both the curse and the promise. The curse and the promise are given together (interwoven) and are not to be separated in thought or proclamation. The curse comes upon all of the creation and all mankind and affects the entire realm of man's dominion. It is not on nature (the ground, plants, animals, etc.) apart from its relation to man. The whole creation groans, waiting in earnest expectation for the appearance of the sons of God[74]—man turning back to God and the original purpose for which God created him. The Fall and redemption both affect the creation.

The curse comes upon all animals. It comes upon some animals more than others, changing their form (to the serpent: "You will crawl on your belly") and their food ("you will eat dust").[75] The curse comes most upon the serpent, the instrument used by the tempter (Satan—the Old Serpent, the Great Dragon, Lucifer, and the devil). It anticipates

---

74. *Romans 8:18–22.*

75. *Genesis 3:14.*

the humiliation and defeat of Satan in the figure of the serpent. Orig-inally, all animals had only green vegetation for food (the creation was very good).[76] After God imposed the curse, some animals became carnivores (devoured other animals for food)—their form was further changed with the change of food. The distinction between clean and unclean animals (those more affected by the curse) reminds man of the curse and man's fallen condition and is a call to stop and think. Later, in connection with this distinction, are the kosher laws, Leviti-cal cleansing, and contact with death, making one unclean—in all of these instances, God is teaching and reminding mankind of the reality of the Fall and the curse (as a call back).

In the promise, God will reverse man's alliance with Satan in believ-ing the lie. "I will put enmity between you [Satan] and the woman."[77] Satan had seduced the woman through a lie, promising enlightenment and fulfillment apart from God. God puts enmity by sovereignly re-storing man to the truth. The enmity arises from the conflict of truth and falsehood, resulting in a spiritual war between belief and unbelief, good and evil, and between the truth and the lie. The spiritual war cannot be fought with the weapons of physical war. "The weapons we fight with are not the weapons of the world. On the contrary, they have divine power to demolish strongholds. We demolish arguments and every pretension that sets itself up against the knowledge of God" (2 Cor. 10:4–5a). The war is being waged in every person (where the war begins), in every sphere of life, and at every level. Spiritual war is, in this sense, a total war.[78] The spiritual war is within a person and among persons, within a church and among churches, within a nation and among nations, and collectively, between the kingdom of God and the kingdom of darkness.

The spiritual war is age-long, between the seed of the woman (all descendants who believe the truth) and the seed of the serpent (all de-scendants who believe Satan's falsehood). The spiritual war is agoniz-ing. The conflict between truth and falsehood is asymmetric warfare. Truth can use only the light of reason; falsehood cannot use reason but resorts to non-rational means through lies, propaganda, and force. The

---

76. *Genesis 1:31.*

77. *Genesis 3:15.*

78. *Romans 7:7–25.*

cumulative failure to use reason to take false thoughts captive results in physical war. Ideologies (pretensions, sleight of hand, and the cunning and craftiness of men in their deceitful scheming) that support physical war should be exposed and demolished, especially in light of the principle of the clarity of general revelation. Only knowing and speaking the relevant truth at the basic level (foundational truths about God and man, and good and evil) can overcome falsehood on which all injustice is based, extending to false teachings and misconceptions of the name of God in idolatry.[79]

The outcome of this spiritual war, which is age-long and agonizing, is that good will overcome evil.[80] The Second Adam who is to come (the seed of the woman—Christ) will spiritually crush the head of the serpent (destroy Satan and his lies). Satan will strike his heel (inflict physical harm). The one who is to come is in the place of Adam (according to the covenant of creation); He will *do* what Adam failed to do: He will hold to the truth and rule to make God known.

The curse brings sorrow in childbearing. Children are born under the Fall in the covenant of creation. They must face the conflict of good and evil. Their hearts must be turned to the truth by God. The conflict of good and evil is manifest between parents and children and between children in the conflict between belief and unbelief. The sorrow in childbearing does not refer primarily to physical pain during childbirth, but the whole process of bringing children into the world in the context of the Fall, the curse, and the promise. The paradigm of sorrow in childbearing manifests in the first children born on earth. Cain did not take to heart Adam's instruction (how sin is dealt with—the need for sacrifice symbolized in the coats of skin), nor from Abel's example, nor from God (who directly called him back to do what is right to be accepted). In unbelief, he was angry and envious that Abel was accepted and he was not. Cain thought he was wronged and slew his brother.[81] We can be certain this brought sorrow to the hearts of his parents.

The conflict between belief and unbelief is the source of all strife on earth. It was and is the source of all violence, murder, and war. It

---

79. Gangadean, *Philosophical Foundation*, 185–198.

80. *Genesis 3:15.*

81. *Genesis 4:8.*

begins in each person and each household: "Do not suppose that I have come to bring peace to the earth. I did not come to bring peace, but a sword . . . a man's enemies will be the members of his own household" (Matt. 10:34, 36). Christ's pronouncement should be understood in light of: "I will put enmity between you and the woman" (Gen. 3:15a). "Consider him who endured such opposition from sinful men, so that you will not grow weary and lose heart. In your struggle against sin, you have not yet resisted to the point of shedding your blood" (Heb. 12:3–4). The promise of redemption (not just the curse bringing sorrow) is also extended to one's household (children) in the signs of the covenant—circumcision in the Old Testament and baptism in the New Testament. The promise of redemption restores the relationship between husband and wife. Having sinned and turned away from God, Adam became a delinquent husband in not leading his wife by the Word of God—one of his first responsibilities as spiritual head. His desire was for his wife without God, and as a result, she ruled over him; he listened to her voice instead of the Word of God.[82] In redemption, Eve's desire will be for her husband, and he will rule over her by the Word of God.[83]

The curse comes on the ground and man. Thorns and thistles reduce the fertility of the earth. "Cursed is the ground because of you . . . By the sweat of your brow you will eat your food."[84] There is stress connected with work in every way. The ground is cursed for man's sake as a call to repentance. Man is to return to the ground by death: "Dust you are, and to dust you shall return."[85] The fullest dimension of the curse is in connection with physical death. Man returns to the ground, if not in some other way, certainly by old age, sickness, and death. As sin increases, the curse increases from toil and strife, and old age, sickness, and death to war, famine, and plague, repeated throughout human history. For example: the curse was increased upon Cain; the life span was greatly reduced after the Flood (900+ to 70); and strife was increased after Babel. The curse is corporate for all men and comes individually on men, groups, and nations.

---

82. *Genesis 3:17.*

83. *Genesis 3:16.*

84. *Genesis 3:17–19.*

85. *Genesis 3:19.*

The curse is not punishment but God's third and final call back to repentance. The curse ends with physical death, a reminder of spiritual death. As natural evil, the curse serves to *restrain, recall from*, and *remove* moral evil. The curse is God's call to stop and think.

Justification: Through Vicarious Atonement

Adam responds to the third call back (the curse and promise) in repentance. Adam shows his repentance to the third call back by naming his wife Eve because she would become the mother of all the living.[86] His naming her Eve shows he decided to obey God by having children in the context of dominion, under the curse of toil and strife, and old age, sickness, and death upon him and his descendants, with hope in the promise that the seed of the woman will crush the head of the serpent. If he had no hope in the promise, his children could rise and curse him for what he brought into the world.

God put enmity between Adam and Eve and the Serpent by turning their hearts from unbelief, self-deception, and self-justification (sin compounded to the third degree) to belief and faith in God's promise. The first step in the order of salvation (the *ordo salutis*),[87] commencing with Adam's repentance, is God's sovereignly changing the human heart by a rebirth, a regeneration, a spiritual resurrection. Regeneration is signified later in redemptive history by circumcision, in which one is to circumcise the heart and not the flesh merely,[88] and baptism, which speaks about a new birth raised to newness of life in Christ.

Man is restored from spiritual death to spiritual life. This life is the life of the *Logos,* which is in all men as light (reason).[89] In sin, man had neglected, avoided, resisted, or denied reason in the face of what is clear about God. The denial of his nature brought spiritual death. By restoring the life/light of reason, man comes to see what is clear about God. The restoration to life brought awareness and conviction

---

86. *Genesis 3:20.*

87. Gangadean, *The Westminster Catechisms,* 191–203; Gangadean, *The Westminster Confession,* 143–180.

88. *Romans 2:25–29.*

89. *John 1:4.*

of death (meaninglessness) due to sin (not seeking, not understanding, resulting in not doing what is right).[90]

God justifies man by covering them with coats of skin. Although the Scripture does not mention justification explicitly, it does mention an act of God. "The Lord God made garments of skin for Adam and his wife and clothed them" (Gen 3:21). In this act, God clothed them with the righteousness of another who has died, representing them in their place as an atonement for sin. In the place of the covering of leaves (to cover guilt and shame signified by nakedness), God provides coats of skin. The coat of skin signifies that the death of another covers their sin/unrighteousness/guilt. Wearing the coats of skin daily was a perpetual reminder of being covered through the death of another. Vicarious atonement (payment for sin by another in one's place) is possible and required by the covenant of creation (fulfilled by the covenant of grace). By vicarious atonement, another in the place of Adam must *undo* what Adam did. There is only one covenant head in the place of Adam. The one who undoes what Adam did is the same as the one who does what Adam failed to do. The one who dies to atone is the one who lives to rule over all. Only by vicarious atonement, under the covenant of creation, does mercy satisfy the requirement of divine justice. God is infinitely, eternally, and unchangeably just and merciful. God cannot deny His justice; mercy cannot set aside justice, as in the case of Islam, where no payment for divine justice is provided.[91]

The covenant of grace in Christ satisfies the demands of the covenant of works in Adam. By representation, there is a three-fold imputation in the covenant of creation: (1) The guilt of Adam's sin is imputed to all he represents (as would his righteousness have been had he obeyed—both are present in the original covenant arrangement). (2) The sin of all in Christ is imputed to Christ as covenant head in the place of Adam. (3) Christ is the Lamb of God, who takes away the sin of the world.[92] In the place of Adam, Christ's righteousness is imputed to all who are united to Him by faith. This act of imputation must be understood in the context of, not apart from, the first two. Salvation is

---

90. *Romans 3:10–11.*

91. Gangadean, "Paper No. 91: Christianity and Islam," in *The Logos Papers*, 479–484; Gangadean, *Philosophical Foundation*, 191–192.

92. *John 1:29.*

by grace alone, through faith alone, in Christ alone, as revealed in the Scriptures alone, and all for the glory of God alone.

Sanctification: Knowledge Through Suffering

Those whom God justifies, He also sanctifies. The goal of sanctification is holiness, which is a devotion to the good as the glory of God. The connection between the holiness and the glory of God is seen in the angelic beings who cry, "Holy, holy, holy is the Lord Almighty; the whole earth is full of his glory" (Is. 6:3). Holiness is manifest in beauty that lasts. "O worship the Lord in the beauty of holiness."[93] As lasting beauty, holiness is true beauty, compared with all else that only appears to be or is a sign of the reality.

Sanctification is a process of cleansing, which begins upon the forgiveness of sin (not before, and not apart from it). "If we confess our sins, he is faithful and just and will forgive us our sins and purify us from all unrighteousness."[94] Sanctification continues throughout one's lifetime and throughout history. It does not continue after death (in some kind of purgatory) or after the end of history (after the Last Judgment). Sanctification ends individually and corporately in the state of glory, completing the process of salvation. Justification is distinct from sanctification but is inseparable from sanctification. Justification is by the imputation of Christ's righteousness in the context of the covenant of creation, which established representation, and therefore imputation. It is not a non-cognitive infusion of righteousness that makes one actually righteous. In justification, one is not yet cleansed of sin; one is accounted as righteous based on the righteousness of Christ, which covers one's sin.

Sanctification is a transformation of the believer through coming to know the truth: "but be transformed by the renewing of your mind."[95] It is a cognitive process involving the understanding in coming to know the truth, which has the effect of transformation (which is not all at once but is progressive over time and throughout history). "Then you

---

93. *Psalm 96:9 KJV.*

94. *1 John 1:9.*

95. *Romans 12:2.*

will know the truth, and the truth will set you free."[96] Most explicitly, Jesus prays in His High Priestly Prayer: "Sanctify them by the truth; your word [*Logos*] is truth."[97] The *Logos* is the truth of the Word of God in its fullness, from foundation to its full expression in the Kingdom/City of God.

The expulsion is the major event in the history of redemption showing the distinction between justification and sanctification, how they are inseparable from one another, and the process of sanctification in which all men (who are justified) share and cannot avoid. Having been justified, symbolized by God's provision of the coats of skin (one's nakedness is covered through the death/sacrifice of another), man is to be sanctified through suffering.

Man is expelled from the Garden to live under the curse, which will lead to death. He is kept from access to the tree of life lest he "eat, and live forever."[98] He is driven from the Garden; there is a reluctance/resistance to suffering (living under the curse) even though he accepted this. There is a guard set against any return: Cherubim and a flaming sword are placed "to guard the way to the tree of life."[99] The suffering of the curse (toil and strife, and old age, sickness, and death) is unavoidable in this life; all must die. Suffering through trials is for maturity and faith, to overcome ignorance and error in foundational beliefs arising from personality and background (part of which is due to being fallen in Adam), and manifested in mood changes (seeking or not seeking; belief mixed with unbelief—e.g., Peter is one moment walking on water and the next he is sinking;[100] one moment he affirms who Christ is and the next, he denies his atoning death).[101]

Foundation, being brought about by sanctification, is necessary for maturity in faith.[102] It brings believers into fruitfulness, unity of the faith, and the fullness of Christ.[103] As a result of sanctification, there

---

96. *John 8:32.*
97. *John 17:17.* Emphasis added.
98. *Genesis 3:22.*
99. *Genesis 3:24.*
100. *Matthew 14:22–33.*
101. *Matthew 16:21–28.*
102. *Hebrews 6:1.*
103. *Ephesians 4.*

is not only growth at a personal level but there will be unity in the Church at a corporate level. All divisions in understanding (of foundational beliefs, of who God is, and the truth of Scripture) will be identified, addressed, removed, and overcome. Foundation is necessary to accomplish the work of dominion. "Be fruitful and increase in number; fill the earth and subdue it"[104] which now includes making disciples of all nations.[105] Man, through the process of dominion, is to attain an understanding of the fullness of the revelation that God has given of Himself in creation and history. The work of dominion ends with rest (the Sabbath) when the earth is filled with the knowledge of God as the waters cover the sea.[106]

—THE LOGOS FOUNDATION
EDITORIAL BOARD
Phoenix, Arizona
February 2024

---

104. *Genesis 1:28.*

105. *Matthew 28:18–20.*

106. *Isaiah 11:9.*

PART I

THE BIBLICAL WORLDVIEW
2003 SERMON SERIES

1

———

WHAT IS FAITH?

On the Nature of Faith, Examples, and Trials

Hebrews 11:1–10

¹Now faith is being sure of what we hope for and certain of what we do not see. ²This is what the ancients were commended for. ³By faith we understand that the universe was formed at God's command, so that what is seen was not made out of what was visible. ⁴By faith Abel offered God a better sacrifice than Cain did. By faith he was commended as a righteous man, when God spoke well of his offerings. And by faith he still speaks, even though he is dead. ⁵By faith Enoch was taken from this life, so that he did not experience death; he could not be found, because God had taken him away. For before he was taken, he was commended as one who pleased God. ⁶And without faith it is impossible to please God, because anyone who comes to him must believe that he exists and that he rewards those who earnestly seek him. ⁷By faith Noah, when warned about things not yet seen, in holy fear built an ark to save his family. By his faith he condemned the world and became heir of the righteousness that comes by faith. ⁸By faith Abraham, when called to go to a place he would later receive as his inheritance, obeyed and went, even though he did not know where he was going. ⁹By faith he made his home in the promised land like a stranger in a foreign country; he lived in tents, as did Isaac and Jacob, who were heirs with him of the same promise. ¹⁰For he was looking forward to the city with foundations, whose architect and builder is God.

WE ARE GOING TO EXAMINE THE TOPIC OF FAITH. Specifically, we will ask the question, *What is faith?* I have wanted to bring to your attention some of the basics in a fuller and more complete way rather than looking at isolated passages. We seek to have this before you, especially as it is summed up in a number of Scripture verses. One of the outcomes is that we will have some Scripture verses to memorize and understand in their proper context.

We want to talk about faith. What is faith? First, we will look at the nature of faith, focusing primarily on the first few verses from the Scripture reading on Hebrews 11. Second, examples of faith by prominent biblical characters. Third, the operations of faith in trials, how can we know whether or not we have faith, and to what extent do we have it?

ON THE NATURE OF FAITH

Keep in mind that we are sinners, and the evidence for this is that we suffer. When God made the world, He made it very good: there was no suffering.[1] Suffering in the world is evidence that there is sin, specifically, the sin of not seeking God, not understanding Him in light of what is clear,[2] and not doing what is right. This is how St. Paul sums it up: he said, "There is no one righteous, not even one; there is no one who understands, no one who seeks God" (Rom. 3:10b–11).

There is sin, and with sin comes death, and death is experienced as meaninglessness, boredom, and guilt. More specifically, it has this connection: that our sin has affected how we understand faith, or how we have emptied the word *faith* of meaning. Death—spiritual death—is present in our understanding of Scripture, and so we want to recover from that. The fact that we have suffering of various kinds indicates that there is sin in us that has affected our seeking and our understanding. We should understand sin is very deep, very pervasive, and that we are often quite insensitive to how deep and pervasive it is. We give a token acknowledgment of the reality of sin, but often, we have to go through a lot of suffering to come to a sense of its true reality.

---

1. God created the world good, as emphasized seven times in Genesis 1: It says, "it was good" (*Gen. 1:4, 10, 12, 18, 21, 25*), and the last time, "it was very good" (*Gen. 1:31*). For a fuller explanation on the goodness of creation, see: Gangadean, *The Westminster Confession*, 75–79.

2. Gangadean, "Paper No. 35: The Clarity of General Revelation (Applied to GR-SR-HC)," 195–200; "Paper No. 41: What Is Clear About God: The Clarity of General Revelation," 225–229; "Paper No. 112: Why General Revelation Is Basic in the Christian Worldview," in *The Logos Papers*, 583–585; Gangadean, The Westminster Catechisms, 111–112, 321–325.2

What this means is that, in the Church, we can expect to see a great deal of misunderstanding of the meaning of *faith*, particularly at the popular level. The Church has emptied *faith* of its biblical content and given it another content that, upon examination, lacks meaning. One of the reasons we get away with letting the meaning of *faith* slip is our lack of critical reflection. In light of this discussion on faith (a fundamental concept), and the reality of sin, one should expect the necessity for corrections.

We have the history of the work of the pastor-teachers to help us, but that history is often ignored. We will look especially at Scripture, general revelation, and Historic Christianity (the work of the pastor-teachers summed up in the creeds), and we will look at our own experience and the experience of others to bring this into focus.

FIRST POINT ON THE NATURE OF FAITH:
Faith Is About What Is Not Seen, About the Future, and About Hope (The Good)

First of all, what is faith? We need to understand that we need to correct common misconceptions, half-truths, and half-falsehoods—sometimes more than half of it is falsehood and less of the truth. **"Now faith is being sure of what we hope for and certain of what we do not see"** (v. 1). Here is the first point: faith is about what is not seen. This is the general topic of faith, and we will be more specific about this as we go. Over and against the seen, faith has to do with what is not seen.

More specifically, faith is about the future because it says here, **"being sure of what we *hope* for"** (v. 1),[3] and hope is in the future. That word *hope* is very rich. **"What we hope for"** sums up all the goodness that we are longing for and hope to have in the future. Faith is particularly connected with the unseen and the future. If we understand **"what we hope for,"** we will see more of the true nature of faith. If we have a faulty hope, a misguided hope, a distorted hope, a truncated hope—and there is a lot of that—then we may think we have faith, but it is not biblical faith. **"Faith is being sure of what we hope for and certain of what we do not see"** (v. 1). Faith is about the future, about the unseen, and the question is: How do we come to know what is unseen

---

3. Emphasis added.

and invisible? People characteristically ask, 'What about the future, in terms of the afterlife, and what about the invisible, in terms of the soul? How do we know that the soul exists? Can we know that? Can we know that there is a future afterlife?' Many people would answer, saying, 'No, you cannot know that; rather, you believe it, and that is what faith is.' Have you heard something like this? That is not what is being said here.

SECOND POINT ON THE NATURE OF FAITH:
Faith Has Support and Evidence

To clarify the meaning of what is being said here about faith, let us get back to the King James: this makes it a little bit plainer, and we can also go to the Greek, which makes it plainer still. "Faith is the substance of things hoped for" (v. 1). It is the "substance" of things hoped for; it is the "evidence," or the proof, "of things not seen." "What we hope for" is about the future and what is invisible, but this is not what you would call, 'blind faith,' and in fact, it is the very opposite of *blind* faith because it speaks about having the "substance" of it and the proof of it. The word for substance is the *hupostasis* or *hypóstasis* (ὑπόστασις). It was translated *substance* because that is how the term has been used historically. We can understand what is meant by way of example: You see this podium before you, and you see the color, and that is evident to the senses, and you see the size, and you can feel the hardness of it, and you might even sniff it and taste it (if you are so minded to), and these are all things that are visible, sensed—visible to the senses. Those are the surface qualities from the senses, but the substance is that which underlies these qualities. Let us say you take away the color, and you take away the hardness, and you take away the size, and the odor, etc., and what you are left with is the substance.

THIRD POINT ON THE NATURE OF FAITH:
Faith Understands the Invisible

Substance, in that sense, is invisible. But it has another connotation: These qualities exist in the substance and could not exist apart from it. We do not have *brown* just floating in pure space. The qualities *inhere* in the substance; the substance supports the qualities, and that is the idea that we are getting at here.[4] **"Faith is the substance"** (v. 1 KJV), the support of that which is yet to come. In that first word—**"Faith is the substance of things hoped for"** (v. 1 KJV)—you have the notion of the underlying support, the invisible-to-the-eye support, but not invisible in terms of the intelligence. Faith is in that which we cannot see, and many people say, 'faith is blind' and 'just take it by faith,' but that is only half of the truth, and some have had that only and not gone on to the other part, which says that it is **"the substance of things hoped for"** (v. 1 KJV)—it is the proof—of what is not seen. God is invisible. Faith in God involves having the proof, the evidence, and the support for that.

Now, perhaps you can begin to see what I was getting at when I said, sin affects our understanding of what faith is. Many people would contrast faith with proof. It is right to contrast faith with the senses— what is evident to the bodily senses—but it is not right to contrast faith with proof, which comes to us through the mind, through reason. By reason, we can grasp what is invisible. Biblical faith involves having proof for the existence of God. If we are short on proof, then our faith needs to grow. Or if we are 'kind of, sort of, somewhat there in the neighborhood,' then we need to do more than that, we need to do better than that.

As we come to ask the question: How do you know if you have faith? Our faith will be tested; there will be trials of faith. How do we know what we hope for? What is your view of the good, of eternal life? Is it heaven, or is it the knowledge of God—the knowledge of God filling the earth? What is eternal life: What do you hope for? At the popular level, it is mostly 'die and go to be with God in heaven.' Jesus said, "Now this is eternal life: that they may know you, the only true God, and Jesus Christ, whom you have sent" (Jn. 17:3). Isaiah said, "the whole earth is full of his glory" (Is. 6:3b) and our task is to glorify God by filling the earth with His glory. What do we hope for? Do we have proof and support for this? Biblical faith is often emptied of meaning and turned inside out because of sin. Sin reverses the order of things. Yet, here in Scripture, we have this description of faith: **"the**

---

4. Gangadean, *History of Philosophy*, 38.

substance of things hoped for, the evidence"—the proof—"of things not seen" (v. 1 KJV).

Faith is about the future. It is about what is not seen. It is about hope, or another way to say it: All you hope for can be summed up as *the good*. I think that is fair to say, and you can certainly raise questions after the service. Faith has support and evidence; this would be a good verse to memorize. **"Now faith is the substance of things hoped for, the evidence of things not seen"** (v. 1 KJV).

The verse goes on: **"This is what the ancients were commended for"** (v. 2). It is the word *presbuteros* (πρεσβύτερος): the ancients. It is **"the ancients"** used in a more general sense. It is not just *elders*, although some have translated it that way. The ancients lived in the past, and we see their history and names mentioned here, such as Abel, Enoch, Noah, Abraham, etc. Please notice, **"this is what [they] were commended for"** (v. 2); this is said several times in this chapter—at least four times explicitly it speaks about being commended for their faith.[5] **"Without faith it is impossible to *please* God"** (v. 6),[6] and if you have faith, it is pleasing to God; it is commended by God. Here, it says, generally, **"This is what the ancients were commended for"** (v. 2). There is a high premium placed on faith, understood as it is stated: with support and evidence—not with sight, but with the understanding. This is reinforced in verse 3. It says, **"By faith we understand that the universe was formed at God's command, so that what is seen was not made out of what was visible."** Here is the visible/invisible theme again. God is invisible, the physical universe is visible, and it is by faith that we *understand*. Notice that it speaks of understanding which involves the use of the mind. We *understand* that what is visible came from what is not visible, that is, by the Word of God. By faith we *understand* that the universe was formed at God's command—the invisible command of God's Word spoken. God said, "Let there be light" (Gen. 1:3). God brought the substance into existence and then formed it: **"was formed at God's command, so that what is seen was not made out of what was visible"** (v. 3b).

Faith involves understanding. We know from general revelation that it does not make sense to say, 'I believe in blup.' Do you believe in

5. *Hebrews 11:2, 4–5, 39.*

6. Emphasis added.

blup? 'Oh yes, I believe in blup.' Do you believe grod is love? What do you mean by God? What do you mean by the basic attributes of God? Can you believe in something, some word, that has no meaning? Can you believe something that is without meaning, that is meaningless? Understanding is particularly directed toward the meaning of things; when you understand, you understand the meaning. When you have faith, you have understanding; again, this involves the intellect, the mind, and the content of faith. Faith is blind to the eyes, visibly, but not blind to the mind. **"By faith we understand that the universe was formed at God's command"** (v. 3a).

St. Paul said in Romans 1:20, "For since the creation of the world God's invisible qualities—his eternal power and divine nature—have been clearly seen, being understood from what has been made, so that men are without excuse." It is the *invisible* qualities that are clearly seen, being *understood* by the things that are made, so that men are without excuse. Notice again, *visible*—from the things that are made—and the word *understanding*, so that men are without excuse. Human beings are held accountable for the clarity of general revelation. We cannot excuse it in the way that many do who fail to see general revelation, saying, 'Well, God knows the faith of every person, and He will accept us.' The Scripture says that it is clear that man is without excuse for not seeing. We cannot make sense of good and evil and human suffering apart from understanding clarity and God's call back. Notice again, spiritual death comes in, and suffering becomes meaningless apart from understanding sin as failing to see what is clear. It may not happen right away, in terms of tradition holding on, but over several generations, words become emptied of meaning. This is where a good part of the Church is today.

Faith has understanding. **"By faith we understand"** (v. 3). Faith involves understanding; it is inseparable from understanding. As truth is inseparable from meaning, so faith is inseparable from understanding.[7]

---

7. Gangadean, *Philosophical Foundation*, 32–45, 121–127; Gangadean, *History of Philosophy*, 3–12, 163–167; Gangadean, "Paper No. 21: Faith and Reason in Christianity," 135–138; "Paper No. 28: Prepare the Way of the Lord: By Faith We Understand," 171–173; "Paper No. 98: Faith and the Word of God: The Object of Faith," 511–514; "Paper No. 128: Abraham's Faith: The Elements of Abraham's Faith in Offering up Isaac," 665–666; "Paper No. 129: Faith and Reason in the Life of Abraham," in *The Logos Papers*, 667–669.

Faith is to reason as truth is to meaning.[8] One cannot believe something to be true while having no understanding of it.

How do we understand? We would say that we understand by reason, and that is what we find in Scripture: that animals are lacking in understanding, and reasoning men are crowned with the light and honor connected with the position of ruling the creation;[9] so it is that which separates us from the animals. God wants us to have faith, to have understanding. This concludes the third point on the nature of faith, that is, faith understands the relation between the visible and the invisible.

FOURTH POINT ON THE NATURE OF FAITH:
Faith Pleases God

Faith pleases God. This is stated in verse 2: "**This is what the ancients were commended for.**" It is stated also in verse 5: "**For before he was taken, [Enoch] was commended as one who pleased God.**" Enoch pleased God by his faith. In verse 6: "**without faith it is impossible to please God.**" Having faith is pleasing to God; it is commendable. Verse 39 sums it up: "These were all commended for their faith, yet none of them received what had been promised." Notice, it is a future hope that is still there, and they had not yet received it, but they were waiting for it. As we go through the list of examples of the faithful, we see that their faith is defined in terms of their future hope: When Abraham leaves Ur of the Chaldees, when Moses leaves Egypt, when Joseph speaks about his bones being carried out and buried—they were looking forward to the hope. We will see this specified further.

Faith is necessary to please God, and you might say it is sufficient to please God; faith pleases God, God wants us to have this. Matthew 13:19a says, "When anyone hears the message about the kingdom and does not understand it, the evil one comes and snatches away what was sown in his heart." This parable is speaking about hearing without understanding—lack of faith—and understanding is being called for and commended by Jesus in this parable. Notice in verse 23: "But the one who received the seed that fell on good soil is the man who hears

---

8. Gangadean, "Paper No. 21: Faith and Reason in Christianity," in *The Logos Papers*, 135–138.

9. *Psalm 8:5.*

the word and understands it." Contrast? Understanding. It is faith that understands—that is what Jesus brings out in this parable.

After the resurrection, Jesus upbraided His disciples. "He said to them, 'How foolish you are, and how slow of heart to believe all that the prophets have spoken! Did not the Christ have to suffer these things and then enter his glory?' And beginning with Moses and all the Prophets, he explained to them what was said in all the Scriptures concerning himself" (Lk. 24:25–27). Christ wants them to understand the Scripture by knowing the explanation from Scripture. Again, in Luke 24:45–48: "Then he opened their minds so they could understand the Scriptures. He told them, 'This is what is written: The Christ will suffer and rise from the dead on the third day, and repentance and forgiveness of sins will be preached in his name to all nations, beginning at Jerusalem. You are witnesses of these things.'" The Christ would suffer and rise from the dead on the third day. The whole of Judaism has bypassed this reality that Christ must suffer, and in doing so, they bypass the reality of the holiness of God, the need for atonement, and that only the Messiah can atone. The ancient people of God have for centuries, as a whole, bypassed this truth. So has Islam, not to speak of others who do not see the difference between the creation and the Creator, such as Hinduism and Buddhism. It is a lack of understanding, a lack of faith. Faith is pleasing to God; He wants us to have this; He works in our lives to bring this about.

FIFTH POINT ON THE NATURE OF FAITH:
Understanding of Faith Is From Diligently Seeking

The understanding that faith requires is acquired from diligently seeking God. "[God] is a rewarder of them that diligently seek Him" (v. 6 KJV). There is no finding of this reward in God apart from diligently seeking. We want to make the connection, not just with seeking, but between seeking and understanding, and between understanding and faith. We have to keep these three together. We cannot have understanding without diligently seeking, but if we diligently seek, we will see it—because it is clear—and we will have understanding, and that understanding is our faith. When we think of faith, we know that faith comes by hearing the Word of God in connection with diligently seeking the Word, and using the means to understand.[10]

SIXTH POINT ON THE NATURE OF FAITH:
The Beginning (Basic) Content of Faith Is About the Existence of God and Our Hope

The sixth point we will make—and there are more points to be made, but at least these will be sufficient for now—is that the beginning, or basic content of faith, is about what? It is not about Jesus Christ. It is not about the Scripture. It is about the existence of God. **"He that cometh to God must believe that he is"** (v. 6 KJV). Secondly, it is about the nature of God and the good: **"That he is a rewarder of them that diligently seek him"** (v. 6 KJV). This we must believe with understanding, with proof, because as stated earlier, this faith that is commended by Scripture is faith with understanding, with proof.

I would like to read a brief passage from the book, *What Is Faith?* by J. Gresham Machen.

> The truth is that in the Epistle to the Hebrews, as well as in the rest of the Bible, we are living in a world of thought that is diametrically opposed to the anti-intellectualism of the present day. According to the Bible, certain things are known about God, and without these things, there can be no faith. To the pragmatist skepticism of the modern religious world, therefore, the Bible is sharply opposed.[11]

This is what I was trying to get at in the beginning of the message: Sin affects our understanding, empties it of meaning, and fills it with new meaning—which makes it possible to claim to have faith when we are quite far from it. "To the pragmatist skepticism of the modern religious world"—Machen is speaking about the Christian religious world—"the Bible is sharply opposed." Machen goes on: "Against the passionate anti-intellectualism of a large part of the modern Church, it maintains the primacy of the intellect. It teaches plainly that God

---

10. Gangadean, *The Westminster Confession,* xvii-xix, 32–37, 88–90, 165–166, 201–204.

11. J. Gresham Machen, *What Is Faith?* (Grand Rapids: Wm. B. Eerdmans Publishing Company, 1946), 51.

has given to man a faculty of reason, which is capable of apprehending truth, even truth about God."[12]

Machen left Princeton Seminary when it went liberal, and he founded Westminster Seminary. He is said to be the father of *fundamentalism*, understood in a positive sense, as against the anti-intellectual form of fundamentalism. There is more that can be read from Machen, but just to touch base, he is talking about this from Hebrews. Machen is saying that faith has content. It is not just faith in a person, but it is belief about the person, about the nature of the person. By faith, we believe *that* He is and *that* He is the rewarder of those who diligently seek Him; it is first doctrine, and life flows out of this.

Faith has doctrinal content, and it is about the existence of God and our hope. Now think about our hope in terms of eschatology. There are the premillennial, amillennial, and postmillennial views, and the larger view that many have held, that 'you die, you go to heaven, and you discover the fullness of blessing.' Whether you take it in the medieval Church, in the form of the beatific vision—directly seeing God in heaven—or you take it in some other form of seeing Jesus, it is not the same as the earth being filled with the knowledge of His glory.[13] What do we hope for? What was the content of Abraham's faith? Why did he leave Ur? How is it that Abraham could endure? Because he had faith in the existence of God and the nature of God. Then, after that, if you believe in the existence and the nature of God, inevitably, if you believe with understanding, you will be moved to seek forgiveness of sin, and you will find this only in Jesus Christ. Faith in God—true faith in God, with understanding (which is a kind of redundancy)—leads to faith in Jesus Christ. In the first section, the author of Hebrews[14] speaks about faith in God, and then he speaks about faith in Christ coming out of this, and this is the order in which it is put in Hebrews.

---

12. Machen, *What Is Faith?*, 51.

13. Gangadean, *On Natural and Revealed Theology*, 9–32; Gangadean, *The Westminster Catechisms*, 321–325; Gangadean, "Paper No. 106: The Good and Heaven: The Good Is Not the Beatific Vision," 547–556; "Paper No. 115: Doxological Christianity," 595–596; "Paper No. 116: The Knowledge of God vs. The Hope of Heaven," 597–598; "Paper No. 117: Knowing and Making God Known," in *The Logos Papers*, 599–601.

14. The authorship of the Book of Hebrews will be addressed in a separate sermon series and commentary. Pastor Gangadean held the view expressed by John Owen in his *Commentary on Hebrews* regarding Paul's authorship of Hebrews.

In conclusion, faith is about what is not seen, the future, and hope connected with the good. Faith has support and evidence. It involves understanding the invisible through the visible. Faith is what pleases God. Understanding is through diligently seeking, and it has specific content in terms of the existence of God and our hope.

ON THE EXAMPLES OF FAITH:
Showing the Nature of Faith

There are examples of faith given in this book. We should classify them to keep them more easily summarized.

Abel, Enoch, and Noah

There are three examples of faith before and up to the Flood. Abel connected with understanding the need for atonement through blood— "[he] **offered God a better sacrifice**" (v. 4a)—and that is over and against Cain. Then there is Enoch, who pleased God and was taken. He had pleased God by faith. He was taken alive from this earth; he did not see death. Notice the kind of contrast there is in faith: The faith that Enoch had, that pleased God, is called attention to, over and against the wickedness of the world. And then: "**By faith Noah, when warned about things not yet seen, in holy fear built an ark to save his family**" (v. 7a). Noah was looking ahead for the promise; he was not looking ahead to dying and going to heaven. At the end of this chapter, verse 39 says, "These were all commended for their faith, yet none of them received what had been promised." What is it that we are hoping for? Sin has affected our understanding. It has emptied a lot of precious truths of their content and filled them with things that are not meaningful. We have to recover those precious truths.

Abraham

There is Abel, Enoch, and Noah, and then there is Abraham. There are three things said about Abraham. One, his leaving Ur of the Chaldees and living in tents as a stranger and alien in the Promised Land that was to belong to him, which he was to receive as his inheritance. We have to ask, why would he leave Ur of the Chaldees, the greatest city of its day? It is like leaving New York City in 1920 and coming out to live in Four Corners, Arizona. You do not do that; the wife does not like it. Are you going to haul all of your furniture out there? When you get there, are you going to tell the people, 'This land is my land, this is not your land?' How long would it take to get the land? How long would it take before Abraham becomes the father of a great nation? Or what is the connection between the great nation and the land, and when will this be? Abraham will die before that, so what is he waiting for? What is the hope and faith of Abraham? It says in Scripture that **"he was looking forward to the city with foundations, whose architect and builder is God"** (v. 10). He is looking for the kingdom of God. That is described at the end of the Book of Revelation—that Diamond City, the completion of human culture, the work of dominion given to man in the beginning, through which the earth is filled with the knowledge of God—all things ordered by the Word of God.

Abraham **"was looking forward to the city with foundations, whose architect and builder is God"** (v. 10). Ur is not that city. Ur has long ago disappeared because it was not built on the truth of God. Abraham had a worldview, a history of the past, of good and evil, of the present, and of what can be expected in the future. This was the faith of Abraham.[15] He knew this, he understood it. He remembered the Flood of Noah, and he saw how that connects in history, rather than simply believing it in some way that is disconnected from the rest of history, and from his worldview. Shem, who went through the Flood, was still living and overlapped Abraham's life by 150 years. We have reason to think that he is the Melchizedek who met Abraham. To him, Abraham offered tithes.[16]

Then we have the birth of Isaac, how long Abraham waited, and the manner in which Isaac was born. Then we will have the offering up of Isaac, and notice how this is spoken of here: "By faith Abraham, when God tested him"—notice that word, we will come back to that—"offered Isaac as a sacrifice. He who had received the promises was about to sacrifice his one and only son, even though God had said to him, 'It

---

15. Gangadean, *Philosophical Foundation*, 124–127; Gangadean, *History of Philosophy*, 163–166; Gangadean, "Paper No. 128: Abraham's Faith: The Elements of Abraham's Faith in Offering up Isaac," 665–666; "Paper No. 129: Faith and Reason in the Life of Abraham," in *The Logos Papers*, 667–669.

16. *Genesis 14:18–24.*

is through Isaac that your offspring will be reckoned.' Abraham"—this is the supreme act of faith, notice how Scripture describes it—"*reasoned that God could raise the dead, and figuratively speaking, he did receive Isaac back from death*" (vv. 17–19).[17] Faith involves understanding; it involves reasoning; it is being sure; it involves proof.

Abraham had to believe in the resurrection of the dead before he left Ur of the Chaldees; he had to believe that he would be heir of the promise, because he would die before it would become a great nation, before they would get to the Promised Land. The question is: Was it just the Promised Land or is it the whole earth? The Promised Land would be the beginning of that, and the whole earth will be full of His glory. What was Abraham looking for? What was his faith? This is what is being taught in the Bible as faith, so let us not yield to something less than this.[18]

Isaac, Jacob, and Joseph

Then we have Isaac, Jacob, and Joseph, blessing their offspring in terms of the future.[19] You know Jacob's whole life, what he sought, how he encountered God at Peniel,[20] and what he waited for. Joseph, when he was dying, believed the promise, that they would be brought back to the land, and he made the Israelites swear that when God visited them, they would take his bones from Egypt to Canaan.[21] Jacob chose to be buried in the field of Shechem, which Abraham bought as a burial place. Jacob affirmed the promise. This is the big picture; there is something that he is waiting for.

Moses

The Patriarchs—Abraham, Isaac and Jacob—and Joseph, affirmed the promise. Then we have Moses, and three things connected with Moses: He chose Christ over the glory of Egypt, suffering with the people of God, and the promise—and the promise was for the despised,

---

17. Emphasis added.

18. Gangadean, *Philosophical Foundation*, 101–127.

19. *Genesis 49.*

20. *Genesis 32:22–32.*

21. *Genesis 50:4–6.*

downtrodden people. What was he looking for? What was his hope? He left Egypt, not fearing the king. He kept the Passover; he understood the holiness of God, the judgment of God, and the covering through the blood. Moses brought the people out of Egypt through the Red Sea. He waited on God and saw God's deliverance, and we should not minimize that, because even up to the very end, they were panicky about it. When they saw the Egyptian army coming, Moses waited upon God, and God parted the sea. These are examples of faith.

Joshua, Rahab, the Judges, and Others—Delivered From and in Trials. Commended Yet Still Waiting (Future/Hope)

Then after these, we have Joshua, Jericho, Rahab the prostitute and her siding with the Israelites, and the Judges, and David and Samuel, and the Prophets—all of these. Some were delivered *in* their affliction—that is, they went through the affliction, without being abandoned; they were sawn in two, they were in sheepskin and goatskin, in rocks and in caves and holes in the earth. Remember Elijah, in this regard; he thought he was the only one left.[22] Isaiah was said to be sawn in two; he endured and he was delivered *in* the trial, while others were delivered *from* the trial. One way or the other, however it pleases God to deliver us, He will deliver us: in it or from it. All of these are examples of faith. This ends now by saying, "These were all commended for their faith, yet none of them received what had been promised"(v. 39)—they died, they went to be with the Lord in heaven, and they are waiting for the work to be completed, and that is the work that is continuing on the earth now. It says, "God had planned something better for us so that only together with *us* would they be made perfect" (v. 40)[23] or complete. They are waiting for us to live out our lives in obedience before God, discipling the nations, taking every thought captive, glorifying God, filling the earth with the knowledge of God—before they can have what they are hoping for. Dying and going to heaven at death is not the end of the process. Those who die and go on are waiting for those who are yet to come, until the work is completed. When it says, **"being sure of what we hope for"** (v. 1), the question is: What do we

---

22. *1 Kings 19:9–18.*

23. Emphasis added.

hope for, and are we sure of it? Faith and hope require proof of what is not seen. From the nature of God, the nature of man, and the nature of the good—we can know these things.

Hope is not a bare conjecture: 'I hope, I hope.' Rather, hope is a certainty, a solidity. This is what enabled the ancients to endure, and this is what they were commended for. Less than that is not going to be commended. You may be saved—even while your work is not done according to the goal, and may be burned with fire—but you may be saved.[24] Our justification is not dependent on our works, rather, it is dependent on faith in Christ. But whether our works endure and are built upon is dependent upon whether they are done with understanding and faith in God.

ON THE TRIALS OF FAITH:
How Do We Know if We Have Faith?

How do we know if we have faith? How do we know if we have *this* faith, and if we do not, how do we get it? Originally, we would know we have faith by being tested. Adam was tested in the Garden to see whether he had faith, whether he had understanding, whether he had been seeking God diligently and had understanding. When he was test-ed, it showed that he believed that "you will be like God, knowing good and evil" (Gen. 3:5b). He did not understand the most basic difference between God and man. God knows good and evil by *creating* the nature of things, while Adam does not and cannot create. We know good and evil by *discovering* it. When we put ourselves to be like God, to know good and evil, to determine it—as the existentialists would say[25]—at that point, we are way, way out of line. We are not determiners of the meaning of things. This is what Adam did: He lost sight of the funda-mental difference between God and man. God is an infinite Creator, and man is a finite creature. When tested, Adam's understanding was shown to be deficient.

Christ, when He was tested, showed His understanding was with-out any lack at all; 40 days without food, in the pain and distress of

---

24. *1 Corinthians 3:10–15.*

25. Gangadean, *History of Philosophy*, 163–170; Gangadean, *Philosophical Foundation*, 121–124.

that, yet keeping a clear eye of what life is, that man does not live by bread alone, but by every word that comes from the mouth of God; and the other temptations all showed His understanding. Both of these—Adam and Christ—were tested when they were without sin, tested to see whether they had faith, whether they had been seeking and understanding. Adam failed. Christ was perfect.

We, in our sin, will also be tested. We will have trials of faith. These trials serve a dual purpose: to reveal to us where we are in terms of our lack of faith and our need to grow in our faith, and also, the pressure of the trial is put upon us so that we might seek God more diligently. Remember, you do not have understanding apart from seeking God diligently: **"he is a rewarder of them that diligently seek him"** (v. 6b KJV). The trials serve both of these purposes.

We might look briefly at some of the passages. "Consider it pure joy, my brothers, whenever you face trials of many kinds, because you know that the testing of your faith develops perseverance" (Jas.1:2–3)—faith is tested. "Perseverance must finish its work so that you may be mature and complete, not lacking anything" (Jas. 1:4). God wants to bring us to maturity, to completeness, to grow up. And then James says,

> Brothers, as an example of patience in the face of suffering, take the prophets who spoke in the name of the Lord. As you know, we consider blessed those who have persevered. You have heard of Job's perseverance and have seen what the Lord finally brought about. The Lord is full of compassion and mercy (Jas. 5:10–11).

We know Job's example is notable. It was a trial of faith. Job was seeing his limits, yet he confessed: "Now mine eye seeth thee. Wherefore I abhor myself, and repent in dust and ashes" (Job 42:5b–6 KJV).

The trial is brought by God, to reveal where we are, and to press us to seek God in this. What happens is that God is revealed at the end of the trial. This is typically the pattern, and Peter alludes to this a number of times. He says, "In this"—in terms of the inheritance kept for you—

> In this you greatly rejoice, though now for a little while you may have had to suffer grief in all kinds of trials. These have come so that your faith—of greater worth than gold, which perishes even though refined by fire—may be proved genuine and may result in praise, glory and honor when Jesus Christ is revealed (1 Pt. 1:6–7).

Notice, the same thing that happened with Job: God's glory was re-vealed. The same happens with us: After we go through the trial, His glory is revealed. Peter also says this: "Dear friends, do not be surprised at the painful trial you are suffering, as though something strange were happening to you"—testing to see whether we have faith and press-ing us to grow and to seek—"But rejoice that you participate in the sufferings of Christ, so that you may be overjoyed"—rejoice and be *overjoyed*—"when his glory is revealed" (1 Pt. 4:12–14). At the end of the trial, we have a breakthrough to a new level of understanding, to seeing the glory of God, even as Job did. The trials come to help us to see where we are and to press us to have faith.

These are some basics of the biblical teaching of faith. We believe that if we have faith, according to Scripture, this is commendable to God. May God help us to take this word to heart, and come to an un-derstanding, which is faith, which is pleasing to God.

2

CREATION AND REVELATION

Five Points on Creation

Genesis 1:1–10, 26–31

¹In the beginning God created the heavens and the earth. ²Now the earth was formless and empty, darkness was over the surface of the deep, and the Spirit of God was hovering over the waters. ³And God said, "Let there be light," and there was light. ⁴God saw that the light was good, and he separated the light from the darkness. ⁵God called the light "day," and the darkness he called "night." And there was evening, and there was morning—the first day. ⁶And God said, "Let there be an expanse between the waters to separate water from water." ⁷So God made the expanse and separated the water under the expanse from the water above it. And it was so. ⁸God called the expanse "sky." And there was evening, and there was morning—the second day. ⁹And God said, "Let the water under the sky be gathered to one place, and let dry ground appear." And it was so. ¹⁰God called the dry ground "land," and the gathered waters he called "seas." And God saw that it was good.

²⁶Then God said, "Let us make man in our image, in our likeness, and let them rule over the fish of the sea and the birds of the air, over the livestock, over all the earth, and over all the creatures that move along the ground." ²⁷So God created man in his own image, in the image of God he created him; male and female he created them. ²⁸God blessed them and said to them, "Be fruitful and increase in number; fill the earth and subdue it. Rule over the fish of the sea and the birds of the air and over every living creature that moves on the ground." ²⁹Then God said, "I give you every seed-bearing plant on the face of the whole earth and every tree that has fruit with seed in it. They will be yours for food. ³⁰And to all the beasts of the earth and all the birds of the air and all the creatures that move on the ground—everything that has the breath of life in it—I give every green

plant for food." And it was so. [31]God saw all that he had made, and it was
very good. And there was evening, and there was morning—the sixth day.

PREVIOUSLY, WE SPOKE ON THE SUBJECT of faith, and we saw that
faith involves support for what is believed, as it is "the substance
of things hoped for, the evidence of things not seen" (Heb. 11:1 KJV).
This is contrary to popular belief, which does not consider evidence and
support. Biblical faith involves understanding: "By faith we understand
that the universe was formed at God's command" (Heb. 11:3). Faith
should be understood in the context of seeking God and understanding who He is. We understand faith in connection with the teachings
of Christ as noted in the previous sermon. Christ opened the disciples'
minds to understand the meaning of the parables, and that the Messiah
must suffer and die and then rise from the dead. Faith is pleasing to
God; this is what the ancients were commended for. It is impossible to
please God without faith. We are to seek God and understand. It says,
"he is a rewarder of them that diligently seek him" (Heb. 11:6b KJV);
in this way, we come to know God. Faith has a specific content: It is
about the existence of God, the Eternal One, and what is eternal. It is
also about our hope and our reward.

In continuing to lay groundwork and foundation for the Christian
world and life view, we come to the subject—the first article of faith—
which is an article from general revelation: That *He is*, that God exists,
that God the Creator exists. We want to look at the theme of *creation*
as part of the worldview. Remember, the biblical worldview may be
summed up in these three words: creation–fall–redemption. Under
creation, we speak about *creation is revelation*. Under the Fall, there is
sin and death. Under redemption, there is the call back to repentance,
justification, and sanctification. All of this is contained in the first three
chapters of Genesis and opened up in the rest of Scripture.

FIRST POINT:
Creation Is Revelation

We want to look at the theme of creation and revelation. What we want
to underscore is that *creation is revelation*. We are trying to support
these points from general revelation, Scripture, Historic Christianity

(the Confession), and our general experience and challenges. In the Westminster Confession of Faith, there are several passages that speak to this point. The very opening words say that God created the world in such a way that it is clear, so that men are without excuse. It says specifically, "Although the light of nature, and the works of creation and providence do so far manifest the goodness, wisdom, and power of God, as to leave men inexcusable; yet are they not sufficient to give that knowledge of God, and of his will, which is necessary unto salvation" (WCF. 1.1). We have a clear revelation, and men are inexcusable for that. Those are the opening lines of the Westminster Confession of Faith. And then it says, "God hath all life, glory, goodness, blessedness, in and of himself; and is alone in and unto himself all-sufficient, not standing in need of any creatures which he hath made, nor deriving any glory from them, but only manifesting his own glory in, by, unto, and upon them" (WCF. 2.2). God manifests His glory in creation, as we see again here: "By the decree of God, for the manifestation of his glory, some men and angels are predestinated unto everlasting life; and others foreordained to everlasting death" (WCF. 3.3). I am trying to underscore here that Historic Christianity (as summed up in the Westminster Confession) speaks of creation, and God's rule is for the manifestation of His glory. That is why we say, *creation is revelation*. This is one of the distinctives of this church—not distinct in contrast to the Confession, but distinct in underscoring it.[1]

The doxological focus answers the question, 'Why did God create?' The Confession answers that question as follows: "It pleased God the Father, Son, and Holy Ghost, for the manifestation of the glory of his eternal power, wisdom, and goodness, in the beginning, to create, or make of nothing, the world, and all things therein whether visible or invisible, in the space of six days; and all very good" (WCF. 4.1). He created to manifest His glory, and His decrees are for the manifestation of His glory. This is not only with regard to creation, but it is the way in which God rules: The decree covers both creation and providence. This is further spelled out: "God the great Creator of all things doth uphold, direct, dispose, and govern all creatures, actions, and things, from the greatest even to the least, by his most wise and holy providence,

---

1. For a fuller exposition of the Distinctives of Westminster Fellowship, see: Gangadean, *The Westminster Catechisms*, 313–356.

according to his infallible foreknowledge, and the free and immutable counsel of his own will, to the praise of the glory of his wisdom, power, justice, goodness, and mercy" (WCF. 5.1). Again, providence—every detail of life, everything that comes to pass, from the greatest to the least—is for the manifestation of His glory. So creation, and with it providence, is revelation. This is the first theme that we must keep in mind when we think of this basic doctrine: *Creation is revelation.*

The last three I will quote briefly. In chapter 6, section1: "Our first parents, being seduced by the subtlety and temptation of Satan, sinned, in eating the forbidden fruit. This their sin, God was pleased, according to his wise and holy counsel, to permit, having purposed to order it to his own glory" (WCF 6.1). In these first six chapters, it is emphasized, again and again, that God does reveal Himself and He creates and rules for that purpose. In short, Historic Christianity affirms that creation is revelation. Furthermore, the first question of the Shorter Catechism, which is about man's chief end, says, "Man's chief end is to glorify God, and to enjoy him forever" (SCQ. 1). "To glorify God," we understand to mean, to come to know His glory, and to make that known. I am citing these because these are summaries of great portions of the teaching of Scripture. Question 46 says, "What is required in the first commandment? The first commandment requireth us to know and acknowledge God to be the only true God, and our God; and to worship and glorify him accordingly." If you go to the Commandments, you find this theme from the beginning: "To know and acknowledge God . . . and to worship and glorify him accordingly." It is the theme of the glory of God and knowing His glory. If we turn to Question 101, the first petition of the Lord's Prayer, we see this theme again: "What do we pray for in the first petition? In the first petition, which is, *Hallowed be thy name*, we pray that God would enable us, and others, to glorify him in all that whereby he maketh himself known; and that he would dispose all things to his own glory."[2] How does He make Himself known? In all of His works of creation and providence. We are to glorify Him in that. Why did God create? To make His glory known. We glorify Him as we come to know His glory and to make that known to others.

---

2. Gangadean, *The Westminster Catechisms*, xv–xxxii.

Whether we go to the Lord's Prayer (the first petition focuses on knowing God, "in all that whereby he maketh himself known"). Or the first commandment, which speaks of knowing and acknowledging God. Or the Catechism's opening question—to glorify God. Or in the Confession, to those sections that I read earlier—1.1, 2.2, 3.3, 4.1, 5.1, 6.1. I hope you can see that from Historic Christianity, it is being affirmed that *creation is revelation,* and we are to know that revelation and make it known.

The first of five points, under the theme of creation, is that *creation is revelation.* I will briefly mention the other four points, and then we will open each up. The second point is that *this revelation is full and clear*—we will look at this in contrast to alternative views. The third point is that *eternal life is knowing God and Jesus Christ whom you have sent.*[3] Fourth, is *the knowledge of God is through the work of dominion.* And fifth, *the earth shall be full of the knowledge of God.*[4]

We hope to look back again on faith and derive our epistemology: biblical epistemology and the nature of faith, the nature of knowing, and how faith involves understanding in contrast to sight. After the epistemological question of faith—how we know, or what faith is, in connection with knowledge and understanding—we are looking at creation: creation is revelation; and then the Fall: sin and death; and then redemption: call back and repentance and faith.

SECOND POINT:
This Revelation Is Full and Clear

To continue: We have talked about the first point under creation, that the *creation is revelation.* We looked at the Confession which summed up the teaching and we will look at some Scriptures. We want to say that this revelation is *full and clear.* In Isaiah 6:3, the angelic beings are crying out before the Lord regarding this revelation. Interestingly, later on, the angels spoke in this same way when they saw Jesus' glory,[5] and

---

3. *John 17:3.*

4. *Isaiah 11:9; Habakkuk 2:14.*

5. This is in reference to *Revelation 5:11–12* when the Lamb of God is given authority to sit on the throne and rule over the created order to bring about the redemption of all things in history.

that is connected with Jesus as Creator, sustainer of all things, redeemer of all things, and heir of all things, as the brightness of the Father's
glory. In that sense, God rules through His Word: our Lord Jesus Christ.

Here is the word of the Scripture on the earth being full of the glory
of God: "With two wings they covered their faces, with two they covered their feet, and with two they were flying. And they were calling to
one another: 'Holy, holy, holy is the LORD Almighty; the whole earth
is full of his glory'" (Is 6:2b–3). The angels see this, and they declare
it. The earth is full of His glory, so we say, this revelation is full. There
is nothing on earth that does not reveal the glory of God. Some have
said that 'this revelation is bare: just sufficient to leave men inexcusable.'
This is not what the Scripture is teaching here: It says the whole earth
is full of His glory. Notice that it is the earth, and it is set in present
tense—*is*, presently, it *is* full of His glory. This is consistent with what
we said before: God created to reveal His glory, and He *rules* to reveal
His glory, and man is to come to *know* that glory—to come to the
knowledge of the glory of God.

This revelation is not bare. It is not merely sufficient for inexcusability; it is certainly sufficient for that, but it is much more than that.
Some people will minimize, neglect, and avoid this revelation, which is
not in keeping with the theme of *creation is revelation*, nor its fullness.

Second, this revelation is not lessened by sin, death, and the curse,
rather, it is increased. "This their sin, God was pleased, according to
his wise and holy counsel, to permit, having purposed to order it to his
own glory" (WCF. 6.1). Sin does not ultimately frustrate God's purpose
of glorifying Himself, but is used by God in His great power and wisdom to *deepen* the revelation—objectively deepen it. Sin subjectively
obscures the revelation—sin in us obscures it—but to someone seeking, it deepens the revelation. Some have tried to neglect and avoid
this revelation by saying, 'Well, not only is it bare, but it is lessened by
sin and death.' That is not true; rather, it is deepened.

Third, God's revelation is not inadequate. That is, the revelation
is not inadequate because we are finite and fallen.[6] Often it is said,
sometimes in Reformed circles, that we are finite and we are fallen,
and therefore we cannot engage with this revelation. It is true that we

---

6. Gangadean, *Philosophical Foundation*, 32–37; Gangadean, "Paper No. 2: Common Ground,"
in *The Logos Papers*, 579–582.

know in part—we do not know comprehensively, but it is true that we do *know* in part, and we will be growing, and ever-growing, in that knowledge. It is not inadequate because of finitude. We are to know, and our knowledge will be finite—it is real knowledge: We *know* in part. It is not that we do not know at all; we know in part and will continue to grow in our knowledge. Finitude has been used as a way of excusing us from coming to know God, but this is not the case.

Sometimes because of our fallenness, we cannot see this revelation. It is true that we are fallen, but that does not mean the revelation is not there. Our failure to see this revelation is due to sin: the sin of not seeking and not understanding. We cannot excuse ourselves from not seeing any more than we can excuse ourselves from not seeking.

In terms of the relation between the two—special revelation and general revelation—in the history of Christian thought, several attempts have been made to put these together. Aquinas said that nature is completed by grace, as if originally, apart from the Fall, man needed some supernatural revelation to engage in his work.[7] If there were no sin, there would be no need for additional supernatural revelation, besides the covenant that God established with Adam, which is certainly supernatural. But there would be no redemptive revelation if Adam had not sinned. So, it is not the case that grace completes nature; that by nature we can go only so far. It is because of *sin*, not because of *nature*, that we do not see what is clear.

Special revelation is not a *replacement* for general revelation. Some will say, 'Now that we have Scripture, everything we need is here, so we do not need general revelation: It is a replacement.' Others will say, 'Because of sin, we cannot see general revelation, so now we have special revelation.' Sin affects our *reading* of Scripture as much as it affects our *reading* of general revelation—just look at all the divisions that there are in the Church. We should say, rather, that it is by the grace of God that we are regenerated, and through the work of the Holy Spirit, we are enabled to see and understand both general and special revelation. When we say, 'this revelation is full and clear,' we are saying it in a way that does not excuse us from minimizing, avoiding, and neglecting this revelation.

---

7. Gangadean, *History of Philosophy*, 121–126.

Special revelation *assumes* the failure to see clear general revelation. Paul certainly makes that point: "since what may be known about God is plain to them, because God has made it plain to them. For since the creation of the world God's invisible qualities—his eternal power and divine nature—have been clearly seen, being understood from what has been made, so that men are without excuse." (Rom. 1:19–20). Here again, we have the theme of faith as understanding, seeing the invisible from the visible, and the need to *understand* the things that are made. Without this faith, without this understanding from seeking God, it is impossible to please God.

Special revelation *assumes* sin, a failure to see clear general revelation. We should add that general revelation is still necessary in order to understand special revelation. In the history of Christian thought, when it is not understood that God is infinite, eternal, and unchangeable—if we misunderstand those attributes—we encounter all kinds of difficulties in reading and interpreting the Scriptures. Recently, there has been a movement afoot in evangelical circles called 'open theism,' where they have tried to make God into something less than infinite, eternal, and unchangeable. Without an understanding of the nature of God, the Scriptures are misread in many ways.

We are restored to seeing that He is. This is a general revelation theme. "For he that cometh to God must believe *that he is*, and that *he is a rewarder of them that diligently seek him*" (Heb. 11:6b KJV).[8] No specific mention there, yet, about Christ and the need for redemption—that will come; it definitely does come, if we understand the nature and existence of God.

Special revelation is not *parallel* or a *republication* of general revelation. In the days of the deists, at their height in their heyday, they said that special revelation just *repeats* what is said in general revelation. 'Some people need it in narrative form, some people can use it in a philosophical abstract form, and for those who cannot, we will give them stories, but it is the same content.' This is not true. Special revelation gives a content that is not in general revelation: It specifically says how we are restored to God from sin and death. This revelation of God, general revelation, is clear, and it is full (not bare), and in saying that, we are not saying it is full so that we do not need special

8. Emphasis added.

revelation; rather, the very fullness of this revelation points us to the need for special revelation.

We are speaking about revelation generally, without distinguishing between special and general revelation. When we say *creation is revelation,* it includes creation *and* providence, which includes redemption, and we are setting this in contrast to an alternative view where God is seen *apart* from His works of creation and providence. This is what the contrast is: not between creation and redemption, but between creation and providence and redemption *in* God's acts—*in* His works—and knowing God *through* His works. *Creation is revelation. This revelation,* creation and providence, including redemption, is full and clear.

We should note some other relevant passages before moving on. We have already spoken of Isaiah 6:3, which says that the earth is full of the glory of God. In Psalm 8, it says, "O Lord, our Lord, how excellent is thy name in all the earth!" (Ps. 8:1a KJV)—*in all the earth.* In Psalm 19, it says, "The heavens declare the glory of God; the skies proclaim the work of his hands. Day after day they pour forth speech; night after night they display knowledge. There is no speech or language where their voice is not heard" (Ps. 19:1–3). The sun, moon, and stars declare that they are finite, that only God is eternal. We have spoken about the kid in Ubangy Bangy—the abused and uneducated kid from Ubangy Bangy—who could know that the sun is finite in size and giving off heat, and could not burn forever, and therefore the sun is not eternal, and therefore it is not to be worshiped.[9] "There is no speech or language where their voice is not heard" (Ps. 19:3). It is clear and full. Recall what is said about this in Romans 1:19–20, which we have already drawn attention to.

THIRD POINT:
Eternal Life Is Knowing God

The first point is that *creation is revelation.* The second point is that *this revelation is full and clear.* The third point now is that *eternal life is knowing God and Jesus Christ, whom you have sent.* Notice how special revelation is included. This is Jesus Christ *whom you have sent.* This is not just Jesus Christ as the pre-incarnate Son of God. It includes Christ's

---

9. Gangadean, *Philosophical Foundation,* 73–80; Gangadean, *History of Philosophy,* 48–50.

coming and the promise of His coming from the beginning: the seed
of the woman.[10] Here we are speaking about both general and special
revelation when we affirm that eternal life is knowing God. In John
17:3, Jesus states what is as close as we can conceive of as a definition
of eternal life. As He is praying His high priestly prayer, He says, "Now
this is eternal life: that they may know you, the only true God, and Jesus
Christ, whom you have sent." John 1:18b says, "but God the One and
Only, who is at the Father's side, has made him known." The Word of
God makes God known. If we go back and look at John, we see how
that Word is eternal, how it comes to us as our light of understanding,
how it comes to us in general revelation, how it comes to us in Scripture, but all of it has been rejected. That Word comes again, incarnate,
that He might forgive our sins and bring us to know God. The only
begotten Son, "who is at the Father's side, has made him known" (Jn.
1:18b). The Son, the one who was sent, comes to make God known.

Let us go back to John 17:4. Jesus said, "I have brought you glory
on earth by completing the work you gave me to do." The work God
gave Christ to do was to make Him known. At the end of that chapter, He says, "I have made you known to them, and will continue to
make you known" (Jn. 17:26a). At the right hand of the Father, Christ
is working as prophet, priest, and king to make God known. *Eternal
life is knowing God.*

Let us consider the implications of this for the present popular
view: Eternal life is not future, particularly connected with heaven. It
is surprising, but most people do think of it that way, that eternal life
is heaven. Eternal life is knowing God; it begins here and now, while
heaven is the future.[11] Heaven, in particular, is the absence of the curse.
Eternal life is not merely the absence of suffering, and it is not what you
might want to sometimes call a direct vision of God, a beatific vision
in heaven: This has been popular and has dominated the Church.[12]
Scripture says God: "who alone is immortal and who lives in unap-
proachable light, whom no one has seen or can see" (1 Tim. 6:16a). In
the beatific vision, we are trying to bypass all of the revelation of God

---

10. *Genesis 3:15.*

11. Gangadean, "Paper No. 116: The Knowledge of God vs. The Hope of Heaven," in *The Logos Papers*, 597–598.

12. Gangadean, *On Natural and Revealed Theology*, 9–39; Gangadean, "Paper No. 106: The Good and Heaven: The Good Is Not the Beatific Vision," in *The Logos Papers*, 547–556.

and creation by coming to see God directly. When we look at the Confession, what is said is that God *created* to make His glory known, He *rules* to make His glory known, He *permitted* the Fall for this purpose, and His *decree* is for this purpose. We are bypassing all that for some direct vision of God in heaven, which is impossible. God is known as He makes Himself known. We cannot see God as He is in Himself, but as He reveals Himself.

Going back to the first theme, *creation is revelation, necessarily*: What God does reveals His nature. It is revelation *intentionally*: That is what He intended to do. When He said it was good,[13] it was good to fulfill His intentions; it was what He wanted to do, and what it did was to reveal His glory. We would add to it *exclusively*: Creation is revelation, necessarily, intentionally, and exclusively. It is contrary to the wisdom of God to give all this revelation and then bypass it in some other way. It is not the case that God is known directly in Himself, but only as He reveals Himself by His acts of creation and providence. This is what we mean by saying that creation and providence are exclusively the revelation of God. We will not bypass all of history to get to this knowledge of God.

Eternal life begins now, and eternal life grows, and it will grow forever. Jesus said, "I have come that they may have life, and have it to the full" (Jn. 10:10b). We are finite beings; we naturally grow. It is consistent with our nature that we will be ever-growing and wanting to grow in the knowledge of God. It begins in this life, and its essence is knowing God, and that continues forever and ever.

This knowledge of God has content. Sometimes, we may want to make up for this lack of knowledge with the presence of God—"I am with you always" (Matt. 28:20b). God is with us in making Himself known, revealing Himself, and illuminating our minds. But one way to see the difference is that this knowledge of God has content. The specific content is God's self-revelation: in all His acts, in all His works of creation and providence, by which He makes Himself known. It is not as if some presence of God is with us that gives us a mystical awareness of a union with God, apart from God's self-revelation and His works. Rather, His presence is with us to bring us to know Him

---

13. *Genesis 1:4, 10, 12, 18, 21, 25, 31.*

as He has revealed Himself. *Creation and providence, including redemption, is revelation.*

FOURTH POINT:
The Knowledge of God Is Through the Work of Dominion

This knowledge of God is through the work of dominion. We have said earlier that creation is revelation, and we have tried to support that, at least from the Confession, and also from a number of Scriptures that go with that. How do we come to this knowledge of the creation? The knowledge of God is through the knowledge of creation, and the knowledge of creation is through the work of dominion.[14] This is what is stated in the beginning. God created them and said, **"Let us make man in our image, after our likeness: and let them have dominion"** (Gen. 1:26a KJV). These are set in apposition, almost as if one is explaining the meaning of the other. Man, the image of God, is the one who *acts* as God to exercise dominion. The word *dominion* has a sense of lordship: master, mastery. We are in the image of God as we rule over the creation. Why is that? Understood that creation is revelation, man is to rule in the creation in order to come to know this revelation.

What does this dominion involve? It involves developing all the powers latent in the creation. It involves both what is called a natural rule and a moral rule. We make that point because many non-believers exercise the work of dominion, in part. Non-believers discover and name the creation, but they do not name it *aright*, ultimately in relation to God; they do name it *in part* correctly, by the grace of God, but they do not continue in it to *see* the glory of God. When we come to see the glory of God, revealed in the creation and history, we are exercising the dominion that God would have us exercise.

In the Scripture, God brought the man to name the creation, and whatever he named each thing, that was its name.[15] Naming involves showing the nature of a thing. When he named her *woman*, because she was taken *out of man*, that has a whole theology with it. When Adam named her *Eve* because she would be the mother of all living, there is a whole theology with it, in light of the promise that God gave. Naming

---

14. Gangadean, *The Westminster Catechisms*, 321–325.

15. *Genesis 2:19–20.*

is not an incidental thing; it is seeing the very nature, the function, of something. From the very beginning, dominion was connected with naming the creation, grasping the nature of things, and seeing how these things reveal and reflect the glory of God, and that is something that we cannot get around because it is clearly there in Scripture. In addition to naming, ruling over it involves increasing what is latent in the creation: developing it, bringing it to maturity, growing and nurturing it to its fullness. This is part of our lordship in the creation, this is part of our rule in the creation, and we do this not for ourselves, but to bring all of these things into their fullness, for the glory of God. There is much development work that needs to be done.

Creation is in time: It goes through a process of developing and maturing, and man is to engage in that. By all the powers within himself, and with nature—that dynamic interaction—he is to know himself and know the creation, and in knowing both, to know God. *Knowledge of God is through the work of dominion.* As we exercise our abilities—our God-given abilities—we come to know what they are. When they are undeveloped, unexercised, we do not see them as they are. It is like an infant in a crib: All that is there within that child is not known until the child grows and comes to maturity, and then we see what really is in the child. It is in this sense that we speak about developing the powers latent in the creation. Non-believers engage in this to an extent, but not fully. We distinguish between a natural rule and a moral rule, but knowledge of God is through dominion.

This work *is not set aside by sin,* but rather, it is *increased.* Romans 6:14 says, "For sin shall not be your master, because you are not under law, but under grace." It shall not have mastery over you, lordship over you, or dominion over you. Understand that you must rule over sin. Our dominion has been increased because of sin, and this is one way in which this manifests: We are to "demolish arguments and every pretension that sets itself up against the knowledge of God, and we take captive every thought to make it obedient to Christ" (2 Cor. 10:5). In the process of taking every thought captive raised up against God, we are exercising dominion; in this case, it is specifically dominion over sin. In our sin, God brings His challenges to our faith so that we might grow in our faith and overcome. Time and again, Revelation chapters

2 and 3 speak about giving life to him who overcomes.[16] At the end of every letter to the seven churches, "To him who overcomes," who exercises dominion to have mastery over that which challenges his faith, his understanding of God, his knowledge of God, He will give rule.[17] Sin does not set aside the work of dominion, but increases it: We are to take every thought captive raised up against the knowledge of God.

Another example of the exercise of dominion is in the work that God has given us to do. At the end of His ministry, Christ our Lord said, "All authority in heaven and on earth has been given to me. Therefore go and make disciples of all nations, baptizing them in the name of the Father and of the Son and of the Holy Spirit, and teaching them to obey everything I have commanded you" (Matt. 28:18b–20a). Notice, sin that is now in the world has to be overcome. The nations have to be discipled. The process of discipling the nations is exercising Christ's authority in teaching and ruling over sin, and teaching after they have come to repentance: "teaching them to obey everything I have commanded you" (Matt 28:20a). This is to establish the Lordship of Christ, the dominion of the Lord. The mission mandate, given in Matthew 28:18–20, is an extension of the cultural mandate given in Genesis 1:26–28. It does not set aside, but instead, it increases the work.

The knowledge of God is through the work of dominion, and now it is through the work of dominion over sin in our own lives, in the Church, and in the culture. As we engage with these challenges sent by God, in His providence, in His wisdom, at specific places where we need to grow, and we engage with that and overcome, we will grow in our faith, without which it is impossible to please God. We will grow in our understanding: By faith we understand. We will grow in our support for our hope; we will grow in our understanding of the evidence of the things that are not seen. We will grow in our reward. He is the "rewarder of them that diligently seek him" (Heb 11:6b KJV). What is the reward? Understanding. The reward is seeking and understanding and doing what is right.

---

16. *Revelation 2:7, 11, 17, 26; 3:5, 12, 21.*

17. *Revelation 3:21.*

FIFTH POINT:
The Earth Shall Be Full of the Knowledge of God

This teaching is given to us from the beginning, in the teaching of the Sabbath. God completed His work of creation, ended His work, and marked that with the Sabbath. Creation is not continuing. Providence is continuing: a new, different kind of work—upholding, directing, and disposing what is created. But the work of creation is completed. Man is made in the image of God and man is to observe the Sabbath in connection with his work of dominion. It means that the work of dominion will be completed: that the whole creation will be named, and it will be named as it should be named to show forth the glory of God. Man is made in the image of God, and the Sabbath is to man a reminder of his origin, that he is created by God, and of his purpose in God, to exercise dominion, and of the hope that the work will be completed. To this day, we still observe the Sabbath, and it is pleasing to God when we observe the Sabbath with understanding. The work we do six days a week is done toward this end: knowing God and making Him known—especially in light of the reality of sin and taking thoughts captive.

A second point, affirming that the earth shall be filled with the knowledge of God, is that after the Fall, the promise was given to Adam, that the seed of the woman will crush the head of the serpent:[18] Good will overcome evil. The work of the tempter, turning mankind away from God, and building on their failure to know God—that work will not succeed, that will be destroyed. We can expect, then, when the works of the devil are destroyed—he is a liar and the father of it—the lie will be removed, and the truth will be in its place. From the beginning, there is in the promise this understanding that the earth will be filled with the knowledge of God. This promise was certainly renewed to Abraham: "in thee shall all families of the earth be blessed" (Gen. 12:3b KJV). There will come a time when all the families on the earth will come to the Lord. Again, in Ephesians 1:22–23 and 4:10, Christ is to fill "everything in every way," and He is "to fill the whole universe." He is to fill it through His body, the Church, which is "the fullness of

---

18. *Genesis 3:15.*

him who fills everything in every way."[19] It is not that Christ is filling everything, but it is through the Church. As we make disciples of all the nations, every name, every authority, is submitted to Christ. This is intended by God, and it will come about.

1 Corinthians 15:25–26 says, "For he must reign until he has put all his enemies under his feet. The last enemy to be destroyed is death." As He reigns for the purpose of making God known, we can expect that the earth will be filled with the knowledge of God.

Lastly, the ancients, and all believers, have been looking for the City of God, the kingdom of God, a city with foundations. We have a vision of the City of God in the New Jerusalem, pictured as a city that represents the completion of all the work of culture, and it is magnificent, beyond our imagination, in terms of its size, dimension, and fullness. The City of God, descending out of heaven from God to earth, that constitutes the new heavens and the new earth, according to the promise of Scripture in Revelation 21, this will come about.

When we think of God as Creator, we think of His purpose, His intention, what the good is, how we are to come to know God, and the hope that we have that God indeed will be known. Without faith, it is impossible to please God. Faith involves understanding. We do not simply say, 'God has created,' and let it go with that, with barely any content. We understand its content, and more than that, we *act* on that understanding. We acknowledge God as revealing His glory and we work to make His glory known.

May God grant us grace to hear and understand His Word, and to obey it.

---

19. *Ephesians 1:23.*

3

SIN AND DEATH

Five Points on the Fall

Genesis 2:8–9, 15–17; 3:1–7

8Now the LORD God had planted a garden in the east, in Eden; and there he put the man he had formed. 9And the LORD God made all kinds of trees grow out of the ground—trees that were pleasing to the eye and good for food. In the middle of the garden were the tree of life and the tree of the knowledge of good and evil.

15The LORD God took the man and put him in the Garden of Eden to work it and take care of it. 16And the LORD God commanded the man, "You are free to eat from any tree in the garden; 17but you must not eat from the tree of the knowledge of good and evil, for when you eat of it you will surely die."

1Now the serpent was more crafty than any of the wild animals the LORD God had made. He said to the woman, "Did God really say, 'You must not eat from any tree in the garden'?" 2The woman said to the serpent, "We may eat fruit from the trees in the garden, 3but God did say, 'You must not eat fruit from the tree that is in the middle of the garden, and you must not touch it, or you will die.'" 4"You will not surely die," the serpent said to the woman. 5"For God knows that when you eat of it your eyes will be opened, and you will be like God, knowing good and evil." 6When the woman saw that the fruit of the tree was good for food and pleasing to the eye, and also desirable for gaining wisdom, she took some and ate it. She also gave some to her husband, who was with her, and he ate it. 7Then the eyes of both of them were opened, and they realized they were naked; so they sewed fig leaves together and made coverings for themselves.

THE FALL:
Sin and Death

WE COME NOW TO THE SECOND of the three basic teachings, or ideas, of the biblical worldview. We come now to the Fall. In thinking about the Fall, we are thinking about sin and death. Earlier, we went over the idea of faith, and we looked at it from three points of view from the Book of Hebrews, but upon reflection and organizing it in ways that are like the other main themes, we thought we could do that in five points on the nature of faith. The first being faith and proof: Faith is the substance of things hoped for, the evidence of things not seen.[1] Second, faith and understanding: By faith we understand that the world was framed by the Word of God, and all the implications of that presently and through history.[2] Third, faith and its content: to believe that He is and that He is the rewarder of those who diligently seek Him. This content is from general revelation and that is basic; it is not just belief *in*, but belief *that*.[3] Fourth, we speak about faith and sin: Faith is what is pleasing to God, and without faith, it is impossible to please God.[4] And fifth, faith and reason: Abraham reasoned that God could raise the dead.[5] These are themes that are of interest and concern to many in the topic's history, so it is appropriate to organize it in a way that speaks to that.

Previously, we spoke about creation, the first theme of the biblical worldview. Let us back up and say that, under faith, we are looking at the whole question of authority and knowledge. From a general revelation point of view, we are looking at the epistemological question. Here, with creation, we are looking at the question of reality, but specifically, we are looking at creation from the point of view of creation and revelation. The first point is: *Creation is revelation.* Secondly: *This revelation is full and clear,* and all the implications of that, especially those of prominent minds of human beings, within the Church and outside the Church. Thirdly: *Eternal life is knowing God* and alternative

---

1. *Hebrews 11:1.*
2. *Hebrews 11:3.*
3. *Hebrews 11:6b.*
4. *Hebrews 11:6a.*
5. *Hebrews 11:19.*

views and ways in which we come short. Fourth: This *knowledge of God is through the work of dominion.* The knowledge of God is through creation, and the knowledge of creation is through dominion; creation includes man being made in the image of God, it includes history, it includes redemption, it includes Christ our Lord being here, and what He continues to do in history. The knowledge of God is through dominion, which includes ruling to make disciples of the nations and taking thoughts captive. Fifth: *The earth shall be filled with the knowledge of God.* Again, another five points, and each of those have significant subheadings that address questions that are relevant that divide the Church, and divide the Church and the world greatly.

We come to the second main theme: the Fall—sin and death. Again, we have organized this into five points, and under each are a number of other points. We will review what these five points are and then go into each. First, the *covenant of creation:* The Fall cannot be understood apart from the idea of a covenant that God made with Adam. I read a little bit about this in chapter 2 just now. Second, there is *temptation:* Temptation came to man, and we will look at its purpose, the agent, and the argument. Third, there was *sin:* specifically sin. Again, this is something about which we are greatly divided regarding the reality of sin, what sin is, and how it has been misunderstood, and we will try to address that. Fourth, the consequence of sin is *death:* We will speak about death and how it has to be understood and how it has been misunderstood. Fifth, we address the question of *theodicy:* 'Why does God permit evil?' We will look at what can be known and cannot be known. We should not try to probe into what cannot be known, but we should know what can be known.

Concisely stated: one—covenant of creation, two—temptation, three—sin, four—death, and five—theodicy.

FIRST POINT:
The Covenant of Creation

God made a covenant with Adam: It is called the covenant of works, or, better, the covenant of creation. This was spoken of in Genesis chapter 2. It is not a second account of creation, but it is an account of the creation in the context of the covenant. There are two covenants in chapter 2, and there is a relation between the two, consistent with the idea of *creation is revelation* and *the visible reveals the invisible*. God makes the covenant of creation by which He binds mankind to Himself in a special relation. The second part of that chapter deals with the covenant of marriage, which is a visible representation of the covenant God made with man.

Chapter 2 is very significant and orderly. We do not have to resort to all kinds of extraordinary theses as to, 'what's going on in Genesis 2?' There is some really crazy stuff that scholars have come up with, like the JEDP theory, where they say that the first chapter of Genesis is representing God as Elohim, the second, Jehovah. They speak of different strands Moses woven together to get these accounts, and it is just nonsense. No, here God is giving an account of the creation in terms of a covenant that He has established between Himself and man. All the details of this can be easily understood in terms of the idea of the covenant.

Representation

In the covenant of creation, what is going on is that we, as human beings, made in the image of God, are finite, temporal, and changeable. In and of ourselves, we are changeable; we cannot be otherwise. Only God is unchangeable: It is an incommunicable attribute.[6] In this covenant, we are being moved from the condition of being changeable in ourselves to where we become unchangeable in the covenant: We will be established in righteousness. It was God's will that mankind be established forever, such as we are now in Christ and will be forever in heaven, so there will be no possibility of falling away. It assumes the reality of the image of God, of the reality of choice. We will be moved, as Augustine said[7] in the ancient world, from a condition where we can sin—*posse peccare*—to a condition where we cannot sin—*non-posse peccare*: changeable in ourselves to unchangeable in God and the covenant. This is a special blessing. It is a condescension on the part of God to bless us, and He will do this by way of covenant, and in this covenant, there is representation.

---

6. Gangadean, *The Westminster Confession*, 47–52.

7. Gangadean, *History of Philosophy*, 113–114; Gangadean, *The Westminster Confession*, 137–142.

Adam represents us, and everything about the account speaks about the centrality of that time, that place, and that person. All the rivers flowed out of Eden.[8] Apart from this, there was no Eden; God made the Garden and put man there. In the middle of the Garden was the tree of life and the tree of the knowledge of good and evil. We are seeing the centrality of the geography and the history of the place. Life was to flow out of Eden along the paths of the rivers. Mankind was to extend the boundaries of Eden to the ends of the world. The vegetation had not been there: This is why God said to the animals that He created when He blessed them, "Be fruitful, and multiply" (Gen. 1:22 KJV), just as He said to man.[9] Just as mankind began small in number and we were to increase greatly, so the animals and vegetation were to increase. Man was to carry that forward. We see the centrality there, and in that centrality, the idea of representation: Everything flows out of this place, and this time, and this is the way it is to be understood.

Probation

Coupled with representation, Adam is the first man from which life flows and represents us, naturally, and this is a source of life, but also covenantly, there is to be probation. The first idea of covenant is representation, and we cannot understand who Christ is apart from Adam. Christ is the second Adam, the last Adam, and He represents us in the place of the first. Christ comes in keeping with the covenant of creation: to *undo* what Adam did by paying the penalty for sin, and to *do* what Adam failed to do, to exercise dominion, to rule in the creation for God. We cannot understand the life of Christ apart from the life of Adam and the covenant of creation. It is very important to understand and keep this in mind.

The second part of the covenant, naturally, is probation. Probation assumes choice: We are made in the image of God, and we operate by choice, whereas animals do not operate by choice. Animals have desires and fulfill them, but it is not with deliberation that they fulfill them. We have freedom in that we can do as we please or otherwise. We have choice, and the choice is between two and only two things:

8. *Genesis 2:10–14.*

9. *Genesis 1:28.*

two ways. This is a constant, and it is a universal: It is constant in all of our lives, and it is universal in every human's life; in every moment of our existence, we have this choice before us. Adam represented us in this choice. We have the choice between good and evil, between life and death. Everything else has to be summed up under this; this is the choice that we have. We will be tested, in the covenant, in Adam, to see which way we will go. From this, we can understand the second point about the test and the temptation.

Manifestation

The third point under the covenant of creation is manifestation. The visible manifests, represents, signifies, and symbolizes the invisible. The invisible God and His attributes are visibly manifested in the creation. The visible makes manifest the invisible, which is a theme represented here, too, and in the Garden and the trees. In the Garden, the two ways are represented as two trees; the ways would exist and do exist, apart from the trees. The two ways are constant and universal: They are in our lives every moment. We are turning toward God, seeking God, or not seeking God. These trees help to make manifest which way we are going in relation to the probation, the test.

First, we have the covenant of creation. Furthermore, this covenant of creation is more *visibly* represented in the relationship between man and woman in the covenant of marriage. The relationship between God and man is spoken of as a marriage covenant. At the end of history, we have the marriage feast of the Lamb. This is perhaps the most telling figure of speech to represent God to us, in our relationship, in the covenant. We have further revelation of this covenant of creation in the covenant of marriage. This is consistent with the theme, under creation, that *creation is revelation,* and the visible manifests the invisible. It is in keeping with the very idea of faith, so that we know the invisible through the visible—in the realm of understanding, in the realm of seeing, in the realm of reasoning, and God wants us to know that. God created to reveal His glory, and He wants us to know that, and it is pleasing to Him that we seek Him out and we know Him. This is all well integrated.

SECOND POINT:
The Temptation

The Purpose

The second point under the doctrine of the Fall, and sin and death, is the temptation: that is, the test. It is natural, if you are called, if you have a choice and you are called to live in a certain way, to make it clear whether you are, or are not, living in that way, and the test serves that purpose. The test serves to *reveal*, not to cause us to sin. It reveals if we are pursuing good or evil; it does not make us pursue good or evil. This is important because when we look at the details of the temptation, we will see that the test and the tempter are merely making manifest what is already going on, particularly as it is symbolized in the trees—not literally in the trees, but what the trees represent: the two ways. The way of life and the way of death. The temptation will show whether we have been going in the way of life, or whether we have been going in the way of death. It makes it manifest in a way that cannot be disputed by anyone. That is, anyone in their right mind: anyone who would engage in dispute, that has reasoning, as against just blubbering, mouthing off, and justifying oneself. The test does not cause the person to fail; it reveals if a person is failing. As a teacher for many years, I have given tests; some people think I am Satan—well, Satan is the tester. And there is a reason why we might make that association, but 'what does it matter?' so long as God is glorified.[10]

The Agent

Satan is the one who tests us. Satan is sent by God. All of that was said to, tongue in cheek, bypass the whole question, 'Why did God allow this to happen?' 'Why did God let Satan do this?' 'Who is Satan?' 'Where did he come from?' and on and on. Those are nonsense questions that are beside the point. What is of relevance is that we are to be tested, and the testing does not cause us to sin, but testing reveals whether we are sinning: that is the point. God, in His wisdom, chooses to use Satan to accomplish this purpose. Satan may have his own purpose, and

---

10. For 45 years, Pastor Gangadean taught and perfected teaching through the Socratic Method and the employment of irony to compel the students to think deeply about basic matters.

God may accomplish many purposes together—'sub-purposes,' so to speak—and many purposes together in one act: this just speaks of the wisdom of God. In terms of other rational beings that He has created, the whole realm of the angelic beings, they too, are implicated in ways that cause the glory of God to be manifest. We do not have to puzzle over this: 'Where does Satan come from?' 'Why did God allow us to be tested?' etc., this is beside the point, once and for all, okay? If you ask me the question in discussion afterward, I will just reiterate what I said. But if you do have questions, ask, even if I reiterate what I said. We will just have to work that out.

Satan comes camouflaged, not announced. It is a surprise test. He does not say, 'I'm Satan, and I'm here to test you.' It does not happen that way. But it serves God's purpose. We tend to cram before the test, but in this case, it is way out of line because it does not work that way with God: It does not work like cramming at the last minute for the test. Have we been walking moment by moment in this choice that is before us constantly and universally? Have we been walking in the way of life? Keep in mind that the *least* turning away is *fundamentally* turning away, so it is not just about the outward end result. God wants to see the disposition of the heart with respect to good and evil. Testing can come at any time—after we have lived a little bit: how long? We do not know, but after a little bit, the test comes to show whether we have been seeking good or evil.

The Argument

The third point is the test itself. The test comes as an argument: There are actual premises and a conclusion. "**For God knows that when you eat of it your eyes will be opened, and you will be like God, knowing good and evil**" (Gen. 3:5). The *for* signifies the premise. The conclusion is, "**You will not surely die**" (Gen. 3:4a). An argument was given to Adam and Eve, and they had to respond to it. An argument can be valid and sound, and I do not want to go into that sort of discussion right now,[11] but they had to engage with the argument. God had said, "**you will surely die**" (Gen. 2:17b). The tempter said, "**You will not surely die**." (Gen. 3:4a). There is a flat contradiction, and in that respect,

---

11. Gangadean, *Philosophical Foundation*, 55–56.

it is a true or false pop quiz, and your life depends on it, and all your kids' lives, forever and ever. Some people think *I* am hard on them.

The test involves an argument. It has a context from what God has said, what is true from general revelation, and what is true from special revelation. From general revelation, it is known, and it can be known, what good and evil is, that there are the two ways of good and evil, and that we must go one way rather than the other. But God also said, **"You are free to eat from any tree in the garden; but you must not eat from the tree of the knowledge of good and evil, for when you eat of it you will surely die"** (Gen. 2:16b–17). The tree is a visible representation of this invisible reality, and the reality is the invisible thing, as seen in the nature of faith. This visible representation is going to reveal our response to the invisible.

There is a context for the argument—what God had said from general and special revelation—and there are terms used in the argument that are known: good and evil. Mankind is to know good and evil, and we will see how we can and should know them, if we had been pursuing the knowledge of God. God spoke, and He used these terms: *death*, *good*, and *evil*, and the assumption is that Adam knew them. God did not provide Adam with a thesaurus and *Strong's Concordance* with all the notes in the back with the numbers where you look up the words and find the meaning; I assure you, God did *not* do that. The assumption then is that they understood the words of God: We must assume this, and we must then ask, 'How is it they would understand those things that are true from general revelation?' Adam had this, we have it, and we are called upon to know it, so the test involves general revelation, as well as special revelation—the special terms of the covenant. We do have the conclusion here in the argument: **"You will not surely die"** (Gen. 3:4a), which is a flat contradiction of what God had said. Here is a test, in the form of an argument, given to man, administered by the tempter: by Satan. The purpose is to reveal our condition. This is the second point. First, under the Fall, is the covenant of creation, and the purpose of this, and the second is the temptation.

THIRD POINT:
Sin

We know what sin is; we *can* know what sin is; we *should* know what sin is from general revelation and experience. Adam had been called to name the creation, and he was engaged in that work before God gave him his wife. "Now the LORD God had formed out of the ground all the beasts of the field and all the birds of the air. He brought them to the man to see what he would name them; and whatever the man called each living creature, that was its name" (Gen. 2:19). Adam was involved in naming, and we should understand what naming is: It goes on throughout Scripture. It reveals the very essence of a being, the nature of things. It is understanding the revelation that God has given of Himself in *that* creature. Naming: grasping the meaning of, the significance of. I hope that there is no question about that. I hope the examples are sufficiently clear from his naming his wife Eve, or naming her Woman, and what that signifies—things that are so lost sight of today, with all of our contemporary education: The nature of man, the nature of woman, the difference between the two, the relation between the two, and the purpose of God and what is involved in saying, 'Yes, I will obey, and I will be fruitful and multiply, and she will be Eve, the mother of all the living.'—under the condition of the Fall, the curse, and sin and death—to go on with that and all that *that* signifies.

Adam is naming, and he can know the nature of things, and he can know that what is good for a thing is based on the nature of a thing. Good for man, created by God, is based on human nature, which is created by God. The standard is structured into the very nature; this is part of saying that the law is written on the heart:[12] It is structured into our being. We are born ignorant, and we need to be taught: This introduces the whole command about authority and what is to be taught by our parents—the fifth command. We can find every command and know every command because it is structured into our very being from general revelation. It is within our very nature, as we live according to our nature. Notice, our naming and understanding the nature of things is to act according to human nature as created by God, and so it is to do what is good for our nature. At the same time, evil is an act contrary to our nature; it is an act that destroys us: It is an

---

12. *Romans 2:14–15; Deuteronomy 30:11–14.*

act of self-destruction. Death comes in because of sin, acting contrary to the nature of things as created by God, one could understand that.

Adam would know what death is and what evil is in the naming of things. If we do not go that way, then we have an extreme puzzle on our hands: Adam is told things that are meaningless to him, empty of meaning, and so how would he know these things? In what sense can we say it is consistent? We know this is the condition in which we were created, with the law of God written on our hearts, as a clear, general revelation.[13] Sin is, first of all, to be understood in terms of acting according to our nature as God created us, or against our nature as God created us.

The second point in understanding sin is spoken of in Scripture in a number of places: It is not seeking, it is not understanding—and it is not doing what is right. Please note three points of sin; it is not just not doing what is right. There is an order between these three: that as we seek and understand, we go on to do what is right. In Romans 3:10–11, Paul sums it up, quoting passages that go back to the Psalms, twice in Psalm 14:2–3: "The LORD looks down from heaven on the sons of men to see if there are any who understand, any who seek God. All have turned aside, they have together become corrupt; there is no one who does good, not even one." And Psalm 53:1–3:

> The fool says in his heart, "There is no God." They are corrupt, and their ways are vile; there is no one who does good. God looks down from heaven on the sons of men to see if there are any who understand, any who seek God. Everyone has turned away, they have together become corrupt; there is no one who does good, not even one.

Thirdly, there is a failure to understand the clear difference between God the Creator and man the creature. There is a clear difference. Paul speaks of this in Romans: what is clear about God so that men are without excuse for not seeing.[14] It is clear in the account of the Garden. Satan came to the man saying, **"you will be like God, knowing good and evil"** (Gen. 3:5b); that is the premise: You will be like God, knowing good and evil—specifically, **"like God"** in regard to knowing good and

---

13. Gangadean, *Philosophical Foundation*, 171–284; Gangadean, *History of Philosophy*, 61–69; Gangadean, *The Westminster Catechisms*, 215–261; Gangadean, *On Natural and Revealed Theology*, 127–139, 166–178.

14. *Romans 1:18–20.*

evil. Notice here the concept of good and evil and what that is, and being like God, knowing good and evil. This raises the question, 'How does God know good and evil?' What is good and evil? Good for man as a rational being, made in the image of God, is to act according to his nature, in the use of his reason: acting according to his nature as a rational being, and finding meaning and understanding by this—and evil is the contrary. We connect that with Romans 1: It is not seeking and not understanding what is clear about God, not engaging reason to see what is clear, to understand.

In this temptation, **"you will be like God, knowing good and evil"** (Gen. 3:5b), how does God know good and evil? He certainly does not know it by discovery. He *determines* the nature of things and *determines* good and evil by creation. God knows good and evil, not by discovery, but by determination. Man cannot create the nature of anything. He can and should know this—in naming the creatures and naming himself, he should know this—he should know he is finite, temporal, changeable, that he does not have the power to bring into being or to change the nature of things. He can act contrary to the nature of things, but he cannot change the nature.

How can you be like God, knowing good and evil? Since the conclusion of any argument rests on the premise—the reason given is taken to be more certain, and we infer the conclusion from the premise—so we go to the premise: **"you will be like God, knowing good and evil"** (Gen. 3:5b). We go to what is more basic, which is, the meaning of that premise. How does God know good and evil? What does that mean? What does good and evil mean? "But without faith it is impossible to please him: for he that cometh to God must believe that he is, and that he is a rewarder of them that diligently seek him" (Heb. 11:6 KJV). Sin is not seeking and not understanding. If Adam had been diligently seeking God, he would have retained an understanding of these most basic things. He is tested now to see whether he has been seeking God, whether he has understanding and has been maintaining and growing in it, or whether he has turned aside from the good as the knowledge of God—intended by God as Creator—and whether he has put something else in the place of God's vision of the good: whether man has determined within himself good and evil, apart from what God has determined by creation.

Adam's eating of the tree of the knowledge of good and evil is an outward revelation of what is going on inwardly: that man has put himself in the place of God to determine good and evil, and that the good is something other than the knowledge of God. Every one of us, universally, constantly, every moment of our lives, are involved in this very choice. No one escapes it. This is *the* choice. Nothing else. *Exactly* the same choice that Adam faced. Are we seeking the knowledge of God as the good, or are we seeking something less than this, other than this, as the good, something we determined to be the good? Are we eating of the tree of the knowledge of good and evil? Are we putting ourselves in the place of God to determine good and evil? What happens automatically, necessarily, when we go this way, is that the whole meaning of good and evil collapses. Because when we separate good and evil from the nature of things, and we say that we are the determiners, that we can determine in any way we please, absolutely, it becomes totally arbitrary. The existentialists, who profess to do this, end up exactly there: in absurdity. Whether they can live honestly with absurdity: they do not, they cannot.[15] Pardon me, but they are idiots. The existentialists who seek to be highfalutin, sophisticated intellectuals are downright idiots; no word can make it plainer, and they lack integrity. I know because I was *there*.

Before my conversion, I had to confront the issue: the honesty of the existentialist position. I could not for a moment, in honesty, live with it—not for a moment. I faced the question of whether I could, as Sartre suggests, drive a car with someone walking along the road, and either drive past them, stop and pick them up, or run them over. For me, it was walking past someone on the stairway and saying, 'I could walk past them, I could say hi to them, or I could trip them up and have them flying down the stairs.' Honestly? Could I regard those choices as equally significant? Did I, could I, do that? No. There was a nature of things which had its demand on me and I could not just say, 'Overcome it.' I could not determine the nature of things. Writing a tome *On Being and Nothingness*[16] is just as meaningful as writing a book called, 'Goosey Goosey Gander' or worse yet, 'Gobbledygook.' But do they do that? If they really faced integrity, would they have said this? Yes, they would. Did they? No, they did not.

A lack of integrity; that is what Adam faced. When you put yourself in the position to determine good and evil, you can go anywhere

---

15. Gangadean, *History of Philosophy*, 163–170.

16. In reference to Jean-Paul Sartre's major philosophical work.

with it; you have lost the difference. When you say, 'all is one,' as in Hinduism, and you have blurred the distinction between good and evil—good and evil are one—what happens to the meaning of it? It becomes meaningless. When you say, 'all is one,' in nature as the naturalists do, what happens? All is natural. You cannot speak about good and evil; you lose the meaning of it. **"For when you eat of it you will surely die"** (Gen. 2:17b)—spiritually. That is exactly what happened. Inescapably, inherently, necessarily, **"you will surely die"**: sin and death. Sin is the failure to understand the clear difference between God the Creator and man the creature. This is the third characteristic of sin.

We now come to a fourth characteristic of sin. So far, we have said that, first: Sin is contrary to our nature. Second: It is not seeking, not understanding, and not doing what is right. Third: It is a failure to understand the clear difference between the Creator and the creature, as in believing that you can be as God. Fourth: Sin is autonomy, putting oneself in the place of God to determine good and evil. When we do not accept God's determination of good and evil, then we have to—we *have to*—put ourselves in the place of God to determine good and evil, and that is the sense of sin as *autonomy*. Many have spoken of sin in terms of autonomy, but we are clarifying and defining it more clearly. Notice, it is seeking wisdom apart from God: a desire to make oneself wise.[17] All the New Age spirituality that comes with seeking wisdom apart from God the Creator, with the assumption that we are all part of God, we are all one, denies the distinction between the Creator and the creature. Denying the distinction between the infinite and eternal Creator, and the finite, temporal, changeable creature is folly; it is sin. We tend to think of the most depraved man as someone killing people, but the deepest depravity comes in seeking wisdom autonomously apart from God: That is the face of evil, that is the face of Satan. Most often, he comes as a college professor in philosophy. He comes as a pastor; he comes as a Buddha; he comes as a Krishna; he comes as a Mohammed. Satan, an angel of light and deception.[18] He does not come as a Saddam Hussein, first and foremost: That is a way down-the-line version of it, after it bottoms out, after it gets into the cesspool. Sin comes claiming to bring enlightenment about good and evil. But

---

17. *Genesis 3:6.*

18. *2 Corinthians 11:14.*

at the core, it is corrupt autonomy, the creature trying to make sense of the world apart from God and ending in death.

Fifth: Sin is unbelief. Specifically, it is unbelief concerning that God *is*, that God the Creator *is*, and keeping that—with understanding—in mind. You could use the words, *God is*, and you could get to the highest mountain and shout it out: 'I believe that God exists!' Mohammed proclaimed that as well. You can cry out, 'Allah be merciful,' and 'God is merciful', and you can see the world through the lens of grace, and you can use these words, and yet they are all emptied of meaning. This is death because of sin. Unbelief is not believing with understanding that God exists and that God is a rewarder of those who diligently seek Him, and not understanding what the reward is: That God Himself is our exceedingly great reward. We embrace this through the knowledge of God as eternal life, and that is the good. All of popular Christianity that thinks we die and go to heaven, that we escape natural evil, and in heaven we have the fullness of blessing—they are missing the knowledge of God filling the earth; they are buying into something less than the truth, and yet their message seems so pious, so nice, so sweet. It goes on so smoothly, but it is not the truth: It is not believing with understanding that God is a rewarder of those who diligently seek Him. I want to emphasize this because it is not unrighteousness first. It is not unrighteousness in the presence of knowledge, which some people speak of as, 'willful, open rebellion.' There are many Scriptures that do not speak of evil in that way.[19] Jesus said, "Father, forgive them; for they know not what they do" (Lk. 23:34 KJV). Jesus did not say to excuse them but to forgive them. It is culpable ignorance. Jesus said, "you will know the truth, and the truth will set you free" (Jn. 8:32). This is over and against those who put down knowledge and say that we sin knowingly, in the face of knowledge. The disciples failed to understand that Christ must suffer, until they stumbled; they should have understood—it was culpable ignorance.[20]

Jesus said, "Sanctify them through thy truth: thy word is truth" (Jn. 17:17 KJV). Paul said, "I did it ignorantly in unbelief" (1 Tim. 1:13b KJV). But he was guilty. He should have known. Culpable ignorance: You were not seeking and that is why you did not understand. This is

---

19. Gangadean, "Paper No. 120: Contra Voluntarism: The Will Is Not Independent of the Intellect," in *The Logos Papers*, 611–647.

20. *Luke 24:13–35.*

sin, and it brings death. It is taking the name of the Lord your God in vain, and God will not hold him guiltless who takes His name in vain.[21] In the face of clear revelation, where God has revealed Himself, when we do not pay attention to this, when we casually ignore it, avoid it, resist it, deny it—God does not hold us guiltless—even if we begin by simply ignoring it—not avoiding it, resisting it, denying it—but just ignoring it. We must diligently seek Him: positively.

We are made in the image of God, we are made for meaning, and all the corruption that comes into our lives is because we do not have meaning; we do not have the reward of knowing Him. The excess that human beings go through, the corruption, the decay of the soul that happens, the depravities, all come down to this: seeking and knowing God and finding your reward in Him. All the sex, drugs, rock and roll—all the kinky sex, all the ritualized forms of sexuality that we may go into to find meaning, to find satisfaction—it all comes back to not seeking God, not loving God. This includes all the suffering that comes pouring into our lives like a tidal wave. All the absurdity of life. What happened with the spacecraft where this piece fell off, and seven astronauts were blown apart? Little things like that: we have to make sense of the world. In the absurdities of life, as well as all the regular aspects of life, we are called to make sense of it, to see it before God. *Creation is revelation.* God reveals Himself in these things.

God is calling us to know Him more. Sin is not merely an act, a power, in the face of having knowledge: It is a failure to know what is clear, and Adam and Eve classically illustrated this. They failed to keep in mind the distinction between the infinite Creator and the finite creature, and so they ate. When they blurred this distinction, when they lost sight of God, it showed that they had not been seeking God. Had they been continuing to name the creation so as to see God and grow in the knowledge of God, they would never have stumbled at this point. The test revealed that they had ceased to seek God, it brought out the fact that they had turned away from good, as God defined it, and determined something else to be good, and they were seeking that. This is a constant condition of sin for all human beings. Adam represented us in this.

---

21. *Exodus 20:7.*

FOURTH POINT:
Death

"For the wages of sin is death" (Rom. 6:23a). **"For when you eat of it you will surely die"** (Gen. 2:17b). There are two kinds of death: physical and spiritual. In Ephesians, Paul says, "As for you, you were dead in your transgressions and sins" (Eph. 2:1): This is spiritual death. Jesus spoke about this in John 5:25 and 28—the two kinds of death: one is spiritual and one is physical. He made that great statement to Martha: "I am the resurrection and the life. He who believes in me will live, even though he dies [physically]; and whoever lives and believes in me will never die [spiritually]" (John 11:25b–26a). There are two kinds of resurrection. Revelation 20:6a says, "Blessed and holy are those who have part in the first resurrection. The second death has no power over them." Death is spiritual. Physical death is a sign of spiritual death. Spiritual death is the death of the soul and all of its activities; individually, it is meaninglessness, boredom, and guilt, and corporately, it is the death of relations, institutions, and culture. Keep this in mind, people of God: Every time we have sin in our lives, it produces death. Sinful disregard and self-indulgence produce strain in relationships—this is part of death. It produces death in institutions, relationships, and marriage: The very institution of marriage is going down the tubes. And in cultures, whole cultures die because of lack of meaning.

Death is present and inherent in sin: **"you will surely die"** (Gen. 2:17b); it is not future and imposed. The lake of fire is said to be the second death—spiritual death. It is a continuation of what is going on in this life. Twice, it says, "The lake of fire is the second death,"[22] and this is referring to spiritual death. Everyone will be raised physically from the dead, but those who are in unbelief will continue in death spiritually. They will be in that lake of fire, which is a symbolic representation of a spiritual condition, which is present in this life and continues on forever.[23] Death comes from sin.

---

22. *Revelation 20:14; 21:8.*

23. Gangadean, *Philosophical Foundation*, 195–197; Gangadean, "Paper No. 147: The Biblical Worldview (Part VII)," in *The Logos Papers*, 747–757.

FIFTH POINT:
Theodicy

Theodicy: Why God permits evil. Briefly, we can say that He permits sin for His glory, to serve the good, the knowledge of God; it is especially to deepen the revelation of His justice and His mercy, which would not be deepened without sin and death and redemption. He does this by enlarging the call upon mankind for dominion: To take every thought captive; sin both reveals and causes us to know in a greater way. There are dimensions about theodicy that are not revealed. Why did God permit sin as against not permitting sin? God acted in permitting sin; the revelation is in that, in connection with our purpose. Some ask the question, 'Why did God create at all?' Or, 'Why did God create me, as against not create me?' His revelation is revealed in what He has created, not in asking the question, 'Why did He not do this act?' We are confined to the revelation that God has made of Himself in His acts, not to the non-revelation that was not in His act. We have to be careful when we deal with this to see that the revelation was deepened and brought knowledge through sin, that this revelation is sufficient, and that should satisfy; we should not be asking, 'Why did God *not* do this?'

We have before us, the main points under the doctrine of the Fall: the covenant of creation, temptation, sin, death, and briefly (partly because we have talked about it elsewhere,[24] at other times, at great length), the theodicy: Why God permitted evil.

Let us reflect on these. If we have questions—serious questions about this—we should ask them and discuss them. If not, we should take this to heart and make it part of our thinking, make it part of our meditation, part of our understanding, part of our faith, which is pleasing to God. Amen.

---

24. Gangadean, *Philosophical Foundation*, 145–161; Gangadean, *On Natural and Revealed Theology*, 141–147; Gangadean, "Paper No. 147: The Biblical Worldview (Part VII)," in *The Logos Papers*, 747–757.

4

CURSE AND PROMISE
The Three Call Backs

Genesis 3:6–24

⁶When the woman saw that the fruit of the tree was good for food and pleasing to the eye, and also desirable for gaining wisdom, she took some and ate it. She also gave some to her husband, who was with her, and he ate it. ⁷Then the eyes of both of them were opened, and they realized they were naked; so they sewed fig leaves together and made coverings for themselves. ⁸Then the man and his wife heard the sound of the Lord God as he was walking in the garden in the cool of the day, and they hid from the Lord God among the trees of the garden. ⁹But the Lord God called to the man, "Where are you?" ¹⁰He answered, "I heard you in the garden, and I was afraid because I was naked; so I hid." ¹¹And he said, "Who told you that you were naked? Have you eaten from the tree that I commanded you not to eat from?" ¹²The man said, "The woman you put here with me—she gave me some fruit from the tree, and I ate it. ¹³Then the Lord God said to the woman, "What is this you have done?" The woman said, "The serpent deceived me, and I ate." ¹⁴So the Lord God said to the serpent, "Because you have done this, "Cursed are you above all the livestock and all the wild animals! You will crawl on your belly and you will eat dust all the days of your life. ¹⁵And I will put enmity between you and the woman, and between your offspring and hers; he will crush your head, and you will strike his heel." ¹⁶To the woman he said, "I will greatly increase your pains in childbearing; with pain you will give birth to children. Your desire will be for your husband, and he will rule over you." ¹⁷To Adam he said, "Because you listened to your wife and ate from the tree about which I commanded you, 'You must not eat of it,' "Cursed is the ground because of you; through painful toil you will eat of it all the days of your life. ¹⁸It will produce thorns and thistles for you, and you

will eat the plants of the field. [19]By the sweat of your brow you will eat your food until you return to the ground, since from it you were taken; for dust you are and to dust you will return." [20]Adam named his wife Eve, because she would become the mother of all the living. [21]The LORD God made garments of skin for Adam and his wife and clothed them. [22]And the LORD God said, "The man has now become like one of us, knowing good and evil. He must not be allowed to reach out his hand and take also from the tree of life and eat, and live forever." [23]So the LORD God banished him from the Garden of Eden to work the ground from which he had been taken. [24]After he drove the man out, he placed on the east side of the Garden of Eden cherubim and a flaming sword flashing back and forth to guard the way to the tree of life.

WE COME NOW TO THE THIRD GREAT theme that constitutes the biblical worldview of creation–fall–redemption. Restoration to God's purpose for us in creation and deepened understanding of His attributes. Redemption must be seen in relation to these first two themes: creation and the Fall, and particularly in relation to the depth, or the fullness, that there is both in creation (in terms of the fullness of the revelation that is given there), and the Fall (the depth of depravity and the fullness of evil). The purpose of redemption is to bring us *out* of sin and death to the goal that was set before us in creation: the knowledge of God. We see that the Fall, in God's providence, in His wisdom, is made to serve His purpose of deepening the revelation of His glory. We must also see redemption, or understand redemption, in the subjective aspect of it: that is, as we who are thinking about redemption are affected by the sin from which we must be redeemed. So, our understanding of redemption is often distorted by the very thing from which we must be redeemed—from sin.

One other point that we must make here is that the Genesis account is a complete account: complete in the sense that all the parts of God's revelation are here. It was the only revelation that the people of God had up through the time of Noah, and beyond that, through the ages— through Babel—and up through Abraham and the Patriarchs, and down to the time of Moses. Essentially, we had a little more revelation at the time of Noah, but there was no new revelation—not much—until the days of Moses. All who were saved were saved by this revelation, and we must understand that it was complete for its purpose of salvation.

That means when we read this, we must read it with understanding. In the Westminster Confession of Faith, a summary of Historic Christianity, which we affirm with our whole heart, Chapter 1.6 says, "The whole counsel of God concerning all things necessary for his own glory, man's salvation, faith and life, is either expressly set down"— literally, verbally, set down—"in Scripture, or by good and necessary consequence may be deduced from Scripture: unto which nothing at any time is to be added." There are two aspects of this revelation: that which is *expressly set down*, and that which is known by *good and necessary consequence*. We read about redemption and understand the completeness of it, in order to see the completeness of this account of redemption, we must use good and necessary consequences—inference, reason—to look at the assumptions and implications of what is being said. This is what is affirmed in Historic Christianity.[1]

If you have further questions about this, look at the Larger Catechism Question 99, which deals with how the law is to be interpreted, and we will see that principle of good and necessary consequences being used[2]—particularly section 6: "That under one sin or duty, all of the same kind are forbidden or commanded; together with all the causes, means, occasions, and appearances thereof, and provocations thereunto" (LCQ. 99). We will be using good and necessary consequences to draw out the meaning.

Adam has sinned. We have seen what sin is: not seeking, not understanding, and not doing what is right. It is not simply not doing what is right, and it is not simply eating of the tree; we saw that they had already partaken, inwardly, of the reality of determining good and evil for themselves, and turned away from seeking God. That which was inward comes to be expressed outwardly, which is in keeping with the whole theme of the visible expresses the invisible. Adam has sinned, and his sin is revealed in his eating the forbidden fruit; it is made known outwardly, objectively, in a way that cannot be denied. Just as our failure to know is there before we take the test, the test reveals a failure to seek, know, and understand. That is the sense of it here, too. Death has been at work in him and he has turned aside from listening to the voice of God. He has turned aside from seeking to know God to seek

---

1. Gangadean, *The Westminster Confession*, 28–32.

2. Gangadean, *The Westminster Catechisms*, 222–225.

wisdom apart from God—"the tree was good for food and pleasing
to the eye, and also desirable for gaining wisdom" (v. 6); against the
Word of God, and apart from God.

One of the first things that happened as a consequence of their disobedience is stated implicitly in Genesis 3:7, "Then the eyes of both of
them were opened, and they realized they were naked; so they sewed
fig leaves together and made coverings for themselves." Here, the implication is that they were naked and they felt *shame*, because in Genesis 2:25 it says, "The man and his wife were both naked, and they felt
no shame." By implication, their nakedness is connected with shame.

THE FIRST CALL BACK:
Shame (Inward/Conscience)

Another implication is that shame is something inward, arising spontaneously, in connection with our conscience—being a witness to us
that we have done what is wrong. Immediately upon eating, their conscience, this God-created conscience, begins witnessing—inwardly, not
outwardly, there will be an outward call—to them and causes them to
feel a sense of shame connected with their nakedness.

You must understand that this is about more than just their physical nakedness which was there before; something has changed, and we
have to infer that what has changed is sin and the *visible* nakedness is
now a reminder to them of *spiritual* nakedness. They are without righteousness. The outward act of eating shows that they did not do what
was right, and that has become evident now. The one reminds them
of the other, and there may be other things that we can infer from it:
Why did he listen to the voice of his wife?[3] Why did he put his relationship with his wife above God? The implications of this, which is a
pattern that has continued in history, is that when we turn away from
God, we turn away to another human being to fill that void. He had
not turned to her in the appropriate sense of being spiritual head and
leading her in the work that God has given them together to do,[4] but
had turned away from that.

---

3. *Genesis 3:17.*

4. *Genesis 1:26–28.*

There is a sense of shame, and shame makes us feel worthless. When we have that feeling, we feel as if we deserve nothing good; we are not deserving of anything good; we are only deserving of things that are bad. There is an element of self-hatred and abhorrence. Job experienced this when he became aware of his sin. He said, "I abhor myself" (Job 42:6 KJV). He hated himself. Job repented in dust and ashes, but Adam and Eve did not. When they felt shame, the sense of worthlessness, a sense of self-abhorrence, instead of understanding it as a call back from God—that we have done wrong, and to acknowledge the wrong, and turn back to God—they avoided the call back by covering it up. They made a significant effort to do so. The sewing together of leaves does not just happen easily. Try it.

THE FIRST RESPONSE:
Self-Deception (Cover-Up)

The sewing of leaves was an elaborate effort they both collaborated in, and perhaps encouraged each other in, and they covered their physical nakedness. The response to the first call back was self-deception, a cover-up. They deceived themselves about their true condition before God: that they were in a condition of sin and that they were experiencing the death of shame, the death of guilt. They could not live in that condition. They deceived themselves about the reality of sin in their lives: that they had not been seeking God, and not understanding, and therefore did wrong. The first call back—inward/conscience, shame—is responded to by self-deception.

How does it proceed from here? Self-deception is not sufficient because as God comes near, in the Garden, they experience fear. They are aware that something has not been dealt with properly before God, and they experience fear and hide from God. This is very interesting because this kind of response comes not only toward God, but also toward others who would bring the Word of God. People feel fearful and try to avoid the presence of one who may call them as God called Adam and Eve. The insufficiency of what they had done becomes apparent.

It should be clear to us, as we think about it, that while you can cover your nakedness, there is one thing you cannot cover, and that is the covering. The covering is always there, and you should be asking yourself, 'What are we covering? Why are we covering this? Why are we doing this?' Notice how both of them are together in this. It is like the title of that work on transactional psychology: *I'm OK - You're OK*.[5] They are probably saying that to each other. All the while, they are noticing this covering that they have on themselves. This is how self-deception works: we *ignore*. There is a deliberate ignoring, and we try to ignore it in a passive way, while not paying attention; we overlook it. The psychology of self-deception is interesting, but it must be kept in mind because it is a serious matter, it is God's call back, and it is going to be one of the things that has to be broken through to get to repentance. We have to overcome the self-deception that is in our hearts about our seeking God diligently.

THE SECOND CALL BACK:
Self-Examination (Outward/the Question)

God comes to man, and He calls, **"Where are you?"** (v. 9b). Think about how ridiculous the situation is: Adam and Eve are hiding from God, who is omniscient. There is a little bit of bad theology here. When God says, **"Where are you?"**, we should not read it in the sense that God, who is omniscient, does not know where they are, as if God is beating around the bush saying, 'Adam, are you there?' Not at all. This is where good and necessary consequences come in. God calls man to answer the question, **"Where are you?"**, not physically, but spiritually. It is a call to self-examination.

THE SECOND RESPONSE:
Self-Justification (Blaming Others)

Adam responds, **"I heard you in the garden, and I was afraid because I was naked; so I hid"** (v. 10). Then God asks him directly, **"Have you eaten from the tree that I commanded you not to eat from?"** (v. 11b). We now have the response to the second call back (the call to self-examination), and the response is self-justification. The first call back was shame and the response was self-deception. The second call was to self-examination, **"Where are you?"** (v. 9b), and the response was self-justification. How so? Adam responded this way: God asks him,

---

5. Thomas Harris, *I'm OK - You're OK* (New York: Harper and Row, 1997).

"Have you eaten from the tree that I commanded you not to eat from?" (v. 11b). Notice how Adam avoids the question. The answer should be yes or no—God did not ask for an explanation. It is either, 'Yes, I ate,' or 'No, I did not eat.' He avoids the question and says, "**The woman you put here with me—she gave me some fruit from the tree, and I ate it**" (v. 12). God did not ask for an explanation, God knows, it is a self-justifying explanation. What Adam does is most serious: He blames another. This is a typical pattern, and this is the essence of sin—not seeking, not understanding, and not doing what is right—and then, in connection with sin, self-deception is added, then added to that is self-justification. In self-justification, we blame others. Here, Adam is blaming his wife. Adam was covenant-head and should be leading, but he has abandoned that and is listening to what his wife said rather than leading in righteousness, and he blames her. But more than that, he blames God: "**The woman you put here with me**" (v. 12a). The implication is that God did not do a wise thing. 'And if you had not put her here, I would have been all right. Why did you put her here?' This is some of the undertone.

Adam blames others and he blames God. It shows how deceitful the heart is. It is deceitful above all else. "The heart is deceitful above all things, and desperately wicked: who can know it?" (Jer. 17:9 KJV). The heart is desperately self-centered, and connected to this self-centeredness is pride: 'I'm okay, I've not done anything wrong.' Self-justification is a tremendous resistance to the truth, and this is our condition in sin and death—and we intensify and increase it through self-deception and self-justification.

The question is: What will it take to humble this desperately wicked, self-centered, proud heart of man that will blame God and blame others in order to justify oneself? We will see that this is where all the dirty fighting comes from. We will talk about that.

What will it take to humble the heart of man? Man has the explicit word, which is a call back outwardly, and he has the inward call back through conscience, and he resists both. It is in light of this that we must understand the third call back. It comes after He calls them back through shame and "**Where are you?**" (v. 9b). They are distinct call backs. "**Where are you?**" came directly from God to man, but now it may be asked by God through others to the person in sin by saying,

'Where are you?' In sharing the message of the gospel, when you begin calling people to repentance, you may ask, 'Where are you?'

THE THIRD CALL BACK:
The Promise and the Curse

This third call back is the curse and the promise together; they must be understood together, and they must not be separated. Many have given the promise without talking about the curse, and some may speak about the curse without talking about the promise. But the curse and promise are *intimately* woven together in this third call back, so they must be taken together.

Where do the curse and promise come in? First of all, God said to the serpent, **"Because you have done this"**—there is a double reference here: the visible and the invisible. Behind the serpent on whom the curse comes, it also comes on the one who used the serpent to camouflage his presence, which is the devil. There is a visible/invisible theme. **"Cursed are you above all the livestock and all the wild animals! You will crawl on your belly and you will eat dust all the days of your life"** (v. 14). This is the curse; it is the beginning of the curse. It comes on the animals. It comes on the serpent. As a result of the curse, two things happen: The form of the serpent has been changed, so it crawls on its belly now (heretofore, it did not), and its food has been changed, **"you will eat dust all the days of your life."** Notice the visible and invisible: eating dust, biting the dust, and the failure, the humiliation, that will come upon Satan. The one who set out to tempt man will bite the dust; he will eat the dust.

The curse is upon all the creatures, all the livestock, and all the wild animals. The curse comes on the serpent more heavily, but it comes on all of them. Creatures are variously affected by the curse, and the curse affects the form and the food of the creatures. When people ask about the Tyrannosaurus Rex, lions, and other creatures, we must understand that they were not originally that way. God created the world good,[6] and the animals were given the green vegetation for food, and it is because of the *curse* that the animals devour each other. It was not that way from the beginning. It is a basic doctrine, but it is missed and

---

6. Gangadean, *The Westminster Confession*, 14–18.

missed and missed and missed and missed. Darwin tried to explain this; it is out of this that he came up with his theory of evolution. He says, 'God did not create the world with all this extravagant waste, or with all of this cruelty, with the animals devouring each other,' so he introduced the notion of evolution to explain this. Darwin's theory is most of all a theodicy rather than a scientific view.[7]

The curse comes in and now we see the promise. The promise is spoken of: **"And I will put enmity between you and the woman, and between your offspring and hers; he will crush your head, and you will strike his heel"** (v. 15). Satan's seduction of mankind through the woman is not going to stand. God said, **"I will put enmity between you and the woman"** (v. 15a). The alliance between Satan and man would not stand; God reverses the order of things. **"I will put enmity."** Here, a spiritual war is established between the woman and the serpent, and between the seed of the serpent and the seed of the woman. Here again, is that double reference of the physical and the spiritual, the visible and the invisible. The serpent literally has baby serpents; he is not referring literally to the snakes, but to the devil and to those who heed the word of the devil: They are the seed of the serpent. Those who hear the Word of God, in contrast to the devil, are the seed of the woman, the sons of God. A spiritual war was set up between those who believe the Word of God and those who do not. **"I will put enmity."** This is not allowing an evil condition to stand, but a reversing of it. The promise begins here.

This spiritual war is going on, and it will go on through generations, **"between your offspring and hers"** (v. 15)—through generations, through history; so we say the spiritual war is age-long, between believer and non-believer. Augustine's book, *The City of God*, speaks about these two cities: the city of man are with those who love themselves more than God, and the city of God are those who love God more than self. This will go on all the way from the beginning to the end of history.

It is a spiritual war that is an age-long and agonizing war. It is a war to the death: The one will *crush* the head of the other, and the other will

---

7. For further exposition regarding the theological elements of the doctrine of evolutions, see the works of Cornelius Hunter, *Darwin's God: Evolution and the Problem of Evil* (Eugene: Wipf & Stock, 2001); *Darwin's Proof: The Triumph of Religion Over Science* (Ada: Brazos Press, 2003); and *Science's Blind Spot: The Unseen Religion of Scientific Naturalism* (Ada: Brazos Press, 2007).

strike His heel. One will inflict a mortal blow, as Christ was killed on the cross, but in doing so, Christ will overcome and crush the serpent, spiritually, and overcome all of his power. It is fundamentally a spiritual war. One side is full of self-justification, fights dirty, does personal attacks: *ad hominem* and *tu quoque*. 'You come short too, look at this,' and imputing motives and, if necessary, using force and killing, even as Cain killed Abel. Cain struck physically, but Abel triumphed over Cain; he testifies to this day, and it stands.[8] It is an agonizing war. But in the end, the one side—the seed of the woman, represented in that promised one—will *crush* the head of the serpent—good will overcome evil. Here we have the promise: There will be a spiritual war, age-long and agonizing, and good will overcome evil through the seed of the woman—the promised one who will come in the place of Adam.

This is the promise. What is the curse? The curse is represented in terms of toil with nature: the ground is cursed, thorns and thistles it will bring forth.[9] It is hard to produce food from the earth. The weather conditions will change. The fertility and fruitfulness of the soil will greatly decrease. This is where you have many plants blossoming, and most of the blossoms die and fail to come to fruition. There is going to be difficulty, and that is going to increase in history. Toil. We experience it when we go to work. In whatever we do, there is toil and there is stress. In addition, there is strife with others. It is spoken of in relation to the woman: **"I will greatly increase your pains in childbearing; with pain you will give birth to children"** (v. 16a). Because of sin, childbirth will be painful. It is not just a physical bringing of the child out of the womb; if that were all there were to it, praise God!—but that is just the beginning of it. **"With *pain* you will give birth to children"** (v. 16).[10] Your very children, this difficulty will be in your very house, between parents and children. Not just mother and child, but parents and children; in pain you will bring forth children. It is particularly directed toward the woman because of her relationship with both her children and her husband. We see the matter being addressed. It is between parents and children, between brother and brother. It is

---

8. *Hebrews 11:4.*

9. *Genesis 3:17–19.*

10. Emphasis added.

between Cain and Abel. It is between believer and non-believer. What we are speaking of is strife.

To Adam, He said, "**By the sweat of your brow you will eat your food until you return to the ground, since from it you were taken; for dust you are and to dust you will return**" (v. 19). Death; it ordinarily comes through old age and sickness. God imposed death upon mankind as part of the curse.

The curse consists immediately, individually, in toil with nature, strife with others, and in oneself—in one's own bones, with old age and sickness, and death. When this is developed and widespread, it becomes famine, war, and plague. Mankind has been afflicted with this. Throughout Scripture, we see these themes in the prophets: War, famine, and plague are explicitly mentioned, and in the Book of Revelation we see war, famine, and plague—instruments by which God rules mankind through the curse, calling man back to Himself. Perhaps you can understand now why we looked back and said this is a third call back, which must be understood in light of the first two call backs and man's response to it. The curse speaks explicitly against the self-deception and self-justification by which we resist dealing with sin. The curse is universal. We must understand that the curse is not original—it was not present in the original creation—everything was good.[11] The curse is not inherent in sin: Spiritual death is inherent, "for when you eat of it you will surely die" (Gen. 2:17b). But physical death is not inherent; physical death is imposed. Physical death is imposed by God to *restrain* man from going as far and fast into sin as he can, to *recall* man from sin, and having been recalled, to *remove* sin that remains in man. Think of the case of Job, sin remained in Job, and he experienced the curse. Some persons are brought down to their knees, humbled low by the curse in their lives, and brought to seek God. Some are restrained by the curse; the lifespan before the Flood was 900 plus years, and after the Flood, it was reduced to 70 plus years; less time, less time to sin; just a sheer, physical, restraint. After the Flood, the fertility of the earth is much more greatly reduced. After Babel, strife was much more greatly increased.

God uses the curse to restrain man from sin, so he does not go and rush headlong into sin and come to that devastation that we had before

---

11. *Genesis 1:4, 10, 12, 18, 21, 25, 31.*

in the Flood. The curse is imposed by God to call man back from sin.
We must remember that the curse is the last, final, and continuing call
back: It shows that God holds us responsible for our sin. The reality of
the curse is where people are; they are concerned about the difficulty in
their work, in their relationships, in old age, in sickness, and death. Psychologically and otherwise, we must reckon with the curse, understand
it ourselves, and be able to bring others to understand it in the context
of the promise. "If we say that we have no sin, we deceive ourselves,
and the truth is not in us. If we confess our sins, he is faithful and just
to forgive us our sins, and to cleanse us from all unrighteousness" (1
Jn. 1:8–9 KJV). We must begin *here* in our thinking, and bring this to
man's attention with the promise.

This is the third call back, and it tells us that we have in us self-deception about how much we are seeking the truth, how diligently we
are seeking God, and self-justification for not seeing what is clear. We
accuse others, blame others, and excuse ourselves. The reality of physical death is there: We must make sense of it, or just say it is nonsense.
It is a great mountain staring every one of us in the face; it is in our
bones, every day.

What happens after this? **"Adam named his wife Eve, because she
would become the mother of all the living"** (v. 20). We must understand that he is obeying God's command to have children, to be fruitful
and multiply, and he is doing so under the presence of the curse, and
all the implications of that. He must give an account to his children
for what he did, and the devastation he has wrought in bringing death
into the world. And how can he, without hope? In naming his wife
"Eve," he is obeying God under the condition of the curse and the
promise. It shows now that he accepts the Word of God, turns back,
and will obey. It shows his repentance, submission and obedience to
God, and his trust in God for the promise: The seed of the woman
will crush the head of the serpent.[12] We have in this statement, **"Adam
named his wife Eve"** (v. 20a), by implication and assumption, that he
repents, has faith, and confesses his faith in this way—that is what we
mean when we speak about good and necessary consequences. What
happens? **"The LORD God made garments of skin for Adam and his
wife and clothed them"** (v. 21); garments of skin. This indicates the

---

12. *Genesis 3:15.*

forgiveness of God through vicarious atonement; through the death of another, he is forgiven.

The coats of skin represent vicarious atonement, which is being taught from the very beginning. He is justified; he is covered through another who is the representative. We have the truth being taught here in Genesis, in redemption, that God calls us back in this way, and when we repent and have faith, He justifies us. Then, lastly, He sanctifies us: having been forgiven of sin and having our sin covered does not mean we have been cleansed from it. God says, "If we confess our sins, he is faithful and just to forgive us our sins, and to cleanse us from all un-righteousness" (1 Jn. 1:9 KJV). This cleansing comes through suffer-ing—he cannot stay in the Garden and eat of the tree of life and live forever. The tree, representing spiritual life, would allow physical life to go on forever—remember the visible/invisible. Adam cannot partake of this tree and live forever. In sin, we cannot live forever. We cannot avoid physical death; we are barred from the tree of life. Furthermore, we cannot stay in the Garden in our sin; we cannot avoid toil. Every-thing is provided for there, so we must go outside, where the curse is dominant, and suffer toil, strife, old age, sickness, and death. Last of all, in our sin, we cannot re-enter the Garden and avoid the curse: We are sealed in that condition; no one can avoid it. The Cherubim are placed in the east of the Garden of Eden, to guard the entrance to it, and the flaming sword is turning every which way. We are doomed, and any attempt to find life, apart from the knowledge of God *through suffering*, is doomed to destruction. We must go through trials of faith, and the sufferings of them, to be cleansed, to grow in the knowledge of God, and to come to the truth of life.

We must remember that this is done because we have to work through not just the sin of not seeking and understanding, but also self-deception, self-justification, blaming others, and fighting dirty. It is a terrible, terrible, dirty conflict given the strife that is there—**"with pain you will give birth to children"** (v. 16), given the self-justification, and given the spiritual war—these three come together. Those who do not believe in the use of reason to see what is clear will not use reason to respond. They will fight dirty, they will fight emotionally, they will do all kinds of abusive things and impugn your motives and call things into question, and when that does not work, they will seek to harm you physically, even to the point of killing you. Remember what happened with Cain and Abel. This is the condition of mankind; it is a universal human condition; we find it in literature, we find it in politics, we find it in economics, we find it in psychology, we find it in philosophy, we find it in religion; it is the universal condition of man in his sin.

We are to understand that the curse is God's call back and understand that the curse is God restraining, recalling, and removing moral evil that remains in us. We are to learn, with Adam, to accept the curse and to live under it. Notice he accepted it in some measure. But if God had not put the Cherubim and the flaming sword there, you could be sure that when he is driven out the front, he will run around, sneak around, and come in through the back way.

We, as human beings, have tried to avoid the curse again and again. Sometimes, we try to avoid the curse rather than sin. We want to get to heaven and avoid the curse rather than come to the knowledge of God. The whole doctrine of heaven has been distorted by the spirit of wanting to avoid the curse. We must watch ourselves, truly repent, humble ourselves, and learn that our good is knowing God. There is no life apart from knowing God, nor is there knowing of God, in our sin, apart from suffering.

God is gracious. Suffering under the curse is not punishment, though perhaps, in a sense, we speak about it in this way. When the curse is intensified, and death has sped up, it may be spoken of as some kind of temporal punishment. But for believers, physical death is not punishment. All will be raised from death physically, and those who are without Christ will continue in spiritual death forever. That is the true punishment: the meaninglessness, boredom, and guilt that there is without God. But in Christ, the seed of the woman, the promised one, there is eternal life—life, and life abundantly. He calls us to come to Him, drink, and be satisfied.

5

SEEKING GOD AND UNDERSTANDING

Ten Points on Seeking and Understanding

Proverbs 2:1–11

¹My son, if you accept my words and store up my commands within you, ²turning your ear to wisdom and applying your heart to understanding, ³and if you call out for insight and cry aloud for understanding, ⁴and if you look for it as for silver and search for it as for hidden treasure, ⁵then you will understand the fear of the LORD and find the knowledge of God. ⁶For the LORD gives wisdom, and from his mouth come knowledge and understanding. ⁷He holds victory in store for the upright, he is a shield to those whose walk is blameless, ⁸for he guards the course of the just and protects the way of his faithful ones. ⁹Then you will understand what is right and just and fair—every good path. ¹⁰For wisdom will enter your heart, and knowledge will be pleasant to your soul. ¹¹Discretion will protect you, and understanding will guard you.

T HE MESSAGE IS ON SEEKING GOD and understanding. I am picking up from the nature of faith; and faith and understanding. What you will hear is summed up in ten points. Perhaps each point should be a sermon in itself, but this is where I am, and this is what is coming, so at least be aware. Not all points will be concentrated on equally; we will particularly concentrate on what is meant by *understanding*. What you will hear are a lot of themes that we have spoken of in the past, but they are put together in a somewhat different way and brought into focus, and this is to get a larger view. What we are basing this on is two passages of Scripture: Hebrews 11:6: "But without faith it is impossible to please him: for he that cometh to God must believe that he is, and that he is a rewarder of them that diligently seek him."[1] Hence, the subject: seeking God. From Romans 3:10–11: "There is no one righteous, not even one; there is no one who understands, no one who seeks God." Again, seeking, but in this case, it is connected with understanding: No one understands, and no one seeks.

FIRST POINT:
It Is by Seeking We Understand

The first point we wish to make is the connection between seeking and understanding, and then we will also get to the necessity for understanding. But first of all, it is *by seeking* that we understand. It seems fairly obvious when stated, but it is possible to think of seeking, understanding, and righteousness as three things side by side; we often divide the human personality instead of understanding the natural unity and order within the personality, and the process that there is.[2] Notice it begins, "believe *that* he is,"[3] and all that is involved in believing: We have talked about the nature of faith. Believing *that* He is the rewarder of those who diligently seek Him.[4] It has to do with our hope, the future, the unseen, and believing *that* He is, which is to understand the invisible God from the things that are made.

We must believe *that* He is and that He rewards those who seek Him, in that, there is a vision of what that reward is, and the implications of the reward connected with seeking *Him*. God said to Abraham, "Fear not, Abram: I am thy shield, and thy exceeding great reward" (Gen. 15:1b KJV). God *Himself* is our reward. We have to understand this and how this is connected with understanding and possessing God in this way. We believe *that* He is and *that* He rewards those who seek Him, understand what that means, and from this we are moved to seek Him. So the believing '*that*' comes before the seeking—some have

---

1. KJV.

2. Surrendra Gangadean, *Man, The Image of God: The Seven Aspects of Human Nature* (Phoenix: Logos Papers Press, Forthcoming 2025).

3. Emphasis added.

4. *Hebrews 11:6.*

raised questions about this and I just wanted to make it clear. It is *by seeking* that we *understand* further and beyond this initial belief '*that.*' This requires an explanation of what we mean by understanding and what we mean by seeking.

A little bit more on this first point: It is by seeking that we understand. We want to underscore that it is *only* by seeking that we understand. It is not that there are other ways to understand besides seeking. To put it more tightly, we would say: Seeking is *necessary* and *sufficient* for understanding, which is why the Scripture makes the point, "he that cometh to God must believe that he is, and that he is a rewarder of them that diligently seek him" (Heb. 11:6b KJV). Notice, in terms of the passage that we quoted from Romans 3, which speaks about seeking and understanding, and what it is to be righteous, but here in Hebrews, all it is speaking about is seeking, "he is a rewarder of them that diligently seek him." We will speak about seeking, understanding, and righteousness—all three aspects of our being and personality—but we will put the emphasis upon *seeking* because that is what the passage does. It is by seeking that we come to understand. We would add further, from the Romans 3:11 passage, that *no one* seeks—that is, no one left to himself (or herself)—*therefore*, no one understands. I am underscoring the connection. The inclination will be to leave these sitting side by side: seeking and understanding and doing what is right. The first point is that by seeking, we understand.

SECOND POINT:
We Deceive Ourselves About Seeking

The Scripture says, "there is no one who seeks" (Rom. 3:11b), so if we are going to come to God and find our reward, we *must* seek. Each and every one who comes to God must seek and come to know Him, and *yet* the Scripture says, no one seeks and no one understands—a stark contrast. Yet we think that we *do* seek God. We deceive ourselves about our seeking God—there is the theme of self-deception coming in. How do we do this? What is meant positively by *seeking*? Outwardly, we can act in certain ways; we can go through a process of activities as duties: We can read our Bible, we can pray, we can do deeds of righteousness, as

Saul of Tarsus did—concerning legalistic righteousness, he was faultless.[5] Many people have read their Bibles, prayed, and practiced the virtues, and yet they have not been seeking God, and therefore, they have not been understanding and gaining their reward. There are people who have been in this congregation who have left, and they regarded things like the novitiate as legalism because they approached it in a legalistic way. Instead of diligently reading the Bible in the spirit of seeking, it was just done legalistically. It may even sink to another level of ritual action. Prayer can become ritual; think of the Rosary being said mechanically, and that is taken for prayer, as against seeking God in prayer.

We have a way—and covenant children, too—of going through the outward motions: going to church regularly, reading the Bible, and, you know, 'I've had my devotions.' And yet it is not accompanied by the spirit of *seeking* to know Him and to understand, and so it is missed. Someone told me this week that 'this is the worst place to be if you are not seeking God,' because we have these requirements connected with the vow that we took, spelled out in the novitiate, and people can go through that and check it off. Then they are going through the motions, and checking things off, and yet not finding their reward and pleasure and gladness in God. Why not? Because they are not *seeking*, and therefore, the reward is not there. There is not seeking, then the understanding is not there, so the reward is not there, and instead, there is emptiness in their lives. People who have been brought up in the faith can testify to this. People who have been attending church, who have been in the church for a long time can testify to this. It is possible to go through the outward motions, which are necessary for understanding, but without the seeking of God, it is not sufficient.

We deceive ourselves about seeking God, not only in outward act but in inward feeling. The Church has been dominated by pietism at times, and certain segments of the Church are particularly focused on piety, with an emphasis on 'holy feelings.' Sometimes it becomes individual, it becomes mystical, and it is very widespread in charismatic circles. There are all kinds of enthusiasms, zeal without knowledge, and feelings that are stirred up. It is almost as if there is a pleasure in having these good feelings, but it is not seeking Him and knowing Him. Both in terms of outward acts and feelings, we could have these things

---

5. *Philippians 3:6.*

and not be seeking and not be understanding. Large segments of the Church have been exposed to this.

Positively, what does it mean to seek God? In Proverbs 2:1–11, we find a number of parallelisms that bring this into focus. Notice: "**if you accept my words**" (v. 1a), that is a start; you accept the Word of God. The second part connected with that goes further: "**and store up my commands within you**" (v. 1b). As it is said elsewhere, "Thy word have I hid in mine heart, that I might not sin against thee" (Ps. 119:11 KJV). Is that a good start? Accepting the Word of God, and memorizing it, storing it up in our hearts. "**Turning your ear to wisdom**" (v. 2a), we listen with our ear, we hear the teaching, the preaching, the work of the pastor-teachers, and those who have benefited from that—we turn our ear and we listen. But we also *apply* your heart to understanding. Turning our ear to wisdom and listening to another is one thing, and applying our heart or applying it to our heart, to put it into practice, is another. We must not be *listening* only: we must be *doing*. We are not to be vain listeners. We accept and we store, we listen and we apply, and we pray: "**if you call out for insight and cry aloud for understanding**" (v. 3). None of this weak, barely audible, prayer. 'Lord! Help! I don't understand, bless me Lord with understanding.' Cry aloud! There is something about uttering it with our voice. I am not inclined to raise my voice about much—I stay pretty low. It takes an effort to raise my voice, it is contrary to my nature. But cry aloud; we cannot get around it. I prefer the groaning method myself.

"**Call out for insight**" (v. 3a)—notice the word *insight*. And notice it says, "**apply your heart to understanding**" (v. 2b)—we are to put it to application. We call out for *insight*. Now someone will try to interpret the word *understand* as just *believe*. There is a difference between those: they are not the same. So the word *insight* disallows us from identifying *believing* with *understanding*.

It says to "**cry aloud for understanding**" (v. 3b): God *wants* us to do this and He wants us to seek. So it says *accept* and *store*, and *listen* and *apply* and *call out* and *cry aloud*. It says to "**look for it as for silver and search for it as for hidden treasure**" (v. 4). Those who went on the Gold Rush, to California or to Alaska, and those who seek for treasure and go deep within the earth, and dangle on the sides of cliffs, searching in the rocks for veins of silver ore—Job speaks about people like that,[6] seeking for wisdom as for hidden treasure—that is how we are to do it. That is what it is to seek the Lord and seek the Lord for understanding. In these four verses, we have two pairs each, from the beginning going all the way through to seeking.

Notice what comes: "**you will understand the fear of the LORD**" (v. 5a)—this is a basic piece, this is the beginning of wisdom. It is not the end of wisdom, but it is the beginning. We are not going to begin, in our sin, without the fear of the Lord. You will understand "**and find the knowledge of God**" (v. 5b). Notice how these three come together in verse 6: "**For the LORD gives wisdom, and from his mouth come knowledge and understanding**" (v. 6). Again in verse 10, "**wisdom will enter your heart, and knowledge will be pleasant to your soul. Discretion will protect you, and understanding will guard you**" (vv. 10–11). These three—wisdom, knowledge, and understanding—are connected, just like *signs*, *miracles*, and *wonders*, describing the same things from three different points of view. *Precepts*, *commands*, and *ordinances*: these kinds of parallelisms are used throughout Scripture.

This is what it is to seek the Lord and not to deceive ourselves about our seeking. First, if we seek, we understand. Secondly, we *do* deceive ourselves about seeking and we should understand what seeking is. "**Search for it as for hidden treasure**" (v. 4b): There must be a *deliberateness* about this; there must be a *pressing* of ourselves. It does not *come* to us; we have to *actively* seek it. Matthew 11:12 says, "And from the days of John the Baptist until now the kingdom of heaven suffereth violence, and the violent take it by force":[7] we have to *exert* an effort, a strenuous effort, to get it. That is seeking God diligently. "He is a rewarder of them that diligently seek him" (Heb. 11:6b KJV).

THIRD POINT:
The Reward for Seeking God Is Understanding God

God rewards those who diligently seek Him—not some*thing* from Him, but *Him*. God said to Abraham, "I am thy shield, and thy exceeding great reward" (Gen. 15:1b KJV). God Himself is the reward. We understand God's self-revelation: In all He does, God reveals Himself. God reveals

---

6. *Job 28:1–11.*

7. KJV.

Himself in His works of creation and providence. He works all things after the counsel of His own will, to the praise of His glory. We are to possess God as our reward in our *union* and our *communion* with Him (some people hear those words and they translate it in a kind of 'mystical presence' sort of way, non-cognitively, as not involving thought). This is how Jesus spoke of it—He spoke of it as *abiding* in Him and He in us and He coming to make His home with us.[8] And He explains what His abiding in us is: "If ye abide in me, and my words abide in you" (Jn. 15:7a KJV). If we grasp His Word in our minds, He abides in us; if we obey His Word, we abide in Him. This is the union and the communion. "Whoever has my commands and obeys them, he is the one who loves me" (Jn. 14:21). We possess God through understanding, we come to know God by union and communion, we *abide* in Him: He abides in us and we abide in Him. God is our reward. The reward for seeking God is understanding God.

FOURTH POINT:
This Reward (The Knowledge of God) Is Satisfying

The reward, which is the knowledge of God, is satisfying; it is more than satisfying: It is *deeply* satisfying. It satisfies our deepest longings, our deepest need, and I will add that it is the *only* thing that has lasting satisfaction. It *is* eternal life. Jesus said to the woman at the well, "but whoever drinks the water I give him will never thirst" (Jn. 4:14a). He gives Himself to us in His Word. As we drink of the water that He gives, we will never thirst again. He says that it will be "a spring of water welling up to eternal life" (Jn. 4:14b). This is the secret spring; if we do not have it, if it dries up, we will find no satisfaction. God and only God knows, in each of our lives, whether it is flowing, whether we are drinking of the fountain, the living fountain, whether we are abiding with God, in union and communion, and coming to know Him. There is no substitute for this.

Jesus said further, in John 7:37b, on the great day of the feast, "If anyone is thirsty, let him come to me and drink." And in verse 38, "Whoever believes in me, as the Scripture has said, streams of living water will flow from within him." It is a spring, in terms of our

---

8. *John 14.*

personal satisfaction and drinking, but it is not only to be a spring for ourselves. It is to be a stream of living waters that will bring life to a thirsty world. It is this water that flowed out from under the threshold of God's temple in Ezekiel;[9] and the water of life that is flowing down the middle of the street in the middle of the City of God,[10] bringing life everywhere it goes. It is to be a stream of living water, as it flows not only from one individual but from the whole Church. God, present, in the Church: abiding in them, and the people of God abiding in Him and growing in that knowledge, that full knowledge. This is the reward of the people of God.

FIFTH POINT:
Without the Satisfaction of Knowing God, We Seek Satisfaction in the World, in Vain

The world cannot satisfy. "Everyone who drinks this water will be thirsty again, but whoever drinks the water I give him will never thirst" (Jn. 4:13–14a). There is *no* satisfaction apart from knowing God. When we go to the world to try to find satisfaction, we inevitably go to excess: We continue to burn in our desires, we are not satisfied, we burn in our lusts, and we go to perversion. Human beings have desires, and they either have those satisfied in God or by the world. You may try to mix it, but that does not go very far. Think about the world and its desires. Think about the culture wars that are raging and what people are saying and what they want. They fight to have the right to abortion. They fight to have the right to engage in sexual promiscuity and sexual perversions. They fight for this, and they cannot find any satisfaction in it. We mentioned the movie *Eyes Wide Shut* and the perversions that were going on there. No satisfaction without God. Everything we try and seek is in vain, and it does become excessive. This is why drugs are present, this is why alcohol is present, this is why we try to drown ourselves in the music of the world and all the longings, and it does not satisfy us, and it only corrupts us more. Without God, there is no satisfaction, we seek it in the world in vain. We hear that Word again with a new, deeper understanding: He is the rewarder of those who

---

9. *Ezekiel 47:1–12.*

10. *Revelation 22:1–2a.*

diligently seek *Him*. We *need* this reward, we *need* this blessing, we *need* this satisfaction, but it comes through seeking Him, and through understanding. Our reward is in knowing Him and growing in our knowledge of God, which is eternal life.

SIXTH POINT:
God Holds Us Responsible for Not Seeking, Not Understanding, and Not Doing What Is Right

The focus, as we have said, is on not seeking. The third commandment is, "Thou shalt not take the name of the LORD thy God in vain; for the LORD will not hold him guiltless that taketh his name in vain" (Ex. 20:7 KJV). He does not hold anyone guiltless who takes His name in vain. The name of God is revealed in His works and in His Word: His written Word. When we lightly and thoughtlessly regard it—when we do not pay attention, when we neglect it—we are taking it in vain. And "the LORD will not hold him guiltless that taketh his name in vain." Neither the one who is disregarding it in the beginning, nor the one who is the most righteous in all the earth; Job was blameless, but he was not sinless, he was not guiltless. God called him further to know through suffering, and Job repented: "I have heard of thee by the hearing of the ear; but now mine eye seeth thee. Wherefore I abhor myself, and repent in dust and ashes" (Job 42:5–6 KJV). God will deal this way with all of His children, to bring them to know Him. He does not hold us guiltless who take His name in vain—lightly and thoughtlessly regarding that by which God makes Himself known. What God does when we take His name in vain is that He gives us up to our depravity, to a darkened mind, hardened heart, to burn in our lusts, to go into depravity. Romans 1:21–32—especially verses 24, 26, and 28—says, "God also gave them up to uncleanness," "God gave them up unto vile affections," "God gave them over to a reprobate mind,"[11] which is the wrath of God given. God is not holding us guiltless when we take His name in vain. This could be the preaching, Scripture, general revelation—all of it. We are to seek Him *diligently*. He is the rewarder of those who diligently seek Him.

---

11. KJV.

God holds us responsible for not seeking and not understanding. We have explained this is the essence of sin, the universal character of sin. We may all sin in different ways: "We all, like sheep, have gone astray" (Is. 53:6a). We have sinned and come short of the glory of God. We have not sought and we have not understood. From there, in terms of our particular ways, we may all go our own way, but this is the universal element: not seeking and not understanding. Remember that you can read your Bible, and you can pray, without seeking God. You can go to church, you can act pious, you can keep legalistic righteousness—which is not a bad thing, but it is insufficient, and we can do this without seeking God and knowing God.

SEVENTH POINT:
We Are to Treat Others as Having the Ability and Responsibility for Seeking and Understanding

God holds us responsible. Point seven is that we are to treat others as having the ability and the responsibility—those go together. We might play on that word, *response-ability*, the ability to respond: We have the ability and the responsibility for seeking and understanding. Spiritual death is the inherent consequence of sin: meaninglessness, boredom, and guilt. More than that, it brings death in all of our relationships and activities. Part of holding others responsible is, on the one hand, to call persons to repentance (recognizing our own need first), but secondly, we cannot and should not try to separate sin and death. In the Garden, when it says, "You will not surely die" (Gen. 3:4a), there is an attempt to separate sin and death, which cannot be separated. When relationships are dying because one person is going on in sin, and the other wants to go on in God, we have to let it die; we should not try to hold on to it. We have to recognize that there is sin and death here. If we try to hold on to the relationship, when there is sin, we are going to go over to the other side and compromise, at least by not being a faithful witness: by shutting up about it and not saying anything more, then by accommodating little by little. If we hang out with the other person, we do what they say, we tolerate what they do, we do not say anything more because we will offend them, and then we begin to accommodate them, and we slide—we slide with them. We cannot separate sin and death. Allowing death to work is part of holding people responsible. We do not impose death, rather, it is there, and we are recognizing it, which is part of holding people responsible.

There are all kinds of degrees, *very fine*, that we see in terms of sin and death. The more we find someone to be unreasonable, in sin—not seeking, not understanding—the more we find we cannot share with them, the more we have to hold back, the less we can be open. We know that there are all kinds of degrees to which this happens. It spontaneously happens; it happens without hardly thinking, it happens so naturally. If a person is not particularly interested in picking up and responding to cues, inquiring, and talking about the things of the Lord, then the tendency is not to talk about it. It is not anything we imposed; we just recognize it. But with some other people, we can talk with about the Lord, we can talk with them about the deep things of the Lord, and that which is deep within our heart. Why is that? We are picking up what is going on. While there is no death in an ultimate sense, sin remains in us, and death is present. This is why Paul says, "O wretched man that I am! who shall deliver me from the body of this death" (Rom. 7:24 KJV). Death remains with sin. It may not reign, as in sin is not reigning,[12] but it is present. We have to reckon with this. God holds us responsible, and we are to treat others as having the ability and responsibility for understanding.

EIGHTH POINT:
God Calls Us Back Through the Curse

We have spoken about the curse.[13] We should recognize, first of all, that almost all deny or neglect the curse, as imposed by God as a call back—almost all deny this. Non-Christians, out and out, and Christians may acknowledge it in some ways, but sometimes say it is punishment. They say that it is part of the original punishment; as against saying that spiritual death is the punishment and the curse is imposed as a call back. We miss the seriousness of the call back, we do not heed it, we let it go and we just grin and bear it. There are times when we are forced to deal with it—without recognizing it as such—when it comes to us as trials, the trials of our faith.

---

12. *Romans 6:12.*

13. Sermon 4: *The Curse and The Promise.*

The curse is, according to Genesis, toil, strife, old age, sickness, and death. In the developed stage culturally, it is war, famine, and plague. We go through wars and then just forget about it. We can get stirred up by war movies. Last night, I saw a war movie about World War II called *Hart's War*. It stirs us for a while, and then we let it go. We have famines in places; it stirs us for a while, and plagues and diseases that are troubling us, and then we go back to the usual.

The curse restrains us from sin, it recalls us from sin and having been recalled, it removes sin remaining. It calls us to stop and think, and that is seeking. In the trials of faith, the fiery trials, it is usually in the trial that we begin to seek the Lord—just spontaneously, without recognizing the theology of the curse as God's call back to us—to break through our self-deception and self-justification about not seeking and not understanding. We just go through life, and that is why we have Psalm 90: Ages and ages pass over cultures and civilizations. This is why there are things like the Book of Ecclesiastes: "Generations come and generations go, but the earth remains forever" (Ecc. 1:4)—time passes. For those who stop and think back and look, I think about the *Elegy Written in a Country Churchyard*, by Thomas Gray. The passing of the day and the recognition of people dying. If you go to the graveyards in England, be sure to go there and perhaps read the Elegy, and think about it. Certainly, it just pushes us to reflect. How old some of those gravestones are. When you go into Westminster Abbey, you see the names of people centuries ago, who are buried there, and where you will be walking, you will see stones on the ground, gravestones there. Certainly it was there in the Church of England in India when we went there. People coming and going and generations have forgotten them, and you wonder about us, and what is it all about? We should live more consciously under the curse; we should not be insensitive. We should not be *morbidly* sensitive: we are morbidly sensitive when we do not recognize the curse as God's call back and a blessing.

Here is a call to seek: which we neglect and avoid, resist and deny. Our lives just pass away as a vapor. When we could have learned from it, we just let it go; we just let our suffering go. When we let our suffering go—on this call back of death—we have really let it go; we have lost it. *Do not waste suffering.* A lot of things are wasted, and then suffering comes to call us back from that, and we may waste our suffering; it is truly a waste. Waste is the word for hell: it is a waste dump, a garbage dump. In the wisdom of God, nothing is wasted, but in our lives, for us, it may be wasted.

God calls us back through the curse. He causes us to seek Him, and in seeking, to understand. When the fiery trials are upon us, we should not shrug it off, not be insensitive, not be hardened, but come to God, to cry out to the Lord. Remember, in Psalm 107:13: "Then they cried to the LORD in their trouble, and He saved them from their distress." Time and again, that refrain came: In trouble, to the Lord, they cried. We are supposed to cry out to the Lord when we are in trouble, and the Lord delivers us. Then we bless the name of God, and we come to know the Lord a little bit more. Because we have so much resistance to seeking, we move forward in our understanding, precept by precept, inch by inch.

NINTH POINT:
Understanding the Meaning and Explanation of God's Revelation

Understanding has content; it has specific content. We can define understanding in terms of its content. When we speak of understanding we mean *understanding the meaning, or explanation, of God's revelation.* One example of this is Romans 1:20: The invisible qualities of God are clearly seen, being *understood* from the things that are made. In that understanding, we have the idea of an *inference* being made, a reason, inferring, enabling us to understand. This is one case of what the word *understand* means in Scripture. Some other examples are: what we read in Proverbs 2 about insight, and from the parables of the Lord in Matthew 13, where Jesus explained to His disciples the *meaning* of the parable of the tares.[14]

Understanding involves understanding the *meaning* of what is explained. This is part of what happens when we meditate on the Word of God day and night: We understand more and more. Understanding has content, and it is particularly the *meaning* of it: What does it mean? In Luke 24:26–27, Jesus is speaking to His disciples after the resurrection, and He says, "How foolish you are, and how slow of heart to believe all that the prophets have spoken!" Notice, "to believe": they are slow *to believe.* "'Did not the Christ have to suffer these things and then enter

---

14. *Matthew 13:18–23.*

his glory?' And beginning with Moses and all the Prophets, he explained to them what was said in all the Scriptures concerning himself." He explained the meaning to them, and then they understood, and then they could believe; this is in contrast to being slow to believe because they did not understand. Notice, after Jesus makes Himself known to them, and He disappears, they ask each other, "Were not our hearts burning within us while he talked with us on the road and *opened the Scriptures to us?*" (Lk. 24:32).[15] Jesus opened the meaning of the Scripture, and what was the effect? As it came into their understanding, their hearts were burning. It says, "he opened their minds so they could understand the Scriptures" (Lk. 24:45). "He told them, 'This is what is written: The Christ will suffer and rise from the dead on the third day'" (Lk. 24:46). Many still do not understand that Christ must suffer and then enter into His glory. All of Judaism has missed this understanding, and as much as they profess to believe the Scripture, they do not understand it. "And repentance and forgiveness of sins will be preached in his name to all nations" (Lk. 24:47). Many do not understand what repentance is, and what the remission of sins is, in the name of Christ. They have a Christ without remission of sin. Karl Barth, adopting universalism, does not speak about the remission of sin that is necessary; he has an atonement without content, without meaning.

We have seen examples from Scripture showing that we must understand the revelation; it has content. The Westminster Confession 1.6 speaks about good and necessary consequences. It says that Scripture is sufficient, either expressly, explicitly, (literally stating it), or by good and necessary consequences may be deduced from Scripture: deduction, inference; it involves understanding. So, understanding involves the use of reason to understand the meaning, and it involves inference. We *infer* what is assumed, we draw implications out, and we understand applications. This is the content of understanding. We said, no one seeks, no one *understands*, no one does what is right.[16] And, "he is a rewarder of them that diligently seek him" (Heb. 11:6b KJV), and the reward is the understanding of God. What is this content? We are specifying it. Some people have tried to empty this of meaning.

---

15. Emphasis added.

16. *Romans 3:11; Psalm 14:2–3, 53:1–3.* Emphasis added.

To put it in somewhat technical terms, as some of the theologians have spoken about it, *notitia*, that is *understanding*, is not the same as *assensus*, which means *assenting* to faith, nor is it the same as *fiducia*, *trusting*, and there is an order between them. *Notitia, assensus, fiducia*, and we will speak about trust in a little while. There have been many attempts to avoid and resist and deny understanding and excuse misunderstanding; fideism is one of these ways, and literalism is another. In literalism, there is an unwillingness to draw attention to the meaning of the term, and just say, 'It means what it says, it says what it means, that is it; God said it, I believe it, that settles it; the good book says it right here.' This is excusing oneself from understanding the meaning of it. What do you mean by sin? 'Sin is sin, what more do you need to know?' Yet Scripture does explain it, and the Confession explains it.

We do a kind of literalism, over and against understanding the implications, and we miss the meaning. Meaninglessness comes in and death comes in. Yet, some people are very proud of this, and they hold to it. We might put it this way from Scripture: *the simple* and *the fool* celebrate an orgy of anti-intellectualism. Look at the simple Christian: The simple Christian resists understanding. Here are some of the Scriptures that are used to say we should be simple Christians: 'Become like a little child.'[17] This passage speaks against *pride,* not to be lacking in understanding. The disciples say, "Who is the greatest in the kingdom of heaven?" (Matt. 18:1b), and He took a child and brought him into their midst and said, "I tell you the truth, unless you change and become like little children, you will never enter the kingdom of heaven. Therefore, whoever humbles himself like this child is the greatest in the kingdom of heaven" (Matt. 18:3–4). Unless you *humble* yourself like a little child. Among us, sometimes in our exchanges on the web, we argue about, 'Who is the greatest?' Watch out for that; humble ourselves, become like a little child, and learn to serve others. So Jesus spoke against pride, not in favor of simplicity.

Here is another verse: "Trust in the LORD with all your heart and lean not on your own understanding" (Prov. 3:5). *Trusting* is in some ways being set against *understanding*, but when you look at the content of this, you begin to see. I had an air conditioning guy come out to my house recently to service my air conditioning, and I trusted this

---

17. *Matthew 18:2.*

guy because he had a license, he had been in business for a long time
so I trusted that he was responsible. I did not understand what he was
doing, and I did not try to understand—that is why I was paying him
100 dollars. I trusted him. I had awareness of the competence of the
company that he works for, which is a company that I have been dealing with for some time, and a trustworthy source recommended it to
me, so the company built up my trust. They had a proven record that
I trusted. And because I trusted, I did not have to understand and go
out there and stand up and say, 'What did you do now? Why did you
do that? How much is that going to cost me? Can I do some of that?'
I trust mathematicians—as far as I can throw them. That is, I trust
them as mathematicians, but as philosophers, I do not trust them.
I can go to them and ask them to work out a problem in their field.
They have competence in that area of mathematics, so I do not have to
understand. When it says, 'trust,' it means that I trust in the character
and the proven ability of the person, not that I have to understand it
myself. I can trust in God without having to understand it myself. I
can trust *that* God works all things together for good[18] because He is
good—and His Word says this again and again—but I do not have
to understand *how* He will work things together for good. I am not
contrasting trust with understanding, in some direct way; rather, I am
speaking about trusting the character based on knowledge of proven
character, from the nature of the being and the act of the being. I do
not have to understand the particulars of how it is done, but that does
not mean that I do not have to understand other things. But the idea
of trust is usually used to promote the *simple Christian* idea.

"My ways [are] higher than your ways" (Is. 55:9). The context of
this passage is in regard to our sinful ways, it does not mean we do not
have to understand. Or, in Philippians 4:7, "the peace of God, which
transcends all understanding," which is much like: 'trusting and not
leaning on our own understanding.' There are times when I have to
figure things out: too often. I wish I had an older person, a shoulder
to lean on, to cry upon. You guys do not know what that is quite like.
In God's providence, I had a mentor when I was 19–25; that is a good
age to have a mentor. I went to him often, and I spent lots and lots of
time with him. But since then, I have not quite had that. It is nice to

---

18. *Romans 8:28.*

be able to go to someone and just give it over and let them figure it out. But when you have a problem, and you have to figure it out . . . and I seem to be always on the steep end of the learning curve here; with electrical, this, that, and the other; you name it, I am always on the steep end. I know that peace when I do not have to figure it out. I do have to trust in the Lord to help me figure it out, to bring that knowledge that I need, or to get me through it. The Lord has been gracious and continually done that.

Another verse that has been used is 1 Corinthians 1:26. "Brothers, think of what you were when you were called. Not many of you were wise by human standards; not many were influential; not many were of noble birth." It says, "not many of you were wise," but some people read that as 'not *any* were wise.' But it says "not many," and it is not against wisdom. Or sometimes the wisdom is spoken against that which is really the wisdom of the world. "The world in its wisdom knew not God" (1 Cor. 1:21), so people say, 'See, where does wisdom get you? Nowhere.' This is the world and its wisdom. There is a wisdom in God that we saw in Proverbs where we are encouraged strongly to seek. Or again, I think you know where this is going, "See to it that no one takes you captive through hollow and deceptive philosophy, which depends on human tradition and the basic principles of this world rather than on Christ"(Col. 2:8). This is a spoiler, this is the ultimate one, right? What the Scripture says is *worldly* philosophy, philosophy after the elements—the *stoicheia*—the fundamental principles of this world, and "rather than on Christ," which is the rest of that Scripture. Those who use that verse to engage in anti-intellectual attitudes and postures are missing it.

There are many warnings against being simple. The simple are to gain prudence.[19] They are not to love their simplicity: "How long will you simple ones love your simple ways?" (Prov. 1:22) There is warning against the simple and the disaster that comes upon them (Prov. 1:32). In Proverbs 22:3 and 27:12, we have reference to the lack of prudence on the part of the simple and the disaster that comes upon them. "The prudent see danger and take refuge, but the simple keep going and suffer for it" (Prov. 27:12).

---

19. *Proverbs 1:4.*

Proverbs 14:15: "A simple man believes anything," they are gullible, and they end up in a lot of superstition, which is not praiseworthy. There is a lot that is said in praise of wisdom—Proverbs 2:1–11, 3:13–20, 4:3–9. Over and against being childlike as we spoke about in Matthew 18:2, it is against pride, not against understanding. 1 Corinthians 14:20 says, "Brethren, be not children in understanding; howbeit in malice be ye children, but in understanding be men."[20] 1 Corinthians 13:11: "When I was a child, I spoke as a child, I understood as a child, I thought as a child; but when I became a man, I put away childish things." Everything encourages us to be mature in our understanding. Hebrews 5:12, "In fact, though by this time you ought to be teachers, you need someone to teach you the elementary truths of God's word all over again. You need milk, not solid food!" Solid food is for the mature.[21] We start off as children but we are to grow and become mature.

We make excuses against understanding and resist it: 'It is too hard, it is not clear, no one knows.' We resist it. Sometimes the arrogant and pompous ways—that thinking that maintains the moral high ground—declare and pronounce upon us: '*narrow-minded* and *intolerant.*' Yet not dealing with the question of truth. Truth is not relevant, as Pilot said, "What is Truth?" (Jn. 18:38a). 'Truth is not relevant because it cannot be known.' They beg the question right off, and they think truth is not relevant. I received something from a member of my family charging me with being narrow-minded and intolerant, and it was based on the claim that 'no one really knows and no one can know. So how dare you?' They are assuming the very thing they should be proving. This is where it gets arrogant and pompous and beside the point. When it becomes sophisticated, as in Jacques Derrida with deconstruction, we have an appearance of sophistication without the reality of it.[22] Derrida pronounces against logocentrism, which is the idea that somehow the structure of the mind is connected to the structure of reality, or, in other words, reason is ontological: the laws of thought are the same as the laws of being.[23] He pronounces against the notion that reason

---

20. KJV.

21. *Hebrews 5:14.*

22. Gangadean, *History of Philosophy*, 173–174.

23. Gangadean, *History of Philosophy*, 35–44, 107–110, 151–162, 167–170; Gangadean, *Philosophical Foundation*, 14–15, 27–31, 73–80, 109–110.

is ontological, and against anyone who would try to affirm truth.[24] In every form, people excuse themselves from understanding: the simple in their way, and the supercilious sophisticated in their way. We can see what is meant by understanding, the call of God to understand, and our reward in that.

TENTH POINT:
The Fear of the Lord Is the Beginning of Wisdom

The fear of the Lord is needed to understand the connection between human suffering—whether it is spiritual death or physical death—and our not seeking. Both are connected with not seeking. The fear of the Lord is to see God as both just and merciful. Remember, Islam speaks greatly about mercy, but they fail to see His true mercy because they deny the atonement of Christ (the expression of God's mercy in Christ).[25] Post-Biblical Judaism speaks about the Day of Atonement, and they miss God's mercy.[26] Liberal Christianity fails to affirm Christ's atonement in paying for sin, and they miss the justice and mercy of God. In its place, they speak about *unconditional love*, which is a kind of indulgent love. They miss the fear of the Lord. It is the fear of the Lord that is the beginning of wisdom. In our sin, to see the connection between suffering, human suffering in every form—inward and outward and circumstantial—and our failing to seek is to have the fear of the Lord, which is what moves us to seek. The fear of the Lord is the beginning of wisdom, or knowledge, or understanding. In our fallen state, the fear of the Lord is there. It is the *beginning* of wisdom; it does not complete it. There is a love, a desire, an attraction, a beauty, and a glory of God, a longing for it, and a desire for it that keeps us going. There is love, on the one hand, that finishes it, and fear that begins it. God calls us to seek Him diligently, in fear and love, so that we might understand and have the reward, the blessing of life: That secret spring flowing in us. Amen.

---

24. Gangadean, *Philosophical Foundation,* 118–121.

25. Gangadean, *Philosophical Foundation,* 191–192; Gangadean, *The Westminster Confession,* 21–27, 37–41, 67–69, 129–130, 236–238; Gangadean, "Paper No. 91: Christianity and Islam," in *The Logos Papers,* 479–484.

26. Gangadean, *Philosophical Foundation,* 193–194.

PART II

THE BIBLICAL WORLDVIEW
2010 SERMON SERIES

6

THE DOCTRINE OF CREATION

Points 1–3 Under Creation

Genesis 1:1–5, 26–31

¹In the beginning God created the heavens and the earth. ²Now the earth was formless and empty, darkness was over the surface of the deep, and the Spirit of God was hovering over the waters. ³And God said, "Let there be light," and there was light. ⁴God saw that the light was good, and he separated the light from the darkness. ⁵God called the light "day," and the darkness he called "night." And there was evening, and there was morning—the first day.

²⁶Then God said, "Let us make man in our image, in our likeness, and let them rule over the fish of the sea and the birds of the air, over the livestock, over all the earth, and over all the creatures that move along the ground." ²⁷So God created man in his own image, in the image of God he created him; male and female he created them. ²⁸God blessed them and said to them, "Be fruitful and increase in number; fill the earth and subdue it. Rule over the fish of the sea and the birds of the air and over every living creature that moves on the ground." ²⁹Then God said, "I give you every seed-bearing plant on the face of the whole earth and every tree that has fruit with seed in it. They will be yours for food. ³⁰And to all the beasts of the earth and all the birds of the air and all the creatures that move on the ground—everything that has the breath of life in it—I give every green plant for food." And it was so. ³¹God saw all that he had made, and it was very good. And there was evening, and there was morning—the sixth day.

WE HAVE BEGUN WHAT WE ARE CALLING Foundation Studies. It is not quite the same as general revelation studies; this is in some ways broader. We will review the creation–fall–redemption material.[1] As we go over the area of creation, we will see how broad and how deep this is and how profound its significance is. I will try to give you snapshots, in slow motion, if possible.

We are doing this in order to get the foundation in place, so we are calling this "Foundation Studies," and we have a number of pieces that belong to the foundation.[2] In the past, we have shown how the idea of the foundation is biblical; it is used a number of times in Scripture.[3]

Previously, we emphasized putting the teaching into practice; that is the one who digs down and builds on the rock.[4] We are always going to be aware of this teaching. There are times when we have to start with what we call the *grammar level*, which is basic pieces of knowledge. Then we go on to a *dialectic level* where we understand the support for it, and we are being asked to know and give the support. Then, we go on to a *rhetorical level* in which we know how to apply it in all situations in a very living way that really communicates and is effective. We recognize different levels in our process of understanding.[5] This distinction has been made (grammar–dialectic–rhetoric), it has been used throughout history in the Western education system, and so we make use of it.[6]

FIRST POINT:
Creation Is Most Basic—It Is Necessary to Understand the Fall and Redemption

Most basic of all, is the doctrine of creation. *Basic* as in basic to all other areas: that is, the Fall and redemption. It is necessary to understand creation in order to understand the Fall. Redemption is being restored because we fell away from what was given to us in the creation. This redemption is continuing, but now it is at a deeper and fuller level

---

1. Appendices A and B.

2. Gangadean, "Paper No. 36: The Pillar and Ground of the Truth," 201–206; "Paper No. 37: The Seven Pillars," 207–210; "Paper No. 62: The Next Reformation," 335–337; "Paper No. 63: Theological Foundation," in *The Logos Papers*, 339–340.

3. *Hebrews 5:11–14, 6:1–3, 11:10; Matthew 7:24–27; 1 Corinthians 3:10–15.*

4. *Matthew 7:25.*

5. The Logos Foundation Editorial Board, *Grammar Catechisms: Philosophical, Theological, and Historical Foundations* (Phoenix: The Logos Papers Press, 2023), xv-xxvi; Gangadean, *The Westminster Catechisms*, 35–45.

6. Dorothy L. Sayers, *The Lost Tools of Learning* (Waterford: Cross Reach Publications, 1948).

because of the reality of sin and overcoming sin. We begin with the doctrine of creation; the turning away from it through sin and death is summed up as the Fall. Redemption is the work of Christ: the second Adam, the last Adam, who comes to *undo* what the first Adam did, and to *do* what the first Adam failed to do. All of what Adam is called to do is given in the doctrine of creation.

We make a number of distinctions when we speak about creation, and I will briefly mention these: We speak about original creation, the purpose of creation, subsequent creation, special creation, man the image of God as the crown of creation, the goodness of creation, and the completion of creation in the Sabbath, and all of that is under point number one of creation. Then we go on to *full and clear, eternal life is knowing God,* etc. Let's think about this briefly.

Original Creation Is *Ex Nihilo*

Original creation is stated in Genesis 1:1: **"In the beginning God created the heavens and the earth."** I have gone along for a number of years, reading this in a way that does not pay close attention to what is being said. I had a certain picture of what was being said here, and by God's grace, I started to pay more attention. I had help from others, particularly D. Russell Humphreys, who wrote *Starlight and Time.*[7] He did a close analysis of this, and I came to think about his analysis and to pay closer attention to what is said in Genesis 1:1.

We distinguish original creation from subsequent creation. When it says, **"In the beginning God created the heavens and the earth,"** what we are to understand is this: God created the substance of the universe. God created the substance out of which the heavens and the earth are made—the sun, all of the stars, as well as the earth. The substance is created and is created as it is said historically: *ex nihilo*, no pre-existing material. Original creation is not formation; it is not formation out of already existing matter; it is creation *ex nihilo*, from nothing.[8] This is not 'being from non-being.' This is matter, or physical energy, from spirit or spiritual power.

---

7. D. Russell Humphreys, *Starlight and Time* (Green Forest: New Leaf Publishing Group, 1996)

8. Gangadean, *Philosophical Foundation*, 141–143; Gangadean, "Paper No. 142: The Biblical Worldview (Part II)," in *The Logos Papers*, 711–717.

Some people hold to creation as formation; we are saying 'no' to that. That means matter is eternal, not created by God. Persons who hold to creation as formation are, generally speaking, dualists. There are many dualists in the history of the world. There is Greek dualism, Persian dualism, Indian dualism, and perhaps also Mormon dualism, if it is possible to understand what exactly is being asserted in Mormonism on this point.[9]

Creation *ex nihilo* from Genesis 1:1, which says that all creation had a beginning, is in stark contrast to every other view under the sun. Outside of this doctrine of creation, every other view says that the creation is eternal. Every other view in the world fails to recognize the idea of the beginning and speaks rather of an eternal cycle. Once we are in an eternal cycle, we are locked in. The view may come out as eternal recurrence, as with Nietzsche, or the Hindus and Buddhists, or all forms of dualism.

According to this view (creation *ex nihilo*), not only did time itself begin, but the physical universe and matter began—it was created—and, in a very important sense, space also began to exist. There is an absolute beginning. That, incidentally, should also be set in contrast to providence, where what is brought into existence is sustained. Genesis begins this way: **"In the beginning God created the heavens and the earth. Now the earth was formless and empty, darkness was over the surface of the deep"** (vv. 1–2). **"Formless and empty"**—it cannot be said that 'In the beginning, God *formed* and the earth was *formless*'—this does not make sense in the language of the text. In original creation, the creation was not yet formed, and it was not yet full.

Subsequent creation is forming and filling. Light had not yet been created, and **"darkness was over the surface of the deep"** (v. 2). I would like us to notice that word: *the deep*. In connection with that, **"the Spirit of God was hovering over the waters"** (v. 2b). What was created was a vast body of water. Some have calculated it to be one light year across: This is the substance out of which the universe was made. It was all together in one place, and notice, **"the Spirit of God was hovering."** The creation is triune, by Father, Son, and Holy Spirit, and once it is

9. In Mormon doctrine, it is claimed that all is matter. See: *Doctrine and Covenants* (131:7–8) "There is no such thing as immaterial matter. All spirit is matter, but it is more fine or pure, and can only be discerned by purer eyes; We cannot see it; but when our bodies are purified we shall see that it is all matter."

created, it must be upheld and brought to completion. The Spirit of God was hovering over the waters, not without infinite thought and intent, and for a purpose.

As soon as we have said these things, we are led to ask, 'Who is God?' The Shorter Catechism is a good place to look: "God is a Spirit [not matter], infinite, eternal, and unchangeable, in his being, wisdom, power, holiness, justice, goodness, and truth."[10] Particularly at this point, we see the infinite power of God, the infinite knowledge of God, that is being revealed in every level of creation, from the smallest to the greatest. The naming goes on at the micro and macro levels. From what scientists are doing to explore subatomic particles by smashing them together in the Large Hadron Collider in Switzerland, discovering what is there, and coming closer and closer to naming all of the parts of the creation, to the largest expanse: galaxies, and clusters of galaxies in the universe beyond our numbering. 100 billion stars per galaxy, 100 billion galaxies; the mind simply staggers. All of these and all their relationships: the finely-tuned universe, in every way. Ten to the millionth power, or, some say, a million to the millionth power: that is how finely-tuned the universe is. When it says, **"God created the heavens and the earth,"** we are speaking about God who is a spirit, infinite in power, and infinite in wisdom and goodness, and we should never forget that. Remember how it was spoken of as comfort to the people of God when they were going to be afflicted greatly through Babylon; they were given a reminder that God is infinite in power. "He stretches out the heavens like a canopy, and spreads them out like a tent to live in" (Is. 40:22b). The heavens are like dust on the scales compared with the infinite power of God,[11] and we think that God does not hear? Do we think that God is not concerned? Do we think that God is not able to uphold us? We come back to the God who has created all things and what great power is displayed in that.

Purpose of Creation

The purpose of creation is to be understood from Scripture, from general revelation, from the creation itself, as well as from what is given to

---

10. *SCQ. 4.* Emphasis added.

11. *Isaiah 40:12.*

us in Historic Christianity, and that purpose is revelation. Creation is revelation, *necessarily*: from the very nature of things, the act of God reveals the nature of God. The eternal power and the divine nature are clearly seen, clearly revealed, being understood from the things that are made, and Romans 1:20 specifies that it started with eternal power. Eternality is the mark above all others. When God reveals Himself to Moses, He says, "I am" (Ex. 3:14): the self-existing one, the eternal one, who is, and who was, and who is to come.[12] Time and again, eternality is singled out as revealing God.

God reveals Himself as eternal in everything that is made, and His eternal power is revealed here. The heavens will be rolled up as a scroll; it can get old; unless it were for the sustaining power of God, the heavens would not continue, but God abides forever. We think the sun is continuing, and God does use it to speak about a high level of dependability: "As surely as the sun rises, he will appear; he will come to us like the winter rains, like the spring rains that water the earth." (Hos. 6:3b). This is the fixity of God's laws. *Creation is revelation, necessarily and intentionally.* There is no gap between what is necessary in the act of God and the intention of God. God intended it to be revelation.

The Westminster Confession says that God created "for the manifestation of the glory of his eternal power, wisdom, and goodness" (4.1), that He rules over what He creates "to the praise of the glory of his wisdom, power, justice, goodness, and mercy" (5.1), He decrees what He does "for the manifestation of his glory" (3.3), and He permits the Fall because He "purposed to order it to his own glory" (6.1).

Creation is revelation, through and through, *necessarily, intentionally,* and we should say, in the wisdom of God: *exclusively.* God does not set aside this revelation for another. It is not as if God could have given it another way and just unnecessarily gave it this way. That brings us to another major point. Original creation is set over and against all who have declared that the universe is eternal, however much they have thundered and declared. Think about Nagarjuna, the Buddhist philosopher, as he thundered, "Never, nowhere, can anything originate."[13] No, God originated the creation. But it is also set over and against those

---

12. *Revelation 1:7.*

13. Gangadean, *Philosophical Foundation*, 115–117; Gangadean, *History of Philosophy*, 107–108.

who have failed to see and appreciate, to understand and celebrate, that *creation is revelation*. They think they can bypass God's revelation and know God directly as He is in Himself in heaven—we must say no to that. *Creation is revelation*. We are called to know God in the way He has revealed Himself through His works of creation.

I should anticipate one point before I go on: God not only created us, but He created us in relationship to Him. As we sang in Psalm 100 at the beginning of our worship, we are His people. "It is he who made us, and we are his; we are his people, the sheep of his pasture" (Ps. 100:3b). He created us, He created us in our being, and we need to appreciate that. Our very being, and all aspects. 'He is my Creator. He gave me being, and He sustains me in being.' Because we are created by God, sustained by God, we are His. Not only that, but we are the sheep of His pasture, in a covenant relationship that He has established with us.

Subsequent Creation

Subsequent creation is that of forming and filling. The God who created this vast body of water next said, after hovering over it, **"Let there be light"** (v. 3). Perhaps we can begin to think about this by thinking about the sun—the way the sun gives light. Energy is being released by a process going on in the sun, and that energy (part of that energy) comes to us as light. God said, **"Let there be light."** God is sustaining the creation, and at the word of His command, He may change that in such a way that new realities are revealed. **"Let there be light."** Notice also that the first thing in subsequent creation (the light) is a visible revelation of God. It is said of God, "God is light" (1 Jn. 1:5). So it is throughout the creation, that the visible creation reveals the invisible God.

After creating light, God created the expanse. This is the expanse of space: interstellar space. Looking at it closely in other texts, clearly, the expanse includes not just the atmosphere but also the stars and the sun set in the heavens. There was an *expansion* of this body of water. **"And God said, 'Let there be an expanse between the waters to separate water from water.'"** (v. 6). Astronomers are discovering the idea of a universe that is expanding and expanding from one source; it is sometimes spoken about as the Big Bang.[14] Perhaps our attention may be drawn to this implication: 17 times in Scripture, it speaks about, "My own hands stretched out the heavens" (Is. 45:12), and in that, the power of God is being revealed to us, and we are learning about that. He created the expanse, separating waters from the waters. He created the dry ground and the plants. He created the sun, moon, and stars to be light bearers; after having created light, these come to be settled in the particular portions of the heavenly bodies. Then, God created the living creatures of the sea. God created the beasts of the earth and the dry land. Then, God created man. God created man in His own image. The Shorter Catechism says "God created man male and female, after his own image, in knowledge, righteousness, and holiness, with dominion over the creatures" (SCQ. 10). The Scripture says, **"So God created man in his own image, in the image of God he created him; male and female he created them"** (v. 27). It does not say here, "in knowledge, righteousness, and holiness," but, other places in Scripture do include these, which is the state in which we were created. We will come back to this idea of the creation of man in the image of God.

Special Creation

All of this is part of subsequent creation. We have listed, broadly speaking, what is created each day, and then specified that this is special creation. Each is created after its kind. Certainly, the living creatures are especially mentioned as each being created "according to its kind" (Gen. 1:11, 12, 21, 24, 25). Nine times, it is mentioned that God created things according to their kinds, and this repetition is to get it to sink into our minds so that we notice. This is said in contrast to the position of evolution, which is a kind of self-creation, where it is claimed that time and chance, or fate and fortune, brought about the things we see. But we are affirming that qualities are irreducible and cannot be reduced to quantity or degree. Special creation is set over and against all forms of reductionism that attempt to reduce everything to one or perhaps two things in the universe. *Each is created after its own kind.* A lot of the battle is being fought fiercely on this point in

---

14. Gangadean, *Philosophical Foundation*, 73–80.

terms of creation and evolution,[15] and much of the Church has given much ground to this. The Catholic Church, coming out of the medieval period, has yielded to theistic evolution, but that is inconsistent with the Scripture, which is our guide. The Scripture says that each is created after its own kind. There are many Protestant groups that have given way to evolution. Many evangelicals say, 'Whatever, what is the big deal? Just say God created and go on.' But the non-believer makes a big deal out of it and uses it to support their faulty interpretation of things. There is in all of creation a great diversity existing in unity.

Man, the Image of God

We return now to the point that man is created in the image of God. He is the crown of creation; he is created to rule. There are many aspects of the image of God, and we need to know, understand, distinguish, and relate all of these aspects in understanding our nature. We speak about the larger aspect: Man is finite, temporal, and changeable in all of his attributes. We speak about the narrower aspect: created in knowledge, holiness, and righteousness.[16] That is where we fell: in the narrower aspect. Do not confuse it with the larger aspect. Man formed is still man and never ceases to be man. He can go from knowledge to unbelief, holiness to unholiness, and righteousness to unrighteousness; that is where we are regenerated. We need to understand the two—the form and the content, and how they operate. Often, our doctrine of man, in his fallenness, has been skewed and made partial and distorted, with great negative effects on the Church. There is a larger aspect and a narrower aspect. In that narrow aspect, there is the triune personality: the idea of prophet, priest, and king—knowledge, holiness, and righteousness—and our diversity in that. And there is the body/soul unity. Sometimes, we struggle to understand what is of the body and what is of the soul. 'These feelings, are they from biochemical changes in my brain, or are they from circumstance? What is the relation between the two?' Also, note that we are a unity: man is a body/soul unity. There is also a failure to understand that, in man, life begins at conception. The Church should bear witness that human life begins at conception

---

15. Gangadean, *Philosophical Foundation*, 86–100.

16. Gangadean, *The Westminster Catechisms*, 133–135; Gangadean, *The Westminster Confession*, 79–83.

and that life goes on forever. The Church has not been a witness as it ought. Particular individuals in the Church may say *some* of this, but the Church has not given a good witness in this area, and as a result, there has been the slaughter of *millions* every year: literally, the slaughter of millions in abortion. This has gone on because the Church has not maintained the truth of the doctrine of man as a body/soul unity. The very life of man is present from conception, and it goes on forever, and those who abort will encounter the one who is so murdered.[17] That should sober us. That should call us to be a witness, so we do not say, 'Oh yeah, whatever,' and just go on and say, 'Yeah, I know that.' We are to address it at the rhetorical level. We witness to it. We use both dialectic and rhetoric. We are to witness skillfully to persons in their need. We discern where people are, and speak that word as God would have us. We do not use the word like a club, but it is sharper than any two-edged sword, piercing and dividing asunder.[18] The sword is doing that work as we use that sword.

We speak about the male/female unity, as one became two, the two are to become one. We are desperately struggling over this. Yes, there was a division of labor from the beginning. Woman would do certain things, man would do certain things, and there are all kinds of implications that go with that. No one can say that that is not original. We fail to understand that male and female are grounded in the very *being* of God, in His image, and that these are spiritual characteristics. We lose a lot of ground; we have had this faulty view of their relationship. We have had gender wars going on for so long now, so many decades, not understanding the relationship between men and women, and instead, each one is doing their own thing; everyone goes their own way.[19] Man does his own thing, and woman says, 'I can do better than you,' and she does; she becomes more autonomous than man. The fallout from this is we have difficulty, in a cynical age, just coming together; everyone is fighting for their rights, and the ordinary process of getting married is distorted because we do not understand our differences.[20]

---

17. Gangadean, *Philosophical Foundation*, 237–239.

18. *Hebrews 4:12*.

19. Gangadean, *Philosophical Foundation*, 236–237.

20. For an explanation of the order that protects marriage, see: Gangadean, *Philosophical Foundation*, 252–253; Gangadean, "Paper No. 138: Concerning Marriage," in *The Logos Papers*, 695–700.

This doctrine plays itself out in the details of our lives and how we relate one to another. Beyond this is our diversity in terms of our history, our ethnicity, our background, including our family background, even things like our birth order, and how that plays out. Beyond this, is the uniqueness of each human being. There are several layers of saying that man is the image of God,[21] and every one of us reflects some aspect of the glory of God in a unique way. We are to appreciate this, thank God for this, and learn to understand it, so that we might come to our fullness in God appropriately. Notice there is an order in human nature, starting from the more basic up to the uniqueness;[22] we do not just say, 'I gotta be me' and forget about all the other things we have in common; this is a gross distortion.

Goodness of Creation

We said man is the image of God, the crown of the creation, and he is to rule over the creation. We spoke about the goodness of creation, that everything that was created was good.[23] Each day of creation was good, and even though it may not say so particularly, it is understood; many times, it is said explicitly, and then it says that all of creation together was *very* good.[24] This means there was no physical death. We read, "**to all the beasts of the earth and all the birds of the air and all the creatures that move on the ground—everything that has the breath of life in it—I give every green plant for food**" (v. 30). We are reminded of this in the kosher foods that are given to man; in the touch of death and the uncleanness: stop and think. In the various forms of the curse that come: we are to stop and think. We do not stop and think—certainly not as we ought to.

The creation was very good; there was no natural evil and no moral evil. There was no old age, sickness, and death. There was no death

---

21. *Genesis 1:26–28.*

22. Surrendra Gangadean, *Man, The Image of God: The Seven Aspects of Human Nature.* (Phoenix: Logos Papers Press, 2025).

23. Gangadean, *The Westminster Confession,* 75–79.

24. God created the world good as it was emphasized seven times in Genesis 1, it says, "it was good" (*Gen. 1:4, 10, 12, 18, 21, 25*), and the last time, "it was very good" (*Gen. 1:31*).

in the beginning, and there will not be any when Christ the redeemer consummates His work in coming again, in the resurrection of the dead—all of this is bound up in the doctrine of creation.

Completion of Creation

The completion of the creation is revealed in the Sabbath: six days of work, then God ended His work, and then He rested. This is the Sabbath day, and the work of providence continues after that. The work of creation was completed, and it ended. We are given the Sabbath to observe. Being made in His image, we are to work. We, mankind together, are to work, and we are to complete this work. When we complete this work, we will rest; this is the most fundamental sense of the Sabbath day.

SECOND POINT:
The Revelation Is Full and Clear

Let us look now at the other points of creation. We have said *this revelation is full and clear*, which is over and against saying it is bare and obscure. I ask you to consider the alternative views and be prepared through study; get this in place, so that when it comes time to teach, you *can* teach rather than needing to be taught all over again. Learn to communicate it effectively. *This revelation is full and clear.* We will see this with twelve points, it is overflowing; it is just running out. Let us think about some of these verses.

Points on Fullness

1. "Thus the heavens and the earth were completed in all their vast array" (Gen. 2:1). The vast array of the heavens, the vast array on earth. This is the doctrine of fullness, a basic doctrine that is repeated in many ways. From the smallest to the largest, in the physical world, nonliving and living, from the details of what goes on in the cell to all the combinations of the parts in a human being. We are, indeed, "fearfully and wonderfully made" (Ps. 139:14). This is all part of the vast array.

2. This revelation is full. "O Lord, how manifold are thy works! In wisdom hast thou made them all: the earth is full of thy riches" (Ps. 104:24).

3. "The whole earth is full of his glory!" (Is. 6:3b).

4. "And in his temple all cry, "Glory!" (Ps. 29).

5. "For thou, Lord, hast made me glad through thy work . . . O Lord, how great are thy works! and thy thoughts are very deep" (Ps. 92:4–5 KJV).

6. "O Lord, our Lord, how excellent is thy name in all the earth!" (Ps. 8:1a KJV). It is revealed in everything that comes to pass.

7. Ephesians 1:23 speaks about "the fullness of him who fills everything in every way." Christ ascended to fill the universe;[25] that is the doctrine of fullness.

8. "In whom are hidden all the treasures of wisdom and knowledge" (Col. 2:3).

9. "For God was pleased to have all his fullness dwell in him, and through him to reconcile to himself all things, whether things on earth or things in heaven, by making peace through his blood, shed on the cross" (Col. 1:19–20).

10. "See to it that no one takes you captive through hollow and deceptive philosophy, which depends on human tradition and the basic principles of this world rather than on Christ. For in Christ all the fullness of the Deity lives in bodily form, and you have been given fullness in Christ, who is the head over every power and authority" (Col. 2:8–10). Do not be spoiled through vain philosophy; we have the fullness in Christ.

11. "In the past God spoke to our forefathers through the prophets at many times and in various ways, but in these last days he has spoken to us by his Son, whom he appointed heir of all things, and through whom he made the universe. The Son is the radiance of God's glory and the exact representation of his being, sustaining all things by his powerful word" (Heb. 1:1–3).

---

25. *Ephesians 4:10, 13.*

12. "He was in the world, and the world was made by him, and the world knew him not" (John 1:10 KJV).

The Revelation Is Clear

All the disciplines of study reveal the Logos, God, including musicology. It is revelation; it is a full revelation. Even with all of this, the heavens cannot contain it: It is an overflow of the glory of God. How glorious God is in Himself. All this says that God is one, and there is no other God besides Him. Nothing is to be put beside to compete with Him, for nothing can compete. He is complete, and this revelation is complete: It is full, not bare. Secondly, it is clear, from Romans 1:20, which says, "For since the creation of the world God's invisible qualities—his eternal power and divine nature—have been clearly seen, being understood from what has been made, so that men are without excuse." The law is also clear, from Deuteronomy 30:14—the law is close, "it is in your mouth and in your heart so you may obey it." From Romans chapter 2, the truth is clear, the law is clear, and this is the law that should be the basis of all of our lives, and we as Christians should be able to enter the public square and speak that law of God clearly from general revelation. This is in contrast to establishing a church—"Congress shall make no law respecting an establishment of religion" (U.S. Const. Amend I)—a particular church, like in England, Scandinavian countries, Italy, or Spain. This is not the same as a religion, one nation under God. There is an identity and a difference that is part of our national boundary. Determined by these truths that are self-evident, that all men are created equal and endowed by the Creator with certain inalienable rights. People who hold to this are holding to what America stands for. All the world is invited to participate. We are not against China becoming part of the United States. We are not against Uruguay becoming part of the United States; if they want to hold to "one nation under God, indivisible, with liberty and justice for all," we welcome that, and we embrace that. Our boundaries are the boundaries of that teaching.[26]

---

26. Gangadean, "Paper No. 101: Rational Presuppositionalism," in *The Logos Papers*, 521–526; Gangadean, *On Natural and Revealed Theology*, 64, 83, 113, 131–132.

Inexcusability of Unbelief

We speak about the clarity of general revelation, and the law by which all of us are to live. The opening words of the Westminster Confession of Faith say, "Although the light of nature, and the works of creation and providence do so far manifest the goodness, wisdom, and power of God, as to leave men inexcusable" (WCF 1.1). These are the opening words of Historic Christianity, in its greatest fullness. The principle is that if there is no clarity, there is no meaning, and there is no inexcusability.

Thinking Is Presuppositional

Thinking is presuppositional, and there are assumptions and implications—we think of the less basic in light of the more basic, and we will not get to clarity unless we do. Someone asked me last night about actual sin and imputed sin and of the Unitarians and where they are. We went back to the more basic and saw that the Unitarians do not even believe in the doctrine of the Fall; let us get that clear, and then we will see more clearly how to deal with these other matters. If we think presuppositionally, we can solve the disputes that divide us.[27] This is true not only from general revelation, but also from Scripture. We speak about contextual interpretation versus literal interpretation and allegorical interpretation.[28] There are many ways in which we bring foreign assumptions to the Scripture to interpret the Scripture. There are many ways that we do not really look at and consider the meaning of the word in Scripture, though we appear to be doing so by cross-referencing and proof-texting—as if those things were sufficient—without a reference to the clarity of general revelation. This is not the way the Westminster divines proceeded; they started with the light of nature (reason) and the works of creation and providence manifesting the wisdom, power, and goodness of God so as to leave men inexcusable. Here we are not talking about what is known by the *sensus divinitatis*, or by common sense, or something spontaneously arising; we are speaking about the inexcusability of *unbelief*, and what is used to suppress

---

27. Gangadean, *Philosophical Foundation*, 185–198.
28. Gangadean, *On Natural and Revealed Theology*, 16–22; Gangadean, "Paper No. 15: Hermeneutics," in *The Logos Papers*, 91–101.

the truth of God, and that men are without excuse for that.[29] We have allowed this to be confused. We have not taken our stand here as we should. This is part of seeing that it is clear.

We speak about the need to consider good and necessary consequences, which is to look at the assumptions and implications of any passage. Going, once again, with contextualism. Perhaps I anticipated this point, but it is *unbelief* that is inexcusable. We are not just accounting for how someone may come to believe, but it is the unbelief that is keeping someone from belief, and the suppression of truth, which is inexcusable.

THIRD POINT:
Eternal Life Is Knowing God

"Now this is eternal life: that they may know you, the only true God, and Jesus Christ, whom you have sent" (Jn. 17:3). Further, He says, "I have made you known to them, and will continue to make you known in order that the love you have for me may be in them" (Jn. 17:26a). This is set in the context of unity, "that they may be one" (Jn. 17:11b). We can rest assured that where there is disunity, it is because there is division regarding the nature of God: We are not knowing God as we should, and we are not, therefore, worshiping God in spirit and in truth, and praising Him as we should. John 1:4 speaks about the life that is in the Logos, that it is the light of men; it says, "the only begotten Son, which is in the bosom of the Father, he hath declared him" (Jn. 1:18b KJV). John 16:12–13, says that the Holy Spirit has been sent to lead us into all truth. And, again, we can speak about faith as understanding in Hebrews 11, and the trials of faith as seen in Abraham, and how he saw, through the trials, the revelation of who God is, with understanding. Scripture says "Abraham *reasoned* that God could raise the dead" (Heb. 11:19),[30] and Jesus said, "Abraham rejoiced to see my day: and he saw it, and was glad" (Jn. 8:56 KJV). Revelation was given, which is part of this knowledge of God that is eternal life.

We are to come to the completion of our faith; we are to come to maturity. In the case of Job, he said, "I have heard of thee by the hearing

---

29. Gangadean, "Paper No. 3: The Principle of Clarity," in *The Logos Papers*, 15–20.

30. Emphasis added.

of the ear: but now mine eye seeth thee. Wherefore I abhor myself, and repent in dust and ashes." (Job 42:5–6 KJV). His heart was satisfied. It was stilled, humbled, quieted, and satisfied. Job, the man of affliction, of deep affliction, is an example for us all. It is this knowledge of God, when Job said, "now my eyes have seen you" (Job 42:5b), this is life for us. Paul says, that "I count them but dung, that I may win Christ" (Phil. 3:8b KJV). He says there is nothing that is worth comparing with the knowledge of God. "I consider that our present sufferings are not worth comparing with the glory that will be revealed in us"(Rom. 8:18). We enter through pearly gates, signifying that it is through suffering that we enter into glory. "One thing I have desired of the LORD, that will I seek after; that I may dwell in the house of the LORD all the days of my life, to behold the beauty of the LORD, and to enquire in his temple" (Ps. 27:4 KJV). The Shorter Catechism says, "Man's chief end is to glorify God, and to enjoy him forever."[31] Question 101 says that we are "to glorify him and in all that whereby he maketh himself known." The first commandment teaches us to "know and acknowledge God to be the only true God, and our God; and worship and glorify him accordingly" (SCQ. 46).

Our "chief end." What could be said more intensely, succinctly? There is so much notice that has been given to our "chief end," which is far beyond what has been given in other catechisms.[32] The Heidelberg begins not with the glory of God, but with man's chief comfort, "What is your only comfort in life and death?" No, we are to glorify

---

31. *SCQ. 1.*

32. Benjamin B. Warfield in his essay "The First Question of the Westminster Shorter Catechism" draws attention to the doxological aim of this question. He states: "No Catechism begins on a higher plane than the Westminster 'Shorter Catechism.' Its opening question . . . sets the learner at once in his right relation to God. Withdrawing his eyes from himself, even from his own salvation, as the chief object of concern, it fixes them on God and His glory, and bids him seek the highest blessedness in Him." He continues:"The Westminster Catechism cuts itself free at once from this entanglement with lower things and begins, as it centers and ends, under the illumination of the vision of God in His glory, to subserve which it finds to be the proper end of human as of all other existence, of salvation as of all other achievements. To it all things exist for God, unto whom as well as from whom all things are; and the great question for each of us accordingly is, How can I glorify God and enjoy Him forever?" Warfield further explains that "The peculiarity of this first question and answer of the Westminster Catechisms, it will be seen, is the felicity with which it brings to concise expression the whole Reformed conception of the significance of human life."

God and, in consequence, enjoy Him. These things are internally connected. Eternal life is knowing God.

From general revelation, we can say the good is the knowledge of God.[33] Good for man as a rational being is the use of his reason to the fullest to understand the nature of things; the nature of things created reveals the nature of God. From general revelation, from Historic Christianity, and from Scripture, again and again, in many ways, we see this truth. These are the things that we want you to get hold of, store up in your heart, and let this be meditated on. Then, you can speak to others and interpret your life and the situations you enter from this perspective.

We have two more points to go. But we will not be able to complete it, so we will simply pause here. The two more are: *the knowledge of God is through the work of dominion*, and the fifth point is a completion of that work, rest, the Sabbath, in which *the earth is filled with the knowledge of God as the waters cover the sea.* That is the doctrine of creation that we must understand and keep in mind if we are to understand the Fall. We must see how intimately connected these points are, and understand creation and the Fall, if we are to understand redemption.

So I ask: Are we going apart from Scripture, beyond Scripture? Is this in accordance with general revelation? Is this in accordance with Historic Christianity? These are the three pieces on which we are resting this teaching.

---

33. Gangadean, *The Westminster Catechisms*, 109–111, 321–325; Gangadean, *The Westminster Confession*, 88–90; Gangadean, *Philosophical Foundation*, 171–177, 208–211; Gangadean, *History of Philosophy*, 61–64; Gangadean, "Paper No. 6: The Good," 29–31; "Paper No. 42: The Moral Law (ML1 Expanded)," 231–235; "Paper No. 106: The Good and Heaven," 547–556; "Paper No. 115: Doxological Christianity," 595–596; "Paper No. 116: The Knowledge of God vs. The Hope of Heaven," 597–598; "Paper No. 117: Knowing and Making God Known," in *The Logos Papers*, 599–601.

7

THE KNOWLEDGE OF GOD THROUGH THE WORK OF DOMINION

The Knowledge of God Is Through the Knowledge of Creation

Genesis 2:15–25

[15]The Lord God took the man and put him in the Garden of Eden to work it and take care of it. [16]And the Lord God commanded the man, "You are free to eat from any tree in the garden; [17]but you must not eat from the tree of the knowledge of good and evil, for when you eat of it you will surely die." [18]The Lord God said, "It is not good for the man to be alone. I will make a helper suitable for him." [19]Now the Lord God had formed out of the ground all the beasts of the field and all the birds of the air. He brought them to the man to see what he would name them; and whatever the man called each living creature, that was its name. [20]So the man gave names to all the livestock, the birds of the air and all the beasts of the field. But for Adam no suitable helper was found. [21]So the Lord God caused the man to fall into a deep sleep; and while he was sleeping, he took one of the man's ribs and closed up the place with flesh. [22]Then the Lord God made a woman from the rib he had taken out of the man, and he brought her to the man. [23]The man said, "This is now bone of my bones and flesh of my flesh; she shall be called 'woman, ' for she was taken out of man." [24]For this reason a man will leave his father and mother and be united to his wife, and they will become one flesh. [25]The man and his wife were both naked, and they felt no shame.

B Y WAY OF REVIEW, WE SPOKE about the five points under creation:

1. Creation is revelation.

2. The revelation is full and clear.

3. Eternal life is knowing God.

4. Knowledge of God is through the work of dominion.

5. The work of dominion will be completed, as spoken of in the Sabbath.

Last time, we went over *creation is revelation*. We distinguished seven points under that, and underneath those seven points, there were several other points. For example, with subsequent creation, we spoke about the light, and the visible revealing the invisible, the expanse in the heavens, the dry ground, and the plants, the sun, the moon, and the stars, the sea and its life, the animals, and man created in the image of God.

We connected these things up with Historic Christianity from the Westminster Confession as well as from the Shorter Catechism. Under *full and clear*, we gave several biblical passages. The whole idea of just proof-texting does not do justice to the teaching of Scripture. It is, at best, a minimal, *a*, not *the*, but *a* minimal entry point to consider further. The method of reading in the Westminster divines is that of good and necessary consequences: looking at assumptions and implications, drawing them out through the use of the light that God has given us.[1]

Under *clear*, we spoke about several points. This is a doctrine that is much disputed, and there is much need for restoration. It is affirmed in the Westminster Confession, in the very opening words. If we went to many churches and asked what this means, we would find not much attention is given to it, and because not much attention is given to it, it is neglected and it is avoided. The implications are avoided because the practice has not been there of showing how it is clear—the eternal power and divine nature—and we have not given attention to this. This goes back to the first point that *creation is revelation*. Perhaps they will say, 'Yes, creation is revelation, but there is much more revelation apart from creation. In particular, there is the direct seeing of God

---

1. Gangadean, *The Westminster Confession*, 28–37.

in heaven.' The beatific vision[2] has been blasting us into the nether world,[3] in our neglect of our calling. The world has triumphed over the Church because the Church has neglected, avoided, and resisted this truth. God calls us back through His Word, through Historic Christianity, and through general reflections on providence to consider this. It is our responsibility to so have this truth in us, that we can easily, comfortably, and quickly, without causing tensions unnecessarily, raise questions for others.

Dominion and the Rhetoric of Witnessing

The paradigm of how to raise questions is the way the Lord did it in the Garden of Eden. When He came to man, He knew exactly where man was, but He asked the question, "Where are you?" (Gen. 3:9b). He was calling Adam to self-examination, and there is a gentleness in raising the point by way of a question. We need to learn to be gentle like God, not casual and presumptuous, not barging in. It is like Matthew 18: We go inquiring, and we go inquiring not with an attitude of already knowing but perhaps really remaining open. We say, 'Where are you?' because we do not *know*. We have the general teaching that no one seeks, and no one understands, so we do not presume someone is seeking, but neither do we want to presume that they are not seeking. We inquire and seek to find out, 'Where are you?' Most of the time, we believe, according to Scripture, that they are not seeking, which will soon be revealed in people's resistance to so many things that are clear.

I was given a recording of a question being asked in a class on black holes; the question was about believing that being can come from non-being. I actually heard the recording, and it was casually assented to, 'Yeah, that is what we believe. But that is a matter for philosophy, and I don't do philosophy. That is not my job; that is not my talent.' No, we are human first, and we need to do foundation work, which is the concern of philosophy. Foundation is connected with *eternal life is*

---

2. Gangadean, *On Natural and Revealed Theology*, 9–39; Gangadean, "Paper No. 106: The Good and Heaven," 547–556; "Paper No. 116: The Knowledge of God vs. The Hope of Heaven," in *The Logos Papers*, 597–598; Gangadean, *Philosophical Foundation*, 40–41, 71–73.

3. In reference to the deplorable state of the Church in relation to the challenges of the Modern and Postmodern world. See: Gangadean, "Paper No. 62: The Next Reformation," in *The Logos Papers*, 335–337.

knowing God, which is another point under creation that we recently covered, and we gave several Scriptures and tried to develop that point.

We come now to *the knowledge of God is through the work of dominion,* and the completion of that work, and then the covenant of creation, which is the first point under the Fall. I am being hopeful again, that we will at least get three more parts covered: two more on the creation, and the first part of the worldview under the Fall. We cannot understand the Fall without the covenant. Your mind should be thinking ahead about the Fall. Who believes in the Fall? Start with Judaism, then with Islam, and then within Christianity? What is the view about the Fall? What is the view on the Fall in general, in Hinduism and Buddhism, in Confucianism, and in Secular Humanism? If, generally, the doctrine of the Fall is not regarded, how can I be a faithful witness to the truth of God? This teaching is not just for me and my two kids and my spouse: It is for the world. "You will be my witnesses in Jerusalem, and in all Judea and Samaria, and to the ends of the earth" (Acts 1:8b). He wants us to bear fruit, and this is part of bearing fruit.

When you hear these doctrines, your mindset should be such that you consider the rhetoric of it. 'How do I apply this to myself? How is it to be applied in the world today, as I rise up and as I sit, as I go out and come in?' These are basic truths, foundational truths, and if the foundations are destroyed, what can the righteous do?[4] What the righteous can do is work to reestablish the foundation. I am not talking about just doing it alone by ourselves but with other believers. One shall chase a thousand, two shall put ten thousand to flight,[5] and three gets us up into a million easily. We are thinking of multiplying our efforts by coordinating and cooperating, not just by going at it solo; going at it solo is the way of the world. I can nuance that some more, but I think it is sufficient, in the context, for you to understand what is being said.

The knowledge of God is through the work of dominion. First point: *creation is revelation.* Second point: *the revelation is full and clear.* Third point: *eternal life is knowing God.* Now we come to the fourth point: *the knowledge of God is through the work of dominion.* That fourth point comes up naturally out of points 1–3. Creation is revelation, it

---

4. *Psalm 11:3.*

5. *Deuteronomy 32:30; Joshua 23:10; Isaiah 30:17.*

is intended to be known, it was *intentional*. God saw that it was good.[6] It was what God intended it to be. And, *necessarily*, every act of a being reveals that being, so God's being is revealed in the creation. There is an absolute difference between the finite and the infinite, the eternal and the temporal. The most basic thing to know about the creation is: "In the beginning" (Gen. 1:1a), the creation began; it is temporal. We should be able to show clearly that these things are temporal. We should be able to show that matter exists.[7] It is not in the mind of God, it is really creation; it is outside of the mind of God. It is not a part of God, it is created as other than God. Matter exists and matter is not eternal.[8] The soul exists and the soul is not eternal, which is over and against all the reincarnation theories that are out there. We need to give a faithful witness here.

Creation is revelation. It is full and clear, not bare and obscure. Eternal life, the good, man's chief end, is to glorify God: to know His glory and to make His glory known. We are not to take the name of God in vain. We are not to casually and lightly hear this, and if it goes in one ear and within two hours we have forgotten it, then we are guilty of violating the third commandment, which is taking the name of God in vain. "Thou shalt not take the name of the LORD thy God in vain; for the LORD will not hold him guiltless who taketh his name in vain" (Ex. 20:7 KJV). When you have not only general revelation and the Scripture given to us and the reading of Scripture, but on top of that, the preaching of Scripture and the explication of it, in light of Historic Christianity, you are getting a lot: we are getting a lot. To whom is given much, much is required.[9] Watch out that we do not become casual and neglectful, and let it go. This is where sin begins: in a casual attitude, in not diligently seeking. Watch for the first beginnings of sin in our lives. Scripture says again and again, be alert, be watchful, "Watch and pray so that you will not fall into temptation" (Matt. 26:41). In the revelation to Moses, He says that He will by no means clear the guilty,[10] meaning that He will not hold him guiltless who takes

---

6. *Genesis 1:31a.*

7. Gangadean, *Philosophical Foundation*, 106–117.

8. Gangadean, *Philosophical Foundation*, 73–80.

9. *Luke 12:48.*

10. *Exodus 34:7.*

His name in vain—particularly that point. The hypocrisy—saying one thing, 'yes, I want to hear,' and appearing to do one thing but doing another—that is just what our Lord Jesus called the Pharisees on, the rulers in His day.

In light of this, we should see that there are all kinds of strong internal connections between points one, two, and three, and point four comes about naturally. First of all, it is explicit in Scripture. It is explicit in a number of ways. The Lord says, "Let us make man in our image, after our likeness: and let them have dominion" (Gen. 1:26a KJV). God is not saying this to man at that time. God, in the communion within the Trinity, is saying, "Let us make man in our image and let them have dominion." There are Greek *substantial* ways of definition in terms of substances, and Hebrew *functional* definitions in terms of function, and we believe that functional definitions are more dynamic, and that is what we have here. Man is the image of God, and the definition is, to "have dominion." That is, God has dominion, man in the image of God has dominion; this is what it means, by definition, to be man. This cannot be underscored more fully. In the very words of God, the very words, the first utterances about man, He says, "Let us make man in our image, after our likeness: and let them have dominion over the fish of the sea, and over the fowl of the air, and over the cattle" (Gen. 1:26a KJV).

It is by definition that man is to have dominion, and by command. The first words of command uttered by God to man are, "God blessed them and said to them, 'Be fruitful and increase in number; fill the earth and subdue it. Rule over the fish of the sea and the birds of the air and over every living creature that moves on the ground'" (Gen. 1:28). Here the essence of things in the definition is coming out in the intention of creating and in the command; notice the internal connection between these notions. By good and necessary consequences, we could say that man is to rule. It is because he is made in the image of God; he is crowned with light and honor, and given a position over the creatures.[11] When you want to see how man has come short, it is often spoken of in this way: that he has become like a brute beast, that he is not thinking. Man without understanding is like the beasts that

---

11. *Psalms 8:5.*

perish.[12] Think of Psalm 73, where Asaph begins by saying that he was envying the wicked. "When my heart was grieved and my spirit embittered, I was senseless and ignorant; I was a brute beast before you" (Ps. 73:21–22).

Man is crowned with light and honor, and that enables man to understand and through understanding, to have insight to rule. By comparison, animals do not have this; they are under man, so man is to rule over the animals, and not only the animals and the plants, but over *all* of the creation. It says that man is to rule over "the fish of the sea and the birds of the air, over the livestock, over all the earth, and over all the creatures that move along the ground" (Gen. 1:26b). It says, "fill the earth and subdue it" (Gen. 1:28). It is broader than just a rule over living beings. "Fill the earth and subdue it." And Christ is to rule until everything is subdued unto Him: *then* the end will come; because He is doing the work that Adam failed to do, *then* the end will come—the resurrection. The last thing to be destroyed is physical death: "The last enemy to be destroyed is death" (1 Cor. 15:26). We can see then, in the Scriptures, what we are called to do: "Be fruitful and multiply" (Gen. 1:28).

The knowledge of God is through the knowledge of creation, and in connection with this, two things were to take place: Man was to take care of the Garden, and he was to name the creation. Before Adam's wife was given to him as a suitable helper, Adam was told to name the creatures, and he did name the creatures. **"Now the LORD God had formed out of the ground all the beasts of the field and all the birds of the air. He brought them to the man to see what he would name them; and whatever the man called each living creature, that was its name"** (v. 19).

Dominion and Naming the Creation

We are going to speak about naming the creation. We have named parts of the creation: eyes, ears, nose, mouth, hands. After we name the hand, then the fingernail, and then you can keep going down to naming the parts of the hand: the skin, the cell, and other layers in the cells, and the parts of the cell. This is naming the creation and extending that

---

12. *Psalm 49:20.*

naming by good and necessary consequences. This is part of what is involved in ruling over the creation. We will speak about ruling more in just a little while.

Adam names the creatures first. Afterward, as he is engaged in his work, he gets married. A guy may say, 'Well, I don't know what the Lord would have me do.' How can you be a suitable helper to an 'I don't know what I am going to do?' 'I can be a suitable helper to *whatever.*' Well, you may be suitable, or you may not be if you do not know what that is.

Adam was engaged in the work, and then he saw the need. Interesting, isn't it? He saw the need in that work, and no suitable helper was found. He was not lonely, per se: He was alone, and **"It is not good for the man to be alone"** (v. 18). *Lonely* is turned more inward. *Alone* is turned outward for the work. The unity of the man and woman is going to be in the work that God has called them to do. If this work is not in place, as it should be, there are going to be all kinds of distortions in the relationship, and it is important to keep this in place.

After God formed the creation in a certain way, consistent with what subsequent creation is—forming and filling—then He formed the man out of the dust of the ground, and then He formed the woman out of man. Subsequent creation is creating by separation: He separated, separated, separated. God *formed* and the man. Whom He formed was to *fill*: "fill the earth" (Gen. 1:28). God loves fullness. I think we do, too. We like to see things brought to completion, not just bare, but full; we have that instinctively in us, being made in the image of God. Then Adam named her **"woman"** (v. 23b). It is interesting that he named her Eve[13] later on. Two different contexts, different concerns. Here, he called her woman, for she was taken out of man. That formation is revealing of so much. We need to meditate on that a great deal. What was one became two, and the two are to be one. **"Bone of my bones and flesh of my flesh"** (v. 23a). In the latter part of chapter 2, this becomes revelational of the covenant that God is establishing between Himself and man. It becomes revelational of the difference between the work of creation and the work of providence. All of mankind, male and female, are involved in God's work of providence. Male and female are in God—as spiritual qualities—aligned, I believe, according to the

---

13. *Genesis 3:20.*

difference between creation and providence. In providence, "God the great Creator of all things doth uphold, direct, dispose, and govern all creatures, actions, and things, from the greatest even to the least" (WCF. 5.1), and all for the purpose of bringing it to its fullness. We are born infants, certainly not full; there is a need to be upheld, ruled, governed, disposed, nurtured, and directed toward coming to maturity and fullness.

After creating, then, and in connection with creating, and necessarily connected with creating, is the work of upholding. We saw that in Genesis 1:2, "the Spirit of God was hovering over the waters." Once the waters were created, providence immediately began—upholding, directing, disposing, governing—preparing the way for what is to come later on. We should not separate creation from providence, but neither should we collapse them; it is a very, very bad move to collapse the distinction, and it is a very, very bad move to separate them. We affirm both creation and providence. It is in providence that we have man, the image of God, upholding, directing, disposing, and governing all the creatures. In connection with God, as in His providential work, man is the one through whom He will accomplish particular ends: for rational creatures, for the revelation of the knowledge of God.

Knowledge of God is through the work of dominion, is explicit in the command to be "fruitful and multiply" (Gen. 1:28). This is assuming that the knowledge of God is through the knowledge of creation, consistent with point one: *creation is revelation: necessarily, intentionally, and exclusively.* By implication—just to make it as sharp and as clear as we can—there is no knowledge of God directly, as He is in Himself: We know God only as He reveals Himself. God is a Spirit, who is invisible, and the invisible is known through the visible. We know the Creator through His work of creation. To think that we know God somehow directly as He is in Himself has been a source of a lot of distortion in the history of Christianity. We know God as He reveals Himself, and He reveals Himself in His works of creation and providence. The work of providence includes the work of redemption, though it is not restricted to the work of redemption. The work of redemption itself must be understood in relation to the work of creation because we are restored to that original condition and more. Deeper.

The knowledge of God is through the knowledge of creation, and part of rhetoric is to consider all the objections that arise in our own hearts and in the hearts of others and to take those thoughts captive. The knowledge of God is through the knowledge of creation; knowledge of creation is through the work of dominion. Creation is objective revelation. The subjective side of this is coming to know what is objectively revealed.

Dominion and Rule: Knowledge Through Development

We know the nature of a being as we see it develop. We know what is in a child as we see the powers within the child become manifest. Yesterday, I heard someone playing the piano. I do not and many others do not have this ability, but this is in that person. This person is majoring in music, and particularly music theory; this person is exploring this area, exercising rule, knowing what sounds express what feelings. There is a logos of the emotions coming to us in music. You know what is in a person as they grow and come to maturity, and you see these things develop. One of the things parents need to do is to be sensitive to what is in their children and not ask all their children to major in philosophy. Do not ask anyone to major in philosophy! I actually tried to dissuade someone, saying, 'Are you nuts?' But if they can overcome that, okay, then they can go with philosophy. We do not want to crush their thoughts but challenge their thoughts. In any case, everyone needs a philosophical foundation, even if you do not major in philosophy.

We are to develop the powers latent in ourselves. We are to develop the infant, the child, into the adult and into maturity. When your child knows how to cook, they are almost ready to leave home. When they can manage their finances, they are almost, almost ready to leave home. When are they ready to leave home? The Scripture says, **"For this reason a man will leave his father and mother and be united to his wife, and they will become one flesh"** (v. 24). How about that? You leave home in a new way, in a full way, in a complete way, in marriage. And you are not alone: you have a helpmeet.

We want to see the young person develop, and we want to see others develop and to see the whole of creation to be developed. We certainly have to provide for ourselves, but that is a minimal take on this. *Minimal* can, I suppose, have implications too, but what we want to do is distinguish between *natural* and *moral* rule. Cain engaged in natural rule. Cain did not engage in moral rule as he should. He did not rule over the error in his thinking concerning God, and the sacrifice, and the nature of God and the nature of sin. "Sin is crouching at your door; it desires to have you, but you must master it" (Gen. 4:7b). We must exercise dominion over it. Cain did not. Cain received six call backs, we should go back and identify those six call backs, which would be an exercise in focusing on the Scriptures and understanding the notion of a call back.

We want to exert moral rule, where we understand the implications and submit our lives to the rule of God in obedience to Him and in everything, as the angels do in heaven. We are to develop the powers latent in the creation. This is not minimalism, but maximalism. But not maximalism where you are having a nervous breakdown; maximalism at a nice, steady pace. It is like running a race; it is like going from the south rim of the Grand Canyon to the north rim. Some people are crazy enough to do that. Some people are super crazy to do rim to rim to rim in one day. Can you believe that? What were these people's parents teaching them? I guess that is one way to show the powers latent in the creation, 'we are going to show this!'

Dominion Is Corporate, Cumulative, and Communal

This work is corporate, cumulative, and communal, and it takes all of mankind to fill the earth and subdue it.[14] As we are filling the earth, as we are going along together, we have to do it peacefully, rather than fight against each other and kill each other along the way. It is cumulative; it accumulates from generation to generation. Certainly, the work before the Flood, marvelous work, great work, was accumulated, not lost. It comes out in the very name, Noah, as it says, "He will comfort us in the labor and painful toil of our hands caused by the ground the LORD has cursed" (Gen. 5:29). Rest, that rest spoken of in Genesis 2:2–3, the work will be completed. This work is corporate, cumulative, and communal. It should develop in us the sense that we need to bring all the people in to get this work done well. We cannot engage with a kind of narrow exclusivism; we need to find ways to reach out to all the world. As our Lord Jesus said, "Go and make disciples of all the nations . . . teaching them to obey everything I have

---

14. Gangadean, *Philosophical Foundation*, 208–211.

commanded you" (Matt. 28:19a–20a). This should become an integral part of our thinking, like breathing in, day by day. The Lord said, "Make disciples of all the nations." How can we do this? How can we make progress today, this day? How can I make progress, with others, toward the goal of making disciples of all the nations? There should not be one day passing us that we do not think this. If you think that I am kidding about this, think about it this way: There should not be one day passing us without prayer. And if you think that I am kidding about that, think about the sanctuary: the showbread, the altar of incense, and the candelabra. The base of the Word of God (bread), and the altar (prayer). And what do we pray? "Hallowed be thy name. Thy kingdom come, Thy will be done in earth, as it is in heaven" (Matt. 6:9b–10 KJV). We have the symbol of the candelabra. We also have the teaching about the firstfruits: Pentecost, the beginning of harvest, ending with the Feast of Harvest, the completion of harvest, where all the nations are gathered in. Pentecost was the beginning of the gathering of all the nations: 3000 Jews from all around the lands, all the nations round about, were coming to the Lord.[15] That was the beginning of the Church. We also believe not just in the Feast of Firstfruits, but the Feast of the Tabernacles. "On the last and greatest day of the Feast, Jesus stood and said in a loud voice, 'If anyone is thirsty, let him come to me and drink. Whoever believes in me, as the Scripture has said, streams of living water will flow from within him.'" (Jn. 7:37–38). This is not just your own thirst being quenched, as with the woman at the well, this is much more than that. It is connected with the Feast of Harvest. This is water flowing out to bring life to all the earth. We believe in that, we are people of the Word of God. This should be second nature to us. We are not to have a minimal, outward understanding of this.

We should think corporate, cumulative, and communal. Before that, we should think that it is continuing, inexhaustible, comprehensive, inalienable, corporate, cumulative, and communal in regard to the good and the knowledge of God. The work of Cain was saved, even the natural rule; he engaged in metallurgy and various forms of cattle raising, and that was passed on through Noah—remember, generally, these things are communicated. We have benefited from China, we have benefited from India, and we have benefited from Muslims

---

15. *Acts 2:41.*

when they were the bearers of world civilization. It happens that now, for the last 300 to 400 years Western Europe has been the bearer of world civilization, and now perhaps particularly America has taken that role, but we have benefited from all who labored before us, going back ages. Think about the alphabet: the Phoenician alphabet. How would you like to be writing in cuneiform? How would you like to be writing in Chinese or Japanese? Conceptually, there is a lot of stuff that goes on when you can put words together in a certain way, and we benefit from that. We benefit from the number zero. Try to count or do math without zero. These discoveries have come: it is corporate, cumulative, and communal. I wonder if one day I will meet the person who came up with zero: I hope I do. I hope this person was not only engaged in natural rule, though it is very possibly so. Would you like to meet this person?

There is a diversity in unity, and we should think about this in connection with the work of dominion. In Adam, that work was lost. In Christ, it is restored. Christ is the second Adam. He not only undoes what Adam did, but He does what Adam failed to do, which is to multiply, fill the earth, and rule over it. How is Christ doing that? Spiritually, by saying, "Go and make disciples of all nations."[16] He is building on the work of Adam: the natural work of parents having children and multiplying. Many of you have parents who are not believers. They contributed something to the kingdom of God—albeit indirectly, unknowingly, unwittingly—but they contributed, and that was a good work. We recognize this, which gets to another question, 'Can non-believers do good work?' We have to expand our notion of what a 'good work' is. Something may, outwardly, in terms of actual form, be a good work. Christ is building on that work. Others have done hard work that you have benefited from. Some of you, I got to know you after you were 18, and all that hard work was done by someone else. I just came in and said, 'Hey, let's talk,' so we started talking. Others do the hard work, and we benefit from that. In coming into Canaan, the Israelites inherited all that the Canaanites had done; they had built cities, dug wells, planted vineyards, olive groves, etc. This is dominion, and it is not wasted, and that includes even our very being. Christ says, "Go and make disciples of all nations." He is not wiping

---

16. *Matthew 28:18–20.*

out all mankind and starting from scratch, and saying, go and make disciples of these. Take the thoughts captive. I suppose that leads quite naturally to the next point.

Dominion Under Sin

Under sin, dominion is enlarged, not decreased; we are to rule over sin; we are to take thoughts captive and make them obedient to Jesus Christ. Remember, He is the Logos who is revealed in all the world; all things were made by Him. "He was in the world, and though the world was made through him, the world did not recognize him" (Jn. 1:10). Any thought raised up against this must be taken captive, including business administration, and justice in the realm of the business world. About five or six of us were sitting around Friday night talking about our affairs in business and the injustices that there are in business, and we can complain on and on. But the Lord said, take it captive, rule over it.[17] Consider what you need to do, get yourself organized, and start to make a change. You are not going to do it alone; you have to do it with others. Get first things in place, build your team, and go after it. We can do it, we are called to do it, we have to do it. Nothing will stop until it is done. On the Lord's Day, we say, "until he comes" (1 Cor. 11:26b), and He will come when the work is complete. "For he must reign until he has put all his enemies under his feet. The last enemy to be destroyed is death" (1 Cor. 15:25–26). Subdue the earth, subdue sin, take the thought captive. Even if they do not come, they must be silenced. Even if they continue to talk on, we are not to go on listening. 'I'm not listening, I'm not hearing you, you're talking nonsense. If you're not going to use reason, why am I morally obligated to listen to you? If you will not give an argument, if you are going to continue to do *ad hominems* and strawmen and begging the question and *post hocs*, red herrings—the whole nine yards—why should I listen to you? Please, I beg you, talk to me, give me an argument; I'm waiting. Listen, look, I'm waiting.' I am sorry, that is getting a bit rough. Maybe, maybe, maybe sometime farther into the process, we have to say, 'I am waiting, I am still waiting . . .'

---

17. *2 Corinthians 10:4–5.*

We can stop the mouths of adversaries. Not literally stop the mouths, but no one will be listening anymore because they are not engaging with the question. Are we to do that? Did our Lord Jesus do that? Look at how our Lord answered the questions that were raised against Him, and then "no one dared to ask him any more questions" (Matt. 22:46b). Once it reached that level, He declared judgment on them: "Woe to you, teachers of the law and Pharisees, you hypocrites!" (Matt. 23:13a). Woe unto you . . . woe unto you. "You strain out a gnat but swallow a camel" (Matt. 23:24b). "You make him twice as much a son of hell as you are" (Matt. 23:15a). "You are like whitewashed tombs, which look beautiful on the outside but on the inside are full of dead men's bones and everything unclean" (Matt. 23:27b). "Look, your house is left to you desolate" (Matt. 23:38). Our Lord Jesus did this; He is our example.

In Christ, we are called to disciple all nations, and in Christ, we are to take every thought captive and stop the mouths of adversaries. We have already spoken about naming all of the creation and extending that naming. This is being done in the work of DNA research and getting the specific DNA footprint. "My frame was not hidden from you when I was made in the secret place. When I was woven together in the depths of the earth, your eyes saw my unformed body" (Ps. 139:15–16a). The fact that some persons have allergies and some do not, and the fact that some persons have asthma and some do not, all connect with this. With an unformed substance, you see, a little move in the DNA here or there, and the child comes out, and the life is shaped in God, in His hands, from His hands to me. The weaknesses and infirmities, and all the particulars, are shaped by the infinite God who knows all these things—that is what we mean. That is what I understand when it is said, 'He's got the whole world in His hands.' How close we can come in an accident to having our nerve severed, and God spared us from that. He has got us in His hands. That is why the picture of Lincoln, *In The Hands of the Almighty*, is so symbolic, so beautiful.

God calls us to the work of dominion, and we are made for it. It is our privilege and our pleasure to engage in it. I have to say this one last point in closing. It is going to require work; it is going to require work to the utmost; it is going to involve all of your effort; it is going to involve all of your very, very, very best effort. When you are doing this, you will be loving God with all of your heart, all of your soul, with all of your strength. One of the metaphors that perhaps stands out more: When Paul is at the end of his life, he says, "I have fought the good fight, I have finished the race, I have kept the faith" (2 Tim. 4:7). It is a race. It is not just that everyone gets rewarded for finishing. It is that you finish in good time, in the best possible time. This is the metaphor. There is the one about the farmer—the hard-working farmer[18]—and there is also one about the soldier[19] that is given to us, to show us something about the way we are to work. Let us get our minds in gear and hear the call: "let them have dominion" (Gen. 1:26 KJV). Praise be to God.

---

18. *2 Timothy 2:6.*

19. *2 Timothy 2:4.*

8

REFLECTIONS ON THE SABBATH

The Completion of the Work

Genesis 1:31–2:3; Exodus 20:8–11

³¹God saw all that he had made, and it was very good. And there was evening, and there was morning—the sixth day. ¹Thus the heavens and the earth were completed in all their vast array. ²By the seventh day God had finished the work he had been doing; so on the seventh day he rested from all his work. ³And God blessed the seventh day and made it holy, because on it he rested from all the work of creating that he had done.

⁸"Remember the Sabbath day by keeping it holy. ⁹Six days you shall labor and do all your work, ¹⁰but the seventh day is a Sabbath to the LORD your God. On it you shall not do any work, neither you, nor your son or daughter, nor your manservant or maidservant, nor your animals, nor the alien within your gates. ¹¹For in six days the LORD made the heavens and the earth, the sea, and all that is in them, but he rested on the seventh day. Therefore the LORD blessed the Sabbath day and made it holy.

W E CONTINUE OUR TEACHING on the biblical worldview: creation–fall–redemption. In the context of this worldview, under creation, we come to point number five. Let me review briefly. The first point is that *creation is revelation*. God created to make His glory known; He rules in everything to make His glory known. When we say creation is revelation, we are saying everything connected with creation, in contrast with what is *not* connected with the creation—that is, the claim of a direct vision of God. First, creation is revelation *necessarily, intentionally, and exclusively*. Secondly, this *revelation is full and clear*, not bare and obscure. Thirdly, *eternal life is knowing God*, as

Jesus said;[1] the Shorter Catechism puts it this way: Man's chief end is to glorify God and to enjoy Him forever.[2] The fourth point is that the *knowledge of God* that is revealed in the creation, *is through the work of dominion* over the creation. And fifth, that *the work of dominion will be completed* in the Sabbath. When that work is completed, what will it look like? This is what it will look like: "the earth shall be full of the knowledge of the LORD, as the waters cover the sea" (Is. 11:9 KJV). Presently, we want to reflect on the Sabbath. Remember that the creation aspect of the worldview is one part only; the second part is the Fall. We will go through that in the weeks to come, and then redemption. Keep in mind the biblical worldview.

THE SABBATH MARKS TIME

The Sabbath marks time. First, it marks that time itself began. The idea that time began is set in contrast to every other view under the sun; those other views deny that God is the Creator, and they mix it up in one way or another. They may use the word *creation*, but it is not creation in the beginning, where everything is brought into being. The Sabbath marks time, the beginning of time itself.

Secondly, it marks time in that God completed the work of creation; creation is not continuing; creation has come to an end. Another work of God is continuing: that of providence. "God the great Creator of all things doth uphold, direct, dispose, and govern all creatures, actions, and things, from the greatest even to the least" (WCF 5.1) to the praise of His glory. It marks the beginning of time and the end of time. Thirdly, it marks time for man: Man is to observe the Sabbath. I say that in the context of the words of Christ: "The Sabbath was made for man, not man for the Sabbath" (Mk. 2:27).

The focus of the creation is the completion of the work. In the Focus for the Week,[3] we are highlighting this work, that the work remains to be completed, and that those who have died and gone on to be with the

---

1. *John 17:3.*

2. *SCQ. 1.*

3. Focus for the Week: "These were all commended for their faith, yet none of them received what had been promised, God had planned something better for us so that only together with us would they be made perfect" (Hebrews 11:39–40).

Lord are waiting for those who remain to complete the work. The focus of the Sabbath is on the completion of the work. God completed His work, and He rested, so man will complete his work and enter into rest.

Sabbath: Requires All Throughout History

Man is made in the image of God, and this image is expressed in the work of dominion, the work of rule over all of the creation. It requires *all* human beings, through *all* of history, to do this work—that *must* be emphasized. This is a creation ordinance: pre-Fall, pre-redemption, it is an ordinance that stands forever. Whatever else comes along will be related to, and fit into, this ordinance. This work was given to all mankind. Scripture says, "Be fruitful, and multiply, and replenish the earth, and subdue it: and have dominion over [it]" (Gen. 1:28a KJV). This means it is going to take all of mankind—when we speak about all mankind, post-Fall, we mean believer and non-believer; we mean *all* of mankind, and we mean *all* of history. This is basic; we must keep it in mind and be reminded of it again, and again, and again.

Sabbath: The Work Will Be Completed

The Sabbath says to us that the work of dominion will be completed, just as God completed the work of creation. Can you say 'amen' to that? So the work of dominion will be completed. Can you say 'amen' to that? We will get a stronger 'amen' on that from you soon.

Rest on the Sabbath affirms our origin and the origin of all things, that God has created all things, and it affirms our destiny. When we start to reflect about the Sabbath, we are to keep in mind our origin and our destiny—that is as basic as we can get.

THE SABBATH DAY ITSELF

The first mention of the Sabbath is in connection with the completion of the work. In terms of the law of God, it occurs fourth, after it speaks about knowing God and worshiping God in spirit and in truth, in commandments 1–3—then it speaks about the Sabbath. Notice, this commandment is first in terms of the ordinances, and in the context of completing the work. As an ordinance, we are told to be fruitful and multiply, fill the earth and subdue it, which is certainly an ordinance. Along with that, we are given the hope that this will be completed, and the reminder of our purpose on earth—our origin and our destiny. Of all the ordinances that exist (by way of observation), this ordinance is the most recurrent ordinance of all. Having said that, it immediately comes to mind that every day there were the prayers connected with the morning and evening sacrifices, and with the reading of the Word. But in terms of the early ordinances, this is the most recurrent. Let us say that we have been on earth, by Ussher's chronology,[4] for about 6,014 years; then if we multiply that by 52, we get roughly 312,000 times in the history of the world that we have had this ordinance observed for one entire day in seven. Each year we observe this ordinance 52 times. In a lifetime, we multiply that 70 times or 80 times, think about the number of times we are called to observe this ordinance of the Sabbath day. The Sabbath is fundamental.

In the Church, there is minimal recognition of the Sabbath day, *minimum*, verging on being emptied of *meaning*. What we want to do is look at the Sabbath in a meaning*ful* way; instead of going in the direction of minimal meaning or no meaning, we want to go the other direction: toward the maximum, to see that it is full of meaning. This is what we want to focus on in our reflections on the Sabbath: to come to the fullness of the meaning of the Sabbath.

Sabbath: Rest From Work

The Sabbath speaks about rest, and rest is rest from work, and it is after work, and it is inseparable from work. In other words, 'if we don't work, we don't rest.' The idea that we somehow enter into that rest without the work just does not connect. God rested *because* He completed His work. Had He not completed His work, it did not make sense to rest. Rest is after work; it assumes work, it assumes progress in our work, and it assumes the completion of our work. We should think about the Sabbath in connection with progress. We observe the Sabbath in anticipation and hope. It is not something added on, it is grounded in the very creation order; it is grounded in God—God worked.

---

4. James Ussher, *The Annals of the World* (Green Forest: Master Books, 2003), 17.

The Sabbath is grounded in God as Creator. Some may speak of God apart from His work of creation and providence. God has all glory in and of Himself, and unto Himself is sufficient, not standing in need. He did not need the creation. He expresses His glory with the Sabbath, and the Sabbath is grounded in the very notion of creation, in God's work of creation, and the completion of that work. The Sabbath for *man* is grounded in God's work of providence, including redemption.

The Sabbath is not something added on. It is a basic principle; it is not 'positive.'[5] The only thing that is 'positive' about the Sabbath is that He completed His work in six days and rested on the seventh. What I mean by 'positive' is 'posited,' declared: what cannot be derived from the nature of things. Why God chose to complete the creation in six days, and not five or eight, is simply something revealed. But that God completed the work (and it would have to be a completion of the work that He would necessarily finish) is evident in the nature of God: He is infinite and the creation is finite, and it does not require an infinite amount of effort to create something finite. Naturally, inherent in the notion of creation, is the completion of it. The principle of work and rest is inherent in things, not added on, not tacked on. The seventh day precept is specific and we will speak about the change from the seventh day to the eighth day in terms of redemption in Christ. So we rest *after* work.

Sabbath: Praise, Worship, and Thanksgiving

On the Sabbath, we are called together, and it is appropriate that we meet together. Why? Because the Sabbath has to do with work, and it is work we have to do together—all of mankind, believer and non-believer, all of history. Did the Israelites inherit cities already built, wine presses, olive groves, and houses? By whom were they built? Non-believers. It takes all of mankind, all of history, to do this. Notice, non-believers do not dwell in the earth; they do not inherit because of their unbelief. They

---

5. Positive in contrast with what is grounded in the nature of things. Positive as posited or declared, for it could not have been derived from the nature of things. Positive is used to designate positive law (agreed upon by convention) in contrast to natural law (deduced from human nature). In the context of the Sabbath, all other aspects of the Sabbath can be deduced from the nature of God, man, good and evil, with the exception of the day that it is to be observed. Yet its change from the seventh to the eighth day is derived from the completion of the work of redemption in Christ's resurrection.

work and leave an inheritance for others. This is a principle throughout. In the days of Cain and his descendants, they lived up to 900 years. They did work, and we inherited that work. Many discoveries in the history of the world have been made by non-believers, and we inherit that. If they believe, they will come in and join in the enjoyment. If they do not believe, they will be cut off from that enjoyment.

On the Sabbath day of rest, we celebrate with praise and thanksgiving to God. We are prepared through the preaching, through the work of the pastor-teachers, for works of service; we are prepared for the week to come. We examine ourselves in light of the preaching of the Word. We confess our sins in repentance and faith, and we renew our commitment to be the Lord's, in worship, on the Sabbath. It is appropriate that we come *together* on the Sabbath, and not individually apart from one another because we do not do this work apart from one another. You did not lay down the asphalt and the blacktop on the road coming down here. You did not build the power plants that provide the electricity and cooling that we have here. Nor did you lay the carpet; we paid for it, but we did not lay it. Many others work, and for many of you, your parents labored to give you nurture and brought you up, and then Christ came in and harvested you for His kingdom and brought you into His kingdom. That is work. *All* are doing work, so it is appropriate—especially for believers—to come together on the Sabbath day and worship together, and to confess that "All that the LORD hath said we will do, and be obedient" (Ex. 24:7b KJV). This is the Sabbath day, hopefully, becoming meaningful.

Sabbath: Fulfilled in Christ

We should note that the Sabbath is fulfilled in Christ. Jesus said of Himself that He is the Lord of the Sabbath. He said, "That the Son of man is Lord also of the sabbath" (Lk. 6:5b KJV). He said, "The sabbath was made for man, and not man for the sabbath" (Mk. 2:27b KJV). The work given to Adam, that Adam failed to do, Christ comes to do as the Son of Man. This is why He was incarnate: that work was given to man. Christ is the Lord of the Sabbath, and all of this is fulfilled in a manner that we will see more of as we look at this principle later on.

The Sabbath is fulfilled in Christ, who is the Lord of the Sabbath, who will bring about the fulfillment of the Sabbath. His first miracle, at Cana of Galilee, was anticipating the consummation of history in the wedding supper of the Lamb, where there is fullness of joy. The disciples got a glimmer of this, and they put their faith in Him. He was showing what He would do, what He would accomplish. He will bring that work to completion in the place of Adam, and He has perfectly obeyed. He suffered, He died. Because of His righteousness, He is raised, and He is seated at the right hand of God, and He is ruling to bring this fullness about. Christ will accomplish, in the place of Adam, what Adam failed to do: to do that work of dominion and bring history to consummation.

The Sabbath Principle Is Basic, Foundational, and Integral

We have already said that the Sabbath principle is basic, it is foundational, and it is integral to all of Scripture. It has to do with our goal, our destiny, our achieving of the good, and the completion of that work. It is throughout Scripture. I am anticipating that now because I am going to Scripture and will begin to list out ways in which we can see it sufficiently. We have to understand this in light of redemption as well: God redeems man. He causes all things to work for the good of those who love Him.[6] As we understand from the Sabbath (in the context of creation as well as redemption) that God is still working for the goal, we can confess and say that no one shall separate us from the love of God that is in Christ Jesus our Lord.[7] Think about it. Remember when Jacob said, "Everything is against me!" (Gen. 42:36b). He had lost his son, and now he had to send Benjamin, but it was not against him, was it? No, all these things were working for him, but he did not see it; he could not see. Jacob, who wrestled with God, whose hip was out of joint, and who said at that time, "I will not let you go unless you bless me" (Gen. 32:26b)—he had to go further, he had to see more clearly. All of the years that Joseph was in Egypt: 22 years before he saw his brothers. 12 years or so in prison. All these things were working together for *good*.

In redemption, God is causing evil to serve the good for those who love Him. We need to get this *deeply* within us. The case of Job. The

6. *Romans 8:28.*

7. *Romans 8:38–39.*

case of Moses: 40 years in the backside of the desert. We are inclined to say, 'All these things are against me.' In redemption, these things work together for good, to forward the purpose, to bring about the end. What did God do through Moses? Look at the revelation that God gave. God was preparing Moses. He was preparing him to further His purpose. This is certainly true of Ruth: She left her family, came to Israel, and became the great-grandmother of David. It is there in Hannah, who is without child and full of anguish; she prayed, dedicated, and made a vow. God raised up Samuel. When Eli's house failed, God raised up Samuel. The Sabbath principle is to be understood in connection with redemption: that all things work together for good. Nothing separates us from the love of God. What it means is that we need to dig down deeper when we are tempted to think, 'Where is the love of God?' We need to dig down and we want to address that when we come to reflections on the Sabbath. How are we to reflect and think about things and think about ourselves on the Sabbath day?

The Sabbath and Eschatology

I want to draw attention to the principle of the Sabbath through Scripture. The fundamentals are all the way through Scripture; they are in the warp and woof of Scripture; you cannot touch any part without it coming out or opening up, because it is so fundamental. This is over and against this tacked-on view of the Sabbath: 'I just do not do certain things on the Sabbath.' We are to look at the Sabbath in a meaningful way in terms of what God intended it to be. We are to reflect on our origin and our destiny.

There are 10 points that we want to list here, and each one of these points has several points under each. The reason for presenting this in 10 points is to help you see that this is vast and full. So when you read the Scriptures, you will keep this in mind and be noticing it in the Scriptures. Once you start looking for it in the Scriptures, it is everywhere. It flies off the page, it hits you in the face—everywhere you turn—and that is what I would like you to see. That is why we are presenting this material to you in this way.

First Point: Sabbath

God blesses the Sabbath in Genesis 2:1–3. He made it holy.

Second Point: Good Overcomes Evil

It comes again in the promise of redemption when it is said the seed of the woman will crush the head of the serpent.[8] This means that there is going to be a spiritual war in which God will "put enmity between you and the woman" (Gen. 3:15a). The spiritual war will be age-long and agonizing, between the devil's seed and the woman's seed, and the outcome of that war is that good will overcome evil. One will crush the other. It will be agonizing: the other side will fight back, to be sure, but one will overcome the other—good will overcome evil.

Third Point: Noah

In the first phase of history, we have the life of Noah, and the naming of Noah: "He will comfort us in the labor and painful toil of our hands caused by the ground the LORD has cursed" (Gen. 5:29). There is rest in Noah. We should let our minds think about this, it should be as if it were yesterday. We should be reminded of what it was like to have all of that first phase of history come to an end. God was preserving the promise through Noah, who was preserving all the work that had gone on. Noah gave us a vast revelation that we are still needing to uncover. Every time you drive by the gas station, you should be thinking of the Flood and Noah, and all that has come out after the Flood. Because of the Flood, we should think about coal and the effects of the Flood. How God preserved. Noah. Rest. God did not just let everyone perish; He planned it and caused Noah to plan for it, too. This is speaking about God's purpose to be accomplished, the principle of the Sabbath—the rest is yet to come. The work that was done before has been preserved.

Fourth Point: Abraham

The promise through Abraham. The nations were scattered in unbelief at Babel, as we see in Genesis 11, and immediately after that is the call of Abraham, the promise to Abraham, in Genesis 12:3b: "in thee shall all families of the earth be blessed." Can you escape that? That is what the Lord is bringing about in His people, in the Church.

---

8. *Genesis 3:15.*

Fifth Point: Moses

We come to Moses and the giving of the law, the tabernacle, the priests, and the sacrifices. First, in the law, we have the tabernacle, the preaching, and the teaching. Secondly, the sacrifices, and thirdly, are the festivals. Principally, I want to draw attention to the festivals. There is not only the annual Passover, the coming out of Egypt spoken of in Psalm 81, but there is also the Firstfruits (Pentecost). It is fulfilled 50 days after coming out of Egypt, at Sinai, where the people are constituted as a nation: the first of all the nations—the Firstfruits. They are being reminded that they are only the first, and all nations are to come, and all nations are called to observe the Feast of Tabernacles: the feast at the end of harvest, signifying all the nations gathered in. It is typical of us to empty things of meaning and to reduce them to their minimum or ritualized meaning, or to fill it with our own meaning. But the biblical meaning is speaking about this. And what happened, what was given to us in the law, in this teaching, is fulfilled in Christ.

The Firstfruits begin when He sends His Spirit on the day of Pentecost. He is anticipating the end of history, and we are fast approaching that end of history. We are at the end of that whole scattering of the nations; we are global now. We are not separated, and the struggle to come together is going to be intense. It is going to intensify, as to what view will dominate as the world seeks to work together. We have come to this point in history *because* of Pentecost—because the Church has expanded, and the Church has enabled some others to do the work of dominion. The work of dominion has especially advanced in Western civilization, and it has gone to the ends of the earth. As a result of that, the leveling effect has occurred: Nations have learned of this technology, development, dominion, and everyone is on their cell phone and 'tweeting' and having connections. We do not give any thought to how this came about, but this is part of that work, and we are global. We are not simply separated as we once were. We are not tribal; we are global. It does not mean the tribes are done away with, but it is now in the global context because of the Firstfruits, because of Pentecost. We are anticipating its completion. Remember, Jesus said at the Feast of Tabernacles, "If anyone is thirsty, let him come to me and drink. Whoever believes in me, as the Scripture has said, streams of living water will flow from within him" (Jn. 7:37b–38). This is not just Jesus' words to the woman at the well, where the water sprang up and we never thirst again. We are giving *out* now, rivers of living water; that is the fulfillment of the Feast of Tabernacles, and that is what Christ speaks of at the Feast of Tabernacles in John 7. Fulfilled in Christ, the Sabbath. It is coming out, all the way through Scripture, every way you touch it.

Sixth Point: David (The Psalms)

Moses, in the law, speaks of this. And what shall we say of David? And the Psalms? They are too numerous; it is everywhere in the Psalms. "All the ends of the earth will remember and turn to the LORD, and all the families of the nations will bow down before Him" (Ps. 22:27). From the Psalter, "On hilltops sown a little grain, Like Lebanon with fruit shall bend; New life the city shall attain; She shall like grass grow and extend" (Psalm 72C).[9] David's prayer at the end of his life, in Psalm 71, speaks about old age and teaching it to the next generation.[10] This is what these persons lived and breathed.

Seventh Point: The Prophets

Isaiah declared that because of the Messiah's rule:

> The wolf will live with the lamb, the leopard will lie down with the goat, the calf and the lion and the yearling together; and a little child will lead them. The cow will feed with the bear, their young will lie down together, and the lion will eat straw like the ox. The infant will play near the hole of the cobra, and the young child put his hand into the viper's nest. They will neither harm nor destroy on all my holy mountain, for the earth will be filled with the knowledge of the LORD as the waters cover the sea (Is. 11:6–9).

It will be done through the one who is crushed for our iniquities,[11] and a highway will be prepared, and all flesh shall see the glory of the Lord together.[12] This is Isaiah, who was sawn asunder; declaring the Word

---

9. *The Book of Psalms for Singing* (Pittsburgh, The Board of Education and Publication, Reformed Presbyterian Church of North America, 1973, 1998).

10. *Psalm 71:18.*

11. *Isaiah 53.*

12. *Isaiah 40:3–5.*

of God, this hope, in the midst of a darkness that was on the land. Jeremiah speaks about the day of the new covenant, and the law written on our hearts:[13] a heart that is deceitful above all else and desperately wicked.[14] Ezekiel speaks about the rebuilding of the temple, and living waters going to the ends of the earth.[15] Daniel said, in the vision of the four kingdoms, that the kingdom of the Lord is being set up in the days of the fourth kingdom.[16] What shall we say about Hosea? "In the place where it was said to them, 'You are not my people,' they will be called 'sons of the living God'" (Hos. 1:10b). Hosea is speaking about the Gentiles being gathered in. And Joel speaks about the Spirit being outpoured in the last days.[17]

Obadiah speaks of Edom's downfall and how the remnant would become holy and would come into their inheritance; how the house of Israel would possess Edom; the victory of the remnant. Jonah: Assyria and Egypt will be my people, "Blessed be Egypt my people, Assyria my handiwork, and Israel my inheritance" (Is. 19:25b). Micah and Nahum, speak about the judgments on the nations. And Habakkuk, in the midst of judgment, just as judgment is coming upon Judah affirms, too, that the earth shall be filled with the knowledge of the glory of the Lord.[18]

> Though the fig tree does not bud and there are no grapes on the vines, though the olive crop fails and the fields produce no food, though there are no sheep in the pen and no cattle in the stalls, yet I will rejoice in the LORD, I will be joyful in God my Savior. The Sovereign LORD is my strength; he makes my feet like the feet of a deer, he enables me to go on the heights (Hab. 3:17–19).

These men were moved by the promise, the fulfillment of the promise, the completion of the promise. What should we say about Zephaniah: it is there, too. It is in Haggai, as he speaks of the latter temple as more glorious than the first. And Zachariah, and Malachi—all of the prophets saw this. They saw the last days, the great and dreadful day

---

13. *Jeremiah 31:31–34.*
14. *Jeremiah 17:9.*
15. *Ezekiel 47.*
16. *Daniel 2.*
17. *Joel 2:28–32.*
18. *Habakkuk 2:14.*

of the Lord, where sinners will cringe before the Lord, hide, and say to the rocks, fall on us,[19] as the kingdoms of this world are brought down because the Church is preaching the Word of God, and causing all the elements of this world to be melted in the fervent heat.[20] This is the Sabbath. This is the promise. It is the same promise given before the Fall: and now Good will overcome evil. You can see how vast that is and how many places you can go through and see it. You can highlight 10 main points in Isaiah alone. We can get the highlights of the prophets in our minds and meditate on it, so it is fixed in our minds that this will be, so that we may give our hearts to this. In this context, you can say, "seek first his kingdom and his righteousness" (Matt. 6:33a). In this context, you can pray, "Thy kingdom come" (Matt. 6:10a KJV). In this context, we can come together on the Lord's Day to worship with God's people, who hold this hope actively before them. This is the context in which we are to come: with this understanding in place, with this faith in place.

Eighth Point: Jesus

Our Lord Jesus gave signs again and again. The first of the signs we have already spoken of in Cana of Galilee. Jesus cleanses the temple, signifying that He will restore the Temple to the place for the worship of God, which is also a sign. The waters flowing out of the innermost being is also a sign. The resurrection is a sign; by His ministry, He spoke about this; He is the fulfillment: "I am the resurrection and the life" (Jn. 11:25a). He is the one who will bring history to consummation by raising the dead. He is the one who is going to reign until all of His enemies are subdued under Him—the last enemy to be destroyed is death.[21] "I am the resurrection" (Jn. 11:25a). He is the Lord of the Sabbath.[22] The Sabbath hope is there in His parables, among all the mixtures of the world: the wheat and the tares, the net. The parable of the mustard seed and of the leaven: the kingdom will start small and will grow, and grow to its completion. The Sabbath hope is in the Lord's

---

19. *Revelation 6:16–17.*
20. *2 Peter 3:10–13.*
21. *1 Corinthians 15:25–28.*
22. *Matthew 12:8.*

Prayer: We pray that God would enable us to glorify Him in all that by which He makes Himself known. And we pray, "Hallowed be thy name. Thy kingdom come, Thy will be done on earth" (Matt. 6:9b–10a). This hope is given in the Great Commission: "go and make disciples of all nations" (Matt. 28:19a). It is given in the sacrament of the Lord's Supper: "Do this, whenever you drink it, in remembrance of me. For whenever you eat this bread and drink this cup, you proclaim the Lord's death until he comes" (1 Cor. 11:25b–26). It is given in His last words, "I am going to send you what my Father has promised; but stay in the city until you have been clothed with power from on high" (Lk. 24:49). He is ascended, He sent the Spirit, which serves as a sign that He is the one chosen by God. "And you will see the Son of Man sitting at the right hand of the Mighty One and coming on the clouds of heaven" (Mk. 14:62b). The Son of Man in heaven, coming on the clouds in great glory, sending the Spirit, and the Church going out to all the earth: This is Sabbath talk. Our Lord Jesus, from the beginning to the end of His ministry, was talking about the promise, and the fulfillment of it, in terms of man's purpose; that in the place of Adam, He will bring it to completion.

Ninth Point: Paul

What should we say about number nine, Paul? "For he must reign until he has put all his enemies under his feet" (1 Cor. 15:25). The Book of Hebrews, which has been historically attributed to Paul, speaks about what the purpose of life is and how Christ will accomplish this. It speaks about the completion of the work. It says, "These were all commended for their faith, yet none of them received what had been promised. God had planned something better for us so that only together with us would they be made perfect" (Heb. 11:39–40). They who have died and gone on to heaven have not received what was promised. It says that explicitly. They were all commended for their faith, yet none of them received what had been promised. This is the explicit Word of God. God had planned something better for us, so that only together with us would they be made perfect, or be made complete. The completion of the work remains. Paul thought in these terms. And what should we say about Peter and Jude?[23] The promise, the hope of eternal life, and man's destiny are there.

Tenth Point: John

What should we say about John, in the Book of Revelation? It is there, as specific as you could possibly want, in the Book of Revelation. In the seven visions, which are near to the reader in every age. Seven different visions of this conflict between good and evil, the curse and the promise working itself out in history, and in every case it ends with good completely overcoming evil.

Remember, the 10 points are a heuristic device for the sake of teaching. It is not absolute that it is 10, not 11; or 10, not 9. It is heuristic. Just relax and do not get upset about it. It is fullness and completion together, and we should be able to see this with what we have talked about: It should be sufficient to make our point.

HOW IS THE SABBATH TO BE OBSERVED?

The Sabbath is fundamental. The Sabbath is not just, 'One day in seven, do not do things.' Meaningfully, it is about our origin and our destiny, and we cannot get around it anywhere in Scripture. How, then, is the Sabbath to be observed? It is a day of rest. It is not a day of vegging. It is not a day of going into a comatose state. It is a day of rest from our work and other days, and it is a day of reflection. We are to stop our work and *think* about our work, what has been accomplished, and what is to come. We are to think about where we are.

Reflecting on progress in oneself, first of all. Then we reflect on progress in the Church, local and at large, and in the world. It is about our origin and our destiny: the goal that we are working towards. Where are we? How are we doing? How am I doing? That is the second sense of reflection on the Sabbath. The first is reflecting about the teaching that has gone on so far. Then, on the Sabbath day, we are to reflect on how we are progressing. First of all, in oneself. I have five sub-points

---

23. Gangadean, "Paper No. 104: Eschatology (Twelve Points)," 539–544; "Paper No. 118: Eschatology (Seven Points)," 603–607; "Paper No. 119: Pauline Eschatology," in *The Logos Papers*, 609–610.

here. We are to be transformed by the renewing of our minds, and that is the general, overarching theme that is over these five sub-points.

Attitude Level of the Sabbath

We are to be transformed by the renewing of our minds. This past week or two, in discussion with others and in challenges of many kinds, this point came into focus more clearly. I think when it says, "be transformed by the renewing of your mind" (Rom. 12:2), there are two levels that we can speak about. A specific truth that has come in, or something more basic than that. That is, in the principles by which we think, there is a change in those principles, one of the principles being the Sabbath: the idea of the goal, that we are goal-oriented, not otherwise, and we will see what the 'otherwise' might be. We need to allow for our thinking to change. What I am getting at here is that we want to talk about change at the level of attitude. Our Lord spoke this way in the Sermon on the Mount when He said, "Blessed are the poor in spirit" (Matt. 5:3a): It is an attitude. "Blessed are those who mourn" (Matt. 5:4a): That is an attitude. "Blessed are the meek" (Matt. 5:5a). "Blessed are those who hunger and thirst for righteousness" (Matt. 5:6a): That is an attitude. And the thing about attitude is this: It is much deeper than simply a belief. It is doctrine applied, and applied in a certain way, habitually, so that there is a disposition in the mind. This is doctrine worked into us at a rhetorical level, not just at the dialectical level where we can quote proofs for it. When it has been applied to our lives personally, and it is now in our attitudes, it is worked in at the rhetorical level. The "poor in spirit" are those who recognize the doctrine of creation, that they are created by God. And as creatures created by God, we are utterly dependent on God for every good that we receive. In this dependence, we are dependent for everything; in ourselves, we are nothing, we are poor, but we have everything in God. It is the doctrine of creation applied, where it is an attitude now.

We want to see change at the level of attitude. When we say, "be transformed by the renewing of your mind" (Rom. 12:2b), we are trying to get to *that* level of attitude, where the doctrine has been habitually applied, so it has become part of the way in which we live. That is what we want to reflect on: reflections on the Sabbath day. How am I doing? How am I progressing towards this goal?

Attitude: The Fear of the Lord

First of all, we sum up this attitude by speaking about the fear of the Lord. This is spoken of greatly in the Scriptures and we can say the fear of the Lord is an attitude. It is not an occasional emotion but an attitude constantly pervading our lives. The fear of the Lord sets the context for understanding the curse as natural evil and seeing the connection between physical death and spiritual death. It is understanding that sin remains in us, that sin is deep, and that sin is serious. Understanding that natural evil is a call back, restraining us, in several ways, from going into greater evil. Remember, God increased the curse after the Flood: we went from 950 years to 70 or 80 years. Many of you have not been touched by this; you are not old enough to be touched by it. You have got to get to somewhere near 40; then you start panicking. You start seeing where it is going. I have heard someone panic about this recently, very definitely. What am I looking at? And what can I say? I felt the panic at 40; that is when I began running 10Ks. 'I'm not going to let this thing get me down.' Continental 10K was my first, and some of you remember that. Dave does, he ran that race with me.

Now, sometimes you come to a crisis; I recently came to a crisis. I went to the doctor, and the doctor looked at my numbers and said, 'crisis—you are over the top, you are filling up, you are beyond the normal limit.' The doctor says, 'This number should be 100, and you're at 101.' All my numbers are just barely over the limit. But the thing about the crisis is that it was building up all through the years, with every choice and decision I made; in all the foods I ate, in all the ice cream that I ate, as modest as it has been, it built up.

Crises do not just occur; the cup does not just overflow; it gets filled up by daily decisions. Today is my 46th anniversary, our 46th anniversary, thanks be to God. My wife has won, and the way it came about was this: We were driving on I-17, coming back home yesterday, and she was not feeling well. We got stuck in traffic because of a fire in the road, about eight miles south of Cordes Junction, and we were stuck there waiting about an hour; prepared as I was, I had a book where I could continue to write my sermon, and I was doing research on the Minor Prophets. Of course, I was too busy that morning and I did not have breakfast, so Patricia went to the trunk of the car, pulled out some food, and she gave me something to eat. She gave me a quarter of a cabbage, raw cabbage. I once saw someone eating raw cabbage in this very building, and I thought this person was nuts. My wife sees me eating this raw cabbage, and enjoying it because my numbers are over the top. I have to change my way of life. Crises come as they have been building up over time, and God is gracious to us, and by the grace of God, I will do better. I am accountable. My wife has wanted me to do this for a long time. She has been persevering and she has won.

Let us get back to the context here: a call back. We may be brought to recognize patterns in our lives that we need to change, and a crisis can bring this into focus. We need to recognize root sin and fruit sin, and not only fruit—we have to deal with the root. We need to recognize the results of spiritual death, the fruit of sin in our lives, and I think many of us are struggling with that. The way we interpret the lives of others, where we may say, 'Others are doing just fine. The ungodly prosper and when they die they leave wealth for their children,' as in Psalm 73, where Asaph writes, "Surely in vain have I kept my heart pure; in vain have I washed my hands in innocence" (Ps. 73:13). Then he came back to the sanctuary and heard the Word of God, "When I tried to understand all this, it was oppressive to me till I entered the sanctuary of God; then I understood their final destiny" (Ps. 73:16–17). What he came to understand is: "Surely you place them on slippery ground; you cast them down to ruin" (Ps. 73:18). He further saw how the wicked were filling the emptiness of their lives with these things. We have to notice this and learn to fear the Lord. Learn to recognize it over and over and over in all walks of life—in every bit of literature, every interpretation. We have to learn to interpret when we reflect on history and the study of history. We have to do a philosophy of history where we can bring this out. In your daily life and all your frustrations, learn to recognize it. Do not simply react, but learn to recognize it. When we see this over and over again, we learn the fear of the Lord, as we see the connection between sin and death, and as we go through the curse in its many, many, many forms, we will learn the fear of the Lord. It will lead us to repentance, where we take responsibility for our lifestyles, our decisions, and our patterns. We will have faith that leads to a new pattern of life.

Attitude: Diligently Seeking God

Second, in our attitude, again, we are to diligently seek Him. This is about being *teachable* rather than being *simple* and going along with the flow, or being a fool thinking we know when we do not. Remember, Job had to repent and grow. We have to use means if we are going to diligently seek Him. We have to honor our father and our mother, to begin with; honor not only our biological father and mother, but spiritual fathers and mothers. In the teaching that comes in the Church, from the Church Fathers, from those who have gone before us in the faith. We have to affirm Historic Christianity, and explicitly, we need to affirm Historic Christianity in terms of the focus. Many affirm the Westminster Confession but miss the focus.[24] Is that in place? If not, then I will have to say that one is not diligently seeking; one is not using the means. We ought to know these things and understand them. With faith comes proof, and with understanding comes a system of thought. Do we have that system in place? Are we putting ourselves where we can get that system in place? Some of us like to grab things and run with it, but we need to be prepared further. We are to be sober and diligent; we are to watch and pray. We are to recognize the trials of faith of many kinds; the curse that comes into our lives, that seeps in through every crack. We have to recognize the role of worldliness—the self-life. We have to recognize the process of challenge and response that is present in these trials of faith, and we are to overcome. Do not give up, do not complain, and do not resent the Lord's chastening. Do not resign, but persevere—fix your eyes on Jesus, who endured—and overcome in seeking God. Get new levels of understanding and overcome, instead of being overcome by it. Overcoming is part of the work of dominion; this is the nitty gritty: overcoming in the daily things of my life, of our lives.

Attitude: Goal-Oriented (Teleology)

We are to have the goal of the knowledge of God. We can understand this by way of contrast. On the one hand, there is thinking teleologically,

---

24. Gangadean, *The Westminster Catechisms*, xv-xvi, xxvii-xxxii; Gangadean, "Paper No. 16: The Historic Christian Faith," 103–114; "Paper No. 17: The Five Solas," 115–118; "Paper No. 18: Salvation by Grace," 119–122; "Paper No. 115: Doxological Christianity," in *The Logos Papers*, 595–596.

which comes from the Greek word *telos*, which means an end, completion, fulfillment of a goal. In contrast to teleology (goal-focused) is deontology, where we say, 'I will do it because God commanded,' without seeing the point of it. 'God commanded the Sabbath, so I will do the Sabbath. I do not get it, but I will do it, He has commanded it.' We are not permitted to get by with that. We are not permitted not to understand. We are not permitted to lapse into a kind of legalism, 'Just do it, period.' We are called to see it in relation to the goal.

Teleology is also contrasted with consequentialism, which elevates happiness as the goal. Happiness is the *effect* of possessing the goal, which is the knowledge of God. This view of knowledge—the earth being filled with the knowledge of God—some may say is particularly prophetic. Well, guess what? In the providence of God, the prophetic ministry comes first, then the priestly, then the kingly: This is the order. There is an order by which one goes about it, and if we try to get change without that order, we are going to miss it. Knowledge is first; the cognitive matter of true and false is first. We are to put knowledge first, rather than mystical experience, which many place first. Are you concerned about economics? We were talking about economics going down into the Grand Canyon. Are you concerned about politics, concerned about economics? But at what level? There is the attitude of the harlot, the worldliness, loving the world, and there is the beast and the power and the exercise of law apart from the law of God, but we have to get back to the false prophet; we have to get back to education. Do you want to change education? Do not go out and think we can just change it in the classroom: We have to change it in the Church, and in the families, and perhaps with homeschooling, and in the curriculum. When enough people do this, then change will begin to manifest. We have to change people's hearts and desires if we want to change the economic system, which involves people's view of the good and their values. If we go out there and try to change these without getting these others in place, we will hit a wall, we will fail, we will give up and resign, and we might get bitter. Fight smart.

Attitude: Foundation in Place

Be sure the foundation is in place, and by the foundation, we mean the biblical worldview. We can sum up a lot in that: creation–fall–redemption.

We are going through that now; we are still on creation, the last point of creation. Three sources: general revelation, special revelation, and Historic Christianity. Just to point out, in terms of using the means to get this in place, in general revelation we are talking about philosophy—which deals with foundational questions. We are not talking only about ethics; we are talking about metaphysics, though they say, 'Metaphysics is dead, we don't do metaphysics here.' What they are really saying is that epistemology is dead. They say, 'We are skeptics, we are in despair, we are without hope of getting knowledge.' We have to back up to epistemology and get back to the more basic. When we begin to get the elements (the *stoicheia*) in place—the Word of God that is self-attesting—we build on that and then we can overcome. John 1:4 speaks about the light that is in all men by which we understand the Scripture and understand general revelation. One cannot leave home without the foundation. One cannot go out to minister without having the foundation.

Attitude: The Fruit of the Spirit

The fruit of the Spirit bears that light in us, first in love, joy, peace, patience, gentleness, goodness, faithfulness, meekness, and self-control. We trust in God, we are thankful, and we are submitted to God when we pray, "Thy will be done on earth, as it is in heaven" (Matt. 6:10b KJV). We are to know and to obey and to submit to the Lord's will in all things, as Jesus submitted when He said, "nevertheless not my will, but thine, be done" (Lk. 22:42b KJV). We should have a certain kind of peace within us because of that, versus fear and worry and complaining; versus the works of the flesh, summed up in terms of the seven deadly sins: pride and envy, wrath (or anger), greed, gluttony, lust and (crowning them all) sloth—spiritual sloth (*acedia*). When we have this in our lives, examining ourselves on the Sabbath day to see how we are doing, and how we are progressing, we will bear fruit in our lives. We will bear fruit as we witness, we will engage with challenges, and we will overcome them. Fight the good fight of faith.

We will also be challenged by the divisions in the Church; if we deal with these in ourselves, then we will be able to engage with the challenges in the Church and *overcome them*. As we deal with it in our lives, and in the Church, and we are engaged with the challenges in the world, *we will overcome them*. The Lord wants us to do that. This is part of the work of dominion. Overcoming is an exercise of dominion in particular challenges that we are facing.

The Lord has called us to overcome, and He has given us the promise of the Sabbath day, that this work will be completed. We need to prepare ourselves to hand it over to the next generation; we have to teach the next generation, and that is not just teaching others now, but as David said in Psalm 71. He asks God to give him strength to teach the next generation; "Even when I am old and gray, do not forsake me, O God, till I declare your power to the next generation, your might to all who are to come" (Ps. 71:18). The next generation is, in a broad sense of the term, our children, and we need to care for them. We need to pass on the teaching to the next generation because, without them, the work will not be completed. It is our desire that the work will be completed: This is what we hope for in the Sabbath.

9

The Covenant of Creation

Genesis 2:4, 7, 15–17

⁴This is the account of the heavens and the earth when they were created. When the Lord God made the earth and the heavens.

⁷the Lord God formed the man from the dust of the ground and breathed into his nostrils the breath of life, and the man became a living being.

¹⁵The Lord God took the man and put him in the Garden of Eden to work it and take care of it. ¹⁶And the Lord God commanded the man, "You are free to eat from any tree in the garden; ¹⁷but you must not eat from the tree of the knowledge of good and evil, for when you eat of it you will surely die."

W E ARE CALLED TO LISTEN, TO SEEK GOD diligently, and to give heed to that by which He makes Himself known. This includes the Word and the preaching of the Word. Let us ask God for grace, each in our own hearts, that we might hear attentively, and might not lightly and thoughtlessly hear that by which God reveals Himself. I want us to think as human beings are to think, which is common to all. Think as the Bereans did: "for they received the message with great eagerness and examined the Scriptures every day to see if what Paul said was true" (Acts 17:11b), this is critical thinking. 'Is it so? Is it indeed so? Where does it say this, and what about this passage and that passage? What about alternatives?' The Bereans were critical thinkers, just in case you were not familiar with them and you wondered where this came from. Listen attentively and be critical, and do not allow anything to get by in the preaching to which you cannot say 'amen.' Everyone is welcome to bring these matters up. One could always write something and give it to me, or one could put it on the communion table, and I will get it.

Christian theism is grounded in the biblical worldview, which is based on creation–fall–redemption. We have covered creation; we have summed it up briefly in five points: *creation is revelation, this revelation is full and clear, eternal life (the good) is knowing God*, that *the knowledge of God is through the work of dominion*, and that work will be completed, signified in the Sabbath—*the earth will be filled with the knowledge of the glory of God as the waters cover the sea*.[1] Is this the view that is around, is this the word on the street? Why not think critically? Search the Scriptures to see if these things are so. We are invited to think critically, we are called to, we are expected to, we are urged to.

We go on to Genesis 2, and here we will speak about the covenant of creation. You should know that the word 'covenant' is not used here. In the minds of some, because the word 'covenant' is not used, it is not *there*—this is a literalist interpretation—and the literalist does not look at context and does not look at the text carefully. We have to ask ourselves, is there really a covenant? What exactly is a covenant? Beside the literalist, is the alternative view: the allegorist.[2] The allegorist finds, through a special system of metaphor and symbolism, some kind of hidden moral meaning. Allegory has been used in that sense, and that may be the most common sense, but we are using the word in a broader sense, referring to the use of an external principle (external to the Scripture) to interpret it. There has been a strong strand of this in the history of Christianity. Higher criticism appeared in the nineteenth century, coming into the twentieth century, and is sometimes summed up as the JEPD theory, signifying that the first five books were not written by Moses. Rather, they are a compilation from different strands (elements) within the Jewish community. There are those who worship God as Jehovah (J), those who worship God as Elohim (E), the priestly element (P), and the Deuteronomic element (D). Meredith Klein has influenced some Reformed circles in speaking about the covenant-making practices in the Middle East, with the Suzerain treaties

---

1. *Isaiah 11:9; Habakkuk 2:14.*

2. Contextual interpretation is opposed both to literalism (which treats context as non-existent or irrelevant) and to allegoricalism (which rejects that interpretation is bound by the clarity of general revelation, or maintains that there is no clear general revelation, or that we cannot know what is clear from general revelation).

between a king and his people. This view of the covenant is primarily connected with Moses, rather than before Moses, in the Garden. There are Reformed folk who speak about covenant theology; they may recognize it as starting in the Garden, and sometimes they will push it back into eternity. Sometimes there are scholastic questions posed about when and how this covenant began. But I want to focus simply (by the grace of God) on the idea of *covenant* in this chapter. I believe that all through this chapter, at least from verse 4—**"This is the account of the heavens and the earth when they were created"**—through the very end of this chapter, is *all* covenant. Covenant is the idea that will help us to hold on to this.

Verse 4b, says, **"When the LORD God made the earth and the heavens."** Up to now, it said, "In the beginning God," but now it says **"the LORD God,"** and they are used together. *Yahweh Elohim*: the Lord God. God, not only as mighty and as Creator, but Lord of the covenant, in a relationship with His people. "The LORD God" gives us a clue as to what is coming. The term "LORD" speaks of God in a particular *relationship* to His people. I say 'particular' because God has a certain relation to His people, but this is in addition to being God as Creator; it is being the *Lord* God.

Purpose of the Covenant

Just to anticipate, the idea of a covenant is, in the broadest terms and arrangement, for a particular purpose between parties. The parties tend to be human, but here it is God and man, and it is a *specific* arrangement for a *particular* purpose. The purpose is to bless man. What blessing could he possibly lack in the Garden of Eden? Adam is created finite, temporal, and changeable, in and of himself, meaning that he can change. God wants to bring him from that stage where, in himself, he is changeable, to *in* the covenant, where he is unchanging—unchanging in the covenant, though changing in himself. God wants to establish man in relationship to Himself so that he will never fall away; this is the blessing. He and all those whom he represents will never fall away. The question is, 'Is there really a covenant here, and is this what it is saying?'

We begin to read in the second part of verse 4; it gives a long dash; This is called an *em dash*, and it is somewhat like a parenthesis; it is giving an explanation leading up to what is coming. What is coming is the Garden and what is leading up to the Garden is what is outside the Garden. The Garden and non-Garden; the Garden and the field. What is the difference? And why is this brought into focus? It says, "no shrub of the field had yet appeared on the earth" (Gen. 2:5a). No shrub of the field, no plant of the field had yet sprung up. "For the LORD God had not sent rain on the earth and there was no man to work the ground" (Gen. 2:5b). We have the Garden that was planted, and outside of the Garden, the field, the earth, which is without shrub. Has that been our picture? Is this a picture being drawn here? Secondly, it says, "but streams came up from the earth and watered the whole surface of the ground" (Gen. 2:6). So there was water. And now it returns back to the original thought: "**The LORD God formed the man from the dust of the ground and breathed into his nostrils the breath of life, and the man became a living being**" (v. 7). God created man in this way, in this particular way. Genesis 1 spoke to us about being created in the image of God to rule in the creation.[3]

More specifically, it is being said in the context of the Garden. Notice how it says that God made him in the image of God: It was one person, male and female, in the image of God. Do not imagine a hermaphrodite; rather, it is an image of God, with these qualities understood as spiritual qualities in a fundamental way. Remember also the principle of *creation is revelation*: the visible reveals the invisible. Keep working on that—these are some basic underlying principles to keep in mind.

Representation

Then God directly, immediately, "**breathed into his nostrils the breath of life, and the man became a living being**" (v. 7b). Man is first created in the image of God, male and female, and this subsequently unfolds. This is to say, in God, there is male and female. We are to understand these characteristics as in God—and these are spiritual characteristics first and foremost—and they relate in God. This is implicit, and a lot of what goes on in terms of understanding man and woman needs to go back to this point. Man is the image of God, and these qualities are in God; they are not just in man, but they are in God first and

---

3. *Genesis 1:26–28.*

foremost, and they come to expression. God is a spirit, and therefore the qualities of God are spiritual, therefore, these qualities are to be understood fundamentally as spiritual. Secondly, the *visible* manifestation of gender difference reveals spiritual qualities. The physicality, the visibility, reveals the invisible; we need to understand this principle and learn to apply it. Man is created as a body/soul unity, not simply a body. God **"breathed into his nostrils the breath of life, and the man became a living being"** (v. 7b). He is not a living being into which a soul is added; that idea has allowed horrible bloodshed. When does a soul enter into the human being? When does human life begin so that it is not okay to abort? No, he is a living being, a body-soul unity, and not a living being into which a soul is put.

Centrality of the Garden

The Lord God planted the Garden, in contrast to what is outside, and He put the man there, whom He had formed. "And the LORD God made all kinds of trees grow out of the ground—trees that were pleasing to the eye and good for food. In the middle of the garden were the tree of life and the tree of the knowledge of good and evil" (Gen. 2:9). We have a picture of the Garden as the center of a world that is without shrubs, without trees, and it is to go out from there. In the middle of the Garden is a special focus: two trees. This further emphasizes the idea of the centrality, the centering. It is out of this visible centering of things that the picture clearly emerges that everything flows from Eden—everything. Life and history flow from Eden, and see how it is put before us: "A river watering the garden flowed from Eden" (Gen. 2:10a). One river that divides into four headwaters—the description of it is as if it is going to the ends of the earth. It is described in the historical names that are used later on; these are probably used here originally and then, from the Garden, transferred after the Flood into rivers. Kind of like York in England and New York, or Amsterdam and New Amsterdam. There is a historical connection with the four headwaters, and the connection is what one would expect: that it is with *water* that life is going to flow and be connected. And those leaving (they must leave because Eden is very limited in size) will continue along the flowing of the water, from the headwaters down. The older you are, the closer you are to the origin. We could almost see time and space working itself out in history in this way; this implication seems to be unavoidable; it seems to be a good and necessary consequence.

It mentions particulars about gold and aromatic resin. Interestingly, gold seems to have been something recognized long ago. Names of places later on (post-Flood) are mentioned, and the names of the rivers are mentioned specifically. The picture that is given here is that all of life in history flows from the Garden. All of it goes back to the very center of the Garden, to the two trees. This idea is central and affects all of life. All of history, plants, and animals, all go out from that source. Remember, the fish were to multiply and fill the sea; the seas were not created full of fish. The earth was not created full of human beings. Two were created, and they were called to *fill*, going all the way back to the opening of Genesis: "the earth was without form, and void" (Gen. 1:2a KJV). Subsequent creation is forming and filling, and it was a blessing of God to continue this in providence. God placed man in the Garden of Eden, and notice, that God placed him there to *work it* and to take *care of it*; we have to understand that. He commanded the man specifically, **"You are free to eat,"** notice that word, "free." *Free* did not originate with Americans; it did not originate in the Western world and it did not originate in the Judaic tradition. It is in the very nature of man. **"You are free to eat from any tree in the garden; but you must not eat from the tree of the knowledge of good and evil, for when you eat of it you will surely die"** (vv. 16b–17).

PROBATION AND MANIFESTATION

There are two trees: the tree of life and the tree of the knowledge of good and evil. One is life, the tree of life, and the other is death: **"you will surely die."** One is spoken of as the tree of the knowledge of good and evil, and we can know from the nature of things that the other speaks about life as the knowledge of God. Two trees, two ways: good and evil, life and death. The knowledge of God versus some other knowledge, something else besides the knowledge of God as the good; defining good and evil independently of the way God has defined it. We have to understand how it is that God defines things. Notice He says, **"when you eat of it,"** or elsewhere, **"[in the day] you eat of it,"** you will **"surely die."** *Surely, necessarily, in the day;* there is a strong connection, an inherent connection. When you go this way, you will die. Sometimes we simply do not think much about it, and we just say that 'this is where death came from.' No, death did not come in here in the physical sense. In the physical sense, death came later.[4]

The Scripture makes a distinction between two kinds of death: physical and spiritual. The Book of Revelation speaks about the first resurrection and the second resurrection.[5] Jesus uttered these words famously, "I am the resurrection and the life" (Jn. 11:25). Read that, go through it, phrase by phrase, and ask: What is being referred to here? Is it physical or spiritual death? In John 5, in John 11, and in many places it is assumed throughout Scripture. "The wages of sin is death" (Romans 6:23a). "As for you, you were dead in your transgressions and sins" (Eph. 2:1). Spiritual death. We do not want to miss this. Can Adam know it? Of course he can know it, and we will see how very clearly. It says in the text, **"you will surely die."** Understood in connection with the eating of the tree and what that signifies, we cannot (necessarily and inherently) separate sin and death.

COVENANT OF MARRIAGE

Then it says that there is one thing that was not good. This should be understood in contrast to everything that God said was good. God repeatedly said it was good, it was good, it was good, it was good, it is good . . . it is *very* good.[6] Now, here it says, *it is not good.* What is happening? That repetition and contrast are heightened in order to draw attention to it. It is *not good* for the man to be alone. Notice, that it says "alone" (Gen. 2:18). It is not lonely; it is to be alone. Very different. Lonely is more self-centered. Alone is defined in relation to the goal: alone in the goal, without a suitable helper. He says, "I will make him a helper suitable for him" (Gen. 2:18b). That is a good term, a great term, a wonderful term, a basic term; we should not use other terms without using this first. A suitable helper is a helper in the context of the work God has given him to do, which can be described as, **"to work it and to take care of it"** (v. 15b); these are two aspects that are related. **"Work it."** That word, **"work,"** did not begin with the West

---

4. *Genesis 3:19.*

5. *Revelation 20:14, 21:8.*

6. *Genesis 1:4, 10, 12, 18, 21, 25, 31.*

and the Protestant work ethic. Work was there from the beginning, as work was necessary for a goal. **"To work it and to take care of it."**

In this connection, God prepares man. God always prepares the way. How does He prepare the way? "Now the LORD God had formed out of the ground all the beasts of the field and all the birds of the air. He brought them to the man to see what he would name them; and whatever the man called each living creature, that was its name. So the man gave names to all the livestock, the birds of the air and all the beasts of the field" (Gen. 2:19–20a). This is a typical pattern of three-fold repetition. This happens often throughout the Scripture. Here we have, name, name, name, and the repetition should get it to sink into us. By repetition, we get it, right? There is something about naming. Now we have two examples of naming, just to anticipate. One is that he has called her "woman" (Gen. 2:23), and he called her "Eve" (Gen. 3:20). These names are full of meaning, and would that we had retained that meaning—history would have been so different.

When Adam named the creatures, one should understand he is not just picking words because, 'Oh, that sounds cute.' Can you see Adam doing cute-talk? The other guys would have smacked him, if there were other guys, right? "He brought them to the man to see what he would name them" (Gen. 2:19b), and in that context, he said there was no suitable helper. Adam was seeing the kinds created, the different kinds, and naming them accordingly. He also saw that there is a distinction between all of these kinds and *man*kind. "But for Adam no suitable helper was found" (Gen. 2:20b). While there are differences according to kind, the difference between all these kinds and man is a more radical distinction than between the alligator and the crocodile, or the alligator and the bird.

Man is given to rule over all the creation, and man is called to recognize this, and it is in this context that we can understand how Adam knew good and evil, and life and death, because when you name something, you understand the nature of it. When we understand the nature of a being, we know that "good for a being is according to the nature of the being."[7] Good for a horse is according to the nature of the horse; good for a rabbit is according to the nature of a rabbit; good for human

7. Gangadean, *Philosophical Foundation*, 171–183; Gangadean, *On Natural and Revealed Theology*, 127–139.

beings is according to the nature of human beings. Adam named the creatures, and in so doing, he would have to grasp the essence—the nature; things do have essences, even if Postmodernism might doubt it, and though this questioning of essences is supplied with all kinds of rhetoric by Nietzsche and others.[8] Adam named the creatures, and that was before marriage because this was his work. He sees what the work involves, and there is no helper, and it is a vast work, and this is just the beginning of the work; this is not all of it. We are still naming the creation; think of the particle accelerator in Switzerland. We are naming the creation; think of the Genome Project. We are naming the creation. When we examine under microscopes the parts of the brain cells, we are naming the creation. When we examine the plants and all their parts, the animals and all their parts, and all their relations, we are naming the creation. This is what we mean by *creation is revelation* and *the knowledge of God is through the work of dominion*. We are developing all the powers latent in the creation. We are to rule over the creation.

No suitable helper was found, and Adam realized this. God caused a deep sleep to fall on him. Interesting that it says "deep" (Gen. 2:21) isn't it? Yes, it was a deep sleep. If it was one of these light sleeps, he would probably try to interfere, like, 'Could you make her a little taller?' Alright, there are too many Adam jokes; let's not go there. You could do that as much as you want to, but let us just keep the focus here. He was placed in a deep sleep, and while he was sleeping, God took one of the man's ribs and closed up the place with flesh. Some people will say, 'Golly, it is one thing if you believe in Adam and Eve, it is quite another thing to believe this rib story. Give me a break!' First of all, initially, on the face of it, that is what it means, and secondly, the visible reveals the invisible. Once you get that in place, you see there is a revelation going on here. One person, one human being, with two aspects of this nature—male and female—becoming two persons. We have to understand the difference between *natures* and *persons*. God is raising reality to a higher level, going from nature to person, because the highest reality is the reality of person. It is one thing to have a unity within your nature, and it is another thing to have a unity of two persons: *this is a higher unity*. You know God, God is just like that, to want

8. Gangadean, *History of Philosophy*, 166–172.

to bring everything to its highest expression. Is that what you would expect from God? Absolutely, and He is revealing Himself in creation.

The woman was formed from the rib and taken out of the man, and "he brought her to the man" (Gen. 2:22b). *He brought her to the man.* This principle is still observed in marriage when the father walks the daughter down the aisle and gives her in marriage. There is a difference between man and woman, and something about this is being manifested here. The man said, "This is now bone of my bones and flesh of my flesh; she shall be called 'woman,' for she was taken out of man" (Gen. 2:23). This is an affirmation of creation: "out of man." However much we try to accommodate ourselves to the teachings of modern science, it is hard to get around, "taken out of man." However much we try to accommodate the naturalistic interpretation of the data, the data cannot be interpreted by these assumptions.

Then it says, "For this reason a man will leave his father and mother and be united to his wife, and they will become one flesh" (Gen. 2:24). Adam and his wife were both naked, and they felt no shame. Let's bring this into focus here quickly. It adds, "leave father and mother," and "be united," and "become one flesh." We can summarize this by saying that what was one person (two natures) became two persons, and the two are to enter into a certain unity, a higher unity, to become one flesh. No, it is not just a friendship, in a general sense, but a unity of the persons, wholly: body and soul. One flesh. All kinds of implications come from this regarding marriage and courtship if we draw out implications by good and necessary consequence. We can say that what God has joined together, let no man put asunder. Body and soul, male and female. This particular man, this particular woman. What God has joined together, let no man put asunder. Sex and love, let no man put asunder. All of these are good and necessary consequences from "one flesh."

Notice now a new level of goodness. At the end of chapter 1, when it says, "it was very good" (Gen. 1:31), it is saying there was no natural evil—animals did not devour each other. Here, in Genesis 2, it is saying something more than that: it says there is no moral evil. Why? How is this seen there? "The man and his wife were both naked, and they felt no shame" (Gen. 2:25). There is no manifestation of death in terms of the shame and guilt that comes in with it. None of that was there, because "it was very good," and this is how God made man.

We are going to the temptation. To understand the temptation, you have to understand *representation*: that Adam is going to represent all of us, and everything is going to flow from Adam's act in the Garden. Adam's act is going to affect all human beings, all through history, down to the very present. That is why we bring babies to be baptized.[9] Every time we bring a baby to be baptized, we are acknowledging the truth of the Fall. The Fall goes back to Adam, it is not just the sin of one man, but through one man, all have sinned. Sinned in what sense? In the sense of imputation. The Bible speaks about triple imputation, by good and necessary consequence. Adam's sin is imputed to us, our sin is imputed to Christ, and Christ's righteousness is imputed to us: *triple imputation*. When someone makes a journey away from Reformed theology, back down that road to Rome, they are turning their backs on this and denying forensic justification and imputation. It is not just Christ's righteousness imputed to us. It is Adam's sin imputed to us, our sin imputed to Christ, and Christ's righteousness imputed to us. We cannot play with this; we should not do that. This issue was settled at the first council of the Church, at Jerusalem, in Acts 15.[10] We do not need the sacraments to be saved; the sacraments were being turned into a work.

We will have to look at representation in Adam. And we will look at probation in the testing of good and evil (and in that probation, the temptation). Then the manifestation in the two trees, in their bodies, the way they see their bodies, and the connection through the bodies as the visible representing the invisible, the soul. And they felt shame connected with their nakedness. This principle must be there: *Creation is revelation*. When we get through temptation, and analyze the temptation, reading it carefully and thoughtfully, we see the nature—the intellectual nature—of sin, which is not seeking and not understanding. Root sin, which is not seeking and not understanding, and not just fruit sin.[11] If we get hold of this, then we can understand death. We will go to temptation, sin, death, and last of all, appropriately and naturally here—why did God permit evil? He permitted evil to serve

9. Gangadean, "Paper No. 140: Argument for Paedobaptism," in *The Logos Papers*, 703–704; Gangadean, *The Westminster Confession*, 299–305.

10. Gangadean, "Paper No. 16: The Historic Christian Faith," 103–114; "Paper No. 60: The Spiritual War (Part II)," in *The Logos Papers*, 329–330.

11. Gangadean, "Paper No. 103: The Noetic Effect of Sin," in *The Logos Papers*, 531–528.

a purpose: the original purpose of creation, which was revelation. Evil serves to deepen the revelation of God, in terms of His justice and mercy. We see now, in Christ, the deepest revelation of God's justice, as He bore the wrath of God on the cross, in our place (representative), for our sin. The mercy of God is that Christ bore it. So, both justice and mercy are joined together. Other theistic religions separate these; they disregard it and separate them, but we cannot do that. We come here to worship God in spirit and in truth, not according to the imagination of our hearts. We have to ask ourselves, 'Is it true that God is infinite, eternal, and unchangeable in His justice and mercy?' God's mercy does not set aside His justice. His mercy satisfies His justice, and there is perfect unity in God. We speak about the simplicity of the divine being. Notice the co-penetration of the qualities of justice and mercy, so the highest expression of one is the highest expression of the other. We are to look at that and stand in awe because so often, we are split apart. 'God, you are being just; you are not being merciful,' because we are not seeing, we are not connecting. Keep your eyes on Jesus. He is the fullness of the expression of the glory of God.

10

THE TEMPTATION

And There Was War in Heaven

Genesis 3:1–7

¹Now the serpent was more crafty than any of the wild animals the LORD God had made. He said to the woman, "Did God really say, 'You must not eat from any tree in the garden'?" ²The woman said to the serpent, "We may eat fruit from the trees in the garden, ³but God did say, 'You must not eat fruit from the tree that is in the middle of the garden, and you must not touch it, or you will die.'" ⁴"You will not surely die," the serpent said to the woman. ⁵"For God knows that when you eat of it your eyes will be opened, and you will be like God, knowing good and evil." ⁶When the woman saw that the fruit of the tree was good for food and pleasing to the eye, and also desirable for gaining wisdom, she took some and ate it. She also gave some to her husband, who was with her, and he ate it. ⁷Then the eyes of both of them were opened, and they realized they were naked; so they sewed fig leaves together and made coverings for themselves.

CREATION–FALL–REDEMPTION REVIEW

WE CONTINUE IN OUR MESSAGES ON THE *creation–fall–redemption* worldview, which is foundational. We come to the temptation in the Garden. This is the second point under the doctrine of the Fall. By way of quick review, remember that these three things go together; every part fits together in a whole, and if they are separated, they begin to lose their force, their substance, their meaning. Keep these three in mind, and all five points under each.[1] Remember, we said that

---

1. Appendices 1–2.

creation is revelation, and do not take that for granted. Many do not think about, do not understand, and do not believe this. *Creation is revelation: necessarily, intentionally,* and *exclusively,* and *the revelation is full and clear. Eternal life consists in knowing God,* knowing God through this revelation, and *knowledge comes through the work of dominion*—knowledge of the creation through the work of dominion leads us to the knowledge of God. How often the Scriptures have spoken about the works of God declaring the glory of God—all the works of God, not just creation, but the way He rules over creation in providence—and the promise that this work will be completed.

We are going to be especially focusing on teleology: the goal and the thinking that goes with that. A good part of our lack of understanding comes when we lose sight of the goal and goal-oriented thinking. The Sabbath clearly speaks about the completion of the work, and therefore the idea of a goal that will be achieved and reached, and how that has to be understood instead of being 'straw-manned' to death by others.

These are the particulars, the broad summary of particulars under creation. Under the Fall, we speak about the covenant of creation; we cannot understand the significance of the temptation and the Fall without the covenant. Then, the temptation. We are going to look at the particulars of the temptation; we will focus on it and try to understand it by way of good and necessary consequences. From the revelation of the details of the temptation, we can come to understand sin (root sin and fruit sin) and understand sin from both general revelation, Scripture, and Historic Christianity. We will also seek to understand death. We cannot take for granted that death is understood; it is often overlooked, misunderstood, and set aside. When we lose the idea of death, spiritual death, we lose the fear of the Lord. We misunderstand God by taking physical death for punishment rather than a call back, and then we run into the problem of evil, and we do not understand. We cannot make progress with the problem of evil, and we end up saying, 'God is just harming us.' I learned recently that Darwin had a ten-year-old daughter who died, and he struggled with that. To understand death is important, including why there is evil and how it fits within God's purpose.

We come now to the Fall. We will talk about the five points under the Fall, and after this, we will speak about redemption: that God calls us back through conscience in the first call back. The response to that first call back is self-deception. He calls us back a second time through the question, "Where are you?" (Gen. 3:9b). The response is self-justification: blaming others. In the whole 'blame game' that is going on, there is an unwillingness to take responsibility, including husbands and wives. They justify themselves for their disobedience, or lack of submission, by blaming each other for their shortcomings; same old, same old; nothing new under the sun. Why should we countenance this, let it go by, and be deceived by it? No, we need to call it for what it is, self-justification. This is the second call back, and now we can understand the third call back. Sin, self-deception, self-justification, and now the curse, but with the curse, the promise—together. The curse is not punishment; the curse is a call back. We understand the content of the curse and the content of the promise, and how that is playing out in history. Then we have man's response to the third call back—faith, belief, understanding, and repentance. He calls his wife "Eve" (Gen. 3:20), which shows his repentance. And we see God's justification of man by covering the man with coats of skin.

Then comes sanctification. To be forgiven of sin is not the same as being cleansed from sin. In the Lord's Prayer, "Forgive us our debts, as we also have forgiven our debtors" (Matt. 6:12) is not the same as praying, "lead us not into temptation, but deliver us from evil" (Matt. 6:13). There is justification and forgiveness, and then there is sanctification and cleansing, and both of those *major* themes summarize so much more; we should learn to think about and understand this, it is part of good and necessary consequences: organizing, summarizing, and connecting things as we should.

Then sanctification through suffering, but our inclination is to avoid and resist this in every way. Christians do this now. They are clothed with the coats of skin, signifying the covering of Christ's righteousness; there it is, from the beginning. It could not be any clearer. And yet, we do not see it.

In Genesis 1–3, we have the whole of the biblical worldview, and what is there expands; what *is* there expands, not what is *not* there expands. This is the organic view of Scripture. It is a seed; everything is in the seed; it grows and expands. This is why we look at creation–fall–redemption as a summary. It was the only revelation that man had for two millennia. It started to increase with Abraham 400 years or so after the Flood, but that was it. If we understand Genesis, we can understand the Book of Revelation. If we do not understand Genesis 1–3, we will not understand the Book of Revelation; we *cannot*. This is part of what we call 'contextual reading';[2] a hermeneutics of context, not literalism, not allegoricalism with some foreign context, but biblical worldview contextualism, from general revelation and Scripture, especially as summed up in Genesis 1–3 and Historic Christianity (as God has enabled us to understand those things in history). So this is where we are, this is what we are building on, this is where we are going.

THE TEMPTATION

We come to the temptation, and let us give some context for it. Remember the covenant of creation. Because of the covenant headship of Adam, the temptation is something unique, but not so unique as to be different or not applicable to us. It is unique as an archetype; *arche* means the beginning, the first of things. It is a type at the beginning that reveals the nature of temptation. We are to understand temptation and the trials of faith, which is another way, from another angle, of speaking about the same thing. Temptations and trials of faith are two sides of one coin. We are to understand our temptations in light of this first temptation. It is the beginning of temptation, *typically* presented to us here; in terms of the outward form, it is typical; the essence is there; it is the very same essence of temptation. If we can understand temptation here, we will understand it elsewhere. This testing is regarding the goal. How well did they understand the goal of life: the good, man's chief end?

I want to underscore that the Confession of Faith and its approach is not what one calls 'proof-texting'; rather, it is by *good and necessary consequences* that we understand meaning. Deriving good and necessary consequences is to derive implications that are not explicitly stated in the text, but assumed and implied. This is what the Westminster Confession says: "The whole counsel of God concerning all things necessary for his own glory, man's salvation, faith, and life, is either expressly set down in Scripture, or by good and necessary consequence may be deduced from Scripture" (WCF. 1.6).

---

2. Gangadean, *On Natural and Revealed Theology*, 9–39.

Some people think when we start doing good and necessary consequences, we go every which way, but that is not true, not if the basics
are in place. There is such a thing as basics, there is such a thing as
foundation. Many people deny it today; they deny it philosophically,
in terms of epistemological foundationalism,[3] but we say 'no' to that;
there is such a thing as foundation. We read about it, we sang about
it in Psalm 87, and it is in Ephesians.[4] We should be alert to this, and
underscore it in the Scripture, wherever we come across the word explicitly, or implicitly. When we read in Ephesians 4 about going on to
maturity, it is speaking about the pastor-teachers laying the foundation. Elsewhere it says this is how you go on to maturity: by getting
the foundation in place.[5]

There is a kind of thinking process that we want to get to, to see
what we are called to do. But it is not a special kind of thinking; it is
just *thinking*. It is one and the same. The Lord wants diligent engagement in thinking as part of loving God with all of our mind, and our
soul, and our strength. With our whole being, we are to respond to the
whole of God. He wants to bring us to the full measure of the stature
of Jesus Christ, that He might fill the universe;[6] this is the doctrine
of fullness. This is part of what foundation is: going on to maturity,
fruitfulness, unity, and fullness. As I read the Scripture again and think
about it further, I am more convinced that this summarizes what the
foundation is to achieve. It is unique, and at the same time, archetypal,
and we are tested regarding the goal.

Man was given a task with the goal before him, and he is going to
be tested in that regard. In contrast to teleological thinking—goal-oriented thinking—there are other kinds of thinking, which are connected
with our personality. There is what is called deontological thinking; it
is connected with the word *deon (δέον)*, from the Greek term for duty,
which has to do with right and wrong and the virtues. Large numbers
of people do natural law ethics deontologically trying to respond to
what we call the hedonist or consequentialist.[7] The hedonists are those

---

3. Gangadean, *On Natural and Revealed Theology*, 3–8.

4. *Ephesians 2:20.*

5. *Hebrews 5:12, 14, 6:1.*

6. *Ephesians 1:22–23.*

7. Gangadean, *Philosophical Foundation*, 172–174.

who hold pleasure as the good; we probably think of pleasure in terms of the word 'fun.' 'We just want to have some fun.' 'Oh, this is a fun thing to do.' 'Come to Vacation Bible School; it is fun.' We are not denying that there is 'fun,' but it is the effect of pursuing and possessing what is the good; not something sought directly. There are consequentialists and deontologists and both have their patterns, and we see both of these in biblical history and Church history. One goes in the direction of right and wrong—rules and regulations, 'do's and don'ts'—and they end up in all the *horrors* of legalism. To speak about the horrors of legalism, you begin to see God as 'just making these rules that are somewhat arbitrary and you do not understand why, and God is going to get you if you don't do this rule.' The Roman Catholic Church is rife with legalistic thinking—you do not see the inner meaning of it. Paul the Apostle was caught up in legalism. And against the legalists, there are the antinomians. Someone said to me, 'Forget it! I don't do anything out of duty; I do it because it is fun.' Where does that lead? 90% of the population is caught up in this antinomy between legalism and antinomianism and the other 10% are being pulled by the current of this too, not thinking teleologically. The Scripture teaches us to observe the Sabbath; we have a goal, and the goal is to see the earth filled with the knowledge of God through the work of dominion. We have to give ourselves to this. And we have to understand right and wrong and the virtues in relation to the good. Good and evil are more basic than right and wrong. Do not lump them together and say, 'whatever.' Someone may be teleologically oriented and still miss it. Sometimes it works this way: 'Let us do what is right—especially the minimum—so we can get to heaven and have fun.' Immanuel Kant did this.[8] Kant added that he could not stand to see someone who is good not being happy, so he brought in God as a postulate of reason to say that God will guarantee the connection between virtue and happiness. What we have is a synthesis between legalism and antinomianism: 'If you're good, God rewards you by making you happy, and God will guarantee it.' But that is not teleology; it is not the goal, and those who pursue a goal, understand it as heaven. Wrong goal.

Under teleology is wisdom. Someone once brought to my attention the question about attending Westminster Fellowship or not attending

---

8. Gangadean, *History of Philosophy*, 151–158.

Westminster Fellowship, and the wisdom of it. Some talk about wisdom, and then the person tried to turn this talk about wisdom into talk about right and wrong. He said, 'What you are saying is that not attending is unwise, and if it is not wise, then it is wrong'—that is how they made this twist. If it is *not wise* then it is *unwise*, not *wrong*. These are different categories; do not confuse them. Wise has to do with the goal: it will further the goal. Take all the particulars of this person's life into account, all the circumstances, and how do we take the next step toward the goal of the knowledge of God? This is wisdom. Some of us have gone after right and wrong, and have lost sight of wisdom; we may speak vehemently about right and wrong, and miss wisdom. We may not think about others who are listening to us, and how they hear us. We may voice our opinion quickly about right and wrong, and not think about how the other person is hearing, and not think about what is wise in this situation. We end up having to clean up the mess caused by this kind of thinking. We should, rather, think teleologically, in terms of wisdom, not deontologically, which moves toward legalism, or consequentially, which moves toward antinomianism.

For two weeks we[9] were away, and we attended another church and heard beautiful sermons that were soteriologically centered—not worldview centered, or doxologically centered, but beautiful sermons. The title of today's sermon, *Temptation: And There Was War in Heaven*, comes somewhat from that experience. We were in Hawaii, and at the church that we attended, there were many military men. Not a word was made of the fight that was going on in that sense.[10] The fight was always spoken of as internal, individual, and personal; it is true, certainly, that there is a fight at that level, but it does not end there. It is individual and corporate in a certain order; this is how we get to the fullness. We speak about the nature of man as common/universal, and the unique/particular as well, in a certain order. We are really talking about the doctrine of the Trinity and the triune nature—that there is a unity of diversity. There is an ultimate diversity, but it is an equally ultimate unity, and they are not side by side. We have to be Trinitarians. When we confess in the name of the Father, and of the Son, and

---

9. Pastor Gangadean and his wife, Patricia.

10. The physical war in Iraq and Afghanistan.

of the Holy Spirit, we need to think about what we are talking about and not see this kind of separation and division.

While there in Hawaii, people were reaching out for the unique and forgetting the common/universal; and a good part of contemporary postmodern thinking is this: reaching out for the unique/particular and speaking in the name of alterity and incommensurability, in these terms, and not seeing what is common, underneath. Some of us may see what is common underneath and let it go. We hear about how 'there are many Christianities,' and 'there are many Buddhisms, and there are many this, and that, and the other.' As against saying no, there is one Lord, one faith, one baptism, one Christianity—there are many *degrees* of understanding which are held more or less consciously and consistently. They quickly flip us and land us right on our backs. Then we say, 'How did that happen?'

When I told people that we went to Hawaii, there was a kind of smile that came on people's faces, a kind of relaxed, otherworldly look. But there is war in paradise, and there is war in Eden, and it comes from the war that is in heaven, which is spoken of in Revelation chapter 12. We cannot forget it. There was war before the white man came; there is a war stretching back in history, and there is not only war but plague and famine. Someone asked me, 'How was your time in Hawaii?' I said, 'Decent.' They shook their heads and played that back to me: 'Decent? What kind of guy are you? Can you not relax and have fun? Turn off your mind for a little bit?' I can say, yes, I did turn off my mind for a little bit—for about a minute and a half. At Waikiki, I was sitting there under the coconut tree trying to relax, you know? I said, something is strange. Wake up, what is going on? No, it is the more the mind is turned on, the more you understand; the more there is a knowledge of God, the more there is joy. 'Can't you have fun?' No, I want *joy*. Some people will transfer joy into fun, and they sing songs like, 'There's a joy, joy, joy, joy, whatever.' What they are talking about is: 'There's fun, fun, fun, fun.' No, joy builds and grows and increases and becomes more joyful. What do you want? Do you think I am weird to want joy more than fun? You think the life of the mind is not joyful? Not better than fun? Richer and more lasting? Come on; let's not go after that one. You know, what God calls us to is joy. So we want to think teleologically, in terms of the goal, and Adam is going to be tested about this.

The temptation is revelational: testing is going to reveal what is in us. It was true originally. It was that way before the Fall (pre-Fall), and subsequently post-Fall. Even with the curse on us, we are tempted. It is really an *a fortiori* situation—an all the more so situation—with the curse. We need to be tested because of self-deception and self-justification, so we can expect it. We can speak about original temptation (pre-Fall), and subsequent temptation.

Currently, we experience them as trials of faith, which are really tests of understanding, for our sanctification. We may experience perplexity and consternation. Paul speaks about this: "perplexed, but not in despair; persecuted, but not abandoned; struck down, but not destroyed" (2 Cor. 4:8b). Perplexed. We do not know what hit us and why. There is such a thing called the old-age truck; the old-age truck hits suddenly, and you can see the tire marks over the body. You still get up and walk, but you walk a little bit slower, and you think, 'What hit me? How did that happen?' Oh, surprise, surprise. It was getting you every day, and all of a sudden, 'What happened?' Why are you perplexed, in consternation, about these things? It shows that we are not understanding basic things that we need to understand, and God is graciously calling us back.

The temptations are always circumstantially relevant. They frustrate our plans and our desires, our short and long-term plans. I hear that cry often: 'I'm trying to serve God, and He is just hitting me right and left, and I cannot understand why.' I have said it. I have been with people at dinner and said it to their face. And I usually come back and say, 'Yes, it is not *my* time, it is not *my* energy, it is not *my* purpose. It is God's.' This is part of the self-life God wants to deliver us from. In reading both Amy Carmichael and Elisabeth Elliott, they speak about this. They speak about how things do not turn out the way we want them to, and we should thank God for that. It turns out *better* than what we want. We do not see it at the time when we were in consternation, but if we come back—if we keep our eyes on the goal, no matter what—we will come to see it.

In the temptation, we are being addressed as rational beings. It involves arguments and reasoning. Satan gave a reason for what was said. We have to recognize that it is a test of our faith. We should notice that a temptation is something inherent in that every time we make a choice, we have to make a choice between, 'is it towards the chief end or not? Is it good or evil?' It is present in every choice we make. Some choices are made almost routinely, so they do not feel like a choice, and we do not experience it as a choice. Sometimes, we come to a crisis of big choices, where we say, 'That's a choice.' But it is really just that we are more conscious of that choice. All the little choices usually add up to a big choice.

We do experience temptations currently, continually, as trials of faith. They are circumstantially relevant, both objectively and subjectively. God knows where we are. "No temptation has seized you except what is common to man. And God is faithful; he will not let you be tempted beyond what you can bear. But when you are tempted, he will also provide a way out so that you can stand up under it" (1 Cor. 10:13). He will not let you be tempted beyond what you can bear. You can bear it, because it is bearable, though He may not remove it completely. Some of you lift weights, and you know what it is to reach your limits. The weight must do its work, and must be of a certain level, to get you to exercise those muscles—otherwise, you are not really getting much benefit. But He will not allow us to be tempted beyond what we can bear. We can say, 'Lord, I cannot bear it anymore, I cannot take it, I cannot stand it.' God knows what He is doing. He is wise. And if we fall under it, we can still cry out to God with our faces in the mud, and someone's foot standing on the back of our neck pushing us further into the mud. It is hard to talk in the mud. You can groan in the mud, and sometimes that is all you can do is groan before God. This is why David said, "a broken and contrite heart, O God, you will not despise" (Ps. 51:17b). He hears the groaning of the prisoner (Ps. 102:20). God is aware, and He especially has His eye on us when we are in that temptation. It is like silver purified in an earthen vessel, seven times. It takes seven times to purify it (a complete number), so He subjects us to temptation again and again and again. This is a matter of degrees, and of being cleansed, and God watches. "Take away the dross from the silver, and there shall come forth a vessel for the finer" (Prov. 25:4 KJV). He watches to see the dross that is skimmed off, and He watches to know when to stop. If you have your eyes on Jesus, God knows. Remember His servant Job? So it is with His servants in every generation. You are not tempted beyond what you can bear.

Temptation is common to man. We can feel isolated in our temptation. Nothing is as common as temptation, trial; but the enemy will try to get us to think that we are all alone in this, and we are being beaten up because we have been bad or we deserve it. No, God loves us, He is treating us as His children. Temptation may be without this kind of outward suffering, but it may be *with*; under the Fall it is usually *with suffering*. Jesus, under the Fall—redeeming those under the Fall—suffered without food for 40 days and 40 nights. The other two temptations did not seem to involve this element. He was asked to presume upon God's grace and cast Himself down, and the other was to worship the devil in order to get what He wanted. Jesus' first temptation certainly had the agony of natural evil to its utmost: 40 days and 40 nights. Some will say, 'Well, that's no big deal for Him.' What about the lashes that He had when He was being taken to the cross and nailed to the cross? Is someone going to say, 'That is okay, no big deal?' Have you been that far? No. Come on. No way. And He was without sin; He did it for us. "The chastisement of our peace was upon him; and with his stripes we are healed" (Is. 53:5b KJV). This is why it says, "Let us fix our eyes on Jesus" (Hebrews 12:2a). No temptation has overtaken you but such as is common to man, and He will not allow you to be tempted beyond what you can bear.[11] This is circumstantially relevant, both objectively and subjectively. He knows where we are. This is also in terms of historically cumulative insight, that which came from much discussion by the pastor-teachers. Where should we be in relation to that? These things are taken into consideration.

THE FALL

Let us look now at an analysis of the Fall in the context of creation, and with an attitude of seeking, to notice and understand the particulars of Genesis 1–3 in context. Notice the particulars, including representation, the covenant of creation, probation, manifestation, and the two trees; the setting is there, and the stage is set. We also have the revelation of the covenant of marriage: what God is trying to do in reconciling the creation to Himself through Christ in the marriage of the lamb.

---

11. *1 Corinthians 10:13.*

The Serpent

On the scene now comes the serpent. **"Now the serpent was more crafty,"** or "more subtle," as the King James Bible puts it, **"than any of the wild animals the LORD God had made"** (v. 1). He is presented here as the serpent, but he is given other names, too, that reveal who he is. In Revelation 12:9, he is referred to as the dragon: the great dragon. He is called Satan—angel of light. He is called the devil—diabolos (διαβόλου): the dung hurler, the slanderer, the accuser of the brothers. We need to have discernment regarding who this tempter is. Regarding the great dragon: on the way home from Hawaii, we saw this movie on the plane flying back. I watched without audio, I did not want to pay money for it, and I thought I could follow the movie well enough. It was titled, *How to Train Your Dragon*. And at the end of the movie, out came the great dragon. Before this, they were, by comparison, mini-dragons. I thought, that is *the* dragon, that is the great dragon.

I think what we have represented here is a threefold aspect of God's created order. The dragon is of all beasts, *the* beast. It uses force to get its way rather than reason. We see this summed up in all of politics without God. But he is also Satan, the deceiver, the false prophet: all of education without God. This other part, (I do not want to force the analogy; I will just leave some of it hanging, and we can talk about it further) he is also the one who is a slanderer, who makes you appear ugly and hideous by saying all manner of evil against you.[12] He throws dung at us; this is not a pretty sight. By the grace of God, we know what this means. We have been experiencing some of this. God was gracious to me and has protected me for the greater part of my life. But lately, I think the Lord has been pleased to lift this and allow slander to be raised up, and I hear the voice of the devil, the *diabolos*, the dung hurler—this is what it is literally: he is hurling *dung* at us. He is accusing us, saying, 'Look at you, you dirty scumbag.' He wants people to think we are a scumbag. In one way or another, this is what the slanderers are saying. Satan rubs it in our faces. The voice of the devil, the dung hurler. We are not ignorant of Satan's devices and will learn to, by God's grace, deal with them appropriately.

Satan is there, and he was there in the beginning, and he is constantly there in these forms. He is Satan, the great dragon, the devil.

---

12. *Matthew 5:11.*

He comes now to the woman. You may want to ask, 'Where did this being come from?' He was created by God. He is finite, temporal, and changeable, like all creatures, and he did change. He was caught in a lie, perhaps because of his beauty, his magnificence. He failed to recognize his creatureliness and became self-sufficient. Left to himself, he turned to himself. He is, first of all, the one deceived. He is a liar and the father of it. He is a slanderer and the father of all slanderers. He is a murderer, Jesus said, and the prince of all murderers. There it is, from the beginning. There is no truth in him, Scripture says. He is created, but he turns away in deception. It is not sudden; you do not have to be a rocket scientist to figure this out. You do not have to be some high archangel to figure it out. "Out of the mouth of babes and sucklings hast thou ordained strength because of thine enemies, that thou mightest still the enemy and the avenger" (Ps. 8:2 KJV). This is so basic and clear; we have to really try hard to get outside of the bounds of God.

Has God Really Said?

Satan is present, but he is the occasion, not the cause. He raised a question: Has God said? The insinuation: Has God really said? Think of the implications of that, psychologically and logically. **"Did God really say, 'You must not eat from any tree in the garden'?"** (v. 1b). Did God really say that? Is that what God meant? Did you hear it right? There is more that we could say about this, but we will move on.

The woman answered, but her answer showed that her understanding was not all that it should be. She said, **"We may eat fruit from the trees in the garden"** (v. 2b). It is more than "may." She goes on: **"but God did say, 'You must not eat fruit from the tree that is in the middle of the garden'"** (v. 3a). There is some ambiguity here. It is not *the* tree in the middle of the Garden. There are specifically two trees in the middle of the Garden, so which one? One of the trees is the tree of the knowledge of good and evil, these are specified by name. **"And you must not touch it,"** which she added, **"or you will die"** (v. 3b), rather than "you will surely die" (2:17b). What grade would you give to her on an exam? I would say maybe a 'C minus.' She is passing. But in terms of her understanding, I would definitely say not an A. Now, people try to say, 'Well, I got the words right.' No, I am looking at your understanding, as best as I can discern it. And some people say, 'Well,

I believe this.' No, you believe those words, but the understanding is not what it should be. This is why I speak about grammatical, dialectical, and rhetorical levels of understanding.[13] Faith has to do with understanding: understanding the meaning. The woman is already lacking in meaning, which is going to be the problem. She has less of the meaning than she should, not utterly without meaning, but she has less of the meaning. This is why the word literally, technically, means *meaning-less*, which is not *meaning-full*. We could adjust the meaning of those terms. We tend to use *meaningless* as *utterly meaningless*, but it is having less of the meaning. This is where the temptation begins because we should be filling meaning more and more instead of having less and less meaning. If we were to ask her about certain things and the assumptions and implications, we would see what is lacking.

We see this in the way people think about and talk about circumcision: that it is outward only. The Scriptures say, "A little leaven leaveneth the whole lump" (Gal. 5:9 KJV); a little lack of understanding is the crack in the door that lets it open, and the tempter will come right through. We are not doing Trivial Pursuit here; we are not playing a game where you say the right word, and then we say, 'Ding, you got it right, you win $300.' We are pursuing understanding. We are tested in our faith, in our understanding. It is by faith that we understand.

You Will Not Surely Die

The tempter comes back and says, **"You will not surely die"** (v. 4a), and here is the devil hurling dung at God by making insinuations about the goodness of God. He said, **"You will not surely die,"** but God said, "you will surely die" (Gen. 2:17b). The devil can quote the Scripture better than we can. He can discombobulate us and throw us for a loop. Then we say, 'Ahh, where do we go from here?'

"You will not surely die" is the central thesis of all of temptation. 'What you are doing is not going to lead to death.' We think to ourselves, 'Oh, I can sin and God will forgive me.' Shall we say, "Shall we go on sinning so that grace may increase?" (Rom. 6:1b). As if there is not a connection between sin and death? If God forgives, what about the death because of sin remaining in you? Are you going to want that?

---

13. The Logos Foundation, *Grammar Catechisms*, xix-xxvi.

Do you think you can separate sin and death? Do you think that you can separate not seeking and not understanding and spiritual death? It does not work that way. Do you think you can be divided within your nature, act contrary to your nature, and not harm yourself? Think again. Do you think that you have no nature? Are you a natureless being? That is what Islam ends up saying about God.[14]

Last night, I saw the second part of 9/11, and my stomach was just churning as I reflected on the manifestation of evil in that form and the lie that it is based on. Shouting "Allahu Akbar," without even knowing what it means to say that God is great. God is great in what sense? Where mercy sets aside His justice? Or, God is both just and merciful and His mercy satisfies His justice?[15] They deny the crucifixion of Jesus, they deny the atonement, and the Church has let that stand for centuries—we have not engaged with that assumption. We talk about Islam without getting to the core issue, so we are not doing what we should do. **"You will not surely die."** That central thesis denies the fear of the Lord. Understanding what death is, *that* is lacking.

The argument is given: **"For God knows"** (v. 5a), there is the reason; he is treating them as rational beings. **"Your eyes will be opened"** (v. 5), you will get more. We are tempted by the idea of gaining 'fullness' without the foundation in place. We naturally desire fullness, but it has to be in the foundation. Believing 'you can be as God, as the Most High'; contrast that with Jesus, "Who, being in very nature God, did not consider equality with God something to be grasped, but made himself nothing, taking the very nature of a servant, being made in human likeness. And being found in appearance as a man, he humbled himself and became obedient to death—even death on a cross!" (Phil. 2:6–8). Let this mind of Christ be in you.

The argument shows Satan's self-deception by denying the essential creatureliness; he denies essences, that we are creatures, and he denies the difference between the infinite God and the finite man. This idea of 'fullness' that Satan offers, is still finite; it is not infinite. There is a lot of confusion in Satan's words, and we can enumerate them.

---

14. Robert Reilley, *The Closing of the Muslim Mind: How Intellectual Suicide Created the Modern Islamic Crisis* (Wilmington: Intercollegiate Study Institute, 2010), 59–90.

15. Gangadean, *Philosophical Foundation*, 191–192; Gangadean, *The Westminster Confession*, 21–27, 37–41, 67–69, 129–130, 236–238; Gangadean, "Paper No. 91: Christianity and Islam," in *The Logos Papers*, 479–484.

The truth of God is inexhaustible. In Hawaii, at the East-West Center,[16] they speak about, 'Whatever you say, you cannot say that we are going to come to a fixed end. Bottom line: no fixed end.' We have said that the central truth about the good is that it is continuing and inexhaustible; no fixed end there. But we get this twisted as if we have to be infinite to get this fullness. No, there is a fullness even for the finite: an inexhaustibility. So you want more? This is how you get more: not by being God, but by being servants of God—filling the earth with the knowledge of God. We saw that faulty reasoning expressed many times; bypassing the fullness does not entail infinitude. We should have fullness, God wants us to attain to fullness, He calls us to the full measure of the stature of Jesus Christ.[17] What we do is substitute the fullness that we are called to—according to our nature—for infinitude: to be as God. What a subtle but absolute difference. How many of us are struggling to even grasp it now?

We can have knowledge of God through the revelation God has given versus the direct knowledge of God in the beatific vision; we are presuming on this difference. Also, the argument calls us to see how it is that God knows good and evil; what is good and evil? In general, we should say that good for a being is according to the nature of that being; we have to get to the idea of natures, which many have denied based on knowledge through experience. We speak against the goodness of God by saying or implying that 'God is holding back from me: He does not want me to be all that I can be.' How often have we felt that? Satan appeals to that in us. 'You can be more. You can be much more. Do not let anything hold you back. This is what you were meant to be. You cannot let that go. You must do this.' Yes, we want more, and we have fullness in Christ, by whom all things were created. We are creatures, and we are members of the body. We have fullness in connection with each other in the body of Christ. It is through the body of Christ that He is to fill everything in every way. He is to fill the whole universe. How is that going to happen? Altogether, I do not know; I sometimes wonder. But it is the earth that is given to mankind to have dominion over. We are given the lie that the ultimate is to be as God, grasping for equality with God, and there is so much pride involved in that.

---

16. East-West Center | www.eastwestcenter.org.

17. *Ephesians 4:13.*

Threefold Appeal

The appeal to the woman is threefold: it is good for food (practical), it is pleasing to the eyes (aesthetic, the beautiful), and your eyes will be opened (gaining wisdom). We see the comparison with what is said in 1 John 2:16, "the lust of the flesh, and the lust of the eyes, and the pride of life,"[18] and the last one is vainglory—boasting. I think it is to be connected with this gaining of wisdom and the position where we think that *we know*, and we seek to rule in connection with that, but it is apart from God. The whole idea, the stupidity of it, as though there is magic—do you think that by eating the fruit you can have knowledge? By doing this, you get that? This is not wisdom. This is not how it happens. This is not according to the nature of things.

She Ate Some

There are a lot of things bound up in *the eating*: taking the outward for the inward without understanding. **"She took some and ate it. She also gave some to her husband, who was with her"** (v. 6). Here is the passive husband again. Right from the beginning, he is standing there, not doing anything, acting like a juvenile. He is wrapped up in her, rather than wrapped up in the good; not leading. Delinquent, our father Adam, **"and he ate it"** (v. 6b). She leads and he follows, because his desire is for her. You want to play that game? Girls, guys? Disaster is there. Do not presume here, not even a little bit.

We said that there is war in heaven. There is war in Eden. There is war in paradise. There is war everywhere, all through history. We are not to presume on that war in paradise; it is a dreadful thing, but it is a good thing in a way. It is good in a qualified way. God established the war: "I will put enmity between you and the woman" (Gen. 3:15a). God is going to reverse the order of things. He will not allow Satan to triumph. Satan is standing in glee: 'Yes, she obeyed me. She heard *my* word over *your* word. It is mine now, you see? They only obey for what they can get. They are not doing it because of who you are.' This is what he uttered regarding Job: "Does Job fear God for nothing? . . . stretch out your hand and strike everything he has, and he will surely curse you to your face" (Job 1:9, 11). Have you heard that line? Again

---

18. KJV.

and again? Satan is in glee, but he does not have the last laugh. "He that sitteth in the heavens shall laugh: the LORD shall have them in derision" (Ps. 2:4 KJV) This is why we began with Psalm 96, about the reign of God.

God rules, even when Satan triumphs in this way. He permits evil, "having purposed to order it to his own glory,"[19] in His infinite wisdom. He shows the freedom of the creature. He shows where it will go if left to itself. He shows that He will glorify Himself and He will glorify His Son Jesus Christ, who will come to take upon Himself human nature, that in Him all fullness might dwell. Satan has another thing coming. Satan does not realize how wise God is. How God will cause his sin to serve God's purpose. How God's truth will be magnified more through his lie, to the praise of His glory. Jehovah reigns!

We should see from this what it is to humble oneself, to become a creature, to become obedient. Christ was obedient even unto death: the death on the cross. There are many ways to die, but this is death on the cross. "Therefore God exalted him to the highest place and gave him the name that is above every name, that at the name of Jesus every knee should bow, in heaven and on earth and under the earth, and every tongue confess that Jesus Christ is Lord, to the glory of God the Father" (Phil. 2:9–11). Christ is Lord. Jehovah reigns.

---

19. *WCF 6.1.*

———

11

SIN

Root Sin and Fruit Sin

Romans 1:18–25; 2:14–15, 21–24, 28–29; 3:9–12

¹⁸The wrath of God is being revealed from heaven against all the godlessness and wickedness of men who suppress the truth by their wickedness, ¹⁹since what may be known about God is plain to them, because God has made it plain to them. ²⁰For since the creation of the world God's invisible qualities—his eternal power and divine nature—have been clearly seen, being understood from what has been made, so that men are without excuse. ²¹For although they knew God, they neither glorified him as God nor gave thanks to him, but their thinking became futile and their foolish hearts were darkened. ²²Although they claimed to be wise, they became fools ²³and exchanged the glory of the immortal God for images made to look like mortal man and birds and animals and reptiles. ²⁴Therefore God gave them over in the sinful desires of their hearts to sexual impurity for the degrading of their bodies with one another. ²⁵They exchanged the truth of God for a lie, and worshiped and served created things rather than the Creator—who is forever praised. Amen.

¹⁴(Indeed, when Gentiles, who do not have the law, do by nature things required by the law, they are a law for themselves, even though they do not have the law, ¹⁵since they show that the requirements of the law are written on their hearts, their consciences also bearing witness, and their thoughts now accusing, now even defending them.)

²¹you, then, who teach others, do you not teach yourself? You who preach against stealing, do you steal? ²²You who say that people should not commit adultery, do you commit adultery? You who abhor idols, do you rob temples? ²³You who brag about the law, do you dishonor God by breaking

the law? [24]As it is written: "God's name is blasphemed among the Gentiles because of you."

[28]A man is not a Jew if he is only one outwardly, nor is circumcision merely outward and physical. [29]No, a man is a Jew if he is one inwardly; and circumcision is circumcision of the heart, by the Spirit, not by the written code. Such a man's praise is not from men, but from God.

[9]What shall we conclude then? Are we any better ? Not at all! We have already made the charge that Jews and Gentiles alike are all under sin. [10]As it is written: "There is no one righteous, not even one; [11]there is no one who understands, no one who seeks God. [12]All have turned away, they have together become worthless; there is no one who does good, not even one."

THE LAMB OF GOD

IN JOHN 1:29, JOHN THE BAPTIST SAID, "Look, the Lamb of God, who takes away the sin of the world!" These passages that I have read are sobering; talk about sin is like that. If we simply end on that note, we are inclined to avoid talking about it. Who wants to go around with this cloud over their heads? But this is not how the Scripture presents it. It presents sin in relation to Jesus Christ. He is the Lamb of God who takes away the sin of the world, and this is not an incidental point that is tacked on to the Scripture. It is at the core of the Scripture, from the beginning to the end. Just to make that a little clearer to you, I will quickly mention, in passing, ten points from the Scripture that illustrate the Lamb of God.

First of all, there are the coats of skin given to Adam.[1] Secondly, Abel's offering that continues to speak: the sacrifice of the flock.[2] Third, Noah observed the sacrifice in bringing the animals that were sacrificed after the Flood.[3] Fourth, Abraham's life came into the sharpest focus when he offered up Isaac,[4] and Jesus said, "Abraham rejoiced at the thought of seeing my day; he saw it and was glad" (Jn. 8:56). He saw what the Father would do, and it was a culminating point in Abraham's life. Fifth, Moses, not only at the altar but at the tent of

---

1. *Genesis 3:21.*

2. *Genesis 4:4.*

3. *Genesis 8:20–22.*

4. *Genesis 22.*

meeting where God meets with the people; the Shekinah is over the mercy seat, in which the blood is sprinkled, in the Most Holy Place, on the Day of Atonement. Sixth, Psalm 22:6 speaks about the sacrifice of Christ and the benefits that came from his sacrifice. Seventh, Isaiah 53 speaks about the one who was crushed for our iniquities, smitten of God, and afflicted. Eighth, John 1:29, which we quoted a minute ago: "Look, the Lamb of God, who takes away the sin of the world!" Ninth, Paul speaks in the same way, in many verses, but this one caught my attention: "May I never boast except in the cross of our Lord Jesus Christ, through which the world has been crucified to me, and I to the world" (Gal. 6:14). Paul also said, "For I resolved to know nothing while I was with you except Jesus Christ and him crucified" (1 Cor. 2:2). Then the tenth point is from Revelation 5:12. This is where it culminates: "Worthy is the Lamb, who was slain, to receive power and wealth and wisdom and strength and honor and glory and praise!" Because He is slain, He is the one who rules. From the beginning to the end of Scripture, we are confronted with Christ, as the Lamb of God who takes away the sin of the world. It is the sin of the world, and we will see how that comes to be applied.

In 1 Corinthians 2:2, which we just quoted, Paul says, "For I resolved to know nothing while I was with you except Jesus Christ and him crucified," that is the focus today. We want to ask ourselves, 'Who is Jesus Christ?' In asking that, we have to consider two things. First, 'Who is Christ?' and 'Who is Jesus?' And second, 'Why was He crucified?' If we weaken, undermine, or compromise the idea of sin in the least bit, if we fail to see inexcusability and the death that comes with it, then we undermine the person and work of Christ and the significance of Scripture. The focus on sin is in order to keep the focus on Christ, as it should be. This is how we speak about sin—in relation to Christ. He is the Lamb of God who takes away the sin of the world. We cannot minimize sin without minimizing the work of Christ. Everyone who has done so—*everyone*, without exception—ends up compromising the person and work of Jesus Christ. It is a matter of degree, and we will see how this plays out. This is why we want to get a clearer idea of what sin is, without compromise, and we hope to do so by the grace of God.

The Christ is the Son of God incarnate. He is the anointed prophet, priest, and king. He comes in the place of Adam. He is the promised one from the beginning. He is the seed of the woman. As Christ, He is the seed of Abraham and the seed of David; Christ comes through that line. Why would such a one be crucified? Why would the Son of God be crucified? Why would the promised one, promised from the beginning, be crucified? If you press persons on this, you will begin to see how the failure to understand sin compromises it. For example, 'Can all men be saved by implicit faith in what is good? By living up to the light that they have?' There is this doctrine of implicit faith, syncretism, and men of goodwill from every faith, that is brought in. There are some who say: 'Those who are at the ends of the earth and have never heard of Christ will get a second chance.' There is the view, which is outside of the framework of clarity and inexcusability, which says that 'belief in God spontaneously arises in persons according to their properly functioning epistemic equipment that is in their minds, and they are then saved by God somehow.' But since we are not talking about clarity and inexcusability, that position slides off into universalism: All will be saved, even without confession of faith in Christ. Some people say, 'In the next life you will have the chance for the gospel to be preached to you, and then you will be saved.' This begins to undermine the whole idea of the call back and what sin is. Why do I need to be preached to in the next life, in any case? If I do not accept the preaching, *then* I am condemned? It does not make sense.

CLARITY OF GOD'S EXISTENCE AND THE INEXCUSABILITY OF UNBELIEF

The only way we can understand the person and work of Christ is to understand sin. The only way we can understand sin is in terms of *inexcusability*. The only way we can understand inexcusability is in terms of *clarity*. This is why we make a big deal about this; this is why you hear this often. Try to justify the notion of sin without the notion of inexcusability, without the notion of clarity, and you will see what happens. Try to get clarity without each and every one (who has come of age) being responsible for seeing it. Try to make progress in the Christian faith without repentance of sin, root sin; it will not go; there will not be a credible profession of repentance.

What is clear is spoken of in Romans. It specifies: "For since the creation of the world God's invisible qualities" (Rom. 1:20a). We know through the eyes of the understanding—not through sense experience.

It specifies further what these invisible qualities are; it is noted; it is in the Scriptures: "his eternal power and divine nature" (Rom. 1: 20). It notices first His *eternal power*, but it includes *all* of His divine nature. There is such a thing as the "divine nature." Of the attributes, it first speaks about power, but even more basically, it speaks about His eternality. This is what is clear: God is eternal, and only God is eternal, and nothing else is eternal. We did not read this *into* the Scripture. We have taken it out from the Scripture. From the beginning of Scripture, the focus has been on the eternality of God: "In the beginning God created" (Gen. 1:1a). Creation had a beginning. God has no beginning. He is the one who is, and was, and is to come: the eternal one. He is Yahweh; "I AM THAT I AM" (Ex. 3:14 KJV), the self-existing one. This attribute marks out God from everything else, and this is what is clear and not just His eternality, but His wisdom and His justice as well. The problem of evil should be easy for Christians to answer,[5] but you see what is happening in the discourse, in Hume's *Dialogues*, as Demea is stumbling all over the place.[6]

The existence of God's nature is clear. Notice it says, "being understood from what has been made" (Rom. 1:20). It refers to a process of understanding and it does not refer to *immediate* knowledge apart from the understanding process. It is "understood from what has been made." As it says, "The heavens declare the glory of God" (Ps. 19:1), and "nothing is hidden from its heat" (Ps. 19:6b). Many have seen the sun and what have they done? They have worshiped the sun, as against worshiping the Creator of the sun.

This is inferred since it is "understood from what has been made" (Rom. 1:20). Some may even minimize this inference by saying that it spontaneously arises, without any thought. This has been recurrent in Reformed Epistemology, which is a craze in intellectual circles, going back to Thomas Reid and his common sense realism.[7] It is what Princeton was built on, what the Declaration of Independence was built

---

5. Gangadean, *Philosophical Foundation*, 145–161; Gangadean, *On Natural and Revealed Theology*, 141–147.

6. David Hume, *Dialogues Concerning Natural Religion* (Cambridge: Hackett, 1998). Demea represents the position of the orthodox believer, speaks analogously about God.

7. Gangadean, *Philosophical Foundation*, 24.

on,[8] and it is why we are in the shape that we are in—because that was inadequate. With self-evident truths, you do not have to make any inference whatsoever, and people have been saying, 'It is not self-evident to me.' We have to speak about what is clear to reason, which is the Word of God in all men.

This is what is clear: "being understood from what has been made, so that men are without excuse" (Rom. 1:20b). This is where we get the two terms: clarity of general revelation and inexcusability. By general revelation, we are speaking first about both the existence and the nature of God. It is not just the nature of God, and then such a being may or may not exist; who knows? No, it is the existence *and* the nature of God; preferably, first, the nature of God, and then the existence of God. If God were not eternal, He would not be God. If God were not the *only* eternal, He would not be God; He would not be higher than other things. Anselm tried to say, "God is a being than which none greater can be conceived."[9] But if we speak in this way, as Anselm does, why could it not be matter? If matter is eternal then matter would be the greatest thing conceivable, because you do not get any greater than being eternal. The dualists went that way.[10]

Let us give attention to the specifics of Scripture here, and the strategic location of this passage in the Book of Romans, which is a systematic statement of Scripture. It is at the beginning of Romans 1 and 2 that Paul seeks to establish the reality of sin. But this is where it begins: with the eternality of God; with His eternal power and the divine nature.

THE MORAL LAW IS WRITTEN ON THE HEART

The second thing that is clear is the law of God that is written on the hearts of all men. According to Romans 2:14–15:

---

8. Gangadean, "Paper No. 20: Christianity, Philosophy, and Public Education," in *The Logos Papers*, 127–133.

9. Frederick Copleston, *A History of Philosophy: Medieval Philosophy* (New York: Bloomsbury Continuum, 1972), 162.

10. Gangadean, *Philosophical Foundation*, 129–137; Gangadean, *History of Philosophy*, 87–105, 111–114; Gangadean, "Paper No. 3: The Principle of Clarity," 15–20; "Paper No. 82: Dualism" in *The Logos Papers*, 427–429.

Indeed, when Gentiles, who do not have the law, do by nature things required by the law, they are a law for themselves, even though they do not have the law, since they show that the requirements of the law are written on their hearts, their consciences also bearing witness, and their thoughts now accusing, now even defending them.

Here it is specifically referring to the Gentiles, but that is not to the exclusion of the Jews, the law as written on the hearts of *all* men. This is not a new teaching; it is certainly there in Deuteronomy 30:11–14. "Now what I am commanding you today is not too difficult for you or beyond your reach. It is not up in heaven, so you have to ask, 'Who will ascend into heaven to get it and proclaim it to us so we may obey it?' Nor is it beyond the sea, so that you have to ask, 'Who will cross the sea to get it and proclaim it to us so we may obey it?'" You do not have to go across the seas to get it, you do not have to go up to heaven to get it and have it come down by way of a special revelation, as it did on Sinai. It did come down on Sinai from heaven, but you do not have to get it in that way. It is near you, "in your mouth and in your heart" (Deut. 30:14). Both Moses and Paul are saying this. Because we are saying it does not mean that it is originating from us, rather, we are recognizing what Scripture is saying.

We have difficulty getting to the law of God, because we do not start with the basics: with the goal of the law, which is the good, which is life. Therefore we have a deontological view of the law and make the law positive. That is, simply posited by God, rather than grounded in the nature of man: in his heart, in the core of his being. Since this is clear, we do not think that we should not know it. We believe that persons who are seeking membership in this congregation should see how the law is clear, and how it is written on the heart; I do not think this is asking too much. We should also ask how it is clear that God, and only God, is eternal. We should all be able to see what Psalm 19 says. We should all be able to see that the soul is not eternal—in contrast to many who try to take that position.[11]

---

11. Gangadean, *Philosophical Foundation*, 71–161; Gangadean, *History of Philosophy*, 47–58; Gangadean, *The Westminster Catechisms*, 111–112; Gangadean, "Paper No. 3: The Principle of Clarity," 15–20; "Paper No. 93: The Logic of Apologetics," in *The Logos Papers*, 493–497.

Suppression by Unbelief

Let us return to Romans 1. People try to suppress the truth about God.[12] That by which they suppress the truth is their unbelief. It does not seem to make sense that there is some other way to suppress the truth unless you kill the truth-teller. That also happens, if suppression does not work. But the truth is suppressed through a lie, through a falsehood: 'This other thing is eternal; this world is self-existing.' 'The jewel is in the lotus (the self-generating forces in the universe),' as the Buddhists say. 'In the beginning was Hiranyagarbha, this golden egg out of which everything came.' This is typical evolutionary thought; the universe is self-generating—no. We should see that this is unbelief that is being used to suppress the truth. Nagarjuna, the Buddhist dialectician, says that never, nowhere, can anything originate, so we can never assert that anything originated.[13] No, Nagarjuna, mere assertion is not an argument; you have to do more; let us go at it and figure it out. It is this unbelief that is inexcusable. It is clear that unbelief is false, and they are inexcusable for their unbelief. Most of the time we address *how* the belief may have originated in us, and we are not addressing the unbelief and the inexcusability in connection with the unbelief that is used to suppress the truth. This is what is clear, as well as the law of God. This should be clear to anyone who has the foundation in place, and the foundation is milk, not meat.[14] This is why it says, "From the lips of children and infants you have ordained praise because of your enemies, to silence the foe and the avenger" (Ps. 8:2). Some people will say, 'Oh, this foundation is deep.' No, the teaching about Melchizedek is deep. The teaching about Melchizedek is going higher, building on the foundation. The foundation is milk. Who here wants to deny milk to the babes? This is what is clear.

---

12. This is where we have disagreements with voluntarists regarding the meaning of suppression. See: Gangadean, "Paper No. 120: Contra Voluntarism," in *The Logos Papers*, 611–647.

13. Gangadean, *History of Philosophy*, 107–108; Gangadean, *Philosophical Foundation*, 115–117.

14. *Hebrews 5:13–14.*

The Meaning of *Clear*

Let us specify a little bit more what we mean by *clear*. Clear means that *all* are responsible, regardless of background. 'My parents didn't teach me, my husband didn't teach me.' No, sorry, it is clear. You stand before God, and you cannot plead that excuse. You are inexcusable. This is not a good excuse. 'My parents hit me upside the head every morning, telling me to worship the sun.' Sorry, this is not an excuse. You can still see this and stand your ground. This is why we put it this way: the abused and uneducated kid from Ubangy Bangy can see what is clear.

All are responsible, and that includes people with PhDs. Having a PhD is no excuse for not seeing this. Most PhDs do not see it, and they speak against it. They have no excuse. So, to the farm boy and the Dread Pirate Roberts, you should see what is clear, farm boy. The educated should see it; all should see it. It is clear. By clear we mean that we are all responsible, but He takes away the sin of the world. All are without excuse: that helps us to see what it means. No one seeks.[15] Then, the second part of this is that *all who seek can see it*; certainly, in Psalm 19, we see this. Thirdly, in terms of clear, you have to shut your eyes to not see. You may have neglected reason, but you may also avoid it, so you have to shut your eyes: you have to stop thinking in order to avoid seeing it; that is how clear it is. "Be ever hearing, but never understanding; be ever seeing, but never perceiving.' Make the heart of this people calloused; make their ears dull and close their eyes. Otherwise they might see with their eyes, hear with their ears, understand with their hearts, and turn and be healed" (Is. 6:9b–10). This is how clear it is. One has to stop thinking in order to avoid seeing this. The third sense is one has to give up one's integrity and become a hypocrite in self-deception and self-justification to avoid seeing this. Integrity is necessary and sufficient for knowledge.[16] Concern for consistency between one's ideas and one's life. But we give it up; we give up on integrity. Jesus charged people with taking the name of God in vain: saying one thing and doing another—hypocrisy. This is the culminating judgment: "Woe unto you, teachers of the law and Pharisees, you hypocrites!" Seven times in Matthew 23. Think about the location in the whole progress of the book.

---

15. *Romans 3:11; Psalm 14:2–3, 53:1–3.*

16. Gangadean, *Philosophical Foundation*, 199–205.

As we think of what clarity means, it is clear that the opposite is contradictory. It is ontologically and logically impossible that being should come from non-being, or that there are square circles, or that something is both eternal and not self-maintaining. Those are contradictory notions because everything that is eternal is self-maintaining. One cannot say that something is eternal and not eternal; this is what we mean by clear.[17] People often ask, 'What do you mean by clarity? Define clear?' We are trying to define what clear means now. All are responsible, all who seek can see, one has to shut one's eyes to not see, one has to give up one's integrity. The opposite of what is clear is contradictory: It is logically impossible and ontologically impossible. This is clarity and this establishes inexcusability. Inexcusability literally means *anapologētos* (ἀναπολόγητος), that is, without excuse, without a reason. That is what the word literally means. *Anapologētos* is related to the word *logos* and "a" means without: without having a reason.[18] There is an inherent connection between sin, as being without reason, and death, which is the consequence of not having reason. It is failing to understand.

SIN: ROOT AND FRUIT

Let us speak further about sin. What is sin? We make a distinction between root sin and fruit sin. In general, the distinction has to do with what is less basic and what is more basic. In the Garden of Eden's account that we have been speaking of, you can see it: They ate the fruit, but there was an argument, and they believed the lie. Behind the lie, they believed "You will not surely die . . . you will be like God, knowing good and evil" (Gen. 3:4–5). There are further assumptions behind this. What is it to know good and evil? The assumptions behind the lie have to do with the focus on good and evil, and being tested regarding

---

17. Gangadean, *Philosophical Foundation*, 3–5, 287–292; Gangadean, "Paper No. 3: The Principle of Clarity," 15–20; "Paper No. 39: Clarity," 217–220; "Paper No. 41: What is Clear About God," 225–229; "Paper No. 102: The Clarity of General Revelation," in *The Logos Papers*, 527–529.

18. *Apologeomai* (ἀπολογέομαι) means to give an account of oneself, to defend oneself, to reason with solid proof, so the negation of that—*anapologētos*—is the condition of being unable to give an account of oneself, lacking a justified defense; this word was frequently used to describe the hopelessness of trying to defend a case in court while lacking an adequate defense, and to refer to something that completely lacks merit.

the pursuit of the good. It involves blurring the distinction between the creator and the creature with regard to knowing good and evil. The good is determined by God, according to the nature of a being, by the act of creation. Good for a being is according to the nature of that being.[19] Good for a horse is according to the nature of a horse. Good for a rabbit is according to the nature of a rabbit. For a human being, it is in accordance with the nature of a human being. Things have natures, which are spoken of as "kinds."[20] Man is different in kind, is distinct, from all of the animals, and that is why no suitable helper was found among the animals. Man is a different category altogether; it is perhaps a different genus.

We know what sin is, and before Adam engaged in the outward sin of eating the fruit, root sin was already present: Adam was already engaged in root sin. His sin had to do with his failure to understand the difference between God and man and to hold on to that distinction; he did not see that the Creator God is infinite and eternal and that finite creatures are temporal and finite. This distinction was lost. We are not saying that he did not have it, but he was finite, temporal, and changeable, and left to himself, he changed. He did not continue to seek and grow in the knowledge he had, so when he was tested, his failure to seek was revealed. The root sin was there, and it was made manifest in the outward eating.

I should mention something that I failed to mention in connection with the covenant of creation. That is, the covenant of the visible reveals the invisible; the covenant of marriage reveals something about the covenant of creation. I did not emphasize that the purpose for marriage is that we were created to know God. Both male and female were created to know God, and the visible is a *sign* of the invisible. Ephesians speaks about marriage as a sign of Christ and the Church. We are established in a permanent relationship with God, which God does by way of covenant. Marriage is not a permanent relationship; it comes to an end. Under the Fall, marriage comes to an end with death: "Until death do us part." But it also says, "people will neither marry nor be given in marriage" (Matt. 22:30) in the final state when the work is completed. Marriage was given in a context. Both men and women are created to

---

19. Gangadean, *Philosophical Foundation*, 171–183.
20. *Genesis 1:11–12, 21, 24–25.*

know God. We should be careful not to make man somehow the me-diator between God and his wife. No, God is the mediator between the husband and the wife. We are created to know God. She is not created to be his helpmeet, she is created to know God. That puts the responsibility squarely on both for their response to God. Both men and women are to respond to God, and she is to submit, in the Lord, to her husband. It is *in the Lord*, not apart from that; when *in the Lord* is missing, left out, we start going astray, and it gets creepy. When we do this, we can be the occasion for the non-Christian to blaspheme.

There is another point I wanted to make about the temptation ac-count: The order was reversed, Adam was not seeking God and the woman was not seeking God. We can say then that sin is rooted in not seeking, not understanding, and not doing what is right. In Romans 3:10–12, there is a relation between these three. It starts with, **"There is no one righteous, not even one; there is no one who understands, no one who seeks God."** But it also says, "he that cometh to God must believe that he is, and that he is a rewarder of them that diligently seek Him" (Heb. 11:6b KJV). If we seek, then we will understand. **"Being understood from what has been made"** (Rom. 1:20), in the context of diligently seeking. Not seeking, not understanding, not doing what is right, in that order, are related. So what is sin? Sin is not seeking. This is the root sin. And not understanding. Left to himself, Adam did not seek. It results in not understanding and in unbelief regarding God the Creator, and the Creator-creation distinction, and the difference between finite and infinite. They did not understand the connection between sin and death, so they believed the lie: "You will not surely die" (Gen. 3:4a). They probably switched into a mode of thinking and being that is noncognitive:[21] to be like the animals. Scripture speaks about us as being like the animals when we do not think. Psalm 49:12b says, "he is like the beasts that perish." Psalm 73:22, "I was senseless and ignorant; I was a brute beast before you." We are to be watchful for those who switch into this noncognitive mode, concerned about neither true nor false. We can identify it in many ways and go into some mystical state, or a descending downward into the animal state, avoiding the engagement with truth and meaning, and trying to make

---

21. Gangadean, "Paper No. 123: Non-Cognitivism," in *The Logos Papers*, 655–656.

those concepts irrelevant. We have to watch for this and for those who seek to avoid God.

Sin as Not Seeking, Unbelief, Autonomy, and Disobedience

The second sense of sin is unbelief with specific content. First is not seeking and not understanding, and then attitude. Thirdly, sin may be spoken of as autonomy, being self-centered in our thinking, as well as in our desires: being self-indulgent—the lust of the eyes, and of the flesh, and the pride of life. Doing what pleases 'me,' and the continuing nature of that. Recognize that this is what we mean when we say that sin remains in us: 'I want to do as pleases me.' 'You know, I've got a part of me that wants to please God, but I've got a part of me that wants to please myself, let's have it both ways!' We try to have it one-time this way, and one-time that way, and be double-minded, and go back and forth. No, we are called to crucify the flesh with the affections and the lusts.[22] We cannot go this way in principle and then in practice: "he must deny himself and take up his cross daily and follow me" (Lk. 9:23b). We cannot be double-minded. We have to work through this.

Last of all, sin is disobedience. The final, full, outward expression of it is that they ate the fruit. And with a play of words, metaphorically, we call that 'fruit sin.' It is not root sin. Unless we repent of root sin, we will not have repented as we should, and we will continue to struggle with fruit sin. Repentance must be followed with fruit in keeping with repentance. We can make this distinction between root and fruit sin. At this point, I think in many ways, we are in a Christian community that does not regard clarity and inexcusability and the obligation to see what is clear. There is no consideration of root sin and fruit sin, and there is no repentance of root sin and coming to see what is clear. The Christian community is not able to be salt and light in the earth.

Applications of Repentance of Root Sin

There are a number of applications. First, sin and repentance, bearing fruit in keeping with repentance, diligently seeking, and perhaps behind that, not doubting that we will surely die. Understanding what death is, seeing it round about us, and fearing the Lord, which is the

---

22. *Galatians 5:24–26.*

beginning of wisdom, moves us to diligently seek. This is one application in connection with understanding root sin.

Second application, if we do not repent of root sin, and we do not understand what is clear, we will not understand what sin is, we will not understand death, and we will talk about hell in place of death. We will not understand why there is evil. We will not see the connection between moral and natural evil; this will not be on the radar. We will be infants, unable to teach when we ought to teach, and we will not come to maturity.

Third application, if we do not get this in place, we will not be faithful witnesses. We will have zeal without knowledge and will soon be turned back in discouragement. When the non-believer raises objections, we will not be able to take the thought captive.

Fourth application, we bring dishonor to Christ if we are not faithful witnesses, and the non-believer blasphemes because of that. Yesterday, a new thought came to me: perhaps some of the slander that has come my way is more in connection with the Church in general. These persons have bad encounters with the Church and they think it is pretty bad. I recently read a little bit about the Religious Wars coming out of the Reformation, and it is evident that we gave the enemy a lot of reasons to blaspheme. Some of that blasphemy comes as slander. Perhaps I need to recognize it as such, and say, 'Yes, we have had it coming.' We have not brought Christ, the Word of God, to the world; we have not addressed Him in His fullness.

Fifth application, we bring division in the Church each time we indulge our little distortions about God, our little idols. When we do not worship God as we should, it brings divisions, apostasy, decay, and collapse. All that I am hearing on the news today is that we are heading into some crisis. We are fighting for the soul of Western civilization. Some people are willing to just try and fight economically, and some politically. Some are *mentioning* theology, but not getting back to the foundation. We see division, decay, and collapse. This is moral law five: "Honor thy father and thy mother: that thy days may be long upon the land which the LORD thy God giveth thee" (Ex. 20:12 KJV). This involves coming to the unity of the faith through the work of the pastor-teachers. We see how people quickly breeze over that. We are saying, 'No more.'[23] I am saying, 'No more,' to this in the process of preparing people for membership; you are going to have to deal with this. Some of you are going to be hearing it within 24 hours; that is, the need to reckon with, 'Where are you in relation to the pastor-teachers, and therefore in relation to the Westminster Confession of Faith?' If these things are not in place, then you are not ready to come to Westminster. If it is in place, you need to act consistently with that, and those who are not teaching according to this need to be set aside. This is coming. Be prepared.

In summary, we can say that sin is to be understood from general revelation, Scripture, and Historic Christianity. Let me try to sum this up. In general revelation, we begin with the definition of good and evil, which we have already spoken about, that it must be in accordance with our nature, not contrary to our nature. Sin is the failure to use reason to understand what is clear and what is revealed in the creation, which is the existence and the nature of God, and the moral law. We said this moral law is clear, comprehensive, and critical, which we can and should see from general revelation.[24] From Scripture, Romans 2–3 speaks about this, and it is exemplified in the Garden of Eden, and in the lives of others, in terms of root sin and fruit sin. It is summed up for us in the Ten Commandments. And the Commandments help us to identify sin. Romans 7:9 says, "the commandment came, sin revived, and I died."[25] And, "Indeed I would not have known what sin was except through the law. For I would not have known what coveting really was if the law had not said, 'Do not covet.'" (Rom. 7:7b). So there again, we see the completeness of it. Psalm 119:96 says, "To all perfection I see a limit; but your commands are boundless." It is summed up in the Ten Commandments.

From general revelation, there is a moral law, which is clear, comprehensive, and critical. The Ten Commandments which are a summary of all that God has required of us, are explicated somewhat in the 613

---

23. Surrendra Gangadean, *The Unity of the Church: That They May Be One That the World May Believe* (Phoenix: Logos Papers Press, 2024).

24. Gangadean, *Philosophical Foundation*, 171–284; Gangadean, *History of Philosophy*, 61–69; Gangadean, *The Westminster Catechisms*, 227–267; Gangadean, *On Natural and Revealed Theology*, 127–139, 166–178.

25. KJV.

laws.[26] In the Shorter Catechism, the Ten Commandments are explicated as a summary of what God requires and the context in which we
define sin: "Sin is any want of conformity unto, or transgression of, the
law of God" (SCQ. 14) and that begins with knowing and acknowledging "God to be the only true God, and our God; and to worship
and glorify him accordingly" (SCQ. 46).

We are going to ask people, in the adherence stage particularly, to
know the Ten Commandments well, and to examine your life in light
of that. We will ask you to know the Lord's Prayer, to be able to pray
in light of the Lord's Prayer,[27] and to develop that habit. We are specifying the stages of our preparation for membership.

The Larger Catechism Question 99 says that when a sin is forbidden, "together with all the causes, means, occasions, and appearances
thereof, and provocations thereunto" (LCQ. 99.6), the opposite is required. Where promises are made, the opposite is threatened. Where it
says that you may live long in the land the Lord your God gives you, it
should be understood that if you do not, then you will not live long in
the land. This is what the political-economic crisis is about. We have
not obeyed. We are not going to stay long here and enjoy this.

The Commandments are exceedingly broad. We can see the seven
applications from general revelation, just as a start.[28] We are told to
meditate on it day and night. We are to pray, "Thy will be done in
earth, as it is in heaven" (Matt. 6:10b KJV), which is to say, completely, everywhere. We are told to make disciples, to teach all to obey *all*
that He has commanded,[29] in all of life. We are told not to go to the
left or to the right[30]—to the antinomies—and many they abound. The
law is over *all* institutions. The law is total, over and against all forms
of totalitarianism. We have increasing government control over more
and more of life, and the bureaucracy of it, the creeping bureaucracy:
that is totalitarianism. The loss of freedom is because we did not set

---

26. Gangadean, *Philosophical Foundation*, 171–284; Gangadean, *History of Philosophy*, 61–69;
Gangadean, *The Westminster Catechisms*, 227–267; Gangadean, *On Natural Revealed Theology*, 127–139, 166–178.

27. Gangadean, *The Westminster Catechisms*, 97–106.

28. Pastor Gangadean is referring to the seven applications derived from each moral law contained in, Gangadean, *Philosophical Foundation*, 165–283.

29. *Matthew 28:18–20.*

30. *Deuteronomy 5:32.*

the limits properly, and we did not bring the Law of God. If we are going to restore this, we have to get the law back in its place. The law is that in light of which sin is to be understood. This is what the Third Commandment is about: not taking God's name in vain. There is hypocrisy that goes with not hearing and not regarding what is revealed in general revelation or the preaching of His Word.

There are some things to keep in mind that cloud this idea of the law: what is to guide us, what the will of God is, and what is right and what is wrong. Conscience is sometimes used as a guide, but conscience is, at best, a *negative guide*: It tells you what not to do. If your conscience permits you to do something, that does not mean it is okay. Because your conscience permits you to drink two cans of Coke, that does not mean it is okay. If your conscience forbids you from drinking any Coke, do not go against your conscience. It is a negative guide. It is a personal guidance for you; your rule of conscience is not to be made the rule for others. Watch out for putting methods in the place of principles. Watch out for this on the women's retreat. Watch out. Do not raise up your 'favorite new book' or 'what has worked for you' as things that are required for everyone. Submit your ideas to the oversight process of much discussion. You can violate someone else's conscience when you make your conscience the rule. Conscience must be instructed. Some of you have unloaded on others about the Sabbath day without having first explained the meaning of the Sabbath. Watch out for that. A rule of thumb is to witness by your life, get to the more basic, and let your life speak. Especially when you are young, before you get the basics in place You are to witness, but start with your life. Francis of Assisi said, "Preach the gospel at all times and if necessary, use words." Put that in context, please. Some say, 'God is leading me to do this.' Watch out for that. How do you know that God is leading you? Are the other basic things in place? Do you know what is permitted, versus what is wise? What is wise is to be understood in relation to the good, all things considered. If you do not have the good in place and you say, 'God is leading me,' you are deceiving yourself. Watch out.

We cannot talk about wisdom, about the will of God, apart from the good or the goal. The law of God from general revelation is universal, perpetual, and total. This is what we must have if we are going to have a law in society. It is not enough to bring out the law from the Ten Commandments or amplify that, as theonomy has done, and bring out the 613 other laws. *That is not the path into the public sphere.* We must respect what God has done, and bring out the law from general revelation. This is the basis of cultures coming together: on the basis of the law that is written in the hearts of men. We have to make a distinction between sin and crime. In our political application, we have to understand that individual freedom is a virtue; it is not the good. Dominion in the sciences is a virtue, not the good. Through dominion and freedom, people can blow up the world or destroy the human race by genetic mutation, all in the name of science.

We have to understand the law in relation to the good, and call others to see that, and not be caught in that kind of distortion. We have to remember Adam's example: How well did he have the good in place? This is a critical point. How well did he have the good in place? He was being tested regarding good and evil, regarding the tree of the knowledge of good and evil. He ate of that which he ought not to; he determined good and evil for himself. This is the first need—to have the good in place—and it is the first to be lost. This was lost in the temptation and trial, and this was revealed to be so. It is appropriate for us in oversight to do testing. The Novitiate is part of this, more of this is needed and more is coming.

It is not just sin, but sin abounding, where it is intensified by self-deception, self-justification, and the divisions there are within the Christian community. It is not just the secularists who are opposing (but they go to the extent of being a mocker and a scorner, and all that goes with that). There is a need, because of sin abounding and the self-deception and self-justification, for those who enter the church to have a credible profession. We are trying to specify what this is, so that before someone comes to church, those who are witnessing can see and understand whether certain things are in place, and on that basis, a person comes. If it is not in place, then we continue to work until it is there: insofar as a person is open to this. And when one comes to church and continues, oversight continues. The second phase, after the inquiry stage, is the adherence stage, and we are spelling that out more. After three months, we can talk about membership. Until then, you may desire membership, but we cannot talk about it. There may be knowledge gained in that time, like a courtship, where you get knowledge of the real situation of yourself and the other. And then, as you go into that last phase of preparing for membership, we are going to ask that you take some time, ordinarily a year, to read the Scriptures; you should be able to read at least half of the Bible during the first year, in preparing for membership. These are the things that we will be asking you in terms of oversight.

Sin is to be repented of. To repent, we have to humble ourselves before God. We have to say, 'I am wrong,' and not indulge in our self-deception, avoiding shame. Remember Job, when he came to see his failure to see, and he said, "I abhor myself." Abhor is a very strong word. I was reading about it in the dictionary, and it is a *very* strong word. "I abhor myself, and repent in dust and ashes" (Job 42:6b KJV). He humbled himself to realize his true state. Some of us need to realize—all of us need to realize—that "The heart is deceitful above all things, and desperately wicked: who can know it?" (Jer. 17:9). Sometimes you want to say, 'Don't you trust me?' The response to that is, 'I don't trust my own heart.' Do you know your heart? Scripture says, "who can know it?" Do not be presumptuous by asking that question or playing on that; please do not. What you should say is, 'Death is upon me, and self-deception remains.' It is the third call back. It is not the first, and it is not the second. It is the third, and we have to work through that. This is our presumption, our attitude, our posture. "Blessed are those who mourn, for they will be comforted" (Matt. 5:4). "Where sin abounded, grace did much more abound" (Rom. 5:20b KJV).

Christ is the Lamb of God who takes away the sin of the world. He knows us; He knows us better than we know ourselves. He loves us, and He died for our sins. This is the only way sin can be removed: by Christ representing us in perfect righteousness, burying our sins in Himself, and His perfect righteousness being imputed to us. Therefore, we rejoice in the Lord our God, and we say: Worthy is the Lamb that was slain: the Lamb of God who takes away the sin of the world.

—————

12

DEATH

The Wages of Sin Is Spiritual Death

Romans 1:18–32

¹⁸The wrath of God is being revealed from heaven against all the godlessness and wickedness of men who suppress the truth by their wickedness, ¹⁹since what may be known about God is plain to them, because God has made it plain to them. ²⁰For since the creation of the world God's invisible qualities—his eternal power and divine nature—have been clearly seen, being understood from what has been made, so that men are without excuse. ²¹For although they knew God, they neither glorified him as God nor gave thanks to him, but their thinking became futile and their foolish hearts were darkened. ²²Although they claimed to be wise, they became fools ²³and exchanged the glory of the immortal God for images made to look like mortal man and birds and animals and reptiles. ²⁴Therefore God gave them over in the sinful desires of their hearts to sexual impurity for the degrading of their bodies with one another. ²⁵They exchanged the truth of God for a lie, and worshiped and served created things rather than the Creator—who is forever praised. Amen. ²⁶Because of this, God gave them over to shameful lusts. Even their women exchanged natural relations for unnatural ones. ²⁷In the same way the men also abandoned natural relations with women and were inflamed with lust for one another. Men committed indecent acts with other men, and received in themselves the due penalty for their perversion. ²⁸Furthermore, since they did not think it worthwhile to retain the knowledge of God, he gave them over to a depraved mind, to do what ought not to be done. ²⁹They have become filled with every kind of wickedness, evil, greed and depravity. They are full of envy, murder, strife, deceit and malice. They are gossips, ³⁰slanderers, God-haters, insolent, arrogant and boastful; they invent ways of doing evil; they disobey their parents; ³¹they are senseless, faithless, heartless,

ruthless. [32]Although they know God's righteous decree that those who do such things deserve death, they not only continue to do these very things but also approve of those who practice them.

W̲E CONTINUE WITH THE FOUNDATION, in Genesis 1–3, summed up as the biblical worldview of creation–fall–redemption. We are on the second part, the second main point: the Fall. We are in part four, and we come now to consider *death*. Remember creation: *creation is revelation*, it is *full and clear, eternal life* (the good, the goal of life) *is the knowledge of God. This knowledge is through the work of dominion*, given to man from the very, very, very beginning, and remaining. The Sabbath is given to us as a reminder of the hope that the work will be completed: that the earth will be filled with the knowledge of God. God established the covenant with man—the covenant of creation—in Genesis 2, and the latter part speaks about the covenant of marriage between man and woman, which is a visible revelation of the covenant of creation. We have the account of the temptation. Remember the words of the tempter: "You will not surely die." Rather, "you will be like God, knowing good and evil" (Gen. 3:4a–5b). Their sin was there already and became manifest in the eating of the tree of the knowledge of good and evil. Eating from the tree is signifying outwardly what man was doing inwardly: determining good and evil from himself, autonomously.

We come to death. Following death, we will come to the understanding of *why* God permits evil, which is known as theodicy: an explanation of why God permits evil. The problem of evil has plagued many and sometimes continues to trouble believers.[1] But as we get these pieces in place, we can answer this question,[2] and the answer is clear, as is all of Scripture, as we proceed step by step. If we miss a step, it is not clear. If we take it step by step, and remember what has gone before, then it is clear.

We come now to death. Briefly, to finish up the narrative and to keep it in perspective before us: after sin and death comes redemption.

---

1. Susan Neiman, *Evil in Modern Thought: An Alternative History of Philosophy* (Princeton: Princeton University Press, 2002).

2. Gangadean, *Philosophical Foundation*, 145–161; Gangadean, *On Natural and Revealed Theology*, 141–147; Gangadean, "Paper No. 7: The Problem of Evil," in *The Logos Papers*, 33–39.

God is going to call man back. The first call back is through shame and conscience, and the response is self-deception: cover-up. The second call back comes through the question, "Where are you?" (Gen. 3:9b), which is a call to self-examination. Man avoids the second call back; he resists through self-justification; the man blames the woman, and he blames God. Then there is a third call back, the curse: toil, strife, old age, sickness, and death, ever-intensifying in history as sin intensifies. With the curse, the promise, and then man's response of repentance and faith. Repentance and faith is seen in Adam calling his wife's name Eve, signifying that he will obey God and do the work: he will multiply and fill the earth. We see God's justification of man represented in the covering with the coats of skin. Lastly, God's sanctification of man is evident in expelling him from the Garden; because of his sin, his self-deception, and self-justification, he is expelled in order to learn, through suffering, to get his mind focused, and to be brought to repentance. In that, we have the suffering of physical death, which has been confused with this point that we are on: death.

SERMON OVERVIEW

First point, note from Scripture that "the wages of sin is death, but the gift of God is eternal life in Christ Jesus our Lord." (Rom. 6:23). Notice this reference to death and life, and notice that this was there from the beginning. We have made a huge shift in the Church from life and death to heaven and hell, and so we have misunderstood the teaching. At the end of Romans 5:21, we also find this reference to life and death and sin: "just as sin reigned in death, so also grace might reign through righteousness to bring eternal life through Jesus Christ our Lord." Sin reigned through death, righteousness through life; we see those words again. As we begin speaking about death, then, we note, and try to clarify what is meant by "the wages of sin is death." To anticipate where we are going, we want to develop this idea of death in connection with the verse, "for when you eat of it you will surely die" (Gen. 2:17b). This is the second point. It is *in the day*, you will *surely die*. The tempter says, "You will not surely die" (Gen. 3:4a). We want to look at the connection between sin and death, and we want to consider the meaning of spiritual death. Third point: What does it mean when Scripture says, "There is no fear of God before their eyes"

(Rom. 3:18)? The fear of the Lord is the beginning of wisdom, that is the fourth point, and there are a number of points under that which will be expanded. Through the fear of the Lord, hopefully, we can be called back to see death, called back to see sin, and come to repentance. Then, last of all, the fifth point: The reason we do not pay attention is that we have this idea that God will forgive us, end of story. 'I know God will forgive me,' people say. Do you really know that? Do you really believe that God will forgive you? Can you believe that God will forgive you and not cleanse you? Do you really believe that God will cleanse you, or are you making grace into something cheap? This is why the focus for the week is forgiveness and cleansing: "If we confess our sins, he is faithful and just and will forgive us our sins and purify us from all unrighteousness." (1 Jn. 1:9). We are taught to pray this in the Lord's Prayer: "Forgive us our debts, as we also have forgiven our debtors. And lead us not into temptation, but deliver us from evil" (Matt. 6:12–13). This is about cleansing in the context of trial and temptation. Those are the five main points, so let us proceed.

FIRST POINT:
The Wages of Sin Is Death (Rom. 6:23; 5:21)

The wages of sin is death.[3] There are two kinds of death. Sometimes, we do not pay much attention to it, and the mind by default goes to physical death, and we think physical death is the punishment for sin. But if we think about it, we soon begin to puzzle over it, and then we shift to hell as the punishment for sin. We want to say 'no' to both of those. The wages of sin is death; there are two kinds of death: physical death and spiritual death. John 11:25–26 is a great passage that is so well known that it is easy to build on it. Notice what it says: "I am the resurrection and the life. He who believes in me will live"—future tense, being raised from physical death—"even though he dies"—*physically*. He will live physically, even though he dies physically. "And whoever lives and believes in me will never die." Is that physical death? No. All of Scripture, and all of our experience, tells us that believers die, so what does it mean? "And whoever lives and believes in me will never die." It can only mean will never die *spiritually*. So, in this verse, Jesus

---

3. *Romans 6:23.*

is speaking of both physical death and physical resurrection, and spiritual death and spiritual resurrection.

In John 5:24–26, these two come out again: "I tell you the truth, whoever hears my word and believes him who sent me has eternal life and will not be condemned; he has crossed over from death to life. I tell you the truth, a time is coming and has now come when the dead will hear the voice of the Son of God and those who hear will live." Those who will hear the voice of the Son of God will live. Then in verse 28–29: "Do not be amazed at this, for a time is coming when all who are in their graves [physical death] will hear his voice and come out—those who have done good will rise to live, and those who have done evil will rise to be condemned."

Paul speaks of spiritual resurrection in Ephesians 2:1 as well: "who were dead in trespasses and sins"[4] were quickened and made alive. Could that be physical death? No, for we *were dead* and were quickened and made alive. Notice, "who were dead in trespasses and sins." Notice the connection between sin and death. It must be spiritual death because of sin. This idea goes on into the Book of Revelation, where it speaks about the first resurrection and the second resurrection. "Blessed and holy are those who have part in the first resurrection. The second death has no power over them" (Rev. 20:6a). Those that take part in the first resurrection, from spiritual death come to spiritual life, and the second death has no power over them. And then it says that the lake of fire is the second death,[5] so the lake of fire must be spiritual death, as we will see more later.

There are two kinds of death: physical and spiritual. From that, we will say that the wages of sin is spiritual death, not physical death; some might try to say that it is both, but we will see it is certainly not both because everyone is raised from the dead physically; *everyone*. Physical death is not part of the wages of sin that continues on forever and ever. We begin to open up this teaching of the Bible on death by looking at the Word and examining it. We have to clarify the meaning and notice where we have been unsure, unclear, confused, and not paying attention. We are called to seek God, to focus, to pay attention, to get hold

---

4. KJV.

5. *Revelation 20:14.*

of it, and to hold on to it, and we are to see the striking contrast that there is between the Word of God and our own word.

SECOND POINT:
In the Day You Eat, You Will Surely Die

There is a connection between sin and death. It is being affirmed in the beginning, that you will *surely* die, no question about it. Yet most people do not notice or pay attention to this, and they doubt it. In the Garden, Adam doubted. The tempter said, "You will not surely die" (Gen. 3:4a). We have to believe the Word of God, or believe the word of the creature. Notice it is *in the day* you eat, not sometime in the future. Some people will try to make this about physical death and say, 'Well, he *began* to die, and he eventually died after 900 years.' We have already made the point that there is a difference between physical and spiritual death, and the wages of sin is spiritual death, not physical death. We have already anticipated the need to account for physical death.

Spiritual death *is* present: You that were dead in your trespasses and sins. It is present, and we want to say that it is not simply present, but it is *inherent* in sin. There is an inherent and necessary connection between sin and death, even for believers whose sins have been forgiven, but who may continue in sin. Paul speaks about this in Romans 6–7: about the death that remains in us as believers. We are not fully conscious and consistent. We have to be continually sanctified; we want to be sanctified, and He wants us to have life and have it to the full.

There is an inherent connection between sin and death, and it is not just present and inherent, but it is continuing forever. The present, inherent understanding of sin and death is in contrast to the future and imposed view. The common view of hell is something that is future, and we will be cast into the lake of fire, which is something imposed upon us. Many have asked, 'What did I do to deserve this? Don't you think it is maybe just a tad too much?' Many persons have had questions about divine justice when it is put in this way. Some have been led to blaspheme the name of God because Christians have misrepresented the justice of God and the truth of God. Spiritual death, which is present and inherent, is not the same as hell, which is future and imposed. We will need to address and clarify this. Some of you are thinking that I am denying the doctrine of hell. We want to understand it first, from the Bible, and then we can see if it is being denied or not. "The wages of sin is death" (Rom. 6:23a). "In the day that you eat of it you will surely die" (Gen. 2:17b). "[You] who were dead in trespasses and sins" (Eph. 2:1b KJV). They continue on in the second death, forever and ever. This is how the Scripture puts it. As a matter of fact, just to anticipate, it speaks about the lake of fire as the second death. It says it *twice*, explicitly.[6]

We are to understand what is called the lake of fire, which is a *figurative* representation, and we will see that in any way we cut it, it is figurative, necessarily, from the Scriptures. We are not dodging and trying to ease something out, and we are not trying to suggest that somehow the punishment is less than we think, or less than it should be. No, we will see that spiritual death as a punishment is much more horrible than we can think. We would wish it were just a lake of fire.

In Romans, Paul speaks of the wrath of God:

> The wrath of God is being revealed from heaven against all the godlessness and wickedness of men who suppress the truth by their wickedness, since what may be known about God is plain to them, because God has made it plain to them. For since the creation of the world God's invisible qualities—his eternal power and divine nature—have been clearly seen, being understood from what has been made, so that men are without excuse. (vv. 18–20).

The wrath of God is being revealed in connection with failing to seek and understand what is clear about God's invisible qualities: His eternal power and divine nature. No question about this. This is what Paul is speaking about when he is speaking about the gospel. This is the gospel that he is not ashamed of. He says, "I am not ashamed of the gospel, because it is the power of God for the salvation of everyone who believes" (Rom. 1:16). This is a gospel that I am not ashamed of: a gospel that begins with the reality of sin and death, and therefore, in that connection, the redemption in Christ Jesus. When we do not have this, it is a distortion of the divine justice and mercy, and I am ashamed of that gospel; I will not own up to *that* gospel. But I will own up to *this* gospel. If someone asks me if I am a Christian, understood in terms of that gospel, I will say, 'If you have a moment, I will be glad

---

6. *Revelation 20:14, 21:8.*

to tell you what I believe.' I will start here: let us speak about the need for Jesus Christ due to sin connected with clarity and inexcusability. **"For although they knew God, they neither glorified him as God nor gave thanks to him, but their thinking became futile and their foolish hearts were darkened"** (v. 21). This is figured into what spiritual death is, the wrath of God. This is how it is coming out. In connection with not glorifying Him as God, our minds are darkened. **"Although they claimed to be wise, they became fools and exchanged the glory of the immortal God for images made to look like mortal man and birds and animals and reptiles"** (v. 22–23). Not each and every one does this. Not every person goes to figures like Zeus or birds, animals, and reptiles. This is a historically cumulative process that is going on. At any time, at any place, people may start out with the knowledge of God and leave it, let it go, let it slip. We will come to that at the end of the preaching. **"Therefore God gave them over in the sinful desires of their hearts to sexual impurity for the degrading of their bodies with one another"** (v. 24). There is the wrath of God; it is manifest in being given over to this sin, to the desires of their heart. The manifestation here is sexual impurity, and it is also greed, lust, and gluttony in terms of some of the appetites. It is also pride, as we will see, and envy, anger, and sloth. God gave them over, and we will see the progression that is going on in this.

Notice that, **"They exchanged the truth of God for a lie, and worshiped and served created things rather than the Creator—who is forever praised. Amen"** (v. 25). The Buddhists would say this, *Om mani Padme Hum*: the jewel is in the lotus, the self-generating force in the universe; the universe is self-creating, which is the same lie as evolution which says that the world is self-creating: given enough chance and necessity—those twin gods that have been worshiped—that is how it came about. They tried to explain the created world in terms of created laws, and they worshiped and served the creature. You may abstract it, or you may personalize it; take your preference, but this is how it has been. They **"worshiped and served created things rather than the Creator—who is forever praised. Amen"** (v. 25). Again, another view in terms of seeking and understanding and putting aside the truth. Now, **"Because of this, God gave them over to shameful lusts"** (v. 26a). A second giving over, a deepening of the wrath of God. First sexual impurity, and now sexual perversion: excess. **"Even their women** exchanged natural relations for unnatural ones. In the same way the men also abandoned natural relations with women and were [notice the words] *inflamed with lust* for one another. Men committed indecent acts with other men, and received in themselves the due penalty for their perversion" (vv. 26b–27).[7] We give up on the knowledge of God, and we go deeper into depravity.

Notice the cumulative effects of sin and how it leads to death. We misunderstand sin and when we do not notice this accumulation, we misunderstand death. "**Furthermore, since they did not think it worthwhile to retain the knowledge of God, he gave them over to a depraved mind**" (v. 28a), and this is the third giving over. This is the wrath of God. He gives them over "**to a depraved mind, to do what ought not to be done. They have become filled with every kind of wickedness, evil, greed and depravity. They are full of envy, murder, strife, deceit and malice**" (vv. 28b–29a). We could go on, but we see this happening time and again in history. Cain manifested this when he murdered his brother, and it became fully manifest in intermarriage and the corruption before the Flood; "the earth was corrupt . . . and was full of violence" (Gen. 6:11). This is how Scripture speaks about sin and death, and the wrath of God, and giving men over to this.

THIRD POINT:
Spiritual Death Is Meaninglessness, Boredom, and Guilt

Since spiritual death is present and inherent, not future, and since the wages of sin is spiritual death, not physical death—how are we to understand it? We have spoken about this in terms of what happens to the inward being of man, and you see that in Romans 1: the mind is darkened. "**Their thinking became futile and their foolish hearts were darkened**" (v. 21b). It is sometimes spoken of in this way: cast them into outer darkness,[8] speaking about the darkness of the mind, the futility of the thinking, the emptiness of that way of life, the meaninglessness of it. Solomon summed it up in this way: "Meaningless! Meaningless!" "Utterly meaningless! Everything is meaningless" (Eccl. 1:2). Everything is meaningless under the sun. Life without God is

---

7. Emphasis added.

8. *Matthew 8:12, 22:13, 25:30.*

empty of meaning. No matter how far you go—and Solomon did go far, with 700 wives and 300 concubines—he still could not get satisfaction; empty. Those who speak about 70 virgins in heaven do not have a clue what they are talking about.[9] Life without God is empty and our thinking becomes futile when we do not understand things in light of who God is. Notice here again, **"were inflamed with lust for one another"** (v. 27). They were inflamed with lust. Burning, burning, burning: that is the term that is used. Unquenchable fire: You can get no satisfaction without God.

Jesus said, "Everyone who drinks this water will be thirsty again, but whoever drinks the water I give him will never thirst" (Jn. 4:13b–14a). This water will be within him like a spring welling up to eternal life, as in the Feast of Tabernacles. It is not only satisfying but bringing satisfaction to a dead and thirsting world. It speaks about where "the fire is not quenched, outer darkness, meaninglessness, the fire is not quenched, the burning, and the lack of satisfaction.[10] One of the preachers who spoke about hellfire more than anyone else was Jonathan Edwards. In the sermon, *Sinners in the Hands of an Angry God,* he speaks about being like a spider hanging by a thin thread of web over the flames, ready to be devoured. Jonathan Edwards also said the seed of hellfire is in the carnal nature of the unbeliever:[11] It is internal. He is using a figure of speech, and we may get caught up in that, but he is making a point: there is an unquenchable fire. The fire is not quenched. The thirst, the lack of satisfaction: boredom is how we sum that up. This is where you get **"inflamed with lust"** (v. 27). This is why we move from sexual impurity to sexual perversion: It does not stop there, and we degrade ourselves. It also says, "their worm dieth not, and the fire is not quenched" (Mk. 9:48). This worm is gnawing; it is the gnawing of conscience and the torment of guilt from the conscience gnawing

---

9. Reference to Islam.

10. *Mark 9:44, 46, 48; Matthew 8:12, 22:13, 25:30.*

11. "There is laid in the very nature of carnal men, a foundation for the torments of hell. There are those corrupt principles, in reigning power in them, and in full possession of them, that are seeds of hell fire. These principles are active and powerful, exceedingly violent in their nature, and if it were not for the restraining hand of God upon them, they would soon break out, they would flame out after the same manner as the same corruptions, the same enmity does in the hearts of damned souls, and would beget the same torments as they do in them." Jonathan Edwards, *The Works of President Edwards: In Four Volumes* (New York: Leavitt & Allen, 1858), 315.

at us. This is what we put aside when we felt shame in the Garden; we avoided conscience as a call back. We can do our best to cover it up with leaves, but we cannot rid ourselves of it: It remains. This is spiritual death. "for when you eat of it you will surely die" (Gen. 2:17b). It was right there from the beginning. There is the worm that does not die. And they knew, and when God came close to them, they hid. The cover-up did not help. We have regret that is going on—blame—and it continues forever. In this way, we are basically saying: 'I am worthless. I am a piece of garbage. I do not deserve anything.' This is what our shame says. It says, 'What you did was worthless.' And the Scripture says, "they have together become worthless" (Rom. 3:12). Not my words. This is from the Scripture, in case you think I am pouring it on thick and adding something extra. Sin—spiritual death—is meaninglessness, boredom, and guilt. It is also spoken of in the Scriptures as a bottomless pit.[12] Here we have the figure of something unending, where there is no worst, no bottom to it. I was reading that poem again this morning by Hopkins.[13] One of the terrible sonnets. It is continuing and cumulative, and there is no escape. What that might be like is too horrific to think about. It begins here, it is inherent in sin, and it is continuing. "The wages of sin is death" (Rom. 6:23a).

FOURTH POINT:
No Fear of God Before Their Eyes

Romans 3:10–12, after saying, "There is no one righteous, not even one; there is no one who understands, no one who seeks God. All have turned away, they have together become worthless; there is no one who does good, not even one," speaks about the words, thoughts, and violence that comes as feet that are swift to shed blood. "The way of peace they do not know" (Rom. 3:17). Romans 3:18, says, "There is no fear of God before their eyes." Notice, it says, "before their eyes." It is right there before their eyes where they should see that it is clear, but they do not see it. They do not see because they are not seeking

---

12. *Revelation 20:1.*

13. Gerard Manley Hopkins, "No worse, there is none. Pitch past pitch of grief" *Poems and Prose* (New York: Penguin Classics, 1985).

and understanding. Let us try to understand this. This is going to come close to home, to each one of us.

First Reason: We Do Not See Good and Evil (Antinomies Regarding Good and Evil)

We do not see and understand good and evil, even as Adam did not, because he did not continue to seek. **"For although they knew God, they neither glorified him as God nor gave thanks to him, but their thinking became futile and their foolish hearts were darkened"** (v. 21). We do not see good and evil and we do not see that root sin is not seeking and not understanding. Remember, we have covered it up with self-deception and self-justification, specifically our not seeking. We like to think we are seeking. I have talked with many people, and one of the first things they say is, 'I'm seeking, I'm seeking.' If you are seeking, how come you do not know what is clear? You are not seeking God; you are seeking something, but it is not God if you are not seeing what is clear. Then come the reasons, the excuses: 'How am I supposed to notice? I have not taken a class in Philosophy 101, right?' God was waiting for someone to offer a class in Philosophy 101 so that you can see what is clear: is that what you think? That does not figure—that is excusing.

One of the ways in which we fail to see good and evil is that we substitute something else for it. The things that we substitute are typically these: antinomies and polar opposites, and there is an attempt at synthesizing these polar opposites. One of these antinomies is to seek virtue as the good or happiness as the good. The view of virtue as the good comes out as deontology—duty for duty's sake—and it comes to expression as legalism. In deontology, we are understanding virtue apart from the good and substituting virtue for the good. Natural law theorists, and there are many, with many 'goods', do not connect with *the good*, with eternal life as the knowledge of God. In contrast to those who are going by 'the law,' and what we think God would require us to do—in this deontological way, without the good in place—is the antinomian. Antinomian is anti-nomos, anti-law, free from the law. They are free from the law as the legalists put it forward, as well as the law as it is in itself. But they look at this distortion—legalism, the straw man—to get around it.

This conflict comes down to us today in conservatives versus liberals. Conservatives sometimes speak about classical education: going back to the tradition and teaching the virtues. Bill Bennett has a book, *The Book of Virtues*, and there is a 'rich tradition' of this in Catholicism. Some Protestants are going to the Catholics to get connected with this and a lot of the popular conservative speakers are from this background. Classical education does *not* get us to the knowledge of God. It did not get us there historically, and that is one of the reasons it fell apart. It was not enough, and to merely return to it is not enough. Many of you have said, 'Well, yes, this classical education is very good compared with alternatives. Compared to the pragmatism of John Dewey and that kind of education, this is a lot better.' Yesterday, I was reading about Great Books college graduate programs, and I am attracted to that. But I am saying that if it is not done in connection with the good, it is going to come short.

The tendency toward virtue and right, and legalism and deontology, apart from the good, ends up in the expression of a 'joyless, grim Christianity.' Both on the side of the Catholics and the Protestants. The Puritans were said to be joyless and grim, and insofar as they slipped into legalism, it became that. 'God is the big foot in the sky, ready to drop on you if you don't obey.' This is one of the ways we miss this, and if you think I am being light, I am going to say that the two greatest conversions in the history of the world, known to us, are from legalism; I will specify more shortly. On the other hand, there are these liberals, progressives, socialists, utilitarians, and pragmatists (John Dewey being a notable figure in that) who seek pleasure and fun and hedonism as the good. This comes into the Church as a health and wealth gospel of prosperity which is as old as the hills in the worship of Baal and Asherah. How many times did the kings of Judah and Israel come along and try to clean it up, and it kept recurring: people go back to it. "They worshiped the LORD, but they also served their own gods" (2 Kgs. 17:33a). Sometimes they try to combine the two—virtue results in happiness—and none less than Immanuel Kant made that move; not coming to the idea of the good.[14]

What should we choose: the law without the good, or the good without the law where the good is pleasure? Which shall we choose? It

---

14. Gangadean, *History of Philosophy*, 153–158; Gangadean, *Philosophical Foundation*, 172–174.

is an antinomy; we do not have to choose between the two. This week, I saw a notable speaker on the news—speaking in the morning, and again late at night—coming to frustration, throwing his pile of papers down on the ground, and inclined toward a great use of sarcasm. He had reached his limits. If it is not sarcasm then there is a kind of cynicism that dominates our lives in our tendency to judge others. We have a tendency to judge others in terms of a narrow law rather than the wisdom connected with the good. Many of the talk show hosts on the radio are following politics and economics without coming back to the knowledge of God, and that is not going to do it: it will not provide the basis. Some have tried to preach the Bible without the knowledge of God, but that is not going to do it either, and rather it will be held in contempt. So here we are in the midst of a decaying society, and no synthesis of the two (virtue and happiness) will settle it.

I spoke just a moment ago about two major conversions. What conversions am I speaking about? A conversion that you heard of last week, St. Paul. Was that one of the great conversions in history? What was he converted from? Judaism, which was legalism. When Stephen spoke in Acts 7, it was getting to Paul, and he fought against the teaching that Stephen brought. But, "it is hard for thee to kick against the pricks" (Acts 9:5b KJV), as Christ would say to Saul. Saul came to see the inadequacy of the righteousness which comes by the law. This is what comes out of Romans: a righteousness from God and Christ, received by faith. Paul's is one of *the* great conversions in history. The second one is Luther's conversion. The same thing had happened in the Church as had occurred in Judaism: It went into legalism again. Luther was tormented when he measured himself up against this legalistic standard. It could not be done. He was honest enough to recognize it. God brought him out of that torment by bringing him to see the righteousness that is by faith in Jesus Christ.

Do Christians sometimes fall into these antinomies? Wealth and prosperity gospel on the one hand, and virtue ethics and legalism on the other hand? Because we do not have the good in place, as Adam got his eyes off of it, we lose the fear of the Lord.

Second Reason: We Do Not See Death (Spiritual Death Is Not the Same as Physical Death or Hell)

Another reason is that we do not see death as it is: that spiritual death is not physical death (we have already addressed this).

Third Reason: We Do Not See the Relation Between Sin and Death

We do not see the relation between sin and death because the relation is one that is gradual and cumulative. It is inherent, but it is gradual and cumulative. Just as life increases, so death increases. "I have come that they might have life, and have it to the full" (Jn. 10:10b). Life is absolute in its beginning, but it is gradual in its increase. Death is absolute in its beginning, but it is gradual in its increase. The picture is, both individually and corporately, of a gradual process. This process is so gradual, because we are temporal and we are growing, that it is imperceptible. Because it seems to be so far removed, we do not notice the connection. We do not see the connection between sin as not seeking and death as meaninglessness, boredom, and guilt, and all the fruit sin that comes out of that, and therefore we lose the connection and lose the fear of the Lord. "There is no fear of God before his eyes" (Ps. 36:1b; Rom. 3:18).

Wrath increases as sin increases as we see in Romans 1:31: "**they are senseless, faithless, heartless, ruthless.**" This is the condition we come into. I see it in families, and I have seen persons I have known for 30 years leaving it off and drifting away, and now their marriages are falling apart, and they are saying, 'What hit me?' I see it in my family; family members over 30, 40, 50 years; a gradual decline that has come to: "**senseless, faithless, heartless, ruthless.**" We do not see the relation between sin and death. Psalm 1:4 speaks about this gradualism: "They are like chaff that the wind blows away," as does Psalm 90:5–6, "You sweep men away in the sleep of death; they are like the new grass of the morning—though in the morning it springs up new, by evening it is dry and withered." At the end of his life, he is blown away like the chaff. They wither and die. But it is also spoken of in moral law five: "Honor your father and your mother, so that you may live long in the land the LORD your God is giving you" (Ex. 20:12), and it speaks of Israel being taken out of the land (the northern tribes), and Judah being taken out of the land. Their removal from the land unfolds over a 300 year period, but it happens.

We do not see the relation between sin and death. We do not see what sin is, and we substitute other things for the good. We do not see what death is, and we substitute physical death and hell. We do not see the relationship between sin and death because of the gradualism and the cumulative effects of it rather than it being full and sudden. It is a kind of romantic idealism: expecting it all to be there right away; it does not happen that way with life; it does not happen that way with death. We might think that if we obey this, we should get this life. We have to move away from this and go back to this gradual process: what we call *rugged-gradual-idealism*. It goes up and down, and we persevere. You could persevere in legalism (deontology), or you could persevere toward the goal (the good). There is no joy in legalism. There is joy in the goal, and with the goal in mind, there is overcoming and growing through the hardships. "Consider it pure joy, my brothers, whenever you face trials of many kinds" (Jas. 1:2). "These have come so that your faith—of greater worth than gold, which perishes even though refined by fire—may be proved genuine and may result in praise, glory and honor when Jesus Christ is revealed" (1 Pet. 1:7). By faith we understand.[15]

Fourth Reason: We Deny Both Spiritual Death and Physical Death

Some miss both the connection between sin and spiritual death and the connection between sin and physical death. The material monists deny physical death as a call back; it is just natural. They deny spiritual death in the sense that there is no afterlife, and they try to fill up the spiritual death now with various forms of pleasure. The spiritual monists, with their teaching about reincarnation, want to suggest that, 'you die, you can come back again and get it, and then come back again.'—as against "it is appointed unto men once to die, but after this the judgment" (Heb. 9:27 KJV). They are trying to minimize the reality of physical death and the significance of it. Then they try to get rid of spiritual death by going into a kind of enlightened state, in which there is no

---

15. *Hebrews 11:3.* For a full explanation of the meaning, see the first sermon in this series, looking at the following section in particular: *Third Point on the Nature of Faith: Faith Understands the Invisible.*

conscious awareness of any change whatsoever. The *enlightened* state is a kind of comatose state—that is the wisdom of the world. And in dualism, the soul goes on without the body; there is no resurrection. The soul is supposed to be enlightened with some kind of platonic enlightenment, some direct seeing of ultimate reality: the forms, the essences (without seeing how it has unfolded in history). So there are a lot of ways in which people—whether in belief or in unbelief, whether those who are believers or non-believers—deny the reality of sin and death and the reality of spiritual death and physical death.

Fifth Reason: We Let Things Slip

Last of all, there are those who let things slip. They have had the truth and they let it slip. "For although they knew God, they neither glorified him as God nor gave thanks to him" (Rom. 1:21a). "Man's chief end is to glorify God" (SCQ. 1). There have been persons here who had this teaching, they did not persevere in it, and it slipped away, and then they begin to lose the idea of the distinctives of this congregation.[16] They lose not just the distinctives of this congregation, but the distinctives of the Westminster Confession of Faith. Some end up saying, 'There is nothing distinctive here at all.' We let things slip. The foundation, as creation–fall–redemption, is there in some vague, generalized, unspecified way, the same way in which everybody agrees that man's chief end is to glorify God. Creation–fall–redemption is there in this general way, but where is the content? It has been emptied of content; it is meaning*less*, not meaning*ful*. So we give lip service—this outward acknowledgment of things—while letting things slip. We do not affirm the historically cumulative insight, and when asked about the doxological focus, we fall silent or say, 'Oh, well,' and then we fall back on the unity of the Spirit—one Lord, one faith, one baptism— rather than pressing towards the unity of the faith: to maturity, fruitfulness, and fullness. We let it slip. This has been recurrent in history. We see it beginning with Adam in the Garden, and then from Adam to the Flood, and then in the wilderness. They knew God, but they did not glorify Him as God. God revealed Himself greatly in Egypt and Mount Sinai, and they ended up wandering in the wilderness. The

---

16. Gangadean, *The Westminster Catechisms*, 311–356.

temple was given through Solomon, and all the glory with it. Then, in 350 years, it slipped. It was 200 years for the northern kingdom and 350 years for the southern kingdom; they let it slip.[17] In Christ's fullness, the brightness of the Father's glory was here on the earth, and they crucified Him; they let it slip again. They did not go on from strength to strength. For these five reasons, there is no fear of God before our eyes—that is, before the eyes of those who let these things slip. We go on and live out our lives the way Moses describes: a thousand years pass, and "Who knows the power of your anger? For your wrath is as great as the fear that is due you" (Ps. 90:11), the same wrath that Paul is speaking about in Romans 1:18. God may let us go thousands of years in our sin and death, and we harden ourselves to His call.

FIFTH POINT:
Cheap Grace

I am not entirely satisfied with the expression "cheap grace." What I am trying to say is what is often said: Let us sin that grace may abound.[18] It comes out this way: 'I know God will forgive me. I know this is sin. I am about to sin, and I know God will forgive me.' In past conversations, I have responded by saying, 'Yes, but will He also cleanse you? Are you separating forgiveness from cleansing?' This is why the focus for the week is forgiveness and cleansing. He is faithful and just to forgive us *and* to cleanse us. Was God faithful and just to forgive Adam? Yes. Was He faithful and just to forgive and to cleanse? Yes. How? After the covering with the coats of skin, signifying that he is covered by the righteousness of another—fully, 100% forgiven—he was cleansed by being expelled from the Garden: driven out of the Garden. He did not go willingly, and we know furthermore that he did not go willingly because God had to set up a double barrier against him. "After he drove the man out, he placed on the east side of the Garden of Eden cherubim and a flaming sword flashing back and forth to guard the way to

---

17. Solomon died in 931 B.C. and Israel was split into the northern and southern kingdoms. The northern kingdom was destroyed by Assyria in 721 B.C. and the southern kingdom was taken into captivity in three stages: the first in 606, the second in 597, and the third invasion in 587, when the temple was destroyed, palaces destroyed, and the walls of Jerusalem torn down.

18. This claim is raised in *Romans 6:1* and then responded to.

the tree of life" (Gen. 3:24). You cannot enter. It is in us instinctively to try to avoid the curse; we avoid living under the curse and learning. We do not want to be cleansed through suffering.

Yes, God is faithful and just to forgive us. Did He forgive David? Yes. Bathsheba? Oh, yes. Blessed is the man whose sins are forgiven.[19] Did God cleanse David? Yes. "Now, therefore, the sword will never depart from your house, because you despised me and took the wife of Uriah the Hittite to be your own" (2 Sam. 12:10). God's cleansing was present in all those difficulties that occurred in his house, including one brother raping his sister, Absalom taking the kingship and then sleeping with his father's concubines in a tent pitched in the top of the palace for all to see. God cleanses us. He forgives us and cleanses us. Do not go that way and just speak about, 'God will forgive.' We deceive ourselves if we think that. God expelled us from the Garden. Do you want to anticipate divorce? Will you say, 'Yeah, it got really rough, and I could not stand it anymore'? If you break your marriage vow and you are the guilty party, are you willing to give up your children? Are you willing to give up your property rights? That is repentance. That is what the Westminster Confession of Faith says,[20] and that is what has been practiced historically. That is what I find people are *not* willing to do. They may say, 'God forgives,' but without being willing to recognize sin—the root sin—and repentance of this, and the cleansing that comes with it. The Church is asked to maintain God's discipline in this way, and we cannot blink on this. If a person does not repent with biblical repentance and accept the consequences for cleansing, then they are regarded as not repentant and not received in the church. This has happened, and people have reacted badly and tried to publish all kinds of slander against the church.

He is faithful and just to forgive us and to cleanse us, and the cleansing is through trials of faith and suffering, to push us to the maximum. The curse has been imposed by God, and this is where you get physical death. It is imposed by God; it was not there originally; it will not be there in the end. God created the world without physical death, and He imposed it because of sin, self-deception, and self-justification. It is the third and final call back. It is not the first call back, but the third

---

19. *Psalm 32:1.*

20. *WCF 24*; Gangadean, *The Westminster Confession*, 263–273.

and the final. It is not a fourth call back. It is the third, final call back, and He intensifies it. How has He intensified it? He first brought in death and then let us live for 950 years. Then He says, 'Okay, you used those 900 years to go deeper into sin, so we are going to have to restrain you more, so we are going to go straight to 70, possibly 80 years.' And when that was not enough, He says, 'Okay, what we will do is we will divide mankind and bring a lot of strife and conflict between mankind': wars again and again and again after Babel. 'And then we will put on plagues and famines. If you continue to harden yourself, then eventually you will be cut off as Pharaoh was in the midst of it.' End of call back. Look at it and read the Scriptures and see how God is calling back Israel. How many times, how many ways? How many times did God call back Pharaoh? Ten times. This is the condition of our heart. The curse is a call back to restrain us from going into evil as far as we can, as fast as we can; it is to recall back to repentance, and then, once we have repented, to remove it. Three different purposes are served by the one act: How wise is God!

The question is, do you accept this understanding as a teaching of Scripture? Do you accept this? And does this lead you to diligently seek God rather than wait for some spontaneous awareness to arise in you? Diligently seek God using ordinary means. This means when you hear this preaching, if these things are not in place, do you just go out and forget about it? Or do you search it out when you come to alternative positions and wrestle with it and not let it go until it is resolved? If you just let it go and neglect it, you are not seeking; you are continuing in sin. And that root sin of not seeking is what the Lord is addressing.

Is the foundation in place of creation–fall–redemption? Is that understanding in place, including all the implications? Is the teaching of the clarity of general revelation in place? Is it manifest by fruit in keeping with repentance and coming to learn? When we are recalled—restrained, recalled, and removed—we are called to repentance, and we are not to neglect it and shrug it off. We are not to let it slip. We are to be diligent in the use of means. Some have not been continuing in fellowship and contact with others in the congregation. I am expecting self-deception and self-justification to excuse it. I am expecting the church to be blamed for it by saying that we are 'not very loving.' What it is, is that the foundation is not in place. They have not lost contact with this church, but with this foundational teaching, and they are excusing it in this way. They are neglecting it, letting go, thinking that it will not accumulate in death. It does; according to Scripture it does; according to the scriptural record it does; according to what I have seen in my experience with those round about me and in cultures and civilizations that I have studied, I have seen it. I taught Eastern civilizations for 10 years—the history of Eastern civilizations. I have seen it in the civilizations, seen it in worldviews. We see the breakdown and attempt to try it again, patch it up, and go again, and more break down, patch up again, and break down again and patch up again; we are still struggling through that.

We are not to neglect it and let it slip. We are to be willing to subject our thinking to the process of much discussion; not interminable discussion because basics are not in place, the basics for discussion, but much genuine discussion. Search it out, otherwise, we are neglecting it and not repenting. Do not excuse it by blaming others. We can expect to overcome when we repent—when we repent of this root sin and come to see the truth about sin and death and learn to fear the Lord and become delivered from those things that bind us and have bound us. Legalism can bind us as much as addictions can bind us. People have been in AA for years and years and years, and they lead in AA and then go off and sin because there has not been repentance. Things that are deep within us from childhood, from when we were one, two, three years old, from the way we were brought up; things have not been addressed, and they continue. Our particular personality bends it off in this way, crooked. We need to back up and deal with those things. Search it out. Diligently seek. Do not expect it to be spontaneous. When we repent in this way, there will be joy in heaven. There will be joy on earth. There will be joy in our heart. The Word of the Lord.

13

THEODICY: WHY IS THERE EVIL?
Moral and Natural Evil

Psalm 90

¹Lord, you have been our dwelling place
    throughout all generations.
²Before the mountains were born
    or you brought forth the earth and the world,
    from everlasting to everlasting you are God.
³You turn men back to dust,
    saying, "Return to dust, O sons of men."
⁴For a thousand years in your sight
    are like a day that has just gone by,
    or like a watch in the night.
⁵You sweep men away in the sleep of death;
    they are like the new grass of the morning—
⁶though in the morning it springs up new,
    by evening it is dry and withered.

⁷We are consumed by your anger
    and terrified by your indignation.
⁸You have set our iniquities before
    you, our secret sins in the light of your presence.
⁹All our days pass away under your wrath;
    we finish our years with a moan.
¹⁰The length of our days is seventy years—
    or eighty, if we have the strength;
    yet their span is but trouble and sorrow,
    for they quickly pass, and we fly away.

¹¹Who knows the power of your anger?

For your wrath is as great as the fear that is due you.
¹²Teach us to number our days aright,
    that we may gain a heart of wisdom.

¹³Relent, O LORD! How long will it be?
    Have compassion on your servants.
¹⁴Satisfy us in the morning with your unfailing love,
    that we may sing for joy and be glad all our days.
¹⁵Make us glad for as many days as you have afflicted us,
    for as many years as we have seen trouble.
¹⁶May your deeds be shown to your servants,
    your splendor to their children.
¹⁷May the favor of the Lord our God rest upon us;
    establish the work of our hands for us—
    yes, establish the work of our hands.

WE COME TO PART FIVE OF THE MESSAGE on the Fall. We read Psalm 90. We will be addressing the question of theodicy: God's justice. This is written by Moses, at the end of his life, after having witnessed the generation that came out of Egypt—age 20 and above—pass away.

God has ordained the preaching of His Word to be an ordinary means, perhaps a primary ordinary means, by which His people are built up in the faith. Part of the preaching involves application, and applications are presenting themselves to us continually as we encounter—as we go out and come in—various forms of unbelief that we need to address, and applications are cumulative. What we experienced this week may connect directly with the previous week. But often, the previous week does not go away. So, we need to give special attention to the preaching of the Word. While there is such a preparation process at Logos Theological Seminary for those who are going to prepare for teaching, all of us are to teach. All of us are to give heed to this ministry of the Word.

We come to part five of the doctrine of the Fall. We covered the doctrine of creation, in five points.

1. *Creation is revelation: necessarily, intentionally, and exclusively.*

2. *The revelation is full and clear.*

3. *Eternal life, the good, man's chief end, is the knowledge of God.*

4. *This knowledge of God is through the work of dominion*, which is to understand and name the creation because creation is revelation.

5. That goal will be achieved in the Sabbath, when *the earth will be filled with the knowledge of God* as the result of dominion on the earth, to the end of knowing God in His works of creation.

In the Fall, we have the doctrine of the covenant of creation, established in Genesis 2. In every way, the centrality of the Garden, the centrality of the center of the Garden, and the two trees radiating out to mankind, are presented. The act that takes place there is going to affect all, and the purpose is to establish man in righteousness—had he obeyed. We see the temptation, the nature of temptation, and our encounter with temptation (as we have spoken about earlier in this series). We see the reality of sin, and we distinguish between *root sin* and *fruit sin*. And then, we spoke about death. The wages of sin is death, and that is spiritual death, not physical death. We made those distinctions last week, and now we come to a question that naturally comes out of all of that: 'If God is all good and all powerful, why is there evil?'

This is perhaps the greatest objection or question that human beings have about whatever they may think about God. This question has appeared in this form through millennia. Many persons have gone on to develop their answer, and have wrestled with it. Darwin certainly wrestled with it when his ten-year-old daughter died, and many have not noticed it, but some have. Cornelius Hunter has[1] and he brought this to light in Darwin's attempt to distance God from evil through an evolutionary explanation of things and thereby mitigate the problem of evil. Many answers have been given, and many answers are inadequate.

The word "theodicy" is a combination of two terms: *theos* meaning God, and *dicy*, which comes from the word *dikē (δίκη)*, which is a Greek term for justice. It is trying to show how God is just in the presence of evil. Everyone must respond to this problem and the responses have been summed up in various ways in different places. Philosophers provide responses, and a notable one is by David Hume in his *Dialogues*

---

1. For further exposition regarding the theological elements of the doctrine of evolutions, see the works of Cornelius Hunter, *Darwin's God: Evolution and the Problem of Evil* (Eugene: Wipf & Stock, 2001); *Darwin's Proof: The Triumph of Religion Over Science* (Ada: Brazos Press, 2003); and *Science's Blind Spot: The Unseen Religion of Scientific Naturalism* (Ada: Brazos Press, 2007).

Concerning Natural Religion; in one section of his book he addresses this problem and provides several solutions.[2] We will touch on that briefly. We will look at the free will solution and will talk about predestination and free will. The common understanding is that if there is no free will, then we cannot speak about evil, and man doing evil. Furthermore, predestination seems to go against free will. Many have wrestled with this. Then, we will go on to provide a solution which we believe is in Scripture, in general revelation, in Historic Christianity, and in the Westminster Confession. We will open this up and apply it so that we might have a perspective on why there is evil.

We should understand what *understanding* is. The Greek term for this is *suniémi* (συνίημι), which means to put together, to connect. Things may be there discreetly, and we have to connect them. So if we are understanding, then implicitly, we have to put things together. The more we put things together in the proper order, the more we understand. We cannot understand why there is evil without understanding creation and the purpose of creation. I talked extensively with someone this week, on two or three occasions, about those who hold to what is called 'the beatific vision' as the end, the good, a direct seeing of God. This person is in close contact with many who hold to the beatific vision, and we went back and forth many times, in many ways, to get it into focus. The view of the direct seeing of God says that 'it *is not* necessary to know God through dominion.' There are all kinds of questions that are raised about man being finite, the good being inexhaustible, and the good being continued from this life to the next as the beatific vision comes in the next life and not in this life. What happens to our work and justifying our moral judgments if the good is in the next life?

All of that comes out of *creation is revelation: necessarily, intentionally, and exclusively,* and *the good is the knowledge of God through dominion,* so in order to come into theodicy and understand this fifth point under the Fall, we have to go back and keep that in mind; if we do not, it will just escape us again, it will just fall flat: It will not do anything and we will be hearing in vain. We have to remember what understanding is. We may put it this way: we start with a worldview, and within a worldview some things are more basic than others, and there is a system connected with a worldview. We have been emphasizing that the

---

2. Chapters 9–11 in Hume's *Dialogues.*

creation–fall–redemption worldview, embodied in Genesis 1–3, contains the foundation upon which we must build if we are to go on to maturity, if we are to go on to unity, and if we are to go on to fruitfulness and fullness. When you find the word "foundation" being used in Scripture, you find these concepts associated with it. More and more, we just have to ask ourselves and be in the habit of asking ourselves and asking each other, 'Is the foundation in place, and to what extent is it in place?' We have spoken about different levels of understanding. A bare, grammatical level (where we perhaps may utter the words), a dialectical level (where we can defend each point), and a rhetorical level (where we can apply it to ourselves and others around us). As I spoke to this person, in the midst of this situation when we are surrounded by 'beatific-visioners' (if I may use that term)—we are to draw them out and draw them back. There are different levels of understanding, and as we have that in place and grow in our understanding, *then* we are in a position to teach. We should not presume to teach without that in place.

DAVID HUME'S *DIALOGUES CONCERNING NATURAL RELIGION*

Let us look at the problem of evil, as it is discussed by Hume. Hume has three persons discussing through this dialogue and one of the persons is Demea, who represents the orthodox position. Hume sets up a trap for Demea by saying that "religion arises from a sense of misery"[3]—as against the truth, as against meaning, as against whether (more basically) religion arises at all. If religion is a belief or set of beliefs used to give meaning to experience, then it cannot arise from experience.[4] Religion may be present from birth, as it was for Adam, and as we grow we spontaneously express autonomy apart from God. Or it may be there by regeneration, new birth, where God restores us to life. This is trap one.

---

3. The full quote is: "It is my opinion, I won, replied Demea, that each man feels, in a manner, the truth of religion within his own breast; and from a consciousness of his imbecility and misery rather than from any reasoning, is led to seek protection from that Being on whom he and all of nature are dependent." David Hume, *Dialogues Concerning Natural Religion* (Indianapolis: Hackett Publishing Company, 1980), 58.

4. Gangadean, *Philosophical Foundation*, 145–147.

I have to acknowledge to you that I got stressed out this week, and I have talked with others who have gotten stressed out, and persons who are wrestling mightily with stress, and I think my stress was due to my deficiency in understanding that the world is full of misery and wickedness. I have said that to myself, but I need to understand it at a deeper level. Think of the word "vile" in Scripture. When we think of the word vile, we think of vile Haman—remember from Esther, "vile Haman"? The word vile is used in Psalm 14, and this is just to bring into focus the nature of evil and how the world is full of evil. Here are the words of Scripture: "The fool says in his heart, 'There is no God'" (Psalm 14:1a; 53:1a). I happened to watch Christopher Hitchens speaking about his cancer and people who are praying for him. Hitchens would be among those who say, 'There is no God.' He is the one who wrote *God is not Great.*[5] Here he is with cancer, and he is speaking consistently with his views. I talked earlier in the week with someone who teaches as an MD and a PhD in economics at Stanford, who met with Hitchens with a few others and he was giving me his impression of Hitchens and of what is going on. I was reading an article in National Review where David Horowitz refers to Hitchens as "a man of unruly contradictions."[6] But the Scripture says here, "They are corrupt" and "their deeds are vile," and in connection with that, "there is no one who does good."

> They are corrupt, their deeds are vile;
>   there is no one who does good.
>
> 2The LORD looks down from heaven
>   on the sons of men
>   to see if there are any who understand,
>   any who seek God.
> 3All have turned aside, they have together become corrupt;
>   there is no one who does good,
>   not even one.
>
> 4Will evildoers never learn—
>   those who devour my people as men eat bread

---

5. Christopher Hitchens, *God Is Not Great* (New York: McClelland & Stewart, 2007).

6. David Horowitz, "Part 1: On the complexities and contradictions of Christopher Hitchens," *Second Thoughts*, National Review (July 5, 2010)." https://www.nationalreview.com/2010/07/second-thoughts-david-horowitz/amp/

and who do not call on the LORD?
⁵There they are, overwhelmed with dread,
    for God is present in the company of the righteous.
⁶You evildoers frustrate the plans of the poor,
    but the LORD is their refuge.
⁷Oh, that salvation for Israel would come out of Zion!
    When the LORD restores the fortunes of his people,
    let Jacob rejoice and Israel be glad!
    (Ps. 14:1b–7).

I was in distress and stressed out because as I encountered evil of many kinds, I was not prepared for it. The Scripture says that the world is full of it.

Hume through Demea and Philo says, "If religion arises from a sense of misery, then the world is full of misery and wickedness."[7] When I am teaching philosophy, I go through a seventeen-point list, about thirteen of which are discussed by Hume, to show how the world is full of evil, including both natural and moral evil.[8] Having done that, Hume drops the trap on Demea: If God is all good and all powerful, how is it that all of this evil exists?[9] Then he provides the solutions. The first solution is that God's goodness is perfect but incomprehensible. This is an appeal

---

7. The full quote is:
    It is my opinion, I own, replied *Demea,* that each man feels, in a manner, the truth of re-
    ligion within his own breast; and, from a consciousness of his imbecility and misery rath-
    er than from any reasoning, is led to seek protection from that Being on whom he and all
    nature are dependent . . . I am indeed persuaded, said *Philo,* that the best and indeed the
    only method of bringing everyone to a due sense of religion is by just representation of the
    misery and wickedness of men. And for that purpose a talent of eloquence and strong im-
    agery is more requisite than that of reasoning and argument. For is it necessary to prove
    what everyone feels within himself? It is necessary to make us feel it, if possible, more in-
    timately and sensibly.
    David Hume, *Dialogues Concerning Natural Religion* (Indianapolis: Hackett Publishing
    Company, 1980), 58.

8. Gangadean, *Philosophical Foundation,* 147–151.

9. Demea says:
    Here, Cleanthes, I find I can relax in my argument. Here I triumph! When we argued earlier
    about the natural attributes of intelligence and design, I needed all my skeptical and meta-
    physical subtlety to escape your grasp. In many views of the universe and of its parts, par-
    ticularly its parts,the beauty and fitness of final causes strike us with such irresistible force
    that all objections seem to be (as I think they really are) mere fault-finding and trickery;
    and then we can't imagine how we could ever give weight to them. But there is no view of
    human life or of the condition of mankind from which we can smoothly infer the moral at-
    tributes of God, or learn about that infinite benevolence, conjoined with infinite power and
    infinite wisdom, which we must discover by the eyes of faith alone. But now the tables are

to the unknown God. This empties the word 'religion' of meaning, that does not go, for it will bring an end to religion. Secondly, in the future, we will know it, in the next life. As if we will know everything in the next life, and to know anything, I must know everything; that is a cop-out. The third solution is that, well, while there is evil in the world, it is not that much, and there is more good than evil. But the question comes back to, why is there *any* evil at all? The fourth solution is that God is finitely powerful, rather than infinitely powerful. This does not work for one who is the Creator. And the fifth: Hume goes through to show that no natural evil is necessary. Hume! David Hume is doing work for us to show that no natural evil is necessary, and he is right. He goes through several claims, and one common claim is: 'To have good you must have evil, to have hot you must have cold, etc.,' it does not work that way. You can have variety without opposition. My favorite example is ice cream, of course. You can have ice cream, and then not have it for a whole year, and after a whole year, you miss it. In the meantime, you have all kinds of desserts. You know how inventive human beings are with respect to desserts, right? You can have variety without opposition. Do not tell me that in order to have pleasure of a particular kind and appreciate it, you must have pain. You can have the absence of a particular pleasure but there can be other kinds of pleasure. As if it were necessary from the beginning of creation. No. He ends by saying that God is indifferent—or not even God, but the origin of things—is indifferent to what is made. You cannot say that God, who is spirit, creating with infinite, deliberate wisdom, is indifferent. These are a number of solutions to the problem of evil, and they all go down under close examination.[10]

THE FREE WILL SOLUTION

Having gone this far, we now introduce the second round. If natural evil is not necessary, then why is there natural evil? The answer commonly given is that natural evil is due to moral evil and moral evil is

turned! It is now your turn to tug the laboring oar, and to defend your philosophical sub-tleties against the dictates of plain reason and experience.
David Hume, *Dialogues Concerning Natural Religion* (Indianapolis: Hackett Publishing Company, 1980), 66.

10. Gangadean, *Philosophical Foundation*, 152–154.

because of free will, so you have what is called the free will solution,[11] and it is a favorite of many believers. The free will solution. 'It is because of free will. Adam chose. He ate the apple.' He did not eat the apple! He ate from the tree of the knowledge of good and evil. So stop it. Do not ever say that again. Adam did eat the fruit. He listened to the voice of his wife and ate of the tree of which God commanded that he should not eat. He did that freely. There are a number of standard, quick objections to consider. Then I will go into the predestination objection because I have been hearing it more from some of the discussions going on in the church.

The first objection to the free will solution says that possibility is not actuality. Free will makes moral evil possible, not actual, like oxygen makes fire possible, not actual. It is necessary, not sufficient. Appealing to free will, you may be free without evil for one minute, two minutes, five minutes and if you are really good, you can be free without evil for 10 minutes! But I know, 'The pressure just builds up inside,' right? 'The longer you go, you just feel an urge to do it'? No, the longer you go, the easier it gets: That is the other side of the story. Free will makes moral evil possible, not actual.

Secondly, if it is actual, it is not necessary. It may in fact have happened, but is it necessary? Could we not have a world without sin? Remember, a lot of philosophers are wrestling with this, and they are going to try their particular kinds of solutions. There are all kinds of discussions about possible worlds, or a logically possible world theory, that explores this.

A third objection is that free will does not have to make moral evil possible. God is free without the possibility of evil. If you say, 'God is not free,' then why are you fussing over the question? God is infinite, eternal, and unchangeable in His goodness—infinite, eternal, and unchanging in His goodness—God cannot do evil. Yet He is free. He does whatever He pleases. So free will does not have to make more evil possible. Man in heaven is free without the possibility of evil because he is so upheld by God that he will never fall away. You believe in the

---

11. Gangadean, *Philosophical Foundation*, 154–156.

perseverance of the saints, right?[12] Free will does not make it necessary for human beings to sin.

Lastly, one can pass from innocence to virtue without moral evil. Adam could have passed from innocence and gone through a test without evil. Jesus passed from innocence to virtue in the wilderness without evil. I remember a professor at the University of Arizona who elaborated a theory about how first-order evil makes second-order good possible, etc. We brought out the example of Jesus, and his response was, 'Oh. Yeah, Jesus.' Jesus passed from innocence to virtue (if you want to put it that way) without evil. Evil is not even necessary in that kind of argument. The free will argument does not go; it does not explain; it does not hold up.

PREDESTINATION AND FREEDOM

Now let us look at predestination; I have roughly organized it in terms of seven, maybe eight points. I will try to number the points to help you to hold onto them. I will try to organize in terms of sources, general revelation, Scripture, and Historic Christianity.

First Point: Definition of Freedom From General Revelation

There is a question of the definition of freedom. What do you mean by freedom? There are two definitions, going back to what is called compatibilism and incompatibilism.[13] That is, 'if you are *caused* to do something, it could not be otherwise. If it could not be otherwise, then you are not free, so maybe you were not caused by anything.'

You should know that I'm reading a book called, *The Closing of the Muslim Mind*.[14] The idea of causality and freedom in God is a big thing. The author traces a connection between the doctrine of God and the will of God absolutely unbound; he shows a direct line from that idea to the current terrorism and the attempt to impose sharia law. It is what you would call divine command theory: something is

---

12. Gangadean, *The Westminster Confession*, 189–195; Gangadean, *The Westminster Catechisms*, 205–207.

13. Gangadean, *Philosophical Foundation*, 66.

14. Robert R. Reilly, *The Closing of the Muslim Mind: How Intellectual Suicide Created the Modern Islamist Crisis* (Wilmington: ISI Books, 2010).

good because God wills it, period. God could have willed adultery. God could have willed murder. This theory is such that nothing in the world has a nature; there are no things with natures as second causes to produce results. There is no nature of things in the world, and God is a natureless being. What it amounts to is that every moment God is creating the world. That is hard to hear, let us just say, it is *big*, and I will need to look into this further. I knew that there were theological voluntarists, emphasizing the will. But I had not realized until I started reading this book, how far they go with it, and how explicit they were with it. In Islam, there is this idea of an uncaused will. Others would say no, determinism and free will are compatible, so there are two different definitions in talking about freedom and causality.

Let me say this, I realize that as I am speaking some of you are going to say, 'What?!' Just get an initial acquaintance level with it, just an acquaintance level where you can say, 'There is a problem here in the definition of freedom and it has to do with causality.' If that much you get on this one point, that is all you need to get at this time, some of you can get more. With regard to freedom and causality, we need to distinguish between first cause, second cause, and uncaused events. Chapters 3 and 5 of the Westminster Confession of Faith, on God's Eternal Decree and Providence, speak about first and second causes. This is not a new concept that I am bringing out. If we get this point clear from general revelation, we can resolve the problem. It is not a small problem; it is a big problem. The Arminian vs. Reformed conflict goes back to this. Is there a conflict, historically? Yes, and it goes back to this. The conflict between Islam and Christianity goes back to this. Is there a conflict? Yes, there is. So do not say, 'Well, I do not need to know this.' There is a big conflict here. We should know its root, and then we can address it from general revelation.

Second Point: The Westminster Confession on Liberty and Ability

The Westminster Confession Chapter 9 speaks of free will. It speaks about the liberty of man.[15]

---

15. Gangadean, *The Westminster Confession*, 47–48.

Third Point: Augustine's Fourfold State Regarding Ability

Augustine distinguishes between liberty and ability. Augustine developed this idea particularly well, and perhaps we can hold on to it in this form—rhetorically, he was very skillful. He spoke about the fourfold state of man in terms of possibility of sin. In the Garden, man could sin; he put it in Latin: *posse peccare*, meaning that man could sin in that first state. In the fallen state, it is not possible for man not to sin: *non-posse non-peccare*—not possible not to sin. Then, in the regenerate state, it is possible not to sin: *posse non-peccare*. In the glorified state, it is not possible to sin: *non-posse peccare*.[16] If you want to impress your friends—especially your girlfriend—learn it in Latin.

What is going on here is to show that *ability* to do good may change from 0 to 100%, but *liberty* remains constant: 100% liberty. Augustine makes a distinction between ability and liberty and shows that freedom is grounded in liberty. That is the point that is coming out through this.

Fourth Point: TULIP[17]

We pick up this same idea in the doctrine of *tulip*: *total depravity, unconditional election, limited atonement, irresistible grace,* and *perseverance of the saints.* Many of you have heard of these points, and this is easier for you to hold onto, but there is a context in which this is stated. Beginning with total depravity; we are dead in trespasses and sins,[18] and therefore God *unconditionally* brings us out of that condition. A dead person cannot do anything to save himself. But it is deeper than *cannot*: a dead person does not want to and is positively resisting because he or she does not want to.

Fifth Point: *Ordo Salutis*[19]

We also have it developed in the *ordo salutis* in terms of Historic Christianity. The *ordo salutis* is the order of the application of redemption. First, effectual calling, where we are regenerated: God's sovereignty

---

16. Gangadean, *History of Philosophy,* 113–114.

17. Gangadean, "Paper No. 18: Salvation by Grace," in *The Logos Papers,* 119–122.

18. *Ephesians 2:1.*

19. Gangadean, *The Westminster Catechisms,* 191–203.

brings us from death to life. It is on the basis of effectual calling that we have a conviction of our sin and death. On the basis of the conviction of sin and death, we have repentance and faith—that is, conversion. So regeneration, then conversion. Then, on the basis of faith, we are justified: the righteousness of Christ is imputed to us and our sins are imputed to Christ. We have justification, and then comes sanctification, where God continues to cleanse us. Then, ultimately, we have full deliverance from any remnants of sin: glorification.

Sixth Point: Contrary Passages

We should notice contrary passages to which persons say, 'What about this passage and that passage?' One of our members recently had written up a statement in the course of his discussion with someone who was raising questions about contrary passages. I remember early in my life I struggled with this question of predestination and this is how it initially came to be resolved. I read in the Book of Revelation that they were praising God for His justice. Remember, we are dealing with theodicy, God's justice. I did not understand, but I saw clearly that they were going to praise God for His justice, so that was one piece of it. The second piece was that as I was wrestling with predestination I thought, 'Well, you know, I am predestinated according to the plan of God but so is Jesus predestinated according to the plan of God.' It is said that He is the Lamb of God, slain from before the foundation of the world.[20] So I thought, 'If predestination makes me an automaton, it makes Jesus an automaton also. And if he is an automaton, I am okay with being an automaton,' end of story—this answer was sufficient in that in heaven I will be praising God for His justice. Since then, further understanding has come, but that was sufficient to get me over that hump. With all the contrary passages, I would say we can fiddle with that in a variety of ways, and I am willing to—you know me—I can fiddle, too. We can talk about it, but generally, I fiddle by getting back to what is more basic.

---

20. *Revelation 13:8.*

SEVENTH POINT:
The Ironic Solution[21]

We come to what we call the Ironic Solution. Here we are going to go for what I think is the epitome of Paul's addressing it: "Shall what is formed say to him who formed it, 'Why did you make me like this?'" (Rom. 9:20b). Have you ever read that in Romans? Would you agree this is a pinnacle point?

What I have been hearing recently is, 'If God predestinates, then I cannot believe unless God regenerates me, and therefore I am not responsible.' Talking about clarity and inexcusability was being undermined by an appeal to predestination. Frankly, that was kind of a new line; I had not thought about it. I thought that clarity and inexcusability stand in any case, but this person was using predestination to undercut it. This is where it came into focus more recently, and we can and should address it.

I think in this solution, we need to recognize that it is *because of evil in us* that we do not understand the problem of evil.[22] It is because of evil remaining in us—not seeking and not understanding—that we do not understand what is clear about evil, what the definition of evil is, and therefore we have difficulty dealing with it. We do not understand the purpose of God because of evil in us—unbelief. Therefore we cannot understand why there is evil. There is a kind of existential dilemma that we should have expected that there is evil in us, and because of that evil in us, evil is hindering us from understanding. We are going to say, 'Of course, that is like a no-brainer, and we should have expected that.' Evil applies to us in our wrestling with the problem of evil.

Why Is There Moral Evil?

If we understand the difference between root and fruit evil—that evil is not seeking and not understanding (in light of what is clear)—we can get started. If we understand *the good as the knowledge of God*, and *the earth is to be filled with the knowledge of God*, we can understand. First of all, why is there evil? Unless we distinguish the two parts, moral evil

---

21. Gangadean, *Philosophical Foundation*, 156–161; Gangadean, *On Natural and Revealed Theology*, 141–147.

22. Gangadean, "Paper No. 103: The Noetic Effect of Sin," in *The Logos Papers*, 531–528.

and natural evil, we will not make much progress. Why is there moral evil? Moral evil serves to deepen the revelation of God's glory. Now think about that. The question in the problem of evil is, 'Why is there evil?', not specifically, 'Why is there moral evil?' Evil serves to deepen the revelation of God's glory. It is put in this way in Historic Christianity: "Our first parents, being seduced by the subtlety and temptation of Satan, sinned, in eating the forbidden fruit. This their sin, God was pleased, according to his wise and holy counsel, to permit, having purposed to order it to his own glory" (WCF. 6.1). What this is saying is that God is sovereign, and God could use evil to serve His purpose. What was His purpose? This is where we go back to the purpose in the creation, and what the good is. The purpose is to reveal His glory. God creates to reveal His glory, and in providence, He rules to reveal His glory (WCF. 4.1). When He permits evil in His providence, it does not set aside the original purpose to reveal His glory. He permits it to *deepen* the revelation of His glory. Evil serves God's purpose in creation versus frustrating it. If we do not know God's purpose of revealing His glory, we are going to miss this, and it is going to be part of the problem of evil. We should know what the purpose of it is. We confess it when we say, "Man's chief end is to glorify God" (SCQ. 1), but we can recite these words and empty them of meaning. We fill in the doxological focus by quoting passages from the Westminster Confession, such as that we are to "glorify God in all that by which he makes himself known" (SCQ. 101), and we can open that up further with, in all of His works of creation and providence.[23] Someone might say, 'That is new,' but it is not new. Connecting these parts may be new. But the parts have been there. This is what understanding is: making the connections. Just as we try to make the connection between the first point of the creation worldview and the last point of the Fall worldview, we are making connections; we are understanding.

Evil serves to deepen the revelation. If it is removed abruptly, the revelation is not deepened; if it is not removed, the revelation is not seen; therefore, evil is removed gradually. Every form and degree of evil (unbelief) is allowed to come to expression in world history, and the cultures of the world are expressions of this. Tribal differences can be explained in light of this: There is a worldview in each which expresses

---

23. Gangadean, *The Westminster Catechisms*, xxviii-xxxii, 3–4, 315–316.

itself in culture, in the details of culture.[24] This is consistent with what the Scripture speaks about regarding the spiritual war that is age-long and agonizing, and good overcomes evil. Evil is allowed to work itself out in history, in every form. It is consistent with what we see in the history of the world: from Adam through Cain, to the Flood, through Babel, Abraham, the Patriarchs, Moses, Joshua, the Book of Judges, to the kingship, through the prophets, to the captivity, and waiting for Christ. Evil is being allowed to work itself out in every degree and combination. God does not remove evil abruptly, which is consistent with the notion of dominion. We are to have dominion over sin. It is not an effortless activity. In our epistemology, four of the five main sources are spontaneous, effortless. Tradition is effortless; common sense is effortless; sense perception is effortless; intuition is effortless.[25] Perhaps because we rely on these, we start to think that all of knowledge is effortless. But the Scripture says, "he is a rewarder of them that diligently seek him" (Heb. 11:6b KJV). It is connected with the work of dominion, requiring all of mankind working together to accomplish this revelation. This effortless model, that we intuitively have in us, is deeply flawed. Is God working in us? Likewise, we have to exercise dominion over sin, and we have to take thoughts captive: We are to demolish arguments that are raised up against the knowledge of God.[26] Like Jedi warriors, we learn to use the lightsaber. We have to be in training for that, right? We have to overcome evil in us, to crucify the flesh with the affections and the lusts, and we have to grow to maturity and become fruitful. Six-year-olds do not have babies (God forbid). Maybe fourteen-year-olds *can*, but hold the line. In terms of custom, it is more like 18 to 21. You do not have to wait until 35, you know? 21 is fine if you have been going according to speed in terms of getting your education, getting prepared, and so on. We come to maturity, and we bear fruit. Exercise dominion.

Get a good grade-school education: especially based on a good childhood upbringing, with a special focus on getting through the two-year-old crisis, which is full of opportunity. Some of us did not make it

---

24. Gangadean, "Paper No. 19: Foundation for Philosophy of History," in *The Logos Papers*, 123–125.

25. Gangadean, "Paper No. 69: Sources of Skepticism," in *The Logos Papers*, 367–368; Gangadean, *Philosophical Foundation*, 22, 24–27.

26. *2 Corinthians 10:4–5.*

through the two-year-old crisis: We are still 30 and throwing tantrums. Oh, we modulate it, you know, but do not take it for granted. This is why in education, we have been pushed logically and ontologically to give attention beyond first grade, and beyond kindergarten. As I spend time with parents, and notice how children behave and how discipline is administered, we are learning about that.

We have to exercise dominion, and one of the first places dominion is exercised is in childrearing. Well, the first place is in marriage, and men bringing the Word of God to their wives. The second place is in bringing the Word of God to their families and to their children. That is for all men, not just guys in Logos,[27] right? But if you are teaching, this is where the teaching begins. Dominion. Does it require work to raise a child? There is never a harder work. I remember this past Monday, I finally got my mind into gear. I said, 'I am here to serve.' It was 100% servant. I was not going to sit down and be able to eat with the others. I was going to stand and cook those eggs and flip those pancakes and just be there like a 100%, full-time servant. It worked. They were served. Parents are like that. This is the origin of slavery. But we are not to be child-centered; we are to be God-centered. Some, because of their upbringing, are child-centered. By way of reaction to their upbringing, everything focuses on the child, rather than getting the child to focus *with us* on the goal. This is going to be a big one. There has been a shift in the climate regarding childrearing. This is all part of dominion, applying it. Moral evil serves to deepen the revelation. It is removed gradually, and we have to take those thoughts captive.

Before we leave moral evil, let us say something about the difference between the root and the fruit. Many people repent of fruit sin: adultery, using drugs, saying a bad word, whatever, and they think that is the end of it. No, no, no, that is not the end of it. To repent of the fruit sin is not the same as repenting of the root sin. Repenting of the root sin is going to take more time to get at it. We have to make that distinction. In the doctrine of repentance, what we need to do is repent of the root sin—not seeking and not understanding and therefore not doing what is right. Many people want to say, 'Well, I repented of that, that is behind me.' No. Maybe that particular expression of the fruit sin, on that occasion, is behind you, but the root is still there,

---

27. Logos Theological Seminary.

and that needs to be cleansed. The Scripture says, "he is faithful and just to forgive us our sins, and to cleanse us from all unrighteousness" (1 Jn. 1:9b KJV).

Why Is There Natural Evil?

We can go on to natural evil, the definition of which is toil, strife, old age, sickness, and death, as we see from Genesis 3. It manifests itself in greater cultural expression in war, famine, and plague. The purpose of this is that we may know God. I counted last night in the Book of Ezekiel, "then they will know that I am the LORD," is said 72 times. God is bringing affliction on the people "that they may know that I am the LORD." The purpose of natural evil is not punishment, but correction, that we may know the Lord. Many times God uses war, famine, and plague as intense expressions of the call back.

We can know from general revelation that natural evil is not original. God created the world good, without natural evil. Natural evil is not inherent in sin, therefore it is imposed. It is not imposed arbitrarily but because of moral evil, but it is not imposed as a punishment. Punishments are inherent. We talked about spiritual death being inherent in sin. Physical death is imposed as a call back to restrain, recall from, and remove moral evil. It is imposed to cause us to stop and think (I will be going over that in great detail when we continue with redemption: first call back, second call back, third call back, justification, and sanctification). It is imposed as a call to stop and think. We know that physical death is not the punishment because *all* are resurrected—believer and non-believer—and punishment is forever; this is one piece that we should be able to hold on to for now. It is imposed to call us to stop and think, and that is exactly what we did not do in sin: We do not seek to understand. This is covered up by self-deception and hypocrisy; we will get back to that in moral law 3: "Thou shalt not take the name of the LORD thy God in vain" (Ex. 20:7a KJV). It is covered up further by self-justification. "The heart is deceitful above all things, and desperately wicked" (Jer. 17:9a KJV), in terms of not diligently seeking and how that is covered up. We are reminded of it in circumcision, applied to children, who need a new heart; and with baptism: children needing a new heart. That heart must be replaced. We are warned about this in the Second Commandment that God visits the iniquities of the fathers unto the third and fourth generation of those who hate Him.[28] When He revealed Himself to Moses on the mountain, He said He will not hold them guiltless who take His name in vain.[29] When we hear and do not put it into practice—hear and do not take it to heart—we have to harden ourselves, justify ourselves, and that gets passed on to our children, through our teaching by example and otherwise, and it is then passed on to grandchildren and great-grandchildren; absolutely, inescapably, it is going to happen. We are going to teach our child by our example, and if our example is that of not hearing and not paying attention to the ordinary means, then it is going to be passed on to the children. This is how the iniquities become visited. Do you want to destroy your child? Don't pay attention; be light and thoughtless about it. Don't stop and think; shrug it off, justify it. It will destroy your children because they are going to pick it up from you. The Word of God says: "visiting the iniquities of the fathers upon the children unto the third and fourth generation."[30] I talk with people coming in, and I often ask about their parents and their grandparents and their great-grandparents, and sometimes their great-great-grandparents. I try to trace the line of where it went off and see how it came down the generations.

We should fear the Lord. Natural evil is imposed to get us to stop and think. It was imposed in Eden:

> Cursed is the ground because of you; through painful toil you will eat of it all the days of your life. It will produce thorns and thistles for you, and you will eat the plants of the field. By the sweat of your brow you will eat your food until you return to the ground, since from it you were taken; for dust you are and to dust you will return (Gen. 3:17b–19).

Physical death is imposed as a call back. It was the third call back, after shame, and after the question, "Where are you?" (Gen. 3:9b), and man avoided it. God forgave man; He clothed them with coats of skin, signifying justification through the death of another—righteousness

---

28. *Exodus 20:5.*

29. *Exodus 20:7.*

30. These words are in *Exodus 20:5*, with very similar words in *Exodus 34:7; Numbers 14:18; Deuteronomy 5:9.*

through the death of another.[31] Then God expelled them from Eden, to live under death.

God is merciful, in one sense at the beginning, death did not happen for 900 plus years—950 was the ordinary lifespan. Men used that lengthy lifespan to go deeper and deeper into evil. Before the Flood, the whole world had gone into evil; they had become corrupt and violent. God wiped out that world in judgment. God permitted evil to reach maximal form then; we have evidence of these things all around us, and we do not pay attention. It is estimated by some, and reasonably I think, that over six billion people were on the earth in the days of the Flood. This is a minimal calculation.

God permitted evil, maximal evil, at that time. We lived under it and used our long lifespan to engage in more and more evil. After the Flood, it was restricted more, eventually to 70 years, but we still went into evil. The whole world went into evil, and we were scattered at Babel by the confusion of tongues. That scattering was reversed under Christ by Pentecost in the ingathering of the nations.[32] With the same means by which they were expelled, by the same means they were gathered back in. Pentecost answers to Babel. It also answers to the Firstfruits; 50 days after coming out of Egypt at Mount Sinai where they were given the law; it was anticipated by the Feast of Ingathering: all the nations gathered in.

We were expelled from Eden.[33] We saw it in Cain: there were many ways in which God called Cain back, and we see it coming down through history. We see it in the prophets, the curse and the promise. We see it in the words of Christ in Scripture, in the Lord's Prayer: "Forgive us our debts, as we also have forgiven our debtors"—forgiveness, justification. "And lead us not into temptation, but deliver us from the evil one" (Matt. 6:12–13)—cleansing and sanctification. We see it in the words of 1 John 1:9: "If we confess our sins, he is faithful and just and will forgive us our sins and purify us from all unrighteousness." God forgave us in the Garden of Eden when He clothed us with the coats of skin, but He cleanses us from the root sin of not seeking, and self-deception and self-justification, by requiring us to live under the

---

31. *Genesis 3:21.*

32. *Acts 2.*

33. *Genesis 3:23.*

suffering of toil, strife, old age, sickness and death. Even when we do not hear that, He intensifies it, and He certainly intensified it for Cain. He certainly intensified it for Pharaoh. This is why we say that the heart is deceitful above all else and we need a new heart; this is why salvation is of the Lord.[34]

We have the teaching of Scripture as to why there is evil. Why is there moral evil? To deepen the revelation. It serves a purpose. Why is there natural evil? To call us back from moral evil, to get us to stop and think. Physical death is the greatest visible reminder of spiritual death, and it has always been that way. The visible reveals the invisible, but it is not punishment. God is gracious in working with us. Our intuitions will not get us there; our intuitions will get us elsewhere. We have to understand this. Our intuitions are putting us toward some kind of ideal world—an ideal world where there will not be suffering—and we take it as punishment, but it is not punishment: it is a call back. I think we can answer the question, 'Why is there evil?'[35] I think we can share our answer with others who ask that question. We may not have covered every form. If there are forms that we have not touched on, please bring them to mind, after the message, after Communion. I would like to know. I hope this message prepares us to deal with questions that arise in our own hearts and in the hearts of others.

---

34. *Jonah 2:9b.*

35. Gangadean, *Philosophical Foundation*, 145–161; Gangadean, *On Natural and Revealed Theology*, 141–147; Gangadean, "Paper No. 7: The Problem of Evil," in *The Logos Papers*, 33–39.

14

THE FIRST CALL BACK: SHAME

Inward Call to Repentance

Genesis 2:25; 3:6–8

²⁵The man and his wife were both naked, and they felt no shame.

⁶When the woman saw that the fruit of the tree was good for food and pleasing to the eye, and also desirable for gaining wisdom, she took some and ate it. She also gave some to her husband, who was with her, and he ate it. ⁷Then the eyes of both of them were opened, and they realized they were naked; so they sewed fig leaves together and made coverings for themselves. ⁸Then the man and his wife heard the sound of the LORD God as he was walking in the garden in the cool of the day, and they hid from the LORD God among the trees of the garden.

G OD CALLS US BACK FROM SIN AND DEATH; in this, His mercy is revealed. This is consistent with what we covered last time on theodicy: the explanation of why evil exists and how God deals with evil. God permits evil, having purposed to order it to His own glory,[1] and He removes evil. He removes it gradually so that evil can work itself out and deepen the revelation, but we need to come to see it, evil must be removed.[2] We are not left in sin and death and we are called back.

As I go through this passage, I would like us to think about how we have read it in the past, and how we hear others round about us read

---

1. *WCF. 6.1.*

2. Gangadean, *Philosophical Foundation*, 145–161; Gangadean, *On Natural and Revealed Theology*, 141–147; Gangadean, "Paper No. 7: The Problem of Evil," in *The Logos Papers*, 33–39.

it, and if there are differences, consider why there are these differences. What is going on? Ask yourself, 'Well, there are differences; is this really true? Is this really the Word of God?' You are to listen attentively, in that sense. Think critically about what is being said. Be concerned about truth and ask yourself, 'Is this the very truth of God in His Word?'

So, we begin. It says, **"The man and his wife were both naked, and they felt no shame"** (v. 25). You wonder why the Scripture would put that in there. But it is there, and there is no question about it. It should jolt you a little bit because you know what? You do not go around naked with your spouse, that is, in the house, you do not both walk around naked. There are times when that might be, but generally, you do not walk around naked, right? Just as the animals ate the green vegetation for food. "[To] everything that has the breath of life in it, I give every green plant for food" (Gen. 1:30b). That was said, right? This tells us that the conditions of creation were good and these things were absent. And now, when we come to the Fall, we read, **"Then the eyes of both of them were opened, and they realized they were naked"** (Gen. 3:7a). These verses need to be put together, not just read separately and disregarded.

What happens now is that we have to, by good and necessary consequences, deduce this, and you tell me if what is deduced from Scripture today is a good and necessary consequence. We need to know that this is part of reading and understanding the Scripture. That is, now they felt shame. They felt no shame before, and now they felt shame. If you have any questions or hesitation about that, please do ask. Scripture is pretty explicit about these two particulars. When you put them together, you can draw this inference; you are almost *required* to. If you do not draw it out, perhaps the burden is upon you to say, why not? Why is this not an inference made by good and necessary consequences? **"So they sewed fig leaves together and made coverings for themselves"** (v. 7b). You know, there are periods, and there are colons and semicolons and commas. This is a semicolon, the thought is continuing over, and it is not ended. The word 'so' is a connector, saying, 'Because of what has gone before, they did this.' **"Then the eyes of both of them were opened, and they realized they were naked; so they sewed fig leaves together and made coverings for themselves"** (v. 7). Of course, we all come to church clothed, we do not go around naked. Some people like to sport their nakedness in all kinds of degrees; different parts of the body are exposed. We say, in regard to that, that you have a *right* to privacy: no one is to require you to take off your clothes, but you also have an *obligation* to privacy: keep private parts private; keep it covered. We do not want to see your nakedness; there is shame connected with nakedness.

We have to put this together. What does it mean when it says, **"the eyes of both of them were opened"** (v. 7a)? There are two possible interpretations. One is that it was a physical opening of the eyes, and the other option is that it was not a physical opening, but a spiritual opening. Which do you think appropriately applies here? Is there a third possibility? Remember, we said the principle is that the visible reveals the invisible—*creation is revelation*—it is there from the beginning. God created to reveal His glory. They saw the fruit of the tree, right? They literally saw it, with their eyes open. It is not that their eyes were closed unless you want to make it somehow so that they could see the fruit, but when it comes to anything else they were blind. That is *reductio ad absurdum,* right? It is ridiculous. Clearly, they could see. Adam was naming the creatures. Or was he blindly naming the creatures? No. It assumes that they were able to see each other's nakedness, and yet they felt no shame. If it said, 'they were both naked and felt no shame, they were both naked and blind?' No, it does not fit there, right? Whichever way you want to cut it—and there may be other ways—this is a spiritual seeing.

Something has changed spiritually. It is connected with the physical nakedness, but they are seeing something in connection with the physical nakedness that they did not see before. What we might say about that is that they were seeing the spiritual nakedness, the lack of righteousness. They were seeing this; they saw it in the other person, and they saw it in themselves. They saw that there was a lack of righteousness. How was that? Because, in the temptation, there was a manifestation. The trees were put there, planted, and named—"the tree of life" and "the tree of the knowledge of good and evil"—to make manifest what was in the heart: this disposition to determine good and evil for oneself. To determine good and evil, to know good and evil in that way, was manifest in the outward eating. The physical nakedness is a reminder of their spiritual nakedness. They were without righteousness; they had disobeyed God. The physical reality is reminding them of the spiritual, and now they are feeling shame in connection with this. Shame is a very powerful feeling. We will be exploring that point as we go along. They engaged in a deliberate act, together, to respond to this shame. What they did is **"they sewed fig leaves together and made coverings for themselves"** (v. 7b). This is a pretty significant effort; the beginning of dominion. Have you ever sewed fig leaves together? Have you sewn any leaves together? It is quite an accomplishment. They somehow connected them, covered their nakedness, and then they tried to go on in this way.

There is another element in the text here: Adam has put his wife before God. God is going to say, "Because you listened to your wife and ate from the tree about which I commanded you, 'You must not eat of it,' cursed is the ground because of you" (Gen. 3:17a). He put his wife before God in a natural way, not in a spiritual way. Perhaps in that natural way, he was particularly regarding her in her physicality. He was led by her and had already given up spiritual leadership. He had given up and had become delinquent. It is said that he was there with her and he said nothing: **"She also gave some to her husband, who was with her, and he ate it"** (v. 6b). This is a very, very basic point that we need to consider. We are being restored from this. "Husbands, love your wives, just as Christ loved the church and gave himself up for her" (Eph. 5:25). No period, no comma, and no semicolon: "to make her holy, cleansing her by the washing with water through the word" (Eph. 5:26). It is speaking of sanctification through the truth. Husbands are supposed to bring the Word, they have this responsibility. It also says that in case the husband does not hold to the Word, the wife is to win her husband without a word, by demonstrating submission with a meek and quiet spirit,[3] which is what the man is to do before God.

Adam listened to his wife and he put her before God. His desire was for her more than for God, and that led him to turn aside. All of this is operating here. As they look at their physical nakedness, it reminds them of their spiritual nakedness, and putting their natural desires above their desire for God. Does that happen often? Did the sons of God see the daughters of men and marry whomever they willed?[4] What was moving them? A natural desire of the man for the woman, or the woman for the man, without reference to God. This was present from

---

3. *1 Peter 3:4.*

4. *Genesis 6:2.*

the beginning, so it was appropriate that the visible was a reminder of the invisible; they were ashamed, and they tried to deal with their shame.

What is shame, and where does it come from? We say it comes from conscience. Conscience is an inner judge within ourselves, not external. It helps us to measure what we do against what we ought to do. Paul says, "For the good that I would I do not"—you see that there is a judgment made here—"but the evil which I would not, that I do" (Rom. 7:19 KJV). We are aware of the standard, and we are reminded of how we come short. Conscience is a judge built into each of us. It is conscience that speaks to us of what God calls us to do, which is to seek Him and to know Him, and to love Him and obey Him. 'I did not do any of that, so my conscience is striking out against me.' Now, we should say that conscience is a judge, and we should not go against our conscience. In that sense, it is a negative guide. Conscience is not a positive guide. If our conscience permits us to do something, that does not mean it is okay. Great havoc has been wrought in the Church by those who have appealed to, 'My conscience is clear.' Our conscience is fallen, affected by the Fall, so just because our conscience permits us to do something, it does not mean we are permitted. But if our conscience says not to do it, then we should not. This is at a subjective level. If our conscience says, 'Do not paint your toenails,' that does not mean it is wrong, but we do not go against our conscience. If our conscience says, 'Do not eat meat offered to idols,'[5] that does not mean it is wrong, but we do not violate our conscience. We have to be careful how we respond to conscience, particularly in our fallen state. It is an inner call back that rises spontaneously. It pronounces its judgment, we feel it, we cannot get away from it, and that is shame.

Adam and his wife felt shame now, without righteousness before God because they had not done what God had said (as was manifest in that they had eaten the fruit). The shame usually kicks in right after you have been satisfied with the act that you do. You want it, you want it, you want it, you have it now, and you realize, 'I should not have had it.' We are blinded by desires, and once they are satisfied, we begin to reconsider.

Shame is to be contrasted with pride. Shame says to us, 'You should be ashamed of yourself.' It is more than just what you did: it is the *doer*

---

5. *1 Corinthians 10:25–28.*

of the act. *You* should be ashamed of *yourself.* Sometimes our parents (our mothers) may say that to us, and we hear that as the voice of our parents. But in Scripture, this is an inner voice. We should not just say it is external and say, 'Get away from me, I do not want to hear it.' We should be ashamed of ourselves. In contrast to thinking we are better, we are great; we should be ashamed of ourselves. There is a self-condemnation. It is before others and before God. Pride comes up in this way: When I think I know, and I do not, I am thinking more highly of myself than I ought. I have chosen this example very carefully. I have been thinking about this for about two weeks, and this is where I want to focus attention finally: 'I think I know when I do not,' versus 'I do not know because I have not been seeking and not understanding.' 'I have been found out with culpable ignorance.' 'I am inexcusable.' Notice the juxtaposition: 'I think I know when I do not'; it is not simply, 'I do not know,' but the juxtaposition of those two. 'I think I know,' 'when I do not.' This is what leads us to this point. We think we know, we think we are wise, and we are not. Scripture says in Romans 1:22, "Professing themselves to be wise, they became fools."[6] The idea of a "fool" is like something worthless. It is put this way in Psalms 14 and 53: "They have become worthless." Worthless means, 'I do not deserve anything good: what I deserve is a kick in the seat of the pants.' I go around with a little tag behind me saying, 'Kick me. I do not deserve anything; I am worthless.' It is the essence of hell, a garbage dump. I become worthless, contrasted with the purpose for which God made me. Shame, self-condemnation, becoming fools, worthless. This inner judgment is there and we have to deal with it, and we do not want to be exposed as a fool. A fool is one who thinks he is wise; he thinks he knows when he does not. I will come back to this idea of being exposed because here, we have a covering and a cover-up. There is a book about transactional analysis in psychology that speaks about this cover-up in the title, which made it popular, *I'm OK—You're OK.*[7] Adam and Eve practiced that. He said, 'I'm okay,' and she said, 'I'm okay,' and they said to each other, 'You are okay! We are okay!' It is interesting how they cooperated in that. We believe the details are given here because it is relevant, it is necessary, it is basic, it is foundational. The rest of

---

6. KJV.

7. Thomas Harris, *I'm OK—You're OK* (New York: Harper & Row Publishers, 2004).

the Scripture is built on this. It is necessary to understand this to understand the rest of Scripture, and so we need to give attention to it.

THE COVER-UP: SELF-DECEPTION

To cover up from one's own conscience involves self-deception. We say that they are being called back through their inner conscience, not outward. There will be an outer call. The next call will be outer, so expect that. The response to this inner call is to cover up, which is self-deception. This is where we get the teaching about sin and self-deception. This is where we get the teaching about first call back, second call back, third call back. We have to ask ourselves, is this being noticed? Have we noticed this in our reading or from others round about us? Is this what others have taught, or have they just passed over it somewhat lightly? If it is passed over lightly, then it is a matter of lightly and thoughtlessly regarding that by which God makes Himself known. We are expressly told: "Thou shalt not take the name of the LORD thy God in vain" (Ex. 20:7a KJV).

There is self-deception. They have to deceive themselves. Why is it that there is self-deception? In some ways, they have succeeded in covering themselves, in deceiving themselves. But you know the covering is there, and certainly they have some memory of what they did, and they have the covering hanging on them, right? They can cover their nakedness, but they cannot *cover* the *covering*. Logically, ontologically, it is the very nature of being in existence, that you cannot cover the covering. No matter how many layers you put on it, there is always a top layer, and you will see the top layer, and you have to do what? What do you do with it? You have to consider, 'Why is that hanging there?' You have to do something in your mind to disregard it, and there is found the self-deception. Notice, they both do it; we not only cover ourselves, but we go along with one another. It is an individual and communal activity. We go along with a cover-up of another. To do this is to *enable* that person, to assist them in their sin, and we should not go along with this. The first thing you will be told is that it is not politically correct to do that. If you do anything to point it out, you are going to have to deal with yourself. You will get a *tu quoque*: you too! What we need to do is deal with it in ourselves first, and having dealt with it in ourselves, remember the Lord's Prayer: "Forgive us our debts, as we also have forgiven our debtors" (Matt. 6:12). As we approach others, we need to remember that we have been forgiven and not get ourselves into a righteous fit.

What we are dealing with fundamentally, in self-deception, is hypocrisy. A lack of integrity is to say one thing and do another. What we are saying is, when we think we know when we do not, and we think we are concerned about truth when we are not, it is staring us in the face. Remember, the original sin is not seeking and not understanding in the face of what is clear about God, as is stated in Romans 1:20. If the basic things about God are not clear, then nothing is clear. If we live consistently with 'nothing is clear,' and we have concern for integrity, we will become nihilists: no meaning, no value, no distinction of any kind. We simply cannot live out nihilism, so we are forced to address it.[8]

God is calling us back. He did not leave us in sin and death. He calls us back first inwardly, through conscience—our very own conscience—and we have to deal with it. We are being called back to repent: to acknowledge that we have done wrong; we are being called to acknowledge it before God and before others, and to do that requires us to humble ourselves. Shame is a kind of humbling. We need to acknowledge that. We should say, 'I am ashamed of myself. I spoke before I thought.' It happens all the time. It happened when I asked someone to bring back my Psalter but it was not actually mine, I spoke hastily. Let us make that an example; let us use that as our favorite example. No one will get righteous indignation about that example. And then if you say, 'Hey, bring back my Psalter,' we know what you mean. But it could happen more seriously than that, too. That was, for me, a slip and a quick recovery, but that could be more serious. Not that that was not serious, to call this person out publicly to 'bring back my Psalter.'

We are also challenged continually to consider our claim that 'I know' by those who believe otherwise. We are making an implicit judgment on those who differ with us, and they are making an implicit judgment on us. The Scripture says, "there are divisions among you, and to some extent I believe it" (1 Cor. 11:18b). One of the reasons for the existence of divisions is "that they which are approved may be made manifest" (1 Cor. 11:19b KJV). Every difference becomes an occasion to say, 'Well, why do I believe this way when the other person

---

8. Gangadean, *Philosophical Foundation*, 3–5, 287–292.

is believing that way?' It is a call to stop and think and go through a process of discussion to see which view is approved and which is not. We are challenged by those who believe otherwise. Let us say one is a theist, and someone else is a naturalist scientist who believes there is no soul, there is no spirit, no afterlife, and there is no God. This is a challenge, both ways. Or, let us say one is an empiricist, believing that all knowledge is through sense experience. Or one is a traditionalist, or one is an intuitionist. One decides to go by common sense pragmatism, and others differ. In each case, we need to deal with the difference. It is an implicit call to say, 'Why do I differ? Do I think I know? Why do I believe this rather than that?' We are being called, and this will get us into the second call back; it will get us to the external voice: "Where are you?" (Gen. 3:9b). We will hold on that for now, since that is the topic of next week's sermon.

THERE ARE MANY FORMS OF SELF-DECEPTION

I would like to list the number which I think holds close to the Scripture. I am going to be listing 10 points. You are probably noticing that in my preaching style, I try to cover a lot of content quickly in a list. If you miss number three, relax, and just keep taking notes as best you can.

Double-Mindedness

First of all, there is double-mindedness. We hold our beliefs more or less consciously and consistently, which means that we have conflicting beliefs within us. Each person has a spiritual war going on within. Remember, "For what I do is not the good I want to do; no, the evil I do not want to do—this I keep on doing" (Rom. 7:19). We want it both ways. We are unstable. We do not want to take up our cross daily and follow Him. We do not affirm the cross, as Jesus said, "Take my yoke upon you and learn from me, for I am gentle and humble in heart, and you will find rest for your souls. For my yoke is easy and my burden is light" (Matt. 11:29–30). The question is: Is this what we want? To learn of the Lord, by taking his yoke upon us? Or are we saying, by maintaining our double-mindedness and resisting that yoke of Christ—in other places referred to as taking up our cross against the self-life—that, 'I really do not want to learn of Christ, rather, I just want to do what occurs to me spontaneously, naturally. I have desires for both things, so I am going to do both.' "For what I do is not the good I want to do; no, the evil I do not want to do—this I keep on doing" (Rom. 7:19). 'And sometimes I do it, and sometimes I don't.' This is a double-minded statement. It means that we are "unstable in all [our] ways" (Jas. 1:8). In all our ways tossed back and forth like the wind of the sea.[9] We ask for wisdom but do not get any if we are double-minded.[10] We have to have an attitude of devotion to get it. We deceive ourselves. How many of us go around and say, 'Hey Bill, I am double-minded, and I love it.' Bill does that, too, because he is covering it up. So double-mindedness—being more or less conscious and consistent—is one form of self-deception. Would you agree? It must be.

Taking God's Name in Vain

We can have sin remaining and fight against it, and that is not quite the same as double-mindedness. We can be more or less conscious and consistent but not double-minded because we are not affirming both. We are resolutely saying no to the self-life and yes to the cross. Even while sin remains in us, by the grace of God, we deal with our self-life daily; we bring it before the Lord in prayer. Another way of speaking of double-mindedness is taking God's name in vain. The Third Commandment: "Thou shalt not take the name the LORD thy God in vain." What do we have to support this? This is where hypocrisy comes from: We say one thing and do another. The Lord says He will "not hold him guiltless that taketh his name in vain" (Ex. 20:7 KJV), and that He will "[visit] the iniquity of the fathers upon the children unto the third and fourth generation" (Ex. 20:5b KJV). Our double-mindedness, our taking God's name in vain, is going to have an effect on our children, our grandchildren, and our great-grandchildren. Instead of going on farther and farther in truth, they will go farther and farther in the error of their ways. If we turn away from clarity and inexcusability, and treat it lightly, what do you think is going to be passed on to our kids? Not clarity and inexcusability. How do we think they will grow up? What do we think is going to happen to that person over 5,

---

9. *Ephesians 4:14.*

10. *James 1:5–8.*

10, 15, 20, 25, 30, 40 years? Our children are going to progress in the same direction that we did. If we turn away from the goal of the earth being filled with the knowledge of God, and do not persist in it, what is going to happen over time? We may outwardly stay with it, and be in a back-and-forth double-mindedness. We deceive ourselves. We sometimes profess things and turn back.

Backsliding

Another term that Scripture uses—and I am trying to stick with scriptural terms as much as possible—is *backsliding*. This is not a term we use much. We place a lot of attention on those coming into the congregation—that they come prepared. We ask others to talk with them and explain this and have them read the Confession, etc., before coming. I think we need to give attention to those who may come and not continue in it, and let it slip. *Backslide* is the term that Scripture uses. We get comfortable in a certain way—comfort and ease—and then we let things slip, and we sink into the pit, imperceptibly, and then we do not know after 10 years what happened. If we do not pay attention to it, we will sink into that pit of woe, because we did not give heed to the Word of God.

Not Coming Into the Light

Another way of expressing this is: not coming into the light, not bringing one's view, or subjecting one's view to critical examination. We should submit ourselves to examination by others, assuming that some of the basics are in place in the others. The Scripture speaks about this in John 3:20. You should know that oversight has a special concern for a person's growth and maturity, and oversight notices those who bring their views and subject them to examination because that is our job: to watch for this. It is not that we are doing any special collection of data; we just notice, we just see it, it just adds up over time, and it becomes pretty clear those who are and those who are not. In the back of our minds, we may say, 'That person is in a dangerous position: not subjecting their views to critical examination and not going through a discussion process.' We begin to groan inside, and we need to do better; we need to be proactive and take steps and bring this to the attention of others. We notice those who do subject their thinking to critical examination.

Lack of Transparency

There is a lack of transparency in our lives. When we cover up, we do not let people know what we have done. We are not saying that we are to broadcast it. One may react against the idea of broadcasting our shortcomings by saying, 'I'm not going to do that.' No, we are not saying there is a need to broadcast our shortcomings, we do not want to get caught in that antinomy. We should let a few who are close to us (including oversight) know what is going on in our lives so that we can be held accountable. Especially those few who are *inclined* to hold us accountable, and if that is not going on, then there is clearly a lack of transparency. Notice, few—by few, I mean about three or four, maybe—who are close to us and at least one from oversight. We know what happens, if one from oversight knows it, then four from oversight know it. So let us count oversight as one, they watch out for you.

Applied to Foundation

Let us apply some of this. How does it apply to foundation? Is there such a thing as foundation? Is it in place in our life? Was it there at one time, but now it is slipping? We should become very familiar and acquainted with foundation and the context of foundation. Let us look at 1 Corinthians 3, where it speaks about foundation in terms of infants, not being mature, and being worldly, as against coming to maturity. Paul speaks about having laid the foundation that others may build upon it.[11] When there are divisions among us, those divisions are a clear mark that the foundation is not in place, or if it was in place at a level of profession, acquaintance, and persuasion, we let it slip. When we ask you the question 'what is the doxological focus,' we do not expect you to go to the Westminster Fellowship Constitution and copy and paste it. All that tells us is that you know where to find it, not whether you studied it. Recently we got a response that was a copy and paste, and I could not believe it. Maybe this person did not understand what they were being asked when we said, 'Please state the doxological focus.'

---

11. *1 Corinthians 3:10.*

When we asked the Logos folks questions over email, we had to say to them explicitly, 'Do not study this before you answer. Do not discuss this with others before you answer. You can think about it for about 24 hours, but answer it by such a time.' We want to see what actual knowledge you have and what is going on. Perhaps at one time, the person could have gotten it, but they have not progressed in it and held onto it and integrated it into their life.

Jesus wants the doctrine to enter into our lives, to get to the level of attitude, where it transforms our attitude. This is why our Lord Jesus taught: "Blessed are the poor in spirit, for theirs is the kingdom of heaven. Blessed are those who mourn, for they will be comforted" (Matt. 5:3–4). *Poor in spirit* and *those who mourn* are getting to attitudes; these are attitudes reflecting an understanding of the doctrine of creation and the Fall. At the end of the Sermon on the Mount, He says that "everyone who hears these words of mine and puts them into practice is like a wise man who built his house on the rock" (Matt. 7:24). He wants to see that we have incorporated this into our lives, to the point where it is the *disposition* of our heart; where our attitude is that of *the poor in spirit*, and of *those who mourn*. This is how we are looking for persons coming to maturity. How does it apply to foundation? Are we saying to ourselves, 'It is in place, or is it not?'

Applied to Distinctives

How does this apply to our distinctives? Is there such a thing as historically cumulative insight, consistent with honoring father and mother and the work of the pastor-teachers (the work of the Holy Spirit through the pastor-teachers) leading us into all truth? It seems to me that some persons just blow by that. When foundation is spoken about, the eyes almost roll into the back of the head, and we miss it. We could be talking to the wall. Is there such a thing as historically cumulative insight in the Christian church? Is it summed up in the Westminster Confession of Faith? Is it there in the doxological focus? Many do not pay attention to historically cumulative insight. If they do, they may not come to the Westminster Confession and if they do come to it, they may not come to the doxological focus.[12] What is going on there? Do

---

12. Gangadean, *The Westminster Confession of Faith*; Gangadean, *The Westminster Catechisms*.

we think we know and we do not know? Do we think we are seeking, but we are not seeking?

Desiring to Teach Without the Foundation in Place

Some desire to teach without having the foundation in place. When for the time you should be teachers, you have need that one teach you the first principles.[13] There is self-deception in this, we do not have the foundation in place, but we want to give advice and teach. Scripture tells us not many should be teachers. I do not like being up here. It is a lot more comfortable to sit in the pew and have someone else do it. It is easy to slip. It is easy to not just slip, but to come short and not even realize it; it is kind of a scary thing. It gives the appearance that I know what I am talking about. By God's grace, we pray and hope that we will not teach error and we will be faithful to the truth. Now, that does not mean that, 'Oh well, I do not desire to teach anybody; I can just relax.' No. It is like saying, 'I do not desire to grow up. I will just relax here in my terrible twos for the rest of my life.' No, we are not permitted to do that, either. We are supposed to grow up and become mature. Two-year-old is cute for a two-year-old, but not cute for a ten-year-old; that is a bit distorted. We need to teach. It says, "though by this time you ought to be teachers, you need someone to teach you the elementary truths of God's word all over again" (Heb. 5:12a). Some desire to teach without the first principles, and some may react by saying, 'I do not desire to teach. Never did, never will, leave me alone.'

Zeal Without Knowledge

There are cases of zeal without knowledge. I have had some terrible times in my life, and this past week, I spent at least twelve hours dealing with a conflict where someone thought they knew and they did not know, and they were making judgments, and it seemed so right. When inquiry occurred, it was not right. They made judgments of others. Again, I am using the scriptural term: zeal without knowledge. I have had contact, through another church (an elder in another church), with those who had been here and are no longer here. I had to bring to the attention of this elder what happened and the zeal that there once

---

13. *Hebrews 5:12–6:1.*

was for "ordination." The discussions we had about 'only Presbyterian ordination is lawful' or 'only apostasy is grounds for beginning a new work.' I had to bring it to the other elders' attention, and those were painful times. Persons who thought they knew but did not. Professing themselves to be wise, they were fools.[14] They could not bring themselves to repent of that. Three parties came up in this discussion from the past. So, this is not a light thing and we need to be careful about zeal without knowledge—Scripture speaks about this.

Membership Vow

Last of all, is the vow. In our vow we say, "In case you should need correction in doctrine or life"—that is, 'just in case'—"do you promise to respect the authority and discipline of the church?"[15] These are the walls and gate built in to protect persons. Jesus is a shepherd; oversight is an undershepherd. Jesus says, "I am the door" (Jn. 10:9). As undershepherds we are like that, we are guarding those who come in and those who go out. Those who go out without respecting the authority and oversight of the church—without submitting their thinking to the process of much discussion—are violating their vow. There would have been a chance to bring out whether they do, in fact, understand what they are claiming or what they would profess, but that did not happen. What happens when one leaves without discussion is that one cuts off discussion with oversight, thereby excommunicating oneself. The church is not excommunicating them; rather, they are excommunicating themselves by leaving without discussion. What the church does is recognize what *is* the case, and what we recognize is that they are in excommunication. One can return, but the point of return is through the elders; it is not through other members. Some have left while still having discussions with this person, that person, and we are friends on Facebook with this person. If we are in Facebook contact with a person who has left in excommunication, we need to change that. By tomorrow, 'defriend' that person because they have excommunicated themselves. Boy, when it gets that specific, we say, 'Whoa!' Yeah, somewhere, the rubber has to meet the road. I think you know

---

14. *Romans 1:22b.*

15. Gangadean, *The Westminster Catechisms*, 355–356.

what I mean. And if you have any questions, please do ask me, I will be in the conference room ten minutes after the service ends.

Hating the Light

Jesus said in John 3:20 that those who are in unbelief hate the light. Again, this is a scriptural expression. He also says, "They kill the prophets" (Matt. 23). You know, they do not kill priests. Priests are nice guys. Priests are like Aaron. Prophets are like Moses. Aaron built for the people the golden calf and said, "These are your gods, O Israel, who brought you up out of Egypt" (Ex. 32:4). Moses came down and broke the tablets. Who likes a prophet? This is why they kill the prophets, right? They confront you with the truth. Nathan the seer said to David, you are the man who has done what you just affirmed in your judgment.[16]

This has been happening for a long, long time. It goes back to the beginning when Cain killed Abel. Abel's actions, just by way of contrast, exposed what was lacking in Cain. God had already not responded to Cain's offering, and Cain did not like it, so he killed Abel. This is how deep this cover-up goes. We do not want it to be exposed. The Athenians killed Socrates. It does not have to be especially Christian. As a philosopher dealing with basic questions, he exposed the ignorance of those in leadership: the artists, the businessmen, and the politicians. Oh, he was really asking for it, wasn't he? So they came against him, and they managed to play on the prejudice against him and get him killed. Do you know why he was killed? The two charges against him were that he was corrupting the youth of Phoenix—I mean Athens. He was corrupting them concerning not believing in the gods of the city: popular religion.[17] The philosopher questioned popular religion, particularly with the youth, and they nailed him on that. Is that new? It is not particularly biblical, but there is a certain amount of light in the process of doing philosophy (or there can be), and Socrates started that process, and they killed him.

The religious establishment was apostate and in hypocrisy, and they killed Jesus. This is true of any religious establishment that drifts away from the Word of God in its understanding of good and evil. Should

---

16. *2 Samuel 12.*

17. Gangadean, "Paper No. 89: History of Religion," in *The Logos Papers*, 467–471.

we challenge the established church and its view of the good as heaven rather than the good as the knowledge of God filling the earth? We will receive that kind of hostility and animosity. Exposed—'We claim we know, we think we know, we do not; we do not want our ignorance exposed; we cover it up. I am okay.' We do not have the shame to say, 'I really don't know,' and to humble ourselves in repentance. Repentance is necessary. This is a call to repentance. It is a call back, which is a call to repentance, and without repentance, *the problem will never go away*. The problem cannot go away until you individually, personally, repent of this sin. We see it going through the years. It could be at 12 years old. It could manifest itself at 22, 30, 42, 55, 60, 70. The problem never goes away. The call to repentance is there; it is about thinking we know when we do not know, and when we should know.

The main work of the oversight is to protect the church in order for the church to do its work and prepare for discipleship. Much of what oversight has to do is deal with the problem of self-deception and self-justification. It started with the sin of not seeking and not understanding. If we begin by acknowledging the curse of God as the third and final call back—which assumes the first and second were not responded to—if we begin with that in place, that the original creation is good, and the curse is in the world now, our hearts will be disposed to say, 'The heart is deceitful above all else and desperately wicked, who can know it?'[18] I need this call back, I am under the curse.' All human beings are under the curse, to restrain those who are non-believers, to recall, to come into belief, and to remove the sin remaining in believers. Job was the most righteous, but he still had the curse. We have to ask ourselves, 'Is this a truth of Scripture?' If it is the truth of Scripture, to this then we say, truly, amen.

---

18. *Jeremiah 17:9.*

15

THE SECOND CALL BACK:
SELF-EXAMINATION
Where Are You?

Genesis 3:8–13

⁸Then the man and his wife heard the sound of the Lᴏʀᴅ God as he was walking in the garden in the cool of the day, and they hid from the Lᴏʀᴅ God among the trees of the garden. ⁹But the Lᴏʀᴅ God called to the man, "Where are you?" ¹⁰He answered, "I heard you in the garden, and I was afraid because I was naked; so I hid." ¹¹And he said, "Who told you that you were naked? Have you eaten from the tree that I commanded you not to eat from?" ¹²The man said, "The woman you put here with me—she gave me some fruit from the tree, and I ate it." ¹³Then the Lᴏʀᴅ God said to the woman, "What is this you have done?" The woman said, "The serpent deceived me, and I ate."

W E NOW COME TO PART TWO OF THE teaching on redemption in the biblical worldview, as it is found in Genesis 1–3. Last time, we saw that upon eating the tree of the knowledge of good and evil, in disobedience to the command of God, the man and his wife felt shame. Shame came connected with their nakedness, and they sewed fig leaves and covered their nakedness. We saw shame as a call to repentance, and it was avoided by sewing these leaves and covering it, but that avoidance involved self-deception. We can cover our nakedness, but we cannot cover the covering; it is there hanging before us, and in our memory—the past and the present—it cannot be covered.

God does not leave man in sin and death. God comes to man and calls man to repentance, and He does so a second time. It is important to notice this progression. It is important to notice that the call to repentance is a part of redemption; both in the manner in which it occurs and the manner in which it continues to occur. Shame continues to be a call back, and when that does not work, or when that is not heeded, God brings the second call back to repentance. It comes differently than the first call. The first call was *inner*. God was not anywhere manifestly present to Adam and Eve upon their eating. It was entirely inward. It was something within themselves, not involving another directly or indirectly. We make a distinction between the *inner* call of conscience and the *outer* call. The outer call begins simply by, first of all, the presence of God.

"The man and his wife heard the sound of the LORD God as he was walking in the garden in the cool of the day" (v. 8a). God's presence was manifest in some way; they heard the sound. We need to take into account that, being a spirit, God has no body; there is the possibility of this being some form of *theophany*, which is a visible manifestation of the invisible God; we are not ruling that out. But whatever it was, something was manifest and they heard the sound of the Lord God as He was *walking* in the Garden in the cool of the day. Their response to this presence of God, the one who had given them the command not to eat of the tree of the knowledge of good and evil—was that they hid, and they hid because they were afraid. We may cover up with respect to our nakedness and try to smooth it over, and cover it up with respect to each other (in ourselves and in the other person), yet when there is any reminder and exposure of it, we become aware of our inadequacy. They heard the Lord, just by His presence, and they were afraid, and they responded in fear to God's presence. What that may mean is they felt, implicitly, that they needed to explain, or give an account of what they did, that they had disobeyed.

To avoid this further, **"they hid from the LORD God among the trees of the garden"** (v. 8b), and this reveals something more about their view of God. Their view of God was already shown to be deficient, their knowledge of God was not what it should be. They should have been seeking it as the first and most important matter of life. They had not progressed in their knowledge of God, they had not held on to what they had, and they likened God to themselves in believing "you will be like God, knowing good and evil" (Gen. 3:5b). They ought to have seen that God knows good and evil not by discovering it, but by *determining* it. He determines it by determining the nature of things by creation and human beings have no capacity to do that. Good and evil is connected with the nature of the thing, and the nature of the thing is something created by God. If we try to deny that, we are denying the truth that was manifest in naming the creatures. When we name the creature, we are recognizing the nature of the thing, what is appropriate for that thing, and what is contrary to its nature is evil for it, harmful for it.

They had lost sight of this knowledge of God. They had the revelation there before them. It was clear, they had not been seeking, they had not been paying attention and they had been neglecting. They were taking the name of God in vain, and they lapsed into idolatry. Idolatry is grounded in any misconception of the nature of God.[1] It later becomes manifest in visible representation or misrepresentation, but any distortion or misrepresentation of God begins in the mind. We see then, in this first sin, the Commandments were being broken. First, the First Commandment: putting yourself in the place of God to determine good and evil.[2] In misrepresenting God as like man—distorting the distinction between the infinite God and the finite creature—they were violating the Second Commandment. The Third Commandment is violated by not paying attention and taking God's name in vain. These commands are broken. Hiding from God is a natural response, and we need to recognize that the human condition is one of *hiding from God*; left to ourselves, we hide from God. The focus for the week is on John 3:20, which says, "Everyone who does evil hates the light, and will not come into the light for fear that his deeds will be exposed." They are hiding, not wanting their deeds to be exposed. Notice what is implicit: not only is it a judgment of their conscience, but implicitly in the very presence of God is the idea of judgment, and fear connected with that. It is not possible to hide from God, is it? It is not possible to hide from the omniscient Creator of heaven and earth; it is ridiculous, and yet this is what is happening. There is no thought this Lord God is the Creator of heaven and earth, who knows all things; we have to

---

1. Gangadean, *Philosophical Foundation*, 185–198.

2. *Exodus 20:3*.

infer that this thought escaped their minds, so they are hiding. The outward act reveals something about the condition of their hearts and the foolishness of their thoughts. But the Lord God called to the man, **"Where are you?"** (v. 9b). Again, we are to understand that it is not that the omniscient God does not know where they are; that would be a foolish interpretation. We may interpret this as though God were like us, saying **"Where are you?"**, but we have already crossed a forbidden line in saying that God is like us in being finite in knowledge. When God says, **"Where are you?"**, He is not asking for information because of some lack of knowledge on His part. He knows exactly where they are. He knows us from before the creation of the world; He certainly knows it now. He knows the exact spot: 'behind the oleander bush, right over there.'

THE DEMAND FOR AN ACCOUNT: WHERE ARE YOU?

Can we picture that in our mind? Can we picture our first parents hiding behind the bushes back there? And it could just as well be an oleander. That must have been a strange sight: our first parents hiding from the Lord. This is what sin does, and we have to say today that human beings hide from God, and it is just as strange a sight. When God calls to man, **"Where are you?"**, it is an external question coming from another person, and it should be understood as a call to self-examination. With that, an explanation is needed of why we are there. We should understand that this question—'Where are you?'—comes to us now. It comes to us through the mere presence of others: their very presence, their very lives, their very differences from us, helps us to become more conscious of where we are. We become conscious that we are here, we are not there; you are there, and I am here. And the question naturally arises, 'Why?' A great deal rests on that question, 'Why?'

Adam does not reply, 'I'm here.' He rather goes to the explanation at one level: **"I heard you in the garden, and I was afraid because I was naked; so I hid"** (v. 10). This is not saying, 'I'm here. Here, Lord. I am right here.' Adam gives an explanation in terms of his immediate consciousness; it does not go far enough. So the Lord asks him (notice how the dialogue is very tightly, naturally connected), **"Who told you that you were naked?"** He asks the question that they knew they would have to face at some point or other: **"Have you eaten from the** tree that I commanded you not to eat from?" (v. 11). At this point, the Lord is asking for an explanation of why they were in fear, in connection with their nakedness and hiding. He is asking for an explanation, a justification; they are to examine themselves and explain why it is that they are where they are. What comes out of the man now is such an accounting. The presence of God, and the presence of others, is an implicit demand for an explanation, an accounting. The words are synonymous. Where are you? Why are you there, rather than here? Why do you believe that rather than this? Why are you conducting yourself in this way, rather than this alternative way?

Remember the case of Cain and Abel. Abel did not have to say anything; what he did, and what God did in relation to Cain and Abel, made a difference, and Cain did not like that. He is called back, he did not hear, and so he wanted to eliminate what exposed him. It was the deeds of Abel that exposed him; it was being in the presence of another, an alternative—someone who was doing what was right. "If you do what is right, will you not be accepted?" (Gen. 4:7a). In the very presence of another, the act is exposed, and then we have to justify the act. What Cain did in anger was to kill Abel and deepen the problem. Here is the presence of another that requires an explanation: 'Why am I doing this, rather than this?', requires an explanation, an account, a justification. It also tells us something from the very beginning of Scripture here, to the end of the Old Testament, to the very end of the New Testament: When God appears, who can stand? Who can stand when He appears? His very appearance requires there to be an accounting: "Have you eaten from the tree?" (v. 11). The man responded to, 'Why have you eaten?' He responds, essentially, to excuse himself from any blame—from being blameworthy—and he does so by not merely excusing himself, but by accusing another, laying the blame on another. There are two parts to this: excusing yourself and putting the blame on another. He claims an implicit innocence, and that he is a victim; he claims victim status. "The man said, 'The woman you put here with me—she gave me some fruit from the tree, and I ate it'" (v. 12). This is the best he could do; it was not good at all, but it does reveal the condition of his heart, and it shows the requirement of an explanation that is imposed and how he responds. The woman did the same when God asked her, "'What is this you have done?' The woman said, 'The serpent deceived me, and I ate'" (v. 13). This looks like an explanation, but we still have to give an account for this deceiving in light of other things.

WE MUST GIVE AN ACCOUNT OF WHERE WE ARE

At the beginning of human history, after the Fall, we have this question, and this attempt to excuse oneself, and that stands over and against the doctrine of inexcusability. They are excusing themselves, whereas the Scripture teaches inexcusability: inexcusability in the face of clarity. We have to ask ourselves, 'How do *we* respond to that?' We might say, 'Well, I have not been taught this,' or 'I was taught wrongly.' Either someone did not teach me this, or they taught me wrongly; my tradition, my upbringing, my parents. This raises the question, 'Am I responsible for knowing? Am I responsible for knowing what I believe? For having a reason for what I believe? Am I responsible when I make a judgment?' She did judge, and the man did judge; they did make a judgment before they ate. People will say, 'How am I supposed to know? I could not help it. Was there a choice?' Yes, there was a choice. I think it is self-evident that it was an act, that no one forced them to act, and that was thinking going on before the act. The question then, is: Am I responsible for what I believe? Am I responsible for my choice, my way of life, for not seeking? Is it really clear? Do I have to justify what I believe? Do I have to justify my choice? Am I responsible for thinking about it? Are there consequences to my choice? When I choose, do I also have responsibility for the consequences? The Lord had said, "[In the day] you eat of it you will surely die" (Gen. 2:17b). Do I now want to say, 'Well, it was not a choice,' or 'It was a choice, but I chose this, not the consequences?' Remember, man is made in the image of God with a capacity to know and to seek.

The doctrine of inexcusability is here from the beginning, and it is here in this account when the man and the woman attempt to excuse themselves when there is no way in which they can do so. Suppose you say that it is not clear, and that nothing is clear. Can I get away with that? It would not be consistent with your actions. If nothing is clear, and you are consistent with that, there would be no meaning. We cannot say, 'It is desirable because it will make me wise.' We could not even speak about wisdom if nothing is clear. There are things that we are assuming, and we are responsible for that. We might say, 'Well, what is God going to do?' It is not so much what God is going to do as what will happen in connection with our sin. God said, "for when you eat of it you will surely die" (Gen. 2:17b). Death comes in terms of meaninglessness, boredom, and guilt. Suppose we want to say, 'Well, that is not so bad,' or 'Why should that be?' Do you need meaning? Are we all of a sudden looking for meaning but we were not then? If we did not care for meaning, and we are in this state now (meaninglessness), why are we objecting? In any case, at any point, if we want meaning, we should seek and understand, because things are clear. Whichever way we cut it, we cannot excuse it. What is the inherent consequence of not seeking? It is not understanding: not understanding the meaning of things. The inherent consequence of sin is meaninglessness; less and less meaning continually, into the bottomless pit.

We must give an account; that is, we must give rational justification of where we are. Why we are here versus there. Why this rather than that? Why do we believe in God versus not believe in God? Or vice versa, why we do not believe in God versus believing in God. We must give a rational justification for that. Why we are Christian, or why we are not Christian. Why we are Christian, or why we are Muslim, or Jewish in terms of historical Judaism. Or why we believe in God the Creator rather than all is one, or *all is dukkha*.[3] Or why we are Taoist or shamanist. We must give a rational justification of why we are here rather than there. Where are you and why? Why we are Catholic, or why we are Protestant. Why we are Baptist, or why we are not Baptist. Why we are Pentecostal, or why we are Historic Christian. Why are we here rather than there? Where are you? We are *called to give an account*. The differences are obvious. We are not living in a vacuum. In time and in space: before they had not eaten, now they have eaten. There is a difference. Why? Why is that difference there, in time and space? 'I am here rather than there,' with Abel. 'I am here, in the line of Cain, rather than in the line of Seth.' Where are you, and why? Is it a choice? It most certainly is. The differences are obvious, and there are others who live in this world, and we are aware of them. Please do not come up with the example that one may be brought up in a tank

---

3. *All is dukkha* is the first of the Four Noble Truths in Buddhism. It means that all is suffering, or, all is impermanent. See: Gangadean, *Philosophical Foundation*, 115–117; Gangadean, *History of Philosophy*, 107–108.

with total sense deprivation, and 'how am I held responsible for that?' We will put that in a special basket and call that a *special basket case.*[4]

There are differences "that they which are approved may be made manifest" (1 Cor. 11:19 KJV). We cannot appeal to our tradition or background to excuse ourselves. That is why we said, 'There is this kid from Ubangy Bangy. He was uneducated, and he was abused, and yet he could see that the sun would burn out.' You cannot tell me you could not know this because of your background. He could see there must be something eternal. Because when we are five or six years old, we ask: 'Where do things come from?' And we also ask the question, 'Who made God?' Thinking a little bit more, we come to the question, 'Is everything made? Did everything come into being?' We may say, 'Oh, no, I did not think about that; therefore it is not natural to think about that.' Others have thought of these things, and so they will rise up in the judgment[5] and say why they thought about it, and we will have to answer why we did not. That would be interesting, wouldn't it?

If I do not give a rational justification—over and against tradition or intuition or "science"—then what I am doing is engaging in self-justification. Those two are contrasted. It is one thing to justify my view by using an argument (rational justification) to "give the reason for the hope that you have",[6] as against justifying myself and my actions as Adam was attempting to do. We could look at an argument aimed at a belief (out of which an action came) rather than simply trying to justify the action and not the belief (for which we are responsible).

In all of these cases—God versus no God, Christian versus non-Christian—we are dealing with our distorted view of God and having to justify that. How can we justify idolatry? How can we justify distortions

---

4. In classroom discussions, this expression is employed to address exceptions only after establishing and mutually agreeing upon the principles. The approach involves considering exceptions in the context of the established rules. Presuppositional thinking emphasizes the need to first establish the foundational principles before delving into discussions about specific applications or exceptions. Addressing these exceptions occurs once the appropriate context and presuppositions have been thoroughly established.

5. *Matthew 12:42*: "The Queen of the South will rise at the judgment with this generation and condemn it; for she came from the ends of the earth to listen to Solomon's wisdom, and now one greater than Solomon is here." *Luke 11:32*: "The men of Nineveh will stand up at the judgment with this generation and condemn it; for they repented at the preaching of Jonah, and now one greater than Jonah is here."

6. *1 Peter 3:15*.

about God? How can we justify the position that God is not both just and merciful at the same time, infinitely, and that God's mercy sets aside his justice?[7] How do we justify that? By denying that God is just? By denying that He is merciful? We cannot justify that.

AM I OBLIGATED TO JUSTIFY MY VIEW OF GOD VS. EVERY OBJECTION?

We have to be thoughtful if we are to justify our views over and against other views. We have to ask ourselves a question: 'Am I obligated to justify my view versus every objection that comes along, every objector? Am I obligated to justify my view versus major alternatives or alternatives in general?' I am not obligated to justify my view versus every objection and objector. Not without common ground.[8] If someone objects at point A, when four or five more basic points are not in place, I am not responsible for responding to this point without these others in place. I wonder if this person is accepting, first of all, that some things are clear, and that the opposite is nothing is clear—nihilism— and if they are willing to live with that. If they are not willing to deal with that, why should I engage them in conversation? If they are not going to be consistent, why should I engage with them? In that case, I am not obligated to justify my view. I am willing to justify my view to anyone who accepts the conditions of justification. The Scripture says to avoid foolish and stupid arguments, "Don't have anything to do with foolish and stupid arguments, because you know they produce quarrels" (2 Tim. 2:23). We have to watch for those who are quarrelsome: those who will keep coming up with some objection or other, without the foundation in place. We have to be careful about those who strain at gnats and swallow camels:[9] those who go after the less basic and the possibilities thereof. Who knows what might come tomorrow,

---

7. Gangadean, *Philosophical Foundation*, 191–192; Gangadean, *The Westminster Confession*, 21–27, 37–41, 67–69, 129–130, 236–238; Gangadean, "Paper No. 91: Christianity and Islam," in *The Logos Papers*, 479–484.

8. Gangadean, "Paper No. 2: Common Ground," 9–13; "Paper No. 50: Common Ground (Part I)," 275–276; "Paper No. 51: Common Ground (Part II)," 277–279; "Paper No. 52: Common Ground (Part III)," 281–282; "Paper No. 53: Common Ground (Part IV)," in *The Logos Papers*, 283–286.

9. *Matthew 23:24.*

without having the more basic in place. I am also not obligated to respond to those who use informal fallacies like slander and strawman and begging the question and quibbles about words. 2 Timothy 2:14 says, "Warn them before God against quarreling about words; it is of no value, and only ruins those who listen." People use the word *living* in a new way: that atoms are alive. If this is a new definition, then we do not want to get involved with those kinds of quibbles. Am I obligated to respond to those who slander? Particularly, am I obligated to respond to anonymous slanderers on the internet? No. How about those who attempt to shift the burden of proof and will the burden of proof on me? If one does not believe some things are clear, and one is unwilling to share in the burden of proof, then do not come thinking you can just dump it on me. I am still responsible, even if someone has not raised an objection, to justify my view. With regard to other positions—even if some persons have not raised them to me—I should consider them. But when someone raises an objection and puts me in a position to respond, they have some obligations, too.

I am not obligated to engage with someone who lacks integrity, but rather to expose it. When they came to Jesus about John's baptism and said, "Tell us by what authority you are doing these things," and said, "Who gave you this authority?"(Lk. 20:2), Jesus exposed their hypocrisy: "I will also ask you a question. Tell me, John's baptism—was it from heaven, or from men?" (Lk. 20:3–4). He exposed their unwillingness to engage with the question and so He said He was not going to answer their question. We do have an obligation to expose their hypocrisy, their lack of integrity. Scripture speaks about those who come in cunning craftiness and sleight of hand.[10] We are obligated to take thoughts captive, so they do not cause the young to stumble. We should see cunning and craftiness and hypocrisy.

I am not obligated to search the latest philosophy journals for a new argument where a new subtlety might come in and wake up every morning wondering whether some new argument by whoever the latest hot shot on the scene might be, to see whether he might have overthrown belief in God. It does not work that way. It does not work in generalities and possibilities, but it works by beginning with the more basic and the certainties of the more basic. I am not obligated to respond to

10. *Ephesians 4:14.*

the anonymous, as against someone in my presence who would identify themselves and raise questions specifically versus in general terms.

I am not obligated to speak about certain truths to persons who are not ready to receive them. I am not obligated to cast precious truths of the gospel to those who will trample them under foot.[11] If they are not willing to accept that there must be something eternal, why should I go further?[12] If they are not willing to apply that to matter, and whether the material universe is eternal,[13] then why should I go further? The Scripture says, "The heavens declare the glory of God; the skies proclaim the work of his hands. Day after day they pour forth speech; night after night they display knowledge. There is no speech or language where their voice is not heard. Their voice goes out into all the earth, their words to the ends of the world" (Ps. 19:1–4). If they are not going to respond to that—the starry heavens above and the moral law within—then why should I go further? Moreover, I want to remind you, warn you, exhort you, particularly those who are involved in taking graduate or undergraduate classes in philosophy: Beware of vain philosophy after the *stoicheia*—after the rudiments of this world—and not after Christ. There is a foundational belief system in Christ; if that is not in place, do not be drawn off where you will get into foolish and stupid arguments. Do not let the praise of this world dazzle you as if this is prestigious and must be taken seriously. Hold your ground to what is more basic. And you know what? If some more basic things are not in place, or the basic things are not clear, then there is no ground to hold, so there is no point in getting into any argument. The Scripture says to avoid foolish arguments.[14] Actually, it says to avoid foolish and stupid arguments. Any argument without common ground in place becomes stupid.

Having said that, I should submit my view to examination; I should come into the light. We are talking about curriculum in Logos and noticing other curriculums. We should submit our view to the light, and others should submit their view to the light and see it, and we should

---

11. *Matthew 7:6.*

12. Gangadean, *Philosophical Foundation*, 61–65; Gangadean, *History of Philosophy*, 40–44.

13. Gangadean, Philosophical Foundation, 71–100; Gangadean, History of Philosophy, 81–85; Gangadean, "Paper No. 90: Christianity and Secular Humanism," in *The Logos Papers*, 473–477.

14. *Titus 3:9; 2 Timothy 2:23.*

see it in terms of the basics, in terms of the goal, the fruit, and man's chief end. Man's chief end is to glorify God and enjoy Him forever.[15] How does this curriculum measure up against that point? Do not dismiss this lightly. This is foundational, and it permeates and penetrates everything. I should submit my view to examination. I should come into the light, rather than hide from it.

JESUS EXPOSES SELF-JUSTIFICATION:
Responding to Objections and Questions

Jesus exposes our self-justification by responding to objections and questions. Notice, He does not always answer the question. He *exposes* our self-justification. There are about seven points I will quickly run through here.

Taxes to Caesar: should we pay taxes, or not? He exposes hypocrisy. They were using the coins with Caesar's image on them, they were implicitly acknowledging his rule, they wanted to catch Him in either saying do not pay taxes, in which case, they accuse Him to Caesar, or in saying to pay taxes, in which case He is a traitor to the nation by acknowledging the legitimacy of Caesar. They were using the coins, so He says, "Whose portrait is this?" (Matt. 22:20). It is Caesar's. "Give to Caesar what is Caesar's, and to God what is God's" (Matt. 22:21b). This should have been obvious to them.

1. The woman taken in adultery. "If any one of you is without sin, let him be the first to throw a stone at her " (Jn. 8:7). You want to apply Moses' law? Let's do that, let's begin with the beginning. They all left.

2. "By Beelzebub, the prince of demons, he is driving out demons" (Lk. 11:15). We should particularly pay attention to this; go back and read it, make a note of it, and read it this afternoon, Matthew 12:23–37. I can identify about eight steps in Jesus' answer, and they get deeper and deeper and deeper. It is in this context that Jesus said, "You brood of vipers." When we get to the "brood of vipers," we know we are near the bottom of the judgment. He says that "every sin and blasphemy will be forgiven men, but the blasphemy against

---

15. *SCQ. 1.*

the Spirit will not be forgiven" (Matt. 12:31). What He used was the law of non-contradiction: "If Satan drives out Satan, he is divided against himself. How then can his kingdom stand?" (Matt. 12:26). "And if I drive out demons by Beelzebub, by whom do your people drive them out? So then, they will be your judges" (Matt. 12:27). They will be your judges in the judgment; they knew, and you should have known. "He who is not with me is against me, and he who does not gather with me scatters" (Matt. 12:30). "You brood of vipers" (Matt. 12:34a). "Make a tree good and its fruit will be good, or make a tree bad and its fruit will be bad, for a tree is recognized by its fruit" (Matt. 12:33). What you are is a brood of vipers, the poison of the asp is under your tongue. He says, "For by your words you will be acquitted, and by your words you will be condemned" (Matt. 12:37). "Every careless word" (Matt. 12:36). We must give an account for every careless word, and we will do it before the judgment seat of the Word of God, the judgment seat of Christ; because God has committed all judgment to Him, that all men may honor the Son as they honor the Father.[16]

3. "And at the resurrection, whose wife will she be?" (Matt. 22:28a). He responds, "You are in error because you do not know the Scriptures or the power of God. At the resurrection people will neither marry nor be given in marriage" (Matt. 22:29–30a). This was the equivalent for them of what the Gettier example is for graduate students in epistemology.[17] How do you define knowledge? Is justified true belief necessary and sufficient?[18] That was the one that they honed for decades and threw it on, but Jesus just demolished it.

4. "Who is my neighbor?" (Lk. 10:29b). The good Samaritan.

5. Is it lawful to do this, that, and the other on the Sabbath? Picking grain or healing? Jesus answered that.

---

16. *John 5:22–23*.

17. The Gettier problem originated in a paper by Edmund Gettier in 1963. "Is Justified True Belief Knowledge?" Edmund L. Gettier, *Analysis*, Volume 23, Issue 6, June 1963, Pages 121–123, https://doi.org/10.1093/analys/23.6.121.

18. For a response to Gettier's challenge to the classical definition of knowledge: Gangadean, *Philosophical Foundation*, 49–50; Gangadean, *History of Philosophy*, 177–179; Gangadean, "Paper No. 72: What is Knowledge? (Concise Version)," 381–383; "Paper No. 73: What is Knowledge? (Expanded Version)," in *The Logos Papers*, 385–390.

6. "By what authority are you doing these things?" (Mark 11:28a). He answers by asking about John's baptism. He answers their questions and exposes their self-justification. They were not really interested in the truth, and He exposed that. They had issues of their own.

7. And then Jesus puts a question to them. Fair enough. You have come at me with seven; now I have got one for you. One for seven is not a bad ratio, right? He says, "What do you think about the Christ? Whose son is he?" (Matt. 22:42a). Did Jesus go for the jugular in that? It is because they are going to condemn Him for saying He is the Son of God. Whose son is Christ? How then did David, in the Spirit, call Him Lord, if He is His Son? He is the Son of Man, the Son of David, and He is the Son of God. Jesus said, "wisdom is proved right by her actions" (Matt. 11:19b). Elsewhere He said, "Ye shall know them by their fruits" (Matt. 7:16a KJV).

WE MUST HAVE JUSTIFICATION:
We Must Give an Account

All of this points to this one truth: we must have justification. It was required of Adam by the very presence of God. It was true then, and it is true in Malachi 3:2, "Who can stand when he appears?" We must all stand before the judgment seat of Christ. We must give an account, and none of us can stand. All of us will be condemned. But for those who are in Christ Jesus, the question is raised: "Who is he that condemns? Christ Jesus, who died—more than that, who was raised to life—is at the right hand of God and is also interceding for us." (Rom. 8:34) It is God who justifies. We have no justification for what we have done. All we have is self-justification, which is like rotten menstrual rags.[19] God is the one who justifies. This is how much we need justification. So the answer to the question, 'Who is he that condemns?' It is God who justifies through Christ.

This has been the deepest longing of the people of God at all times. When Job was being put through it, he came to this point when he said, "I know that my Redeemer lives, and that in the end he will stand upon the earth. And after my skin has been destroyed, yet in my flesh

---

19. *Isaiah 64:6.*

I will see God; I myself will see him with my own eyes—I, and not another. How my heart yearns within me!" (Job 19:25–27). Job had a vision of his Redeemer, standing on the earth, and he had a vision of his resurrection. Because he said, "And after my skin has been destroyed, yet in my flesh will I see God" (Job 19:26). Therefore, behold the Lamb of God, who takes away the sin of the world.[20] Our sin is laid upon Jesus Christ, and Jesus' righteousness is given to those who put their faith in Him. We stand before God, not by self-justification, but in the justification that we have in Jesus Christ. Adam and Eve covered themselves. They knew they needed a covering, but that covering was worthless: the works of their own hands. Rather, they were covered by God, with the skin of the animal; it was slain by God, signifying none other than Jesus, who is the Lamb of God: smitten of God and afflicted, crushed for our iniquities, by whose stripes we are healed.[21] We are covered by the righteousness of our Lord Jesus Christ. Blessed be the name of the Lord.

---

20. *John 1:29.*

21. *Isaiah 53:4–5.*

16

THE THIRD CALL BACK:
CURSE AND PROMISE
Origin, Form, Purpose, Presence, and Response

Genesis 3:14–20

¹⁴So the LORD God said to the serpent, "Because you have done this, "Cursed are you above all the livestock and all the wild animals! You will crawl on your belly and you will eat dust all the days of your life. ¹⁵And I will put enmity between you and the woman, and between your offspring and hers; he will crush your head, and you will strike his heel." ¹⁶To the woman he said, "I will greatly increase your pains in childbearing; with pain you will give birth to children. Your desire will be for your husband, and he will rule over you." ¹⁷To Adam he said, "Because you listened to your wife and ate from the tree about which I commanded you, 'You must not eat of it,' "Cursed is the ground because of you; through painful toil you will eat of it all the days of your life. ¹⁸It will produce thorns and thistles for you, and you will eat the plants of the field. ¹⁹By the sweat of your brow you will eat your food until you return to the ground, since from it you were taken; for dust you are and to dust you will return." ²⁰Adam named his wife Eve, because she would become the mother of all the living.

ORIGIN OF THE CURSE (CONTEXT)

WE COME NOW IN OUR SEQUENCE in preaching to the third call back: that of the curse and the promise. Let us think about the origin of the curse in terms of the context. We speak of this as the third call back. First of all, it is a call to repentance, so it assumes sin. We have gone over this reality of sin in the Garden of Eden; it is the failure to seek God and to pursue the knowledge of God, failure to understand good and evil, and failure to do what is right. It is disobeying by eating of the tree of the knowledge of good and evil; putting ourselves in the place of God to determine good and evil, rather than understanding good and evil as something determined by God—by the act of creation—creating each thing after its kind. We should understand that good for a being is according to the nature of that being (the kind that it is) and act accordingly. In the work of dominion, we are to develop the powers latent in the creation to show forth the glory of God.

Sin is an act contrary to our nature as rational beings; it is a failure to seek and understand; it is to neglect, avoid, resist, and deny reason in the face of what is clear. It is unbelief: failure to believe what is true about God; believing that you can be like God knowing good and evil. It is the failure to see that God is the infinite Creator and we are finite creatures. It is disobedience, expressed in the eating of the tree, and all of that is summed up in autonomy: putting ourselves in the place of God. Autonomy is self-centered existence; this is what we have been called to repent of. We may confuse sin with simply the expression of it, which is called fruit sin, and not deal with the root; here, we are called to repent of root and fruit.

This is the third call back and presupposes the first and the second. The first had to do with shame, the cover-up, and the self-deception that occurred in that cover-up. The second had to do with the question, "Where are you?" (Gen. 3:9b). Through another calling us to examine ourselves—to give an account for what we believe and to justify it—we end up in self-justification and justifying ourselves by blaming others. Remember, the reality of shame is subjective, and guilt is objective— before another. Shame is within ourselves, and guilt is the objective reality of having done what is wrong before God.

God does not leave us in that state. We see how increasingly desperate is becoming the whole reality of not seeking and understanding God in the face of what is clear about God, the self-deception about our seeking and the self-justification, to the point of blaming God. This is a rejection of the Word of God, and it will manifest itself ultimately in the rejection of the Word of God incarnate, in crucifying the Son of God. This is where the self-justification is leading. We should not minimize, undermine, and think it is other than this. It was manifest in Cain killing Abel. It was manifested throughout history in so many ways.

We are in a desperate condition, and God does not leave us in that condition, but with the first call back (inward) and the second (outward) having failed, what else remains? How else can man be called back? Not by the repetition of the first or the second, but by a third, which is in the circumstance affecting his very being. This third call back is the *final* call back; there is no fourth call back. It is the third coming after the first and second, and this must be remembered, and it is a final call back. Existentially, this is the call we have to face continually. Having avoided and resisted the first two, we have only this remaining. This is the point at which the call back is occurring for us as human beings, including believer and non-believer, insofar as sin remains. There is no second chance after this call back; when this call back ends—and it ends with death—there is no possibility to say, 'Maybe there will be a second chance for another call back.' No, it is the third and the final call back.

THE FORM

The form that this call back takes is described for us in the passage from which we read. It comes in three expressions: first, to the serpent, then to the woman, and then to the man.

On the Serpent

"So the LORD God said to the serpent, 'Because you have done this, Cursed are you above all the livestock and all the wild animals! You will crawl on your belly and you will eat dust all the days of your life'" (v. 14). This is the curse; the word is explicitly used; we cannot miss it for that reason. It is on the serpent, but not only on the serpent; it is on all the livestock and all the wild animals and all the animal life. It is from this that we begin to get the distinction between those that are more cursed and those that are less cursed, and in light of this, a reminder of the distinction between *clean* and *unclean*, as this develops in Scripture.

This curse now has an effect. The effect is that it changes the very form of the creature and the food of the creature, as seen in this expression, **"You will crawl on your belly."** The implication is that this was not the manner in which the serpent moved; it affects the form of the creature: **"and you will eat dust all the days of your life"** (v. 14b). This is connected with the very crawling on the belly that is closest to the dirt, **"and you will eat dust."** Remember, it is on the serpent and the tempter that is using the serpent; so we have to see a double application—a double intended meaning—as it applies to the serpent, and as it applies to the tempter in the serpent.

All of the animals have been affected by the curse—some more, some less—and we believe the beginning of the change in the animals goes back to this. The animals are not now, today, as they were in the beginning. Animals did not devour each other for food; the very structure of their being was affected: their teeth and jaws are now structured for devouring each other for food and this goes back to this Edenic curse.

One may say, 'Why did God curse the animals? What did they do? They are innocent.' One may also ask, 'Why did God curse the ground?' It is in relationship to man. Man is called to rule over these creatures and develop the powers in the creation. It is to be understood in relationship to man. Man is going to rule over the animals and the ground, and this is like his city being bombed: 'What did the city do?' The city did not do anything, but man used that to further his sinful purposes, and it was affected by the curse.

The promise comes here, likewise. Just as the curse comes, so comes the promise. It says, **"I will put enmity between you and the woman"**: that is, between the serpent (the tempter) and the woman. How is this the promise? This is a reversal of what had occurred before: the woman was seduced by the serpent to his side and had come into an alliance with the serpent over and against the purpose of God. God is not going to allow that alliance to stand. God said, **"I will put enmity between you and the woman,"** it is not only there but **"between your offspring and hers"** (v. 15a). Remember, there is a double application here that speaks about their offspring: particularly of the devil, the serpent, that old dragon—Satan. It speaks about those who are his offspring; it is not just speaking about baby snakes and human children, but it is speaking about those who believe the lie of the devil: They are the children of the devil. Sometimes the Lord speaks of unbelievers as a "brood of vipers"; John the Baptist and our Lord Jesus spoke in that way.[1] Speaking about them, He says, "You belong to your father, the

---

1. Matthew 3:7, 12:34, 23:33.

devil," because you believe his lie; "When he lies, he speaks his native language, for he is a liar and the father of lies" (Jn. 8:44). Those who believe the truth of God are the children of God: "He who belongs to God hears what God says. The reason you do not hear is that you do not belong to God" (Jn. 8:47). We have this contrast of the enmity between those who are following unbelief and those who are following the teaching coming down through the woman. Those in the state of enmity against this falsehood are believers. **"Between your offspring and hers"** (v. 15) is something that is going to go on through the generations; it is not just the first child. This is going to go on through history.

This enmity involves a spiritual war, and it is not fundamentally physical; it is fundamentally spiritual. It may come to express itself physically, as we will soon see, but it is a spiritual war going on through the ages. What will be the outcome of this war? It says, **"he will crush your head."** It switches to a singular—"He"—the seed of the woman, one person, who is particularly to come. In His coming, He will overcome *you*: **"he will crush your head, and you will strike his heel"** (v. 15b). This is a conflict between belief and unbelief, so it is a conflict that is going on in believers. We should note that, at some level, it is in believers. "For the sinful nature desires what is contrary to the Spirit, and the Spirit what is contrary to the sinful nature. They are in conflict with each other, so that you do not do what you want" (Gal. 5:17). It is also between oneself and others who are in unbelief, insofar as they are in unbelief. It may be fundamental unbelief, in which case the person is a non-believer, or it may be unbelief remaining in the believer; there will be conflict. Enmity may be in one's own household. **"I will put enmity"**; it is a spiritual war that is age-long and agonizing. In the statement, **"he will crush your head,"** is a picture of a spiritual defeat: a destruction of the lies of the devil; this will come about; a destruction of all of the lies in a fundamental sense and all its application. Everything that is raised up against the knowledge of God will be destroyed. Paul explicitly speaks about the spiritual war in this sense in 2 Corinthians 10:3–5:

> For though we live in the world, we do not wage war as the world does. The weapons we fight with are not the weapons of the world. On the contrary, they have divine power to demolish strongholds. We demolish arguments and every pretension that sets itself up

against the knowledge of God, and we take captive every thought to make it obedient to Christ.

There is this battle being described by Paul—in case you have any questions about it.

Christ is going to reign and subdue all things to Himself until the last enemy is destroyed, at which point the end will come, and then the resurrection of the dead will take place. The last enemy to be destroyed is death, which will be destroyed by the resurrection of the dead.[2]

There is a conflict between belief and unbelief; between those who follow the Word of God as reason and those who do not—those who are non-rational, anti-rational. Once we start fighting in a non-rational, anti-rational way, we inevitably use non-rational means, which are psychological manipulation or the use of force. It is expressed in this: **"and you will strike his heel."** From the very beginning, it has been like this. Cain struck Abel; Abel's witness against Cain could not be resisted. He had nothing to say, all he could do to overcome was to strike him. When it came to our Lord Jesus, when they could resist Him no longer by any word or argument, when they were exposed,[3] they struck and brought about His physical death.[4] But even in that, even in physical death, our Lord Jesus triumphed over them; God's purpose was accomplished.

There will be a spiritual war that is age-long and agonizing, and good will overcome evil. The Sabbath day, as we said, is our first eschatological expression; it is speaking of our origin and our destiny. When anyone speaks in the news and books and articles, and so many ways, about our origin not being of God, the Sabbath day is a reminder and gives a falsehood to that: No! God created, God rested, and we are reminded of it. It is clear; you have to deny reason to avoid seeing it. We see these persons, in their hearts, being foolish, darkened, and expressing nonsense. Sometimes at the very pinnacle of their lives, at the height of their glory, they speak nonsense. We saw that this week; I received over five or six responses to this Hawking book[5] that is being advertised. I

---

2. *1 Corinthians 15:24–26.*

3. *Matthew 22:46.*

4. *Luke 22:2.*

5. Stephen Hawking and Leonard Mlodinow, *The Grand Design* (New York: Bantam Books, 2010).

went to the bank and my banker said to me, 'Have you heard?' I had a
book with me and he saw that I had it and he made connections about
that. It is all over the news, and people are noticing it. But Hawking is
speaking nonsense, and I hope you can see the nonsense.[6] When they
can speak no longer, and they are exposed, the only thing they can do
is resort to force. They strike back physically to end it.

On the Woman

The curse and promise come not only there. It comes to the woman:
**"I will greatly increase your pains in childbearing; with pain you will
give birth to children"** (v. 16a). This is the curse. This pain is not only
in the process of physically bearing the child in the womb and delivering the child; there is certainly pain there, more or less, but there is
pain in the whole process of bringing up the child. The child has his
own will; the child is self-centered—going astray. That is why the child
is baptized, or used to be circumcised, and that reminds us of that self-
will, and there is a lot of pain in having to deal with that continually. If
it is not dealt with properly, early, it just grows more and more. Even
if it is dealt with properly, it has to be cultivated continually. There is a
lot of pain in bringing up children who are in sin; who may outwardly conform but inwardly resist, until God applies grace to the heart to
turn their hearts to hear. I think everyone can testify to this; I do not
think there is any doubt about this.

There is also a promise; this is not often read as a promise, but I
believe it can and should be read as a promise. **"Your desire will be
for your husband."** There is nothing forced about this. **"Your desire
will be for your husband"** (v. 16b), and in that context, **"he will rule
over you."** This should be understood in light of the earlier reversal:
"I will put enmity" (v. 15a). God is making another reversal, and it
is not something forced, as some might be tempted to read it; we can
see that as a result of the desire of their nature, it is natural that he will
rule. What had happened earlier was that his desire was toward her,
and she ruled over him. Remember Solomon: As he got old, he clung
to these foreign women that he married; his desire was for them, and
they ruled over him; he followed their word. This is how it operates,

---

6. Gangadean, *Philosophical Foundation*, 78–79.

so God is reversing this order, which should be understood as a promise. Remember the intermarriage before the Flood: "the sons of God saw that the daughters of men were beautiful, and they married any of them they chose" (Gen. 6:2). Their desire was for their wives, so their wives ruled over them; they followed the word of their wives, to please their wives; we naturally want to please those toward whom your desire is. But it is saying that our desire should be toward God: that we might be holy by being devoted to and delighting in His will, and He will rule over us.

On the Man

The curse comes to the man. To Adam he said, **"Because you listened to your wife"**—there it is—**"and ate from the tree about which I commanded you, 'You must not eat of it'"** (v. 17a). It is a contrast. It is not that you listened to your wife as against listening to yourself, but that you listened to your wife instead of listening to me (God). Because of this, **"Cursed is the ground because of you"** (v. 17b). It is for your sake, because of you, because of your sin, and for your sake to call you back from sin, **"through painful toil"** (v. 17b). There is that word again: **"with** *pain* **you will give birth to children";**[7] **"through** *painful* **toil you will eat all the days of your life. It will produce thorns and thistles for you, and you will eat the plants of the field"**(vv. 17b- 18).

We see now that not only are the animals cursed, but the plant life is cursed by the curse on the ground, and there are thorns, being aborted fruitfulness; these were not there before. **"Through painful toil you will eat of it all the days of your life. It will produce thorns and thistles for you, and you will eat the plants of the field. By the sweat of your brow you will eat your food until you return to the ground, since from it you were taken; for dust you are and to dust you will return"** (vv. 17b–19). This is, physical death. Dust you are—physical existence—and to dust you will return. We are speaking now about the form of the curse. We can summarize what has been said here as *toil* with nature, *strife* in our relations one with another, both from the enmity between believer and non-believer, but even within your home. It is not just between believer and non-believer, but within your home:

---

7. *Genesis 3:16,* Emphasis added.

"**in pain you will give birth to children**" (v. 16). We are looking at the conflict that arises from within the home. There is strife, *old age, sickness,* and *death*—physical death. What leads up to this is the breakdown of the body in various ways: in sickness, as you get older, and eventually the complete breakdown of the body in physical death. Toil and strife with others, and in one's very being: old age, sickness, and death.

As humans increase, and as sin increases—individually and corporately—the curse also increases. When the curse increases widely, that *toil becomes famine.* The many causes of famine: drought, locusts, and war sometimes increases famine. Then the *strife becomes war*; it breaks out into war. Think again about Cain and Abel. Then, *sickness can become widespread as plague.* All of this leads to physical death. We find in the prophets a reference to these three occurring time and again, explicitly in those words: "war, famine, plague," or "famine, war, plague;" several times in the prophets, these are expressed in just those terms.

THE PURPOSE OF THE CURSE

Not Original, Not Inherent, Not Punishment

What is the purpose of the curse? We have said that the curse is not punishment. First of all, it is not there originally; it is not natural. We can know that from general revelation, that God is all good and all powerful. 'Why is there evil?' And the answer is, originally there was no evil: moral or natural.[8] The curse, physical death, is not original. This is forgotten by all non-believers, and forgotten by most believers. If we go around and ask if natural evil is original and we get an, 'Oh yeah, I guess not.' It is taken as 'That is just the way it is.' It is good to be reminded that it is not original. And it is not inherent in sin; what is inherent in sin is spiritual death, not physical death. Therefore, we reason that it was imposed; it did not come from God originally; it did not come by man from his sin; it certainly was not brought by man in any other way. It was imposed, and in his nature, it was imposed by God. It is imposed not arbitrarily—for no reason whatsoever—but

---

8. God created the world good as is emphasized seven times in Genesis 1, it says, "it was good" (*Gen. 1:4, 10, 12, 18, 21, 25*), and the last time, "it was very good" (*Gen. 1:31*). For a fuller explanation on the goodness of creation, see: Gangadean, *The Westminster Confession*, 75–79.

because of moral evil: due to sin. It is not imposed as punishment; therefore, it is imposed as a call back. We will see that the wages of sin is death—spiritual death—as we see, "You that were dead in your trespasses and sins" in Ephesians 2:1. This is spiritual death; there are two kinds of death: physical and spiritual, and physical death is not the punishment.[9] We also know that all human beings will be raised from the dead and that there is such a thing as the *second death*, and that continues on forever; this is the second death; spiritual death is the punishment for sin. Again, we need to see whether this is in place: not just barely in our thinking, but integrated into our thinking, where it is coming down into our attitude and our habits of thought.

Natural evil is imposed, therefore, not as punishment, but in this context, as the third call back. It is a call back from sin plus self-deception and self-justification. It is a call to stop and think. There are many stop-and-think incidents throughout Scripture. Parents sometimes do this with their children: 'timeout, you are grounded, stop and think.' The point is not just to *stop*, but to *stop and think*. Think about what? The moral wrong that there is, and the root of it in not seeking and not understanding, as well as how we have avoided this and justified it. Stop and think.

The curse has multiple applications depending on to whom it comes. It *restrains* sin in all human beings; with old age, sickness, and death, we just cannot sin with the same vigor. It is harder to get out of bed and do good, and it is also harder to get out of bed and do evil. Although it is a lot easier, all told, to do evil at least initially. It restrains us. It is not as though it restrains us so that we are not going to do evil forever and ever on this earth. We had 950 years, and we did evil all the way, maxed out, and death restrained it: 'All right. Enough. Stop.' Then, our lifestyle was shortened to 70 years or 80.[10] It restrains, at least in that sense. When you are ill in various ways, like you have an ingrown toenail, it just makes you want to lie there and not do anything. I remember earlier this week, I had one of those rare days when I was moving, and I was not aware of my body. You know what I mean? This is no humbug burden from having a body; I just felt great. And usually,

---

9. Gangadean, *Philosophical Foundation*, 145–161; Gangadean, *On Natural and Revealed Theology*, 141–147; Gangadean, "Paper No. 7: The Problem of Evil," in *The Logos Papers*, 33–39.

10. *Psalm 90:10.*

it is just hauling around this body: "Brother Ass,"[11] as it is called. It is a burden. Then, within 36 hours of that, illness came in; fall allergies started to wreak their havoc on me, and for the last four days, I have been working through and struggling with this. My voice normally goes out with allergies; I had about four medications and different applications to contain it and hold it down. But thank the Lord: The voice did not go out. In cases like this, I just have to rest. I could not do a number of things. Of course, I did not have much evil planned. Usually, we do not have to plan evil; that spontaneously arises; we go on, and then, 'Oops, I did evil again; there it is. I said that word and should not have said that word; that was not the right way to communicate to my spouse.' I have also talked with couples, and this is just something that happens when we are around others: we speak words that we wish we had not spoken.

The curse is to restrain us, and it is to *recall* us from evil. It is a call to repentance; there is a specific term—we are to repent of root sin, as well as fruit; and while we repent and we are forgiven, we still need to be cleansed from sin, and this cleansing process is lifelong, so the curse remains with us all our lives: We all get old, sick, and die, and all through this we are being called. There are times when we are being called more than other times. I am noticing, for example, that Job was particularly called at a certain time, more than other times. What Job said is, "the thing which I greatly feared is come upon me" (Job 3:25a KJV). As I reflected on it this week and talked with others about it, I saw that this is what is going on with others. I have seen that it can hit somewhere after 25, and it comes on usually in full strength by the time you are 30, and it lasts about a decade: the valley of the shadow of death. If we are exercised by it, if we come out struggling; we can come out in a good place, we will come out of it in a good place. It can be pretty intense at times. What is happening is the Lord is delivering us from what we greatly fear: all of our insecurities, we may call them, but they are fears, given our personality, our lack of knowledge of the good, our background—the way we process things. What we fear. The Lord brings us to face our fears. We might have to ask ourselves, 'What do I greatly fear?' It is not just what you fear now, but what you fear

---

11. A reference to Francis of Assisi, who referred to the burden of having a body as "Brother Ass."

as it goes back in your life, and what were the crisis points in your life, and what was happening then, and learn to think about this and see what is underlying, and see the root underlying sin in terms of knowing and understanding this may have been affecting you, and learn to overcome. Remember, if you do not repent of root sin, it will remain, and it will remain with us until we die, and it will continue to hinder us. The curse is a call back. It *restrains, recalls from, and removes moral evil*; it is not punishment.

The Curse Is Always Accompanied by the Promise

A second point to note about the curse in terms of His purpose: it is always accompanied by the promise and always should be accompanied by the promise. See how they are intimately related: "**Cursed are you above all the livestock and all the wild animals**," and "**I will put enmity between you and the woman.**" "**Greatly increase your pains in childbearing**," and "**Your desire will be for your husband.**" And then, earlier, "**the seed of the woman will crush your head**" (Gen. 3:14–16)— the promise is made in terms of the one who is to come. These are not to be separated. We are not to have the curse without the promise, or the promise without the curse. Existentially, this is where it begins. We need to start from where we are, under the curse, and work back.

Sometimes, a person is severely under the curse. Some may think: 'This terrible thing is happening to you because you sinned against God.' That comes out sounding ugly. Instead, we are to say: 'All of us have sinned, and all of us are being called back.' At this time, the severity is particularly being noticed, but all of us are being called back. Do not ever fall into that position as against what Jesus said, "Do you think that these Galileans were worse sinners than all the other Galileans because they suffered this way? I tell you, no! But unless you repent, you too will all perish" (Lk. 13:2–3). That is the context. Sometimes it may be that God's glory may be revealed: "His disciples asked him, 'Rabbi, who sinned, this man or his parents, that he was born blind?' 'Neither this man nor his parents sinned,' said Jesus, 'but this happened so that the work of God might be displayed in his life'" (Jn. 9:2–3). We have to keep some of these things in context as we think about it.

This summer, I watched two post-apocalyptic movies: I saw *The Book of Eli*, and I saw *The Road*. I saw *The Road* two days ago, and I commented: I said, 'When you see this, you are very thankful that you have a chair to sit on, and that you have people beside you who are not ready to eat you. You got up, you had breakfast, and you are not scrounging in all kinds of strange places and grabbing for food.' What I did not like about these movies, mostly, is that they had the curse in an intensity without the promise. When the curse comes in its intensity, the promise also comes in its intensity, and that is the point we are to keep in mind. When the curse came in its full intensity—and no time is more intense than the time of Noah—the promise was there, in Noah. He came through the Flood bringing the results of dominion with him, so we did not have to start over from scratch. I do not think there is a more intense time. I was thinking about those who deny the curse—those who deny the Flood—and I was led to compare in my mind those who deny the Holocaust, and I am thinking, 'How are they different?' Which is worse: a Flood denier or a Holocaust denier? The evidence of the Flood is with us in a way that the Holocaust is not. Some might not only deny the Flood, but deny the curse: 'This is just natural; this is just the way things are.' Everyone who deals with the problem of evil and comes out in a wrong formulation is denying the curse; we will see that all mankind is inclined to this. Curse deniers. Denying of the call back, and probably there is a sequence in our thinking that leads to that; I want to look at that in a little bit. The curse and the promise are not to be separated.

The curse as a call back assumes, presupposes, and requires the promise. Since the curse is a call back, the call back assumes that there is forgiveness, and if there is forgiveness, then there must be some account of how God, who is infinitely and eternally just, can forgive sin. Justice says, 'Let them go, give them up,' and mercy says, 'Bring them back.' So the curse is clearly in the category of mercy: a call back. How can God be both? There is only one way in which you can know this, God's will to forgive and how God can be both, and this is by Scripture. The whole point of Scripture is redemptive revelation, to show how God is both just and merciful to man in his sin. It is not merely teaching the law again; it may be the law is given, given the hardness of the heart, but it is primarily a redemptive revelation, showing how we are to be saved from sin and death.

PRESENCE (EXISTENCE) OF THE CURSE

The presence of the curse is here for all of us to see in that everyone dies, and everyone has to deal with this question of death. The curse has been intensified; speaking now about the presence of the curse—its existence and intensity—everyone dies. But it has been intensified, especially after the Flood; the lifespan was reduced greatly, from over 900 years to maybe 70 years. It has been intensified precisely because when human beings are given extended longevity as before the Flood, they may not heed the curse, and we have said that as sin increases, the curse intensifies. It was there again at Babel: Mankind was divided. To constrain human beings from going as far as they can, the curse was intensified at Babel through strife.[12] Then, universal history leaves off, and you can pick up with a particular history. We will pick up on that in a little bit.

RESPONSE TO THE CURSE

What is our response to the curse? We have spoken about the origin, the form, the purpose, the presence, and now point five: The response to the curse.

Adam's Response

First, let us look at Adam's response to the curse. In verse 20, we read, **"Adam named his wife Eve, because she would become the mother of all the living."** Under the curse, which is *in all*, and with the promise, which is *for all*, Adam repents of his sin, believes in the promise, and obeys. All of that is summed up in calling his wife's name *Eve*, **"because she would become the mother of all the living."** He is going to be fruitful and multiply on the earth.

He has to consider this: He has been the occasion now—or the cause, you might say—of the curse on himself and all of his offspring. What will his children think of him? When they are living under the curse, what will they think about the one who brought in the curse? It is very easy to think that they will curse him. Who would want to

---

12. *Genesis 11:8–9.* Through the confusion of languages and scattering over the earth, divisions among mankind arose and with it wars.

bring children into the world who will rise up and curse us? Many people think that because of suffering in the world, they do not want to bring children into the world; apart from whether the children will rise up and curse them, they believe it is just a bad environment: Old age, sickness, and death is a bad environment into which to bring children. There is no getting around it. Adam has to consider this, and he remembers the promise, and if he just remembers the curse and says, 'I want to end it here,' he would not inherit the promise, because it is through the seed of the woman that this promise would come and he will crush the head of the serpent. He believes in the promise that good will overcome evil, in the context of the curse and sin and death, because believing in that shows his faith. He has faith in the promise and that it will come to pass, as God has said. Adam reveals his faith, and it is expressed in these words: **"Adam named his wife Eve, because she would become the mother of all the living"** (v. 20). He will obey, under the curse, for the promise. Adam, with the third call back, repents and believes. He had not done this the first time or the second time. This is not the end of the story; there is more to follow, and we will see how it works out. That is, in the next two segments of the series, God's two-part response to man's repentance and faith.

The Non-Believer's Response

This is how Adam responds to the curse. How do non-believers respond? We could cite a few. Cain did not respond to the call back; he hardened himself, and the curse intensified on him more than on others. Esau had the call back; he experienced a kind of remorse; he wanted the blessing in an external sense; he sought it with tears. It was not that he understood the blessing; he wanted it, but more in a material sense. He never had the blessing because he had not sought it with faith. His unbelief is evident in his disregard: selling his birthright and marrying non-believers, unlike his brother Jacob, and that showed where he was. Esau and his descendants continued in that until they were finally wiped out when they were rejoicing that Babylon was destroying Jerusalem's walls; Obadiah said that Edom would be destroyed, but Jacob will possess their inheritance.[13] Pharaoh responded to the curse as it intensified upon him, and he hardened himself to the point where he was cut off.

These are just a few examples. Buddhism recognizes old age, sickness, and death. It begins with those three visions, but Buddha does not interpret it in a biblical framework. He said, *all is dukkha*—nothing is eternal, nothing is permanent—as against God is eternal, He created things that have permanence to them, even though they are not eternal; Buddha tried to find his solution to evil. Darwin tried to find his solution to the problem of evil naturally:[14] evil was just there from the beginning; it could not be God. He distanced God from the creation, and this was occasioned by the death of his ten-year-old daughter. Freud gives the explanation in psychological terms about the suffering that there is in the world, and this is natural for human beings; they sublimate, and think of some kind of deliverance in this when they cannot deal with it properly. I would say that it would not be hard to think that Stephen Hawking, who spoke this week about how you do not have to bring God into the picture to explain the universe, that he too is struggling with the problem of evil; his body is affected by affliction, and he is perhaps bitter and resentful, and thinking there is no God, and he may despise those who think there is a God, and so he speaks about evil as natural. Not only is evil natural, but everything is natural; the whole universe is natural, even if you have to give up your reason and say it came into being from nothing.[15] We see how men, at the pinnacle of their lives—he is in his sixties now, and probably writing his last book—are speaking, the whole world is listening, and he is uttering foolishness. We see how his mind is darkened; he is not noticing the obvious. He speaks of gravity as if it is a thing in itself, as against the relation between things, and tries to explain the relation as the source of the origin of the things. God leaves us to go in our way when we fail to recognize what is clear about Him.

---

13. *Obadiah 1.*

14. For further exposition regarding the theological elements of the doctrine of evolutions, see the works of Cornelius Hunter, *Darwin's God: Evolution and the Problem of Evil* (Eugene: Wipf & Stock, 2001); *Darwin's Proof: The Triumph of Religion Over Science* (Ada: Brazos Press, 2003); and *Science's Blind Spot: The Unseen Religion of Scientific Naturalism* (Ada: Brazos Press, 2007).

15. Gangadean, *Philosophical Foundation*, 73–80.

The Believer's Response

What about the believer? The believer is inclined to forget about the curse and is to be reminded. Even in his best state, without sin, he is to be reminded: He was reminded by the Sabbath day of his origin and his destiny, the knowledge of God through the work of dominion, and the hope that it will be achieved.[16] How shall we evaluate mankind's remembrance of his origin and destiny—even believers, who may remember the origin, but forget about the destiny and hope that there is? Human beings forget. The curse can be seen in the wilderness[17] when the Israelites had many calls, and continued in unbelief; Psalm 95 speaks about 40 years of grieving for that generation in the wilderness. We sang of it in Psalm 90—the opening Psalm today. We sang of it also in Psalm 119I, which is the focus for the week: "It has been very good for me that I was humbled low. It through affliction was that I Thy statues came to know."[18] What about the curse? They forget that too, so in the Law of Moses, in the teaching concerning the tabernacle and the priestly work, there are a lot of expressions where man is called to stop and think: when he encounters uncleanness in the world, both spiritually in himself and the curse on the creation. When he encountered, in his reproduction, the uncleanness of the mother who has to experience that for 30 or 60 days. And with the child and the circumcision or baptism. In the foods that he eats, he is being reminded of it. When he had skin diseases that the priests examined, they saw he was unclean, and he was to stop and think. In his contact with physical death, in various forms, he is unclean; he is to stop and think. In the law, we are being reminded again and again of this, and how we are to think about it.

Our Lord reminds us of our need for forgiveness and cleansing. "Forgive us our debts, as we also have forgiven our debtors. And lead us not into temptation, but deliver us from evil" (Matt. 6:12–13). He reminds us of this in the context of the first, second, third, and fourth

---

16. The Sabbath (*Gen. 2:2–3*) was given prior to the Fall (*Gen. 3*).

17. This reference of the people of God in the wilderness is not to be taken as claiming that they were unbelievers. But as believers in whom unbelief remains, when facing the curse, we continue in our unbelief.

18. Psalm 119I, *The Book of Psalms for Singing* (Pittsburgh, The Board of Education and Publication, Reformed Presbyterian Church of North America, 1998). From *Psalm 119:71*– "It was good for me to be afflicted so that I might learn your decrees."

petition, which has to do with the curse. "Give us today our daily bread" (Matt. 6:11). There is an element of toil in making a livelihood and in finances. We need not only bread but healing; it says healing is the children's bread.[19] We desire to have protection from harm in various ways; we pray for that in the Lord's Prayer, in the context of the first, second, and third petitions. "Our Father in heaven, hallowed be your name, your kingdom come, your will be done on earth as it is in heaven" (Matt. 6:9b–10). In that context we pray: Give us this day our daily bread, and for the forgiveness of sins and for cleansing. We see the Lord says that the Church is to be salt and light, and if we are not, we are to be cast out.[20]

We see it in the law of Moses and the curses that were spoken of in Deuteronomy 27–28: How we will be the tail and not the head if we are disobedient, and how war will come in from a strange people, from a distant land, and they will come in and conquer. We are reminded of what happens when we do not give heed to our father and mother and the historically accumulated insight that comes through them or should come through them; if we do not give heed to this, then we do not live long in the land that the Lord our God gives us. The curse comes upon us through being oppressed in the land or removed from the land, where the very existence of the nation as such ceases. We cannot take it for granted that the time and boundaries of the nations will continue. They are dissolving now, in this time; we are hearing it from the news every day. Those who are multinationals want to dissolve the bond; they do not want to enforce immigration laws, as if national boundaries are not significant, and the identity of nations and people are not significant. There are those who are moving in and asserting their position, who want to subject a nation to foreign laws, and who are making more and more demands, and using force if necessary. Do not take it for granted that the time and boundaries will remain. And do not think that because this happens day by day, slowly, you just do not do anything about it. The Church has to be salt and light. There are divisions in the Church. If we can start at least with being faithful witnesses (whatever the response may be) to those who are closest

---

19. This is a common saying that has been connected with Jesus' statement, "It is not right to take the children's bread," from *Matthew 15:26* and *Mark 7:27*.

20. *Matthew 5:13*.

to us; yes, within the Westminster Confession of Faith; yes, whether the doxological focus is in place; yes, whether Psalmody is in place; and then go out from there to others. Within Protestantism, there is the distinction of the Baptist position and their view of the Covenant and God's promise. And with the Pentecostals. If we can clean this up, maybe we can speak more believably to the Catholics about their view of the good, the nature of evil, and hope; do not think that you can avoid this and that you are not to seek first the kingdom of God in these basic matters.

We are being called back to stop and think. The apostle speaks of this in terms of *trials of faith*. In Hebrews 12:5, we are warned not to despise the chastening of the Lord, nor faint when we are rebuked of Him in these trials. Do not make light of it, do not despise it, do not resent it, and do not become bitter under it. Watch out lest the root of bitterness spring up and defile many. We are suffering for a variety of reasons; there is every kind of reason that we may suffer. How are we to respond? This is God's call back to *us*. We are to process it for ourselves, particularly with respect to self-justification about the good, and self-deception, and not seeking diligently, and not understanding good and evil. It says, "No discipline seems pleasant at the time, but painful. Later on, however, it produces a harvest of righteousness and peace for those who have been trained by it" (Heb. 12:11). We need to watch ourselves in this matter. Let us all watch ourselves and exhort one another, in our afflictions and troubles, and not to resent and despise and become cynical, or whatever it may be, but to submit under the mighty hand of God as chastening—recognizing His love, knowing that He is working all of these things together for the good of those who love Him.[21] We are not to be caught up on whether we love God or are faking it; we are to be exercised to discern good and evil and to give ourselves to what is good. We are to recognize that there is a lot of division within Christianity, and we are not to go for the least common denominator and say, 'Well, that is what we have in common, that is what it is.' No, that is not the unity of the faith that the Lord calls us to.[22] We are accommodating ourselves to a lot of misconceptions about

---

21. *Romans 8:28.*

22. Surrendra Gangadean, *The Unity of the Church: That They May Be One That the World May Believe* (Phoenix: Logos Papers Press, 2024).

God in that. We are to particularly give heed to the word that has already come down to us, through the pastor-teachers, summed up in the Confession, and focus on the doxological focus.

The curse is a call to all of us to stop and think. Physical death is the greatest reminder of spiritual death; it is a natural symbolism, connection, where physical death symbolizes spiritual death. The blindness of the eyes, the dimming of the hearing of the ear, unable to hear spiritually; our impotence, the crippling in our arms and legs, and Jesus healed all of those, showing that He is the one who not only takes away the curse, but He restores us to life in Him through His Word and Spirit. We are to give heed to this and not be discouraged, and turn in repentance, particularly at the level of root sin, in our understanding of good and evil, and to give ourselves to this. Let us keep this in mind as we come to the Lord's table, and let us turn our Psalters now to Psalm 25A as we prepare our hearts for coming to the table.

17

JUSTIFICATION

*The Possibility, Vicarious Atonement,
and Imputation*

Genesis 3:17–21

¹⁷To Adam he said, "Because you listened to your wife and ate from the tree about which I commanded you, 'You must not eat of it,' "Cursed is the ground because of you; through painful toil you will eat of it all the days of your life. ¹⁸It will produce thorns and thistles for you, and you will eat the plants of the field. ¹⁹By the sweat of your brow you will eat your food until you return to the ground, since from it you were taken; for dust you are and to dust you will return." ²⁰Adam named his wife Eve, because she would become the mother of all the living. ²¹The Lord God made garments of skin for Adam and his wife and clothed them.

RESPONSE TO THE CURSE AND THE PROMISE:
REPENTANCE AND FAITH

LAST TIME WE FINISHED THE curse and the promise, we did not speak about the response to that in any great detail. The response to the curse and promise is repentance and faith. We believe this is shown in Genesis 3:20 when it says, **"Adam named his wife Eve, because she would become the mother of all the living."** We want to show how this involves repentance and faith and what God's response to man's response is.

What is repentance? It is a change of thinking, manifesting itself in a change of conduct. Not just feelings; it is thinking, *metanoia, noūs* 'mind', and the prefix *metá*, a change of mind, or a change of thinking. From the root word, "metá," we get metamorphosis, a change of form. It begins there and does not start in the emotions but in the thinking. We are to think about what has happened in the past, the direction Adam has been going, and the direction that he should go, along with the conduct connected with that. We spoke about these call backs, these calls to repentance. We want to get in mind what repentance is. It is a change of thinking; he thought this was the way to go, but he now sees this is not the way to go. It is wrong; this is the way of death. This is the way to go; this is the way of life. It is more than that, and we have tried to open it up, but it is at least that. In connection with repentance is also faith; just as the curse and promise cannot be separated, so repentance and faith in the promise cannot and should not be separated. They are distinct, but they are inseparable.

The question is, (1) *How is repentance possible?* This is the first question that we will address. Then, a question is generated by that—(2) *How is forgiveness possible?* This is the second point to be addressed. (3) *Is the debt to be canceled or paid, if so, by whom?* This is the third point that we will cover. And (4) *how?* This has two parts because we will see that forgiveness has two parts and is symbolized in the garments of skin with which God clothed them. There are two parts to point four, (4a) *how?* By means of vicarious atonement and (4b) *how?* By means of imputation.

HOW IS REPENTANCE POSSIBLE?

First, how is repentance possible? We think of what has happened in the Fall of man, that man has not been seeking and not understanding. Scripture says the wages of sin is death,[1] and that is spiritual. It is revealed in the act of eating of the tree of the knowledge of good and evil. When they became aware of shame, they covered it up. It is not an incidental act; this is very deliberate. It involves a certain amount of ingenuity and deliberate effort to make coverings of leaves and to cover themselves. In every specific thought, action, deed, and putting it together, there is a deliberateness of what they want to do. We have to see that deliberateness as revealing the state of mind and

---

1. *Romans 6:23.*

the self-deception that is involved in it. We see that the man and his wife, left to themselves, turned away, and did not continue to seek. We saw the depth of that misunderstanding in believing "you will be like God, knowing good and evil" (Gen. 3:5b), what is involved in terms of the understanding of good and evil, and the pursuit of it. They put themselves in the place of God to determine good and evil and denied the distinction between the Creator and the creature, not keeping in mind and understanding what the good is. All of that is involved; all of that is here in the story.

We might say by way of a short preparatory remark: One might think, 'That is getting a lot out of a little,' and I am saying not at all. This is a characteristic way in which we should interpret, but we ought to be careful not to run off in any and every direction. Stay within bounds. Think about how you came into existence, one cell, and in that cell, the DNA information is all there of your coming into existence; your very being should speak to you about this way of interpreting. It is called *the organic seed form understanding of Scripture.* It is all there; every bit of it is there in the DNA. If you think that is very small, there are a lot of things a lot smaller than the atoms out of which the molecules are structured in this quantum world. That is one point.

Secondly, you might say, 'It's not clear.' Again, that is not true; things can be very clear, and we do not see it. Jesus said to His disciples after being on the Mount of Transfiguration: Pay careful attention to what I am telling you; the Son of Man is going to be betrayed into the hands of men, and they could not hear it.[2] Now, perhaps after the fact we can see it, but we are blameworthy for not seeing it. Jesus later said to His disciples, "How foolish you are, and how slow of heart to believe all that the prophets have spoken! Did not the Christ have to suffer these things and then enter his glory?" (Lk. 24:25–26). When we look back we realize, 'Oh, yes, it is *obviously* there.' In that sense, it *is* there, and it is *obviously* there. This is what we are going to try to bring out by the grace of God. Of course, if you think, 'He has taken liberties with the text,' please come and tell me. If you do not feel like telling me this, you can approach it by saying: 'I don't see how that follows; could you explain it further.' It is perfectly all right; this would be a gentle way, so you should not feel that you have to reprove your

---

2. This is a paraphrase of *Matthew 22b–23* by way of illustration.

pastor; you are inquiring, which is perfectly all right. I invite you to and encourage you to do so.

This is the condition of their hearts and not only the sin of not seeking and not understanding, but the self-deception and the deliberateness of that, and they are going deeper into the pit, especially connected with shame, avoiding the shame of not seeking and not understanding. In what is further exposed, "Where are you?" (Gen. 3:9b), we see the self-justification, and we spoke about that. Human beings are going deeper and deeper into the pit. How is repentance possible? Why would they not see what is clear originally? Why would they not turn around and avoid this pit? Why would they go further and resist to the point of blaming God? Blaming each other (after they had been mutually covering up for each other) and blaming God—this is a desperate state to be in. The mind is darkened. They are without meaning. They do not understand good and evil, and they do not understand the distinction between infinite and finite. They do not know the infinite God knows where they are in their hiding. It is so bold and presumptuous to blame God. This is what is revealed. I believe it is clearly here in Scripture for us to see.

How can we think that they will repent? We have to understand that God is the one who is seeking them out. God is the one who is bringing salvation, and God is the one who is revealing how He will bring salvation. The very first words of the promise are given to us in these words, "I will put enmity between you and the woman" (Gen. 3:15a). If we stop and think about these words, and what is involved, we will begin to see how it is that repentance is possible.

Repentance begins with an act of God, putting enmity between the serpent and the woman. What is involved in that? It should be understood that the enmity involves a change for the better. The serpent and the woman (who had believed the serpent) were on one side now, and they were both in enmity against God. When God says, "I will put enmity between you and the woman," it means He is not making a change in the serpent, but in the woman; the serpent will continue to have that enmity, but the woman will be changed, so that what she formerly loved, she now hates. There is an inward change that God puts, and He puts it there in a particular way; we want to look at this further. "I will put enmity." John 1:12–13 says, "Yet to all who received him, to those who believed in his name, he gave the right to become children of God—children born not of natural descent, nor of human decision or a husband's will, but born of God." We are born again, not of natural descent, but born of God. This comes out in the next passage: "between your offspring and hers" (Gen. 3:15), your seed is the seed of the serpent, and her seed is the seed of the woman, who are also children of God. Being children of God, they are born *of* God and not of man. As we see in John, it says, "born not of natural descent, nor of human decision or a husband's will, but born of God" (Jn. 1:13). "Yet to all who received him, to those who believed in his name, he gave the right to become children of God" (Jn. 1:12), this is adoption: to become children of God. Then it says that these children of God, who are children by adoption, were born. It is not that you are born when you become a child of God, but you are adopted to become a child of God "children born not of natural descent, nor of human decision or a husband's will, but born of God." The emphasis seems to be: this is an act of God, not an act of man. This is why it is put this way, "I will put enmity" (Gen. 3:15a). This enmity is going to come within one's own house. "I did not come to bring peace, but a sword" (Matt. 10:34b).

We should also see the doctrine of election implicitly present in the next statement. First of all, God sovereignly does this. He does not do it for all; He does it for some. He says, "between your offspring and hers" (Gen. 3:15). We are not talking about baby snakes here. We are talking about being children of the tempter by virtue of believing the word of the tempter, and children of the woman, in enmity against that, believing the Word of God. When God says, "I will put enmity," *some* will believe, and will be at enmity with others who do not believe. God is going to do this sovereignly. All of those who are in conflict with one another are children born of the woman, but not all have that enmity against the word of the devil.

Nothing that we can do will bring about regeneration. We concern ourselves with curriculum[3] and struggle as much as we can to get it into focus to the very best we can, to improve over every other curricula

---

3. Pastor Gangadean is referring to the Logos Foundation Ministries designed to provide a doxological education from kindergarten through lifelong education, which includes The Logos Curriculum, Logos Preparatory Academy, Logos College of Liberal Arts, Logos Paideia, Logos Theological Seminary, Public Philosophy Press, Logos Papers Press, and The Logos Study Center. All are designed to instill the foundation necessary for maturity, fruitfulness, unity, and fullness.

that we are aware of, and we need to keep (especially and fundamentally) the goal in mind. The goal of man's chief end is to glorify God and enjoy Him forever, to glorify Him in all that by which He makes Himself known, in all of His works of creation and providence—it is that simple, by keeping the *goal* as the knowledge of God. This is what Adam turned away from. The good is no longer the knowledge of God, and the earth being filled with the knowledge of God; he turned away to something else as the good. Even when we teach this to our children as much as we can, from the earliest stages, from before they are one, it is not going to change their hearts. This is something God has to do. God said He will do it, and He will do it sovereignly, "I will put enmity between you and the woman" (Gen. 3:15a). Not by changing the serpent to make the serpent the enemy, but by changing the woman, to change her heart to believe. The enmity will be between some of her offspring and others of her offspring, whom God determines sovereignly.

It goes on in the next line in the promise, "he," singular, the seed of the woman, "will crush your head" (Gen. 3:15b). In that is pictured a decisive defeat. To have your head crushed—and we are not talking about snakes being crushed. 'Every time you see a snake, kill it!' No, that is not what we are talking about. We are talking about the tempter that was present in the snake; his head will be crushed, and the works of the devil will be destroyed. "For this purpose the Son of God was manifested, that he might destroy the works of the devil" (1 Jn. 3:8b KJV). He, the Word of God, will destroy that work in a particular way. We will see that soon. In the process, "he will strike your heel" (Gen. 3:15b), the conflict is between belief and unbelief, between the Word of God and what is not the Word of God; the Word of God in its completeness and fullness, first coming into us as the light of life, as reason.[4] The conflict is between the rational and the non-rational. This is how the non-rational fights—emotionally, characteristically with slander, and if the slander does not get you, they will try to bring about your destruction, to kill you. As exemplified in Cain and Abel, "strike your heel." It is ultimately manifest in the seed of the woman who was struck on the cross. "None of the rulers of this age understood it, for if they had, they would not have crucified the Lord of glory" (1 Cor.

---

4. *John 1:4.*

2:8). In that blow, God triumphed, Christ triumphed. We will look at this further in just a bit.

How is repentance possible? How does this change come about? God brings it about, and I would like to read a few questions from the Shorter Catechism, starting with Question 29. "How are we made partakers of the redemption purchased by Christ? We are made partakers of the redemption purchased by Christ, by the effectual application of it to us by his Holy Spirit." So it is God the Holy Spirit who is going to bring about what God has said, "I will put enmity." Question 30, "How does the Spirit apply to us the redemption purchased by Christ? The Spirit applieth to us the redemption purchased by Christ, by working faith in us, and thereby uniting us to Christ in our effectual calling." Notice this term is introduced: "effectual calling." This third call was an outward call (as it came to Cain as well), but it was effectual because God had worked in the woman and the man to put this enmity and to turn the heart. Now the question is, "What is effectual calling? Effectual calling is the work of God's Spirit, whereby," notice these terms, "convincing us of our sin and misery, enlightening our minds in the knowledge of Christ, and renewing our wills, he doth persuade and enable us to embrace Jesus Christ, freely offered to us in the gospel."[5] What we are saying is that the promise that is given here—"I will put enmity between you and the woman, and between your offspring and hers; he will crush your head, and you will strike his heel" (Gen. 3:15)—is the reality of the gospel in seed form—It is all here. This is what the Spirit is enabling Adam and Eve to see and understand.

One last question from the Shorter Catechism because this is going to explain what comes after. "What benefits do they that are effectually called partake of in this life? They that are effectually called do in this life partake of justification,"[6] this is the next thing we will see on the basis of repentance and faith: justification. We will see *how* this comes about. "Adoption"; they are given the rights and privileges of being children of God. "Sanctification"; we will see sanctification spelled out as the next main point after justification. "And the several benefits, which in this life, do either accompany or flow from them."[7] We are going to sing

---

5. *SCQ. 31.*

6. *SCQ. 32.*

7. *SCQ. 32.*

in closing, blessed is the man whose sins are forgiven.[8] Think about all who are still in their sins (relatives and friends), and ask yourself: Is it a blessing to be effectually called? Is there a greater blessing?

This turning of the heart by the work of the Holy Spirit is sovereignly done according to God's eternal plan in election. There comes to be an awareness of sin and death as such, and the Catechism calls it "misery."[9] The emptiness of life without God. It is not so much the misery of natural evil, but the misery of spiritual death. The emptiness, the lack, the torment of guilt against which they are working desperately. It is there, they become aware of it as such, both sin and death as such. Furthermore, they have a conviction of death as being due to sin. This is a distinct aspect. Sometimes, it is referred to theologically as *notitia*, the notion of it, the concept of it. Then there is an *assensus*, where you assent to, and you agree to, in your understanding, the connection between the two. Everyone who comes to Christ, at some point, must experience this. Even if you are regenerated from your mother's womb (and you can be), you must come to an awareness and conviction of sin and death, that you might embrace the promised one, Christ, as He is offered to us in the Scriptures. Everyone must come this way, so we need to look at our experience to see when we became aware of our need for Christ. When did we become aware of the sin and misery of life? When did we become aware that we cannot go on in that way, we do not want to go on in that way, and we desperately need to turn around? We did turn around; when? Can we identify that? Can we share that with others? We should be able to.

Then there is a change of mind and a change in conduct. We are enlightened in the knowledge of the one promised, and we act on it; we trust in the promise, and we act on it. This is the third stage in speaking about saving faith, *fiducia*. It is first *notitia*, where we are aware of sin and death as such. *Assensus*, where we agree that 'my misery is due to my sin, not to be blamed on anyone else, not to be excused, it is my sin, I did not seek God, and because of that, I do not have God in my life, and I am in this miserable state, and I deserve to be cut off from God forever and ever and ever unless I am forgiven. How can I be forgiven?' Until that has been worked out, we will not be able to

---

8. *Psalm 32.*

9. *SCQ. 31.*

trust in the promise. These are the distinct states that can be applied to understand the working of the Holy Spirit, and the Spirit works *by* and *with* the Word. The promise is not to be separated from the curse. We have to understand sin, death, and the promise for there to be repentance of sin—these are not to be separated.

Adam did come to see this, and he chose to obey, and he revealed his choice to obey. Scripture says, **"Adam named his wife Eve, because she would become the mother of all the living"** (v. 20). He will obey, under the curse, *in* and *for* the promise. This is, for the promise to come about, he must obey. Because there is a promise, and he wants to get hold of that, he is going to obey. Remember, it is under the curse. Adam is aware that he has brought the curse on the creation, himself, and the generations to come. It is the ongoing conflict and death that he brought on. There is no question that his action is affecting all and that he is a representative head—he is aware of that. This means he is aware that the curse is going to affect his offspring, and without the promise, either he has no children, or he will try to continue on with the promise. What will happen is that his children rise up and curse him, curse him because he brought the curse on them. Who would want to do that? It is no small thing for him to obey under the curse. That is why I said *in* and *for* the promise.

HOW IS FORGIVENESS POSSIBLE?

This raises another problem. The first one is: How is repentance possible? The second is: How is forgiveness possible? Is sin against God? Does sin involve incurring a debt? Christ said, "Forgive us our debts, as we also have forgiven our debtors" (Matt. 6:12). The Scripture, at times, speaks about the one who has been forgiven an amount such as ten thousand talents or a hundred denarii, etc., and the one forgives, and the other does not.[10] Sometimes, it is spoken of in terms of debt, and it is appropriate for us to think about that. The question is, there is a debt that is owed because of sin, how is the debt dealt with? There are two possibilities, the debt is either *canceled* (set aside), or the debt is *paid*. It is not even possible to think about the debt being set aside for two reasons. (1) If someone owes me ten dollars, and I set it aside

---

10. *Matthew 18:21–35.*

and I forgive what they owe me, I suffer the loss of what is owed to me. It is inescapable that I would have to suffer that loss. One way or another, this has to be dealt with. (2) Here is the problem, if the debt is merely canceled, not paid, then we have mercy setting aside the requirements of justice. So, the two possibilities are that mercy *sets aside* justice, or mercy *satisfies* the demand of justice.

I have given the story at other times about someone caught drunk driving: $50,000 fine or five years in jail, he cannot pay and he throws himself at the mercy of the court. What is the court going to do? Is the judge free to change the law? He would not be doing what he is called to do as a judge. But the judge can, from his own resources, pay the $50,000 and let the guilty party go free because the debt is paid. The demands of the law are met—they are satisfied. But since it is satisfied by another, it is *mercy*. In this way, *mercy must satisfy justice; it cannot set it aside.* Someone has to pay it, who will pay? How can they pay? It must be paid. Can I pay for it? No, I have nothing. I am a debtor, I have nothing to pay with. I am in the hole. I cannot go to my bank account and pull anything out; I am a debtor with nothing to pay with. Can someone else pay? Adam's sin is such that it affects all—all are debtors. There is no one else that can pay; no other human being. The question remains, staring us in the face, demanding an answer: *How is forgiveness possible? How can the debt be paid? Who can pay that debt?* Remember when Abraham was called to offer up Isaac: "Take your son, your only son, Isaac, whom you love" (Gen. 22:2a). He realized that Isaac was circumcised, which means he needed a new heart. It was when he was eight days old, which means the sin of Adam comes down through Abraham to Isaac, and Isaac cannot be the burnt offering. Nevertheless, God was calling him to offer up Isaac, and God was revealing to Abraham something very significant about how this debt would be paid.[11] It is being revealed more now with Abraham than before with Adam—this is the way the Scripture unfolds. In every period, the promise is unfolded more and more. When we come to Isaiah, we see much more, but it is *the same promise*, one exact same promise as from the beginning, organically present.

---

11. *John 8:56.*

BY WHOM? THE SEED OF THE WOMAN

How is the debt paid? By whom and how? Adam already has the promise and it is the promise concerning the seed of the woman. This one will be human; He will be born of a woman. What this one is going to do is going to benefit others, as Adam's act affected all in him, this other one who is going to crush the head of the serpent—His act will affect many. This one who is to come (the seed of the woman) is not Adam. Adam is not in a position to correct this; it is another one. The question is, who? By what woman? Is it Eve? Perhaps she thought so. When Cain was born she said, "With the help of the LORD I have brought forth a man" (Gen. 4:1). Cain was a murderer; he was of the seed of the serpent, and he did not repent; he did not understand his sin. So, by whom? Adam should also have known about theodicy; that God permits sin to deepen the revelation of His glory and God will remove sin. Sin will not be removed quickly; it will be removed eventually. We also see that implicitly, in the words "between your offspring and hers," in the offspring to come, we see that implicitly, **"she would become the mother of all the living"** (v. 20b); history is going to go on. This is a process that will go on in history; that is why we say that it is *age-long and agonizing.*

Who is this seed of the woman? It is a human and must be a man to represent man, and He *does* represent in that He brings benefit for all affected by Adam. He is the one to come, and He is in the place of Adam. It is from this that we say that the covenant that God established with Adam is continuing to operate, and it is still in effect. Remember, the purpose of the covenant was to raise man from the condition where he is changeable in himself, to where he is unchanging in the covenant; to be established in righteousness—that still has to come about. God has not changed His mind about blessing man through the covenant. That will of course be done by Him and all that He brings into being. This one who is coming now, "the seed of the woman," who would bring covenant blessings by being representative, is going to be in the place of Adam. He must *undo* what Adam did, and He must *do* what Adam failed to do. He is the new representative head. The seed was not Cain, but neither was it Seth; it was through Seth, it was through Noah, it was through Shem, it was through Abraham, it was through Judah, it was through David, it was through those who returned from captivity, it was through Zerubbabel, and was preserved until Christ would come.

HOW? THROUGH VICARIOUS ATONEMENT

By whom? When we come to Isaiah, it is said, "The virgin will be with child and will give birth to a son, and will call him Immanuel [God with us]" (Is. 7:14b). This seed of the woman is explained more now as being born of a virgin, and now we understand that the imputation of sin that came through Adam (through man) is not present in Christ who is born. Adam is a covenant head who is not involved in this birth, but this one is human. A virgin shall conceive, bear a son, and call His name Immanuel, God with us. "For to us a child is born, to us a son is given, and the government will be on his shoulders. And he will be called Wonderful Counselor, Mighty God, Everlasting Father, Prince of Peace" (Is. 9:6). We are told, as the Scripture unfolds, of who this one is, through which line He will come, of what He will accomplish. It said, "Of the increase of his government and peace there will be no end" (Is. 9:7a). As a result of His rule,

> The wolf will live with the lamb, the leopard will lie down with the goat, the calf and the lion and the yearling together; and a little child will lead them. The cow will feed with the bear, their young will lie down together, and the lion will eat straw like the ox. The infant will play near the hole of the cobra, and the young child put his hand into the viper's nest. They will neither harm nor destroy on all my holy mountain, for the earth will be full of the knowledge of the LORD as the waters cover the sea (Is. 11:6–9).

This one is going to *undo* what Adam did and is going to *do* what Adam failed to do.

We know more about who the seed of the woman is, the covenant head who will *undo* and *do,* and we know more as we look into history who it is not. This one is both the Son of Man, and He is the Son of God. This is why revelation is necessary: to reveal to us how God will forgive sin.

How will He forgive sin? How will He bring about this forgiveness? We have already said that the Holy Spirit is working to establish that enmity, which involves a change of heart—spoken of as regeneration, being born again. It is spoken of in the sacraments, signified in circumcision (having a new heart), and baptism (the work of God sovereignly). How will He accomplish redemption? The revelation of this comes to us in Genesis 3:21, "**The Lord God made garments of skin for Adam and his wife and clothed them.**" God made garments of skin. What was made with the garments? The skin was put together in a form that they could wear, and God Himself made it. The skin comes from the animal that is killed. Introduced here is the notion of a sacrifice. Later on, this comes to be called *vicarious atonement* in theology. This is the first part of how God brings forgiveness and justification. Sin has to be paid for, and it is paid for by another. This other is represented in terms of a sacrifice, a lamb that dies, or an animal that dies. Later in Scripture, we are told in Isaiah 53:5–6, "But he was pierced for our transgressions, he was crushed for our iniquities; the punishment that brought us peace was upon him, and by his wounds we are healed. We all, like sheep, have gone astray, each of us has turned to his own way; and the Lord has laid on him the iniquity of us all." "Look, the Lamb of God, who takes away the sin of the world!" (Jn. 1:29b). This is what is being pictured for us in the seed of the woman who will *undo* what Adam did and pictured for us in the sacrifice. "By his knowledge my righteous servant will justify many, and he will bear their iniquities" (Is. 53:11b). Here is the case where our inequities are put on another and this other is slain, "smitten by him, and afflicted" (Is. 53:4b). God required that His justice be satisfied and He is teaching us *how* this will be and by whom it will be.

HOW? BY IMPUTATION

The second part to this is that they are covered with the garments of skin. The animal was slain, it died in our place, and it was cut off from the land of the living. It is what we deserve, to be cut off from the life of God forever and ever, to be left in that state forever and ever, to descend into the pit of woe, a bottomless pit, in meaninglessness, in boredom, and in the torment of guilt. Another is cut off; another is forsaken in our place. Our Lord Jesus experienced this, certainly when on the cross, He cried out, "My God, my God, why have you forsaken me?" (Ps. 22:1a). Not only does He bear away our sin, but the garments are made. By contrast, we are clothed, signifying our struggle to deal with our unrighteousness and making garments of leaves for ourselves. Garments of skin are provided, still signifying the need for righteousness, but now we are covered through the righteousness of another, to which nothing at any time can be added. Christ perfectly obeyed God, whereas Adam did not, and each of us has come short. He obeyed even unto the point of death, the death of the cross, and He was obedient all of His life. When He was 12, His mother did not understand, nor His father Joseph, that He should be about His Father's business. He went and submitted Himself to them.[12] He lived obediently under the law, the law meant for sinners; He humbled Himself to become a man. The infinite gap between God and man is much greater than myself and an act, He humbled Himself and became a man, and He continues to be a man, the Son of God who is the Son of Man. He humbled Himself and became obedient, He was born in a lowly estate, in a manger. He submitted to circumcision meant for sinners, He submitted to baptism meant for sinners, He endured the temptation in the wilderness, He lived obediently in the face of three years of thorough examination by all of Israel. He lived a perfect, sinless life—Jesus our Lord.

It is in that righteousness, even to the very point of death, that He said, "Father, into your hands I commit my spirit" (Lk. 23:46). He died trusting in His Father, though fully recognizing the blow that came upon Him when He was forsaken. Jesus was *thoroughly* obedient in every last detail. It is His righteousness that is put down to our account, which we receive by faith—by which we stand before God—accepted. We are accepted in the beloved, the Son of God, whom He loves. Adam and Eve wore these skins continually. They were being taught continually as they wore the garments of skin: Is it the animal? Or is it another? They knew the promise, the seed of the woman, another to come. They would know that it could not be by an animal; it had to be by the seed of the woman to come. Just as Adam's unrighteousness was imputed to all who are in him by natural generation, just as our sin is imputed to Christ, as a Lamb of God who takes away the sin of the world, so too now, the righteousness of Christ is imputed to all those who are united to Him, by faith. There is not an infusion of righteousness here; there is an imputation of righteousness. It is not

---

12. *Luke 2:41–52.*

one act of imputation; it is the third act of imputation. No one can or should in any way doubt this and try to add works to grace in any sacramental theology.

The covenant of grace fulfills the covenant of works. We should just speak about this one that has been graciously fulfilled by God Himself in sending His Son, and it is not set aside; it is fulfilled. Where sin abounded, grace did much more abound. We need this as we see ourselves struggle with sin and see others struggle with sin. We need to hold on to this, that we are accepted by God on the basis of the righteousness of Christ, and God is faithful and just not only to forgive us but to cleanse us from all unrighteousness. This is the next, the last, the final piece in the teaching on redemption, that of sanctification. We have affirmed that this is one of the blessings that flow out of our effectual calling. "I will put enmity between you and the woman, and between your offspring and hers; he will crush your head, and you will strike his heel" (Gen. 3:15), and **"The Lord God made garments of skin for Adam and his wife and clothed them"** (v. 21). Praise be to God for His grace. In closing, let us turn to Psalm 32C and let us sing.

18

SANCTIFICATION

Knowing the Truth Through Suffering

Genesis 3:22–24

²²And the LORD God said, "The man has now become like one of us, knowing good and evil. He must not be allowed to reach out his hand and take also from the tree of life and eat, and live forever." ²³So the LORD God banished him from the Garden of Eden to work the ground from which he had been taken. ²⁴After he drove the man out, he placed on the east side of the Garden of Eden cherubim and a flaming sword flashing back and forth to guard the way to the tree of life.

SANCTIFICATION IS DISTINCT FROM JUSTIFICATION

WE HAVE COME TO THE LAST PART of redemption, the final part of a fifteen-part series on the biblical worldview. This worldview is found in Genesis 1–3. It is the foundation on which everything else occurs in the rest of the Bible, and it is to be the foundation in our lives. We are to heed it so that we can go on to maturity, fruitfulness, unity, and the fullness that there is in God, which He intends for us.

Last time we talked about justification, and this was revealed to us in God's response to Adam's repentance and faith under the curse: "Adam named his wife Eve, because she would become the mother of all the living" (Gen. 3:20). This is on the assumption that Adam repents and accepts correction and the curse is God's call back to him. He repents by adhering to the promise and is waiting for its fulfillment. Upon being justified, in which case his sin is covered, God makes provision to cleanse man from the sin that remains. This represents two aspects of salvation—first, forgiveness, and second, cleansing. Forgiveness connected with justification is one part of that, and it is a one-time event. God clothed Adam with the skins once, the animal died once, the animal paid the price. In his repentance and faith, he is forgiven and has faith in God's promise. Adam is forgiven, and he is clothed with the righteousness of this perfect sacrifice.

What happens once in justification is distinct from what happens (ongoing) in sanctification for the rest of our lives. Forgiveness is not the same as cleansing, but both (together) constitute the salvation that is in our God. The imputation of righteousness is not the same as *actual* righteousness. Our sin is imputed to Christ; He bears our sins. He is not *actually* a sinner, He does not have sin in Himself, so we can make the distinction between *imputed* and *actual,* by which we are forgiven. We can distinguish between imputed sin and actual sin, and understand that if actual sin is removed, there is no actual righteousness. Without actual righteousness, death remains. I do not say that death *reigns.* As Paul speaks of it in Romans 7, it may reign in our members.[1] We believe this is the condition of the believer with sin remaining in them, and Paul speaks about this as death continuing. There is an inseparable connection between sin and death, but Christ has broken the power of this. We do not want to remain in this condition of having sin and death remaining in our lives. We cannot split our belief in Christ as Savior in terms of forgiveness, and as Lord in terms of obedience, putting away the sin of disobedience. *Salvation involves both forgiveness and cleansing.*

After the covering, then comes the cleansing. In some understandings, these two are not distinguished. Justification is thought of as an *infusion* of righteousness. During the Reformation, this sacramental theology that speaks about infusion through the sacraments was challenged and set aside. Luther wrestled with it; he saw that if it is a matter of righteousness infused by the sacrament, then when we sin, the sin sets it aside, and we can never have peace on that basis. Luther himself was greatly troubled; the more conscious and consistent we are in our understanding of justification and sanctification, the more we will see the error of infused righteousness.

---

1. *Romans 7:7–25.*

After the covering, then the cleansing. This can be seen in Genesis 3, which marks the distinction between these two: justification and sanctification; forgiveness and cleansing. It is in Genesis 3 in the acts of God: God covered them with skin, He pronounced the curse upon them, and God expelled them from the Garden to live under the curse. 1 John 1:9 says, "If we confess our sins, he is faithful and just and will forgive us our sins and purify us from all unrighteousness." Many persons in Protestant circles have blurred the distinction between forgiveness and cleansing; they have said, 'I will sin, and I will ask for forgiveness, Christ will forgive me, I will ask the church for forgiveness, the church will forgive me, and I will continue in the church with that fruit of sin under my tongue.' It does not happen that way. The person who tried that found out it does not happen that way, and a number of persons have tried it only to find it does not happen that way. They need to be ready to repent and accept the teaching of repentance connected with the Westminster Confession of Faith that the adulterer is as if he were dead.[2] In the Old Testament, he was dead; he was stoned to death. In the New Testament, it is as if he were dead, and some were unwilling to accept that. When you are dead, you do not have custody over the child. When you are dead, you do not have property rights, it all goes to the innocent party. This teaching has been the source of a lot of attacks against the church. The worst type of name-calling and vileness has come because of this. Do not neglect the distinction, and do not allow others to neglect the distinction. When people come into the church, we have to remind them more thoroughly and carefully that both are true: justification/forgiveness and sanctification/cleansing.

We see the example in the Scripture in Genesis, in John[3] (which we just spoke about), and in the Confession.[4] This distinction is there in the Lord's Prayer, "Forgive us our debts, as we also have forgiven our debtors." He also has said, "lead us not into temptation, but deliver us from evil" (Matt. 6:12–13). This is not just evil out there, but the evil remaining within. We are praying for forgiveness and cleansing in the Lord's prayer. It is there in the Lord's prayer, not only in Matthew 6 where it is recorded, but also in the Lord's prayer in John 17:17:

2. Gangadean, *The Westminster Confession*, 263–273.

3. *1 John 1:9*.

4. *WCF 24*.

"Sanctify them by the truth." Christ is praying for those who believe in Him. He is praying for His disciples that they might be sanctified. Notice how that sanctification becomes manifest: "That all of them may be one . . . that the world may believe" (Jn. 17:21). Until we have the unity as is between the Father and the Son and the Holy Spirit, sin remains. Have we overcome the division between, 'I am of Paul, I am of Apollos, I am of Cephas?'[5] It says you are mere men; you are carnal, you are infants and immature.[6] This has to be dealt with, we should not take the divisions among us lightly. This is God's call to us to stop and think and Paul says, "No doubt there have to be differences among you to show which of you have God's approval" (1 Cor. 11:19). We have to ask ourselves, am I contributing to the division? Have I departed from Historic Christianity as a start, or is Historic Christianity wrong? Is this held without much thought? Has it gone through much discussion and been held correctly? This is part of the work of the Holy Spirit in the Church.

SANCTIFICATION IS BY THE TRUTH

Sanctification is also in the Ten Commandments, as we will see, especially in the Tenth Commandment, which speaks about covetousness and discontent, and we will be focusing some attention on that. It is in all the Commandments, which are the standard of righteousness. If sanctification is the removing of sin, then any coming short of the Ten Commandments will have to be addressed. Divisions manifest coming short, but we can examine ourselves in light of the Commandments. There are sins of commission, as well as omission. We see this in the case of Job where there was sin of *omission*. God was cleansing Job. There is also the sin of *commission*, as in the case of David with Bathsheba. In both cases, there is a call for truth in the inward part,[7] deep within. If sin is not seeking and not understanding and not doing what is right; if sin is neglecting, avoiding, resisting, and denying what is clear about God; if sin is unbelief, misunderstanding; if sin is disobedience; if sin is autonomy, where the self-life is central; then we are called to put

---

5. *1 Corinthians 1:12.*

6. *1 Corinthians 3:1–4.*

7. *Psalm 51.*

aside sin, all of it. God desires truth in the inward part and wants us to be one, as the Father, the Son, and the Holy Spirit are one. I hope, if we may have neglected this in terms of not paying attention to it, it will come back to mind now as in the preaching, and we will give heed to it. There is a connection between the unity of the people of God, and the Word of God going to the ends of the earth. That they might be one that the world might believe.[8] If we can overcome sin, in ourselves and in the church, we stand a chance of dealing with it in the world. Judgment must begin at the house of God[9]—God desires truth in the inward part.

I want to make the connection as clear as possible that sanctification is through the truth; the truth, the whole truth, and nothing but the truth, nothing else. The centrality, the importance of truth, is here in sanctification. Christ said in John 17:17, as we put in the focus for the week, "Sanctify them by the truth; your word is truth." And in the call to worship, "you will know the truth, and the truth will set you free" (Jn. 8:32). Nothing else at all will bring about sanctification; truth is *necessary* for it and *sufficient* for it.

We said this is truth in the inward part. We speak about dealing with sin by way of repentance, and repentance involves confession of sin as such and naming it. This repentance begins in our thinking. Repentance is *metanoia*, a change in one's *thinking*. It is not simply at the level of words that are spoken; it is going deep within, so it is a habit of the heart. It is a disposition, and it is an attitude. Jesus expressed this by saying, "Blessed are the poor in spirit" (Matt. 5:3a), this is how the doctrine of creation translates. We are creatures utterly dependent on God. We have nothing of our own; we are poor in spirit. The doctrine of redemption: "Blessed are those who mourn" (Matt. 5:4a); It is a disposition of the heart, it is an attitude. Those who hunger and thirst after righteousness, this is a disposition of the heart; this is an attitude. Attitude is the level that we are speaking of, where we speak about truth within us, "Surely you desire truth in the inner parts; you teach me wisdom in the inmost place" (Ps. 51:6). This is why David said, "Cleanse me with hyssop, and I will be clean; wash me, and I will be whiter than snow" (Ps. 51:7). Snow is white, but in the heart of

---

8. *John 17:21.*

9. *1 Peter 4:17.*

every snowflake, there is something impure around which it is formed. This is what is entailed in being whiter than snow; God desires truth in the inward part.

A few Scriptures that should be noted are John 17:17 and John 8:32, which I have mentioned already, likewise Romans 12:2. In light of all that has gone on before, Paul beseeches us "to offer your bodies as living sacrifices, holy and pleasing to God—this is your spiritual act of worship. Do not conform any longer to the pattern of this world, but be transformed by the renewing of your mind" (Rom. 12:1b–2a). Again, the mind, we are transformed as we behold His glory. "And we, who with unveiled faces all reflect the Lord's glory, are being transformed into his likeness with ever-increasing glory" (2 Cor. 3:18a), but here particularly, I want to note Romans 12:2. It has a very specific concrete expression in our Lord Jesus Christ: we are to be *conformed* to our Lord Jesus Christ. All things work together for good to that end.[10] To be like Him, the Word of God incarnate. These are some Scriptures that we can keep in mind which focus on sanctification through the truth.

We also said that the law of God is the standard, and we are to give heed to this law, all of it. We are to be reminded of it continually. The picture of being reminded of the law is having it in a box on your forehead. To have it wrapped on your hands and to have it on the fringes of your garment; to remember all the Commandments, and to have it on your doorposts. As you go out, as you come in, rise up and sit down, you are talking about this. You meditate on it. The law summarizes all that God requires of us, and it is summarized by our Lord: "'Love the Lord your God with all your heart and with all your soul and with all your strength and with all your mind'; and, 'Love your neighbor as yourself'" (Lk. 10:27). This is for all of life, it is to be done "on earth as it is in heaven" (Matt. 6:10b).

We are to be cautious in two ways about some of the standards that may creep in. We may make our conscience the standard. Our conscience may not be well-informed by the law, and we may hold up things that we think are the standard. We may think we may be doing superlatively well, or better than others, and hold that up as a standard, but we may end up imposing a standard which is other than biblical and actually less than biblical. Remember the righteousness of

---

10. *Romans 8:28.*

the Pharisees. They thought they were great. Remember the righteousness in the Catholic Church that speaks about supererogation. I could obey over and above the law and accumulate merit for the church, which will be dispensed in the sacraments, the visiting of saints, and the display of parts of their bodies here and there (relics). The use of that kind of teaching—the saints having merit and being set apart as holier—all of that is a false understanding of the law. It is pharisaical, legalistic righteousness, and it does not reflect the wisdom of God in terms of what the real goal is. Jesus especially spoke against legalistic righteousness, over and against the tax collector and the harlot, because there is an element of pride behind the attitude of legalism. There is not the same element of pride in the prostitute, and that is what He was addressing. We may think that we are being righteous, and we are not, so we have to be careful when we begin to approach the law that we do not make our conscience the standard and impose it on others. Just because your conscience permits it, does not mean that you can do it; that has wreaked havoc in the church. Conscience is, at best, a negative guide for *you*. If your conscience tells you not to, then you do not do it; it is not a positive guide. We do not impose our conscience on others—it is both a negative guide for you, and you do not impose it on others. When we speak about the law of God, we recognize areas of *adiaphora* that are to be approached as a matter of wisdom, and wisdom is a much higher standard than legalism. Wisdom keeps the good in mind; legalism does not see the good—the earth being filled with knowledge of God. Wisdom seeks to answer how to take the step from here to there to go farther in the good. Legalism does not; wisdom is a much higher standard and more consistent with the law.

TRUTH THROUGH SUFFERING

This truth that we must have in the inward part comes to us through suffering. It is expressed in three ways in Genesis 3:22–24: God banished man from the Garden. Think about that word: to be banished. It is—'you have to go, and you cannot come back'—firmly set, banished. But more than that, God *drove* them out of the Garden, so they were banished from the Garden to live under the curse. Remember we spoke about outside the Garden; there are no plants, and the ground is watered in a certain way. All of life is concentrated there and from that place, four rivers go out. The whole centrality of the Garden: In the center of the Garden there is the tree of the knowledge of good and evil and the tree of life. Adam is driven out of the Garden, and he is kept from coming back in. All three of these are right here in this passage. This tells us something: even the forgiven person, the person who holds on to the promise, when the curse is pronounced, is reluctant. We are resistant to cleansing in the same way that we are toward death, we have the fear of death. We are to guard our lives and not just expose ourselves to harm. There is a certain fear that drives that. It can become overexposure quickly. We must be careful to preserve life, but not at any cost with this sense of fear, the fear of death that dominates.

God drove the man out and placed Cherubim on the east side of the Garden. We do not know how many, but it was sufficient. The Cherubim are the guardians of the holiness of God. The Cherubim appeared again in the Most Holy Place, with wings outstretched over the Shekinah presence of God over the mercy seat. They are guardians of the holiness of God, and man must be holy, must be sanctified, if he is going to approach God. The Cherubim are placed there in addition to "a flaming sword flashing back and forth to guard the way to the tree of life" (Gen. 3:24b). We see that man is banished, he is driven out, and he is kept from coming back in. This tells you about the disposition of our hearts, and we need to look at this. We see the ways in which the world responds to suffering, and how the believer *should* respond to the suffering of the curse.

We should know that this is no small thing; we have every reason to believe that the Garden did not simply disappear from the face of the earth when they left it. The Garden continued. We do not believe the Garden is still on the face of the earth, we believe it was wiped out with the Flood. But until the Flood, it remained, and until the Flood, the geography remained, and until the Flood, the rivers flowing out continued. Everyone who went out along those rivers would have been able to trace them back to the Garden. This warning to man remained for mankind—for all mankind—until the Flood. The Cherubim, we believe, remained. We do not have any reason to think that after 200 years they reasoned, 'I think they've gotten the point, they won't sneak back in. This is getting old; let's pull back the sword.' No, they have not gotten the point. Imagine the impression that left in history. They may get the point that they will not get back in, but just in case someone might come back and report, 'I was by the Garden this morning, and I did not see those Cherubim. I did not see a flaming sword. What do you think? Should we try?' You bet they will try. After 900 years, some of these guys are dying off, saying, 'Oh, I remember that, you know we can't get in there, but the tree of life is there. If somehow we can get in there, we will get the ultimate source of potency in life that will remain unendingly.' The Garden, the Cherubim, and the flaming sword were a witness to the people.

THE REALITY OF THE CURSE

There is a connection between suffering, the truth, and sanctification. We must be sanctified. It is by the truth, and the ordinary way in which we get to truth (given our autonomy; not seeking, our self-deception, our self-justification, and our casualness) is through suffering, living under the curse. Resistance is futile; you cannot avoid it. That does not mean you just run into it. It means you live under it before God, seeking to obey the call to dominion, and holding on to the promise. The reality of the curse is revealed in toil and strife, and old age, sickness, and death. It is not the only way; it manifests itself further from time to time in war, famine, and plague, and it is increased in history. Lifespan was 950 years on average and went down to about 70. We were all together in one place, of one language, rushing off into sin again, but God prevented that through Babel. The differences have become the occasion of our identity, our identity differences, and idolatry connected with that, which are the occasion for strife. Some of you know strife in terms of your parents and siblings, brother and sister, and some of you know strife in terms of children. There is sibling rivalry between the children, there is no lack of strife, and we see strife in places of work. Oftentimes, we live relatively isolated lives. It is one way to have peace; 'let's just avoid it.' There is strife in the church, and sometimes when one church seeks to move ahead in one way, another church begins to say, 'cult.' Isn't that wonderful, your brother and sister in Christ making those kinds of claims about you? You may be mainline Historic Christianity—that does not mean anything. You may be the one who gives the most reasons in the world—that does not mean anything. 'Cult!' Don't you love it? Strife. That does not count for all the stuff that is said on the internet; that is just said personally, so welcome to the world of sin and strife and toil.

How are you doing with your work? How about your income? How is the weather outside? 'Horrible! We are breaking records! I cannot believe that this is happening!' Believe it! Things have gotten worse, so we should expect a little more scorching from the sun. 'Oh yeah? Well, I know some places where it is not so scorching.' Well, you get other kinds and forms of the curse there. Difficulty in working? You are ready to cry your eyeballs out, given this 'dumb job.' But thank God you at least have a job where you get a paycheck. Strife at work, and you are barely hanging on, and many people are competing with you for work. You have to go through the grind, as day after day, year after year, year in and year out, there is no let-up. You are born, you get a college degree, you go to work for so many years, and you get old, then you die, and that is it; your story is over. Perhaps they can put you on display, like Jeremy Bentham, whose body is on display in a glass case.[11]

If somehow you get around toil, and you manage to buy your way out of strife by buying an island, where you have large acreage, where no one even gets close to you to make any noise or any sound, you have your own property, your own yacht, and you can go out there, you could manage to get away. Everyone wants that, just to get away every once in a while, right? If you are wealthy enough, you can get away from toil and strife, but this one you are not going to get away from: *old age, sickness, and death.* Some persons managed in God's providence to die fat and flourishing.[12]

We have the reality of the curse; we cannot avoid it. Gregory Peck got old, James Stewart got old, you see, you don't even remember these guys, do you? Clark Gable, do you think Madonna is not going to get old? And what's his name? Brad Pitt? Who else? I am not even sure they should be mentioned here.

We have the curse—toil, strife, old age, sickness, and death. We are always worried about war and famine, the economy, and 10% unemployment, and in some places between 16 to 18%. In some segments of the economy, it is more than that, and in some parts of the world, it

---

11. Jeremy Bentham's body is preserved on display at University College London.

12. For a full reference, read *Psalm 73* as Asaph reflects on the prosperity of the wicked and comes to see the error of his thinking.

is greater than that. Poverty, connected with that, scraping by, malnutrition connected with that, this is a kind of famine. Then wars sweep through in tribal areas, and one tribe preys on the other and wipes them out. They have this belief that if you kill your victim and eat their heart, somehow you get their strength; a weird, perverse thing. In Rwanda, Hutus and Tutsis were at each other. In Bosnia, they were at each other. The Irish and the English were at each other. There is no limit; this includes India and Pakistan over Kashmir; they were just at each other, and it seems to be a never-ending civil war in every nation. This spiritual war is going on in a person, between persons and families, in a church, between churches, in a nation, between nations, and ultimately between the kingdom of God and the kingdom of darkness. Sometimes, it breaks out into physical war.

RESPONSE TO THE CURSE: THE WORLD

We have the curse with us, and we have to respond to it. Let us consider the world's response, and then the believer's response. I believe that the best way to summarize the world's response is to think about the Tenth Commandment. You shall not covet. You shall not covet anything that is your neighbor's, your neighbor's wife, your neighbor's house, your neighbor's property, or car. There is a lot of coveting, and so that is one response. 'I'm as good as that person; I deserve as much. I don't think they did anything particularly to deserve it. They just ripped off the system. You know what? We should have a government that will redistribute wealth so everybody is equal.' This is envy in connection with coveting, the idea that victim status must be redressed by the government and that the government is going to somehow bring justice in the world—justice as defined in terms of the equality of outcome: Marxism. Socialist thoughts still abound in many areas in many parts of the world, in our politics, and a good part of what is going on in our nation between the left and the right is over socialism and a kind of individualism. There is class warfare, envy between the rich and the poor, and all that goes with that to justify it. That is not an appropriate response. We are to watch ourselves.

Envy may rise from the attention given to another person, or the honor given. Iago had enough to eat in Shakespeare's play *Othello*, but he envied the position given to another person rather than to him. He brought about the destruction of Othello in lying, scheming ways. The Pharisees envied Jesus, and they killed Him. Many envied Paul and tried to stir up trouble for him. One may see the success of another and it reflects on them; 'How come we are not having this kind of success? It must be that this person is cheating, mesmerizing, confusing, seducing, and corrupting the youth.' They are not using reason, and all these corrupted youth, 'they are not using reason; they are psycho followers or something.' That is the latest theory. I'm not making this up; I'm just reporting. So instead of seeing, 'Maybe I've not addressed the question of clarity and inexcusability, and maybe this is what people are hearing,' there is a denial, and it might provoke certain kinds of responses. 'We have been here 35 years, faithfully, and we have 15 people in our congregation; what's the deal? We are faithful, aren't we? So, this church over here must be corrupt.' It is this kind of thinking that occurs.

I should say that we do not say, 'We have about 100 people here, and that church down the road has about 25,000. What are we doing wrong?' We do not say that, we are not ready for 25,000. Maybe after we get our act together, God will add another 10, 20, or so, and we can handle that. Furthermore, we do not desire 25,000 members; we desire 25 million. No, we are not going to settle for this, we want the whole world. We are not in competition with other churches, we want to share with them Historic Christianity, and let everyone go and bring about the change in the world. We do want the foundation in place.

Stoicism is a response, we harden ourselves to just endure, not in hope, but to just endure. This is not an appropriate response; a number of persons go that way. There is resentment and bitterness that may come, "do not despise the LORD's discipline and do not resent his rebuke, because the LORD disciplines those he loves" (Prov. 3:11–12a). "For whom the Lord loveth he chasteneth, and scourgeth every son whom he receiveth" (Heb. 12:6 KJV). Think about Job; Job wanted to plead his case before God. 'Something is wrong here.' I just got through reading Job again last week; that book is so great, and that book is so rich. I started sketching out the arguments, P then Q then R (P $\supset$ Q $\supset$ R); and I said, 'Wow there is an argument here; this is really tight!' They are responding to arguments, and we can trace the theme piece by piece in every response. To think it is traditionally said that Moses wrote the Book of Job. Whoever wrote Job, that person is my friend.

You do not have to meet someone to be friends with them, you have this feeling of, 'Wow, we are together in this.' Most of my friends are dead—Moses, David, and Abraham. Abraham, I love Abraham; I feel at home with Abraham. Abel is there; I don't know, for some reason, I don't quite connect with Adam. I have to get over that. Noah—he did a stupendous work. He endured and came through the Flood. Moses—he has a special place. You get connected with these persons who have suffered for the sake of the kingdom, a great cloud of witnesses. We do not go into resentment and bitterness but submit to the hand of God. How does the world generally respond? With envy, stoicism, in resentment and bitterness, and discouragement, without hope.

One of the things that I am learning is that we are to *overcome* in our trials, which means that what was thrown at us, instead of becoming a stumbling block, becomes a stepping stone. To put it in the colloquial, 'when life gives you lemons, you turn them into lemonade.' This is how you overcome and not get discouraged. Sometimes we have to struggle and work with it for a while, but we should not lose hope in discouragement. 'Kids today,' have you ever heard that remark? 'Young people today, young people outside of this church today.' We might do well to remember that the younger people are the same in every age. Let us find a way to work with these persons. They are made in the image of God. They may have been messed up, screwed up, or lacking some things; they are human, address them in their humanity, find ways to connect with them, grow and overcome. 'Bloom where you are planted.' The Lotus sometimes grows out of brackish water, producing a beautiful flower. We labor in the Lord, but not in vain.

Sometimes we turn to self-indulgence. 'I deserve this. I'm going to treat myself well, I'm going to celebrate my this, that, and the other.' We celebrate ourselves into all kinds of self-indulgence and harm ourselves with that. This is not the way to respond to the curse. Cynicism is around these days because there is a lot of breakdown. There is a lot of sin in the world, and people who are sometimes idealists see the sin, and they are not going to be taken in by it, and they want to note it and sometimes point it out; they have their resistance up against sin. Cynicism is common; there is a 'despair.com' website that celebrates it. It is kind of funny how they turn cynicism into an opportunity, and they are selling 'despair.com' coffee mugs and so on; it is a new thing. You do not want to be taken in by cynicism. Cynicism sees sin but does not see grace, and the Scripture says that grace is greater than all of our sin. "Where sin increased, grace increased all the more (Rom. 5:20b). We need to learn to see that, and if we do not, we are not seeing clearly; we have tunnel vision, we are not truthful. Do you get the sense that Paul the Apostle was a cynic? No, you do not get a hint of that. Do you think that Jesus was a cynic? Then be like Jesus.

Then there is fatalism, a resignation to the curse. There are the others who react to fatalism and have a utopian view: 'We will bring it about even if we have to kill you.' And they usually do. 'We will cleanse the world once and for all from all hindrances to our purpose and plan.' Whether it is socialism, Marxism, whether it is national racism like the Nazis, or it could be religious, using force, the terrorist ideology. Fatalism is not the way to go. We are rugged gradual idealists; we are not romantics, we are willing to work hard; we are not going to yield to sloth. Remember the Ten Commandments? I believe I recently summed up some of this for you. If I have not, I will have to come back and do it another time.

What I just did was to pull from the moral law given in general revelation, Moral Law 10, responses that are inadequate.[13] What is adequate? We must have faith, that is, understanding the basics, understanding sin and death, and what death is (not 'hell'), and what sin is in terms of those five points. If I have not made those five points clear, let me quickly mention them: First of all, not seeking, not understanding, and not doing what is right. Then, in the second point, we develop not seeking in terms of neglect, and avoiding, resisting, and denying reason in the face of what is clear: an act contrary to your nature. Number three, we developed not understanding as unbelief. Sin is unbelief, failing to believe. Fourth, we developed unrighteousness as disobedience. We saw all three of those as autonomy, so our faith requires us to understand sin and death, the suffering that is connected with it, and how both contribute to this kind of response to suffering. Some of it is to fill the void of emptiness, the aching emptiness, and we try to get more and more and more, and we lie and steal and kill and cheat; this happens a lot on Wall Street. We institutionalize it; we have paid advisors; lobbyists. The indication that lobbyists are not being on the up and up is that they are not being transparent. Be transparent, and

---

13. Gangadean, *Philosophical Foundation*, 277–283.

that is the first step. Truth and justice go together; the truth, the whole truth, and nothing but the truth. They have been able to avoid justice.

RESPONSE: THE BELIEVER IS PREPARED FOR SANCTIFICATION

There is this desire to fill the emptiness, but there is also pain from circumstantial evil or natural evil, and both of those are suffering. What is the response of the believer to suffering? Jesus, in John 13, as He is about to leave His disciples, tells them what is going to happen. First of all, Judas is going to betray Christ, and Peter is going to deny Christ. Then John 14:1 begins, "Do not let your hearts be troubled. Trust in God; trust also in me." Then, in 16:13, John speaks about the Holy Spirit coming, and He is spoken of as a counselor, the spirit of truth. "But when he, the Spirit of truth, comes, he will guide you into all truth." Remember, we need to have truth in the inward part. While suffering should call us to focus our attention, unless the Holy Spirit is there, we will not notice the promise; we will separate the curse from the promise, and we will not have the truth in place. The Holy Spirit, the Spirit of truth, is coming. This is particularly dramatic and strategic, in that Jesus is about to go to the cross, and He is about to leave His disciples, and he is preparing them for what is coming. They are forgiven, but they need cleansing. He is preparing them for that. John 13–17 should be read with that in mind.

Christ Prepares the Disciples

In John 14:27, Christ speaks about peace: "Peace I leave with you; my peace I give you. I do not give to you as the world gives. Do not let your hearts be troubled and do not be afraid." John 14:1 says, "Do not let your hearts be troubled," God calls us to peace, in connection with the work of the Holy Spirit being present with us, and bringing truth into our hearts. The same is said in John 15, that we should bear fruit. Peace is connected again with the Spirit coming in verse 18: "If the world hates you, keep in mind that it hated me first," and in verse 26: "When the Counselor comes, whom I will send to you from the Father, the Spirit of truth who goes out from the Father, he will testify about me." It speaks of truth again. John 16:1: "All this I have told you so that you will not go astray." Again, in verses 7–13a:

> But I tell you the truth: It is for your good that I am going away. Unless I go away, the Counselor will not come to you; but if I go, I will send him to you. When he comes, he will convict the world of guilt in regard to sin and righteousness and judgment: in regard to sin, because men do not believe in me; in regard to righteousness, because I am going to the Father, where you can see me no longer; and in regard to judgment, because the prince of this world now stands condemned. I have much more to say to you, more than you can now bear. But when he, the Spirit of truth, comes, he will guide you into all truth.

At the end of the chapter, John 16:33, Christ ends by saying, "I have told you these things, so that in me you may have peace. In this world you will have trouble. But take heart! I have overcome the world." We are to be like our Lord Jesus and recognize the presence of the Spirit working in us, as the Spirit of truth, amid our trials to help us to overcome.

Then in John 17, He prays that high priestly prayer for the sanctification of His people, and the unity and the joy that comes from that. So clearly, our Lord Jesus, in this strategic time, is speaking to His people about the work of the Spirit, sanctification through the truth, and being at peace. What is the Christian's response to the world? We are to have the peace of God in connection with knowing the truth, by the working of the ministry of the Holy Spirit.

Paul, Peter, James, and John Prepare Believers for Sanctification

Paul speaks about peace in Romans 8:28, "And we know that in all things God works for the good of those who love him, who have been called according to his purpose." In verses 38–39, Paul says, "For I am convinced that neither death nor life, neither angels nor demons, neither the present nor the future, nor any powers, neither height nor depth, nor anything else in all creation, will be able to separate us from the love of God that is in Christ Jesus our Lord." Paul is reckoning with the suffering that we will have in the world, whether it is through strife or other ways, but it is more than that. He speaks about "trouble or hardship or persecution or famine or nakedness or danger or sword"

(Rom. 8:35). He says, "To this very hour we go hungry and thirsty, we are in rags, we are brutally treated, we are homeless" (1 Cor. 4:11). Philippians 4:11–12 says, "I am not saying this because I am in need, for I have learned to be content whatever the circumstances. I know what it is to be in need, and I know what it is to have plenty." Our Lord Jesus knows both. Paul speaks about the peace of God filling our hearts in terms of thinking about what is noble and true and just and right.[14] We are to have joy in connection with peace as against discontent. In Hebrews 12:3–13, the author, who is believed to be Paul, says that we are not to be discouraged when we are chastened by the Lord.

James 1:2–4 "Consider it pure joy, my brothers, whenever you face trials of many kinds." In 5:10–11, he speaks about Job as an example. Peter, in 1 Peter 1:7, speaks about how fiery trials that are to try us are more precious than gold that perishes. Think it not "as though something strange were happening to you. But rejoice that you participate in the sufferings of Christ, so that you may be overjoyed when his glory is revealed" (1 Pet. 4:12b–13). John speaks of it in 1 John 1:9.

Christ, Paul, James, Peter, and John are leaving the scene, and they are preparing the hearers for that ongoing work, not of justification, but of sanctification. To have peace, we are going to have to go through suffering, but we are to have peace in the midst of our suffering. In the Book of Revelation, John certainly speaks about the curse and the promise together in all of those visions. And what shall we say about the prophets, who have this vision of the curse and the promise? It is all through the Bible from the beginning to the end, this teaching about sanctification through suffering. Suffering restrains sin, it recalls us, and for those who are called back, it restores us, and focuses our attention, with the work of the Spirit, to get to the truth by which we are sanctified. What remains, Paul says, is faith (the understanding of how God works), hope (that this will indeed come about), and love;[15] these three remain. We can overcome our enemies and those who may say all manner of evil against us in responding by way of love to seek their good. I do not mean that in some kind of emotional, romantic sense, but it may be that we pray that God will humble them through suffering, that they may bow and learn that the Lord is God, that they

---

14. *Philippians 4:8–9.*

15. *1 Corinthians 13:13.*

may fall into the pit they have dug, but not that they would perish there. Rather, we pray that through this, they would be humbled and come to repentance.

Our response to the curse, in faith, hope, and love, is love and what comes from love—joy, and the peace of God, the peace about which our Lord Jesus spoke. This is what is before us, and we do not have to be discouraged; we can be patient and wait upon God, seek Him and overcome, and find ourselves in a new place of peace and joy. Thank God for His Word to us, and this concludes our discussion of the worldview of creation–fall–redemption. Let us stand and sing from Psalm 73C.

APPENDICES

THE BIBLICAL WORLDVIEW
CREATION–FALL–REDEMPTION
Concise Version

CREATION

1. Creation is revelation: necessarily, intentionally, and exclusively.

2. This revelation is full and clear.

3. Eternal life is knowing God.

4. The knowledge of God is through the work of dominion.

5. The earth shall be full of the knowledge of the Lord as the waters cover the sea.

FALL

1. The covenant of creation: representation, probation, and manifestation; the covenant of marriage.

2. Temptation: the purpose, the agent, and the argument.

3. Sin: not seeking, not understanding, and not doing what is right.

4. Death: two kinds of death: physical and spiritual; the wages of sin is spiritual death.

5. Theodicy: why is there evil? Evil deepens the divine revelation.

REDEMPTION

1. The first call back: shame (inward/conscience).

   The first response: self-deception (cover up).

2. The second call back: self-examination (outward/the question).

   The second response: self-justification (blaming others).

3. The third call back: the promise and the curse.

   > The promise: spiritual war, age-long and agonizing; good will overcome evil.

   > The curse: toil, strife, and old age, sickness, and death; war, famine, and plague.

   The third response: repentance and faith (names his wife Eve).

4. Justification: forgiveness of sin through the death of another (the coats of skin).

5. Sanctification: cleansing from sin through suffering (the expulsion).

———

THE BIBLICAL WORLDVIEW
CREATION–FALL–REDEMPTION
Expanded Version

INTRODUCTION

The biblical worldview of creation–fall–redemption in Genesis 1–3 is foundational for all of life.

Foundation is necessary to go on to maturity, fruitfulness, unity of the faith, and fullness of the knowledge of God.[1]

Foundation is laid in one's life at every level of learning: grammar, dialectic, and rhetoric; at the levels of knowledge, understanding, and wisdom. It must be factually remembered, in order; it must be rationally justified, at every step; and it must be applied, with social virtuosity.

ON CREATION

1. Creation is revelation: necessarily, intentionally, and exclusively.

  i. Necessarily: A being is revealed in its acts; the acts of God in creation and providence reveal the nature of God.

  ii. Intentionally: Creation is good; it was what God intended; God created to reveal himself and rules to reveal himself.

---

1. *Ephesians 4; Hebrews 6.*

   iii. Exclusively: There is no knowledge of God without revelation; there is no revelation apart from the works of creation and providence.

2. This revelation is full and clear.

This revelation is full.

   i. The whole earth is full of his glory.[2] The length, breadth, depth, and height of God's glory is seen in his filling everything in every way.

   ii. The vast array of the creation, each after its kind, and the multitudes of human beings in history are a full revelation of God's glory.

   iii. Providence of the Fall and of redemption are a full revelation of God's justice and mercy; nothing more is added to what is full.

This revelation is clear.

   iv. The eternal power and divine nature are clearly revealed in the things which are made; the law of God is written on the hearts of all men.[3]

   v. The clarity of general revelation makes the unbelief of mankind without excuse.

   vi. Clarity is opposed to all forms of skepticism (no knowledge is possible) and to fideism (belief without proof/understanding).

3. Eternal life is knowing God.

   i. From general revelation: the good for man as a rational being is understanding creation and providence, which reveal God; the good is the knowledge of God.

   ii. From special revelation: eternal life is knowing God;[4] it begins in this life and grows unendingly in the next life.

---

2. *Isaiah 6:3.*

3. *Romans 1:20; 2:14–15.*

4. *John 17:3.*

iii. From Historic Christianity: man's chief end is to glorify God and to enjoy him forever;[5] to glorify God is to know his glory and to make his glory known.

4. The knowledge of God is through the work of dominion.

i. The knowledge of God is through knowledge of God's self-revelation in the creation unfolding in providence/history.

ii. The knowledge of the creation is through the work of dominion. In dominion, man is to be fruitful and multiply and fill the earth and rule over it.[6] The work of dominion is corporate, cumulative, and communal. It requires all of mankind, working together through all of history, to be achieved. Dominion requires naming (grasping the nature of) all beings in all their parts and relations, and developing this nature/essence, the excellence/glory in all beings, so as to make known the glory of God. The outcome of the work of dominion is the City of God.[7]

iii. The work of dominion under the Fall and redemption requires making disciples of all nations and taking every thought captive which is raised up against the knowledge of God.[8]

5. The earth shall be full of the knowledge of the Lord as the waters cover the sea.

i. Man is the image of God; as God's work of creation and providence is revelation, so man's work of dominion brings knowledge of God as Creator and Ruler.

ii. As God completed the work of creation, man will complete the work of dominion.

The Sabbath day of rest is instituted by God to remind man of his origin and his destiny in eschatological hope.

---

5. *SCQ. 1.*

6. *Genesis 1.*

7. *Revelation 21.*

8. *Matthew 28:20; 2 Corinthians 10:4.*

   iii. The work of dominion will be completed when the earth is filled with the knowledge of God as the waters cover the sea.[9]

ON THE FALL

1. The Covenant of Creation

   i. Purpose of the covenant: to establish mankind in a permanent (positive) relationship with God.

   ii. Representation: all of life and history is centered in the Garden of Eden; the act of one man, Adam, will affect all.

   iii. Probation: Adam is to be tested concerning his pursuit of God's purpose for mankind: the knowledge of God through the work of dominion.

   iv. Manifestation: the inward, invisible choice of good and evil is manifested in the outward act of obedience regarding eating from the two trees.

   v. The visible covenant of marriage between man and woman reveals the invisible covenant of creation between God and man.

2. Temptation

   i. The temptation is a test of one's faith/understanding of good and evil (both objectively and subjectively).

   ii. Neither the tempter nor the test is the cause of sin, but rather the outward occasion that reveals sin.

   iii. The test comes in the form of an argument addressed to the understanding: a reason (premise): "for you shall be as God knowing good and evil" is given to support the conclusion: "you shall not surely die."

   iv. Eve was deceived: she justified her act on the basis of seeking wisdom apart from any reference to God.

---

9. *Isaiah 11:9.*

v. Adam had turned back: he had ceased to seek the knowledge of God as the good for himself and for his wife. He failed to keep in mind the clear difference between God the Creator and man the creature with respect to knowing good and evil. He determined good autonomously by what pleased him.

3. Sin

i. From general revelation: sin is an act contrary to one's nature as a rational being, made in the image of God; it is to neglect, avoid, resist, and deny reason in the face of what is clear about God.

ii. From special revelation: sin is not seeking, not understanding, and not doing what is right;[10] the root sin of not seeking and understanding leads to the fruit sin of not doing.

iii. Sin is unbelief as lacking understanding, which leads to the outward act of disobedience; because of the clarity of general revelation unbelief is inexcusable.

iv. Sin is disobedience; the outward act of eating of the tree of the knowledge of good and evil reveals the inward reality of determining good and evil for oneself.

v. Sin, in its essence, is autonomy:

a. It is putting one's self in the place of God to determine good and evil.

b. It is doing what is right in one's own eyes.

c. It is doing whatever pleases oneself.

d. It is being a law unto oneself.

e. It is lawlessness—not being subject to the law of God in any area of life, beginning with the first form of the Word of God to man as the laws of reason.

---

10. *Romans 3:10–11.*

4. Death

   i. There are two kinds of death—physical death and spiritual death.[11]

      The wages of sin is spiritual death, not physical death. "In the day you eat you shall surely die."[12] "The wages of sin is death."[13]

   ii. Spiritual death is present and inherent in sin, not future and imposed; it is not hell conceived of as a literal, physical lake of fire.

  iii. The inherent consequence of moral evil is self-destruction of the soul; it is meaninglessness, boredom, and guilt, increasing without end; it is spiritual death.

  iv. Spiritual death is spoken of as darkness (of mind), burning (of desire without satisfaction), torment (of conscience), as a bottomless pit, and as the second death. The lake of fire is (symbolically) the second death.[14]

   v. Physical death is imposed by God as a call back from spiritual death.

5. Theodicy

   i. Moral evil as unbelief serves subjectively to obscure and objectively to deepen the revelation of God (particularly the divine justice and mercy).

  ii. If moral evil is removed abruptly, then the revelation will not be deepened; if moral evil is not removed, then the revelation will not be seen.

      Therefore, moral evil is removed gradually.

  iii. Moral evil as unbelief is allowed to work itself out in world history in every form and degree of admixture with belief.

      In the spiritual war between belief and unbelief, which is age-long and agonizing, good will overcome evil.

---

11. *John 5:25, 28; 11:25; Ephesians 2:1.*

12. *Genesis 2:17.*

13. *Romans 6:23.*

14. *Revelation 20:6, 14; 21:8.*

iv. Natural evil (as toil and strife, and old age, sickness, and death, and war, famine, and plague) is imposed by God to restrain, recall from, and remove moral evil; it is a call to stop and think; physical death is a call back from spiritual death.

v. Physical death as a call back is mercy; it requires special revelation as redemptive revelation to show how God is both just and merciful at the same time.

ON REDEMPTION

1. First call back: shame. Response: self-deception.

i. The outward effect of sin: their eyes were opened and they realized their nakedness.

ii. The inward effect of sin: in one's thoughts, feeling shame from one's own conscience is the first call back to repentance from sin.

iii. In the body/soul unity, the visible reveals the invisible; under sin, physical nakedness is a reminder of spiritual nakedness.

iv. Outward response to the shame of nakedness: shame is avoided by making a covering of leaves, yet the covering is still seen and still reminds.

v. Inward response: by self-deception a person avoids acknowledging the sin of not seeking and not understanding what is clear about God.

2. Second call back: call to self-examination. Response: self-justification.

i. The second call back by word goes beyond the first: it is outer and from another vs. inward and from within oneself.

ii. The second call back comes by word, from God, as a question: "Where are you?"

iii. The question, coming from God who is all-knowing, is a call for Adam's self-examination, not a call for his self-disclosure.

iv. From hiding in guilt and fear, man is called to confession of sin: "Have you eaten from the tree of which I commanded you . . . ?"

v. Man's response: man justifies himself by blaming both the woman and God: "The woman whom you gave to be with me . . ."

3. Third call back: the promise and the curse.

i. The promise consists in establishing a spiritual war between belief and unbelief, which will be age-long and agonizing, in which good will overcome evil; the seed of the woman, in the place of Adam, will do what Adam failed to do.

ii. The curse in the third call back is in deed, beyond word: it is imposed by God on all mankind throughout history through Adam's representation.

iii. The curse consists of toil and strife, and old age, sickness, and death; at times the curse is intensified corporately to war, famine, and plague.

iv. The curse is not punishment, but mercy; it is the final, continuing call back from sin and self-deception and self-justification.

v. The suffering of natural evil, imposed through the curse, serves to restrain, to recall from, and to remove moral evil; it is a call to stop and think.

4. Justification: God's response to man's response: repentance and faith.

i. Adam accepts life for mankind under the curse, with hope in the promise of redemption.

ii. Adam calls his wife's name Eve, the mother of all the living; he chooses to obey in repentance, with faith in the promise.

iii. God clothes Adam and Eve with garments of skin: vicarious atonement, through the sacrifice of another in the place of Adam, will undo what Adam did.

iv. Under the covenant, there is triple imputation: Adam's guilt is imputed to all whom he represents; the guilt of all who accept the promise is imputed to the one promised in the place of Adam; the righteousness of the one sacrificed is imputed to all who believe.

v. Wearing the garments of skin vs. the covering of leaves is a continual reminder of God's justification (the forgiveness of sin and provision of righteousness) through the one who is to come in the place of Adam.

5. Sanctification through the truth.

i. Sanctification is the cleansing from sin; it assumes one has received God's forgiveness of sin and his justification.

ii. Sanctification is by knowledge of the truth;[15] this knowledge comes through suffering under the curse; natural evil serves variously to restrain, to recall from, and to remove moral evil in every form.

iii. Man is driven from the Garden of Eden, to live under the curse, to be cleansed from sin and self-deception and self-justification.

iv. The call back through the curse cannot be avoided; the way to the tree of life is guarded; all born of Adam must die physically.

v. Sanctification for those who are justified continues until death; it is incomplete until death and ends with death.

---

15. *John 17:17.*

INDEX

ABOUT THE AUTHOR

DR. SURRENDRA GANGADEAN (1943–2022) was a Professor of Philosophy at Phoenix College and at Paradise Valley Community College for 45 years. Additionally, he taught from the pulpit at Westminster Fellowship for almost 30 years and taught courses at Logos Theological Seminary for over 25 years. Courses he taught include: Introduction to Philosophy, Logic, Ethics, Philosophy of Religion, Eastern Religions, World Religions, Introduction to Christianity, Introduction to Humanities, Philosophy of Art, The Great Books, Philosophical Theology, Biblical Worldview, Biblical History, Church History, Systematic Theology, Biblical Hermeneutics, and Existential Hermeneutics. He received an M.A. degree in Literature from the Arizona State University, an M.A. degree in Philosophy from the University of Arizona, and a Ph.D. in Natural Theology from Reformed International Theological Seminary. He presented academic papers and public lectures on Natural Theology and the Moral Law. Dr. Gangadean was the organizing Pastor of Westminster Fellowship church, and President of The Logos Foundation, which serves academic education in Liberal Arts and Theology.

www.ingramcontent.com/pod-product-compliance
Lightning Source LLC
Chambersburg PA
CBHW020430130626
46549CB00001B/61